The Therapeutic Dialogue

THE THERAPEUTIC DIALOGUE

A Theoretical and Practical Guide to Psychotherapy

Sohan Lal Sharma

Foreword by Thomas Szasz

University of New Mexico Press

Albuquerque

Library of Congress Cataloging-in-Publication Data

Sharma, Sohan Lal, 1927–
  The therapeutic dialogue.

  Includes bibliographies and index.
  1. Psychotherapy—Philosophy.   2. Psychotherapy—
Social aspects.   I. Title. [DNLM: 1. Psychotherapy—
popular works.   2. Social Environment—popular works.
WM 420 S531t]
RC480.5.S4446   1986   616.89′14   86-885
ISBN 0-8263-0883-X

Contents

Foreword

Thomas Szasz

The mental health disciplines are undergoing profound changes. According to most experts, the engine that drives these changes is science producing "advances" in diagnosis, exemplified by DSM-III, and "breakthroughs" in therapy, exemplified by the antipsychotic drugs. I disagree. The celebration of DSM-III and the enthusiasm for neuroleptics are, in my opinion, only elaborate rituals to sanctify "mental illnesses" and their "treatments" as bona fide illnesses and treatments. The engines that drive the current changes in mental health practices are, I believe, mainly economic and social.

We are too close to this scene to be able properly to evaluate what is happening. Soon enough, historians of mental health will study our present beliefs and practices and pronounce their verdict upon them, just as we have judged the beliefs and practices of those who have gone before us.

One thing seems clear: psychiatrists are fleeing the ship of psychotherapy and are busy boarding, or rather reboarding, their mother ship, medicine. The reasons for this are also economic and social. The preoccupation with studying DSM-III instead of the lives of persons called "mental patients" is a symptom of this process. Since health-care services are increasingly paid for by third-party providers (mainly and perhaps ultimately the government), professionals who want to feed at this trough have a fresh and all but irresistible incentive for classifying human misery as medical malady. "The decision of the APA to develop DSM-III and then to promulgate its use," writes a Harvard professor of psychiatry, one of America's most distinguished leaders in mental health, "represents a significant re-affirmation on the part of American psychiatry of its medical identity and its commitment to scientific medicine."* Maybe so. But I doubt it. I believe it represents the APA's latest strategy to seduce private and public health-care providers into treating "mental illness like any other illness" and the psychiatrist like any other doctor.

Appearing at this juncture in the history of health care, Professor Sohan Lal Sharma's book on psychotherapy is an especially important contribution. His work provides an excellent up-to-date account of what the complex and ever-so elusive enterprise called "psychotherapy" is about. In addition, with this work Professor Sharma embraces, revalues, and imparts fresh dignity to psychotherapy at precisely that moment when psychiatrists are discarding, devaluing, and demeaning it.

I believe that by rejecting psychotherapy, psychiatry is committing professional suicide. At the same time, freed of psychiatric entanglements, psychotherapists will have more freedom to develop and nurture a form of human helpfulness whose exercise has become a burden and an embarrassment to both doctors of divinity and doctors of medicine.

Real psychotherapy—that is to say, the humane and egalitarian "cure of souls," rather than the condescending paternalism of psychiatry or the pretentious pseudo-science of psychoanalysis—is not about to disappear from the American scene. It will only change hands. Professor Sharma's book should facilitate this change.

—Thomas Szasz
Syracuse, New York

---

*Gerald L. Klerman, A debate on DSM-III: The advantages of DSM-III, *American Journal of Psychiatry* 141 (April 1984): 539.

Preface

While discussing the books on the reading list with the students in the psychotherapy class that I have taught for many years, I go over each book and briefly discuss its contents. Routinely, for many years I would tell the students the weaknesses of the books on the reading list. One semester, as I finished my presentation, a couple of students raised their hands and asked, "If you think all of these books are so inadequate, why don't you write your own?" That was the provocation to write this book. I have no doubt that future authors will discuss my book as I have discussed those of my predecessors.

I have practiced, supervised, taught, and lectured on psychotherapy for over two decades in various institutions in more than one country. Owing partly to such experiences and partly to my dissatisfaction with the existing texts, I decided to put my thoughts on psychotherapy in a book and to make it as thorough as I could.

Literature on psychotherapy is vast, amorphous, and frequently subjective; sifting through and distilling it took me approximately four years. Had I known it would turn out to be such a lengthy and consuming process, I might not have attempted it.

I have looked at approximately 30 percent more of the literature on psychotherapy than I have cited in this work. I chose not to include it for various reasons. Some writers present only their personal and subjective opinions about a certain aspect of psychotherapy; other writers offer essentially a recapitulation or a summary of a certain trend of thought in the field of psychotherapy which contributes little to the existing knowledge for example, writings of various psychoanalysts on transference, or "resistances", certain writings on race and psychotherapy, and so forth. Some writers offer studies which are empirical in nature but tend to bog down in the minutiae of methodology and design, adding little to the concepts, contents, or the techniques of psychotherapy.

Although many books deal with "principles of psychotherapy," to my knowledge very few are solidly based on empirical foundations. Hence, a beginning therapist frequently feels that he may be trying to master a belief system or an ideological system and grows discouraged. For this reason, I have attempted to present the general principles of psychotherapy that have some empirical or social basis. I feel there is a place for such a work, especially for the beginning therapist and the practitioner who may not have the time or the inclination to dig out the empirical studies on various aspects of psychotherapy. I hope this work will provide the reader with a relatively concrete framework for the art and the science of psychotherapy.

It is a truism by now that no one can write a book on psychotherapy without projecting his biases in the text. Given my bias, reflected in the title of this book, I have tried to be as objective as possible, and have struggled to extract certain implicit or explicit principles which may have some empirical and/or social basis.

I am well aware of the fact that this work does not cover many of the areas or aspects of psychotherapy with which every beginning therapist has to struggle—focusing during a session, the guidelines for selecting a theme for the session out of a plethora of themes that the client presents in the beginning of a session, and so on. However, owing to limitations of time and space, I had to make a choice between covering the aforementioned topics and certain other ones such as the medical model and its relation to psychotherapy, dropping out of therapy, and so on. I consider these topics more important to cover because they are rarely discussed in the existing textbooks, although they are frequently talked about by therapists.

The book is divided into two parts. The first part, Chapters 1–4, discusses the theoretical and philosophical assumptions and the models of psychotherapy; the second part discusses the techniques. It is necessary for a student or a practitioner to have some familiarity with these assumptions of therapy and with the models of therapy before the discussion of techniques or the principles of therapy can be initiated. I believe the techniques of psychotherapy (what one does with the clients) are predetermined by the theoretical and by philosophical assumptions and the models of psychotherapy that a therapist explicitly or implicitly espouses.

Generally, most writings on psychotherapy focus upon the client—his diagnosis, his psychopathology, his resistances, his manipulativeness. I have, however, attempted to focus upon the role of the therapist in the process of psychotherapy. The major thrust of my focus is on the social forces (including the client) as they impinge upon the role of therapists and how such forces may affect the therapist in his work. I believe that it is crucial for every therapist to be aware of the social forces, for in many ways they shape the structure of and the interaction within the psychotherapeutic process. It should be clear to the reader that I attach a considerable importance to the social aspects of psychotherapy, both for the client and the therapist. I do not subscribe to the commonly held notion that psychotherapy is "neutral," like a medical technique. Rather I believe that psychotherapy is more akin to socioideological or even sociopolitical trends and movements which prevail at a particular time in a certain culture.

The reader may find some repetitiveness in this work. To me, such repetitiveness is the result of my attempt to carry the reader through the process of psychotherapy from the first session to termination, during which time many of the clients' life-themes, feelings, and conflicts reappear in various forms. Thus, in psychotherapy, as every experienced therapist knows, there is a certain repetitiveness which I have tried to reflect in this work.

It may be somewhat baffling to the reader to notice that sometimes the text uses the word *patient*, as well as the word *client*. Both pertain to the individual who goes to psychotherapy. I have used the term *patient* either when I am quoting other writers, or when I am closely transliterating the writing of those who use the term *patient*. When I present my own ideas, I have consistently used the word *client*, for I believe with Carl Rogers that this term at least attempts to avoid the implication of sickness that a therapist is accustomed to attributing to those who come to psychotherapy.

A few remarks are necessary about the use of the pronouns *he* and *she* in this work. I have consistently used *he* for both the therapist and the client, other than where it is not warranted by the text. I am well aware that approximately two-thirds of the therapists are male, while the same proportion of "out-patient" clients are female. Perhaps, therefore, I should have used *he* for the therapist and *she* for the client. But that leaves out the large number, growing each year, of female therapists.

It is a difficult task to change the historically established male-dominated language. I would have preferred to use a neutral term such as *one* but was advised that it is not a preferred mode of expression. I thought of using the *he/she–his/her* format, as some writers have done, but felt that this approach becomes too cumbersome and distracts from smooth reading. So I have used familiar male-dominated language, even though it does not represent the "reality" of the psychotherapy enterprise as it exists today.

Numerous people have helped me in completing this work. I can hardly thank them all for their assistance and help. I do, however, wish to single out some of them for their continuous encouragement and support, without which I do not believe I would have been able to complete this work.

Ron Leifer, M.D., of Ithaca, New York, has been consistently interested in and encouraging about the progress of my manuscript throughout the four years I have worked on it. He looked over every chapter of the manuscript, gave constructive suggestions, and brought to my attention many pertinent works which otherwise would have escaped my notice.

In spite of her busy schedule, Joyce Ballard Wexler of Los Angeles was generous enough to take an objective and critical look at the manuscript. She brought many points to my attention which I had neglected to cover in this work.

Professors Robert Kloss and John Leggett of sociology departments at California State University, Sacramento, and Rutgers University, New Brunswick, New Jersey, gave many suggestions from a sociological perspective.

Paulette Lathom, of Davis, California, was my typist, editor, and critic. She did the final typing of a major part of the manuscript but could not see it through because she began work on her Ph.D. and did not have time to complete the rest of it.

Morgana Richardson, California State University, San Francisco, was my undergraduate assistant who did the bulk of the library work and obtained for me some obscure articles that I might otherwise not have been able to consult.

In spite of her full-time job, Helena Bennett, California State University, Sacramento, offered to type the final version of the last three chapters of the book.

Linda Hays of Sacramento looked at the manuscript from a lay person's viewpoint and gave numerous suggestions with regard to the clarity of the presentation and the writing style.

I also thank Diana Jackson of Sacramento, and Rupa Sahni of New Delhi, India, for their support and encouragement.

Finally, I wish to thank the members of the Sharma Center for Psychological Services, Sacramento—Chuck Meyers, Michael Parks, Doris Effman, Vince Newland, John Leonard, Carol Fecci-Rogers, and the late Robert Lewis—all of whom regularly looked at the manuscript, tried to make sense out of what I was trying to convey, and helped me put my writing into a coherent style.

I am also thankful to innumerable students and clients from whom I have learned a great deal about the psychotherapeutic process, about the pitfalls that await a therapist, and about myself.

Part One

Theoretical and Conceptual Aspects

1

Who Goes to Psychotherapy: Understanding the Client in the Referral Process

The question, "Who goes to therapy?" has many dimensions, each of which has profound implications for therapy and requires the therapist's careful consideration. These dimensions include whether the client is voluntary or nonvoluntary, male or female, Anglo or ethnic minority, and middle class or lower class.

Various attempts have been made to categorize the clients who go to psychotherapy. Howard and Orlinsky (1972) have classified three distinct groups of adults who seek psychotherapy. They are: (1) "young adults in relatively affluent circumstances, generally college educated, verbal and intelligent;" (2) "persons who tend to be distinctly less affluent, of working-class or lower-class status, and more often than not adults (over thirty), women, sometimes married, . . . often less than high school education. This group tends to be less culturally sophisticated, less verbally communicative, to be judged as more seriously impaired, . . . and to contain those of the non-white population who receive therapeutic treatment." The third group "has been relatively hidden from the awareness of the mental health profession . . . because this type most frequently seeks and receives help from religious rather than secular sources. . . . This group appears to consist of persons who tend to be middle-aged, of various classes but most typically middle class (businessmen and their wives), more often than not women, with families, Protestant, and less frequently college educated."

This schema of grouping clients offers little help to the therapist. It fails to tell the therapist what his role with the clients in each of these categories is going to be. Furthermore, it doesn't tell the therapist what to expect of the client and how to proceed with him.

Some practitioners of psychotherapy maintain that clients belong to one of four categories: (1), those who have had a disturbed or turbulent family background; (2), those who are anxious or in conflict or develop "symptoms"; (3), those who are friendless and lonely and who are frequently frightened by such existential experiences (Schofield 1964; Wheelis 1958); and finally, those who are caught in the stresses and strains of life and are unable to cope with such stress. This method of grouping begs the question. If prospective clients had not had disturbed family backgrounds, were not anxious, friendless, and lonely, or were not experiencing stress in their lives, they would not go to a therapist.

From a therapist's point of view, it is more productive to group clients according to the social forces that bring them into therapy. This method of grouping delineates the social role of the therapist in relation to the client, and at the same time projects the parameters of psychotherapy.

One could say that four groups of people seek therapy. First, there are those who seek therapy voluntarily and define themselves as clients. Such future clients believe that something is wrong with them or that they have a problem for which they should seek treatment. Second are those who seek therapy under duress and pressure from others. For example, a spouse may be told to seek therapy or else the partner will seek a divorce. Third are those who are forced to attend therapy, such as inmates in a mental hospital, or those who come to therapy under court order. Fourth are those who seek therapy because it is fashionable to be in some form of therapy. We shall discuss each of these categories and the relation of the therapist to the client in each.

Types of Clients Seen by the Therapist

Volunteer or Self-Defined Clients   For volunteer clients the decision to seek therapy is not as simple as it may appear on the surface. A future client goes through a series of steps before he enters a therapist's office. He takes some of these steps successively and others simultaneously. Nonetheless, these steps follow a rough pattern. First comes formulation of the problem: the conflicts and difficulties of a future client should be formulated in such a way that the client believes it is appropriate to go to a therapist (Kadushin 1969). Many potential clients do not formulate their problems in this way. They blame other people and external agents for their difficulties. For example, husbands may blame their wives, or vice versa. One may say that his troubles are caused by other people who send electrical signals to control his thoughts. Such persons do not seek therapy unless forced to do so. A 1962 study by Srole, et al. surveyed the emotional well-being or "mental health" of midtown Manhattan residents. The study estimated that about a quarter of the population was psychiatrically impaired. But only one-fourth of those judged impaired had ever been to a psychotherapist. In other words, although the psychiatric team judged many to be in need of help, only a quarter of them had formulated their difficulties in a way in which they felt that it might be necessary to seek therapy. In comparison, a little less than 10 percent who were judged unimpaired went to a psychiatrist or psychologist. Members of this group did formulate their problems in such a way that they felt they needed psychotherapeutic help, although the psychiatrist didn't think that they did.

To view one's troubles within the psychiatric framework and ideology seems to be the first condition for a person to seek therapy. And for a client to continue in therapy, he should have at least a moderate level of verbal skills, and the ability to use these skills to examine himself. He must have an interest in and concern about his intentions and feelings (McSweeny 1977). If either condition is lacking, the probability of an individual seeking psychotherapy voluntarily and continuing with it is slim.

Somatization of Emotional Conflicts   Another step that a future client frequently takes, one generally not mentioned in the literature, is an attempt to attribute the conflicts, dilemmas, and inadequacies of his life to his bodily processes and organs. Reasons for this step are understandable. First, emotional and interpersonal conflicts generally make a person tense. This tension is experienced by the person as physiological. If the interpersonal conflicts continue over a period of time, a person begins to interpret such tensions as "physical symptoms" and begins to believe that they may be caused by a physiochemical imbalance or malfunctioning of a body organ. Second, it is generally less threatening for a person to "somatize" his emotional and interpersonal conflicts and complain about his physical symptoms than to face his problems and dilemmas of ethical choices. A person is not held responsible (even by himself) for his physical and somatic symptoms, whereas he is held accountable for his interpersonal relationships and life activities. Thus, it is not unusual to find a predilection among the future clients to transform or translate their troubles into some form of somatic complaint or physical symptom.

Myers and Roberts (1959) found that "most neurotic patients believed that their physical health was deteriorating and that they were about to develop an illness before they ever sought psychiatric assistance. Specific physical symptoms of a functional nature also appeared. The most frequent complaints were headaches, chronic fatigue and gastrointestinal difficulties such as constipation, diarrhea, indigestion, nausea and vomiting. Palpitations of the heart were also common and were interpreted as symptoms of heart or lung disease." Later studies confirm such findings (Strupp, Fox, and Lessler 1969).

In a study of prepaid health plans, Cummings (1977) found that "sixty percent or more of the physician's visits are made by patients who demonstrate an emotional, rather than an organic, etiology for their physical symptoms." Other studies show that "a large proportion of persons who seek medical care are under some form of emotional distress; in many cases, no organic cause for physical symptoms can be demonstrated. Conversely, persons suffering from mental disorders and emotional problems tend to be high utilizers of medical services" (Olbrisch 1977).

After an extensive review of the literature on this issue, Rosen and Wiens (1979) conclude that

significant life adjustment difficulties would be associated with high use of medical services. Whether one selects samples with a diversity of psychological problems, or with specific disturbances and investigates medical use in general, or with respect to a specific physical disorder, the results generally support this thesis. The greater the emotional disturbance, the poorer the functional recovery, the greater the probability of multiple medical consultation and surgeries, or more extensive the medical use.

A thirty-five-year-old white male, father of two teenage children, called the clinic for psychotherapy. He was a heavy-construction worker. He was having marital difficulties and also problems with his sexual potency. Six months prior to the call, he had lost his job and at that time had decided to become a schoolteacher. To obtain his teaching credential he had been taking night courses. His wife was a schoolteacher. Their marriage was not stable. He had suspected that his wife was having an extramarital affair, but she did not confirm it until he lost his job. He was seeking therapy because he wished to understand what role, if any, he had played in bringing all this upon himself and his family. However, before he came to the clinic, he made an appointment with a urologist to find out whether there might be a physiological reason for his impotence. Two weeks later he told the therapist that although the urologist was unable to find a physical cause for this trouble, he would prefer to wait and see how the home situation developed before coming in for therapy.

It should be observed that the socioeconomic class of the future client plays an important role in the process of somatization of psychological troubles.

Before contact with psychiatry, many neurotic patients in both classes (lower-class and lower-middle-class) considered their symptomatology as an expression of an organic illness. However, by the time they reached treatment there was a significant class difference in the predominant types of presenting complaints. Class V patients (lower-class) usually present themselves with somatic symptoms, whereas class III patients (lower-middle-class) present their complaints more frequently in terms of psychological or interpersonal difficulties (Myers and Roberts 1959).

In studying a larger sample of anxious neurotic outpatients, Derogatis et al. (1971) conclude that "a substantial inverse relationship exists between social class and somatic symptomatology with patients of higher social status manifesting substantially lower distress levels on this dimension than their lower-status counterpart." Extending and refining their study of the relationship between social class and psychological disorder, they caution that unless the symptoms of anxiety and somatization are prominently included in a test measuring psychopathology, the typical relationship between social class and psychological disorder will not be observed (Derogatis et al. 1975).

Discussion with Others   After the problem is formulated by the future client so that he feels that he may require help, he generally talks to other people about his troubles and conflicts. In one study, from 80 to 90 percent of those who applied to the clinics for help had talked about their troubles to friends and relatives (Kadushin 1969). The same holds true for married couples.

Before a couple decides on marital therapy as a last resort before seeing a lawyer, they have already been through despair, frustration, loneliness, depression and anger. They have made frantic efforts to recapture old sexual feelings, made repeated efforts at reconciliation and gotten advice from family and friends and perhaps tried individual therapy (Framo 1978).

Such discussions about their troubles and anguish may be initiated either by the future clients or by others. When friends and relatives talk to the future client about his troubles, they give various kinds of advice. Such advice is generally presented in the form of "do something about your problem." Hence, one could say that there is social pressure to recognize the problem and/or behavior deviance and to take action, to go to a therapist. Such discussions give a certain social support to the prospective client seeking psychotherapy; they also function as a warm-up for the forthcoming therapy (Kadushin 1969).

Various surveys show that between 35 and 40 percent of the prospective clients first consult a clergyman about their troubles (Gurin et al. 1960; Ryan 1969; Kulka, Veroff, and Douvan 1979). This suggests that more than one-third of the people who go to a therapist view their troubles not as medical problems, but rather as value conflicts and ethical dilemmas, or as symptoms of a "troubled soul." Approximately 40 percent of the prospective clients first consult a physician about their troubles (Gurin et al. 1960; Ryan 1969). The clergyman and physician are the two major sources that funnel people into the mental health network.

Friends and relatives of the prospective client also direct the future client as to where to seek help. Generally, friends and relatives are familiar with the place or person to whom they send the prospective client; sometimes such familiarity is based upon their own experience as patients. Hollingshead and Redlich's 1958 figures show that for upper- and middle-class "neurotics," approximately 17 percent of the referrals to outpatient agencies are made by friends and relatives. The rest are referred by public agencies—police, courts, other mental health agencies—and by "mental health" practitioners.

Reading   In addition to these steps, a future client initiates others, whether simultaneously or successively, before he seeks therapy. Generally, once one feels that he has a problem, he reads about it

(Kadushin 1969). Among the clients of the sophisticated clinics that cater to the middle and upper class, such as psychoanalytic clinics and university clinics, approximately 90 percent of the clientele claims to have read something about the field, their problems, and psychotherapy in general. Even among those groups that are not as educated, reading popular-magazine articles about one's troubles is not uncommon (Kadushin 1969).

Shift in Identity   By the time the prospective client comes to a therapist he has struggled with his troubles, has attempted to learn about them, and has tried to straighten himself out. He has clearly not been successful in his struggle or he would not be seeking therapy. In this struggle, he is generally liable to distort the active role he plays in generating his conflicts. The prospective client begins to develop a low self-esteem and sometimes a feeling of defeat; going to a therapist is usually an admission of one's inability to manage one's own life. Thus a certain amount of defensiveness and misperception is likely to characterize a client's narration and perspective on his relationships with others and himself (Raimy 1975).

Once a person has decided to apply to a clinic or to see a therapist, psychologically he is no longer the same person; his self-image changes from that of a self-reliant individual to one who needs help and who cannot manage his own life (Kadushin 1969).* Furthermore, a certain shame and a perjorative connotation are attached to consulting a therapist (Scheff 1966, Rabkin 1972). Kadushin (1969) states that "even among applicants to a sophisticated clinic like University Psychoanalytic Center, 90% said 'yes' to our question, 'Do you think that some persons think there is something wrong with a person who goes to a psychiatrist?' Though 'something wrong' is ambiguous, popular usage points to a perjorative connotation. . . ."

The reason for this negative image is that a psychiatrist, or an expert, determines who is "mentally ill" or "crazy" and who is not. Without a therapist there would be no "official" way to know who is disturbed and who is not, or who should be labeled "mentally ill."

Self-effacement is further engendered in the client because whatever his "presenting complaints" and problems are, they are generally not taken by the therapist at their face value. Rather, the inferred psychological state is taken as the therapist's reality (Kadushin 1969).

---

*See also Clausen (1981) who discusses the self doubts of the ex-hospitalized mentally ill.

For example, if a male client says he is having sexual troubles with his wife, the therapist may infer that the client's attachment, attraction, and/or conflicts with his mother may be the "real" cause of the client's sexual troubles. His sexual problems with his wife must derive from his attachment or hatred for his mother. Usually the presenting difficulties are taken as defenses or as unreliable reporting of facts. The sophisticated client, as studies suggest, is vaguely aware of the fact that his presenting difficulties are not being taken at face value (Begley and Lieberman 1970). Therefore, the beginning of therapy may be a self-effacing situation for the client.

The general notion that mental illness is like physical illness is only partially accepted by a certain strata of society. Sarbin and Mancuso (1970) state that "a review of the studies of the public attitude toward mental illness and mental health demonstrates that the moral enterprise of promoting the 'mental illness' metaphor has failed. The general public has not been persuaded that illness is an appropriate metaphor for deviant behavior," and further that "more financially secure and higher educated persons are more likely to use a mental illness orientation toward deviant behavior and unhappiness."

In general, going to a psychotherapist is not experienced by the client in the same way as going to a physician for a physical illness. A patient does not feel embarrassed or humiliated about going to a physician, for it means to the client and to others that a part of his body is not functioning properly. The patient is rarely held accountable for the malfunctioning of his body. In contrast, going to a therapist reflects that one's way of life—that is, one's social-interpersonal behavior—is unacceptable. This is a reflection upon the social being or social identity of the person, for which one is held accountable by others (Szasz 1962).

Yet, at the same time, a client who voluntarily goes to therapy shows a certain fortitude and moral stamina. In spite of his low self-esteem, inner feelings of humiliation, and implied indictment of his way of life, he is willing to confront the problem and to change. This dual aspect of the client's motivation—diffidence and low self-esteem as well as moral courage—becomes an integral part of psychotherapy.

Those Who Go Under Duress   Another group of clients includes those who go to a therapist under threat, duress, or pressure. There are numerous examples of such clients: a wife or a husband who goes to see a therapist because directly or indirectly the spouse has conveyed to the partner that divorce is the alternative; those who go to a therapist because the court has ordered therapy instead of jail; those who are sent by a probation officer as a condition of parole.

Under all such conditions, clients have mixed feelings about therapy. Others expect them to be in a therapist's office although they may not wish to be there and may not want to assume a client's role. Hence, they resent being in therapy. Often they look for any opportunity to drop out of therapy. (See Chapter 6.) Each client has his own method and reason for dropping out.

A young homosexual who was arrested by the vice squad was ordered by the court to seek therapy or go to a correctional institution. It was implicit in the court order that psychotherapy would change his homosexual orientation to a heterosexual one. The young client began weekly therapy. Soon, he started to miss appointments without advance notice. A few weeks later, the client came to therapy and announced that he had gotten engaged to a woman; therefore, he was no longer a homosexual. Thus, he believed he had fulfilled the condition of the court order.

This kind of client attitude and behavior often provokes the therapist's resentment; such behavior runs counter to the assumptions of therapy itself—that the client should show commitment or involvement in the process of therapy.

If the therapist wishes to work with such clients, it is his task to generate some motivation in the client. In other words, the therapist should try to make the external motivation of therapy internal to the client. Different authors have suggested various devices and techniques for this purpose (Swanson and Woolson 1973; Enright 1975).

It is not unusual for a therapist, directly or indirectly, to intimidate such clients into therapy. It should be mentioned, however, that no therapist of integrity should use intimidation, badgering, or any other form of implied threat for this purpose. But persuasion, explanation, and open discussion may be useful in clarifying the client's motivation for therapy.

Institutionalized Clients Another group that a therapist is likely to see in therapy are those clients who are confined to institutions, mental hospitals, rest homes, juvenile detention homes, and jails. A therapist is likely to see such clients either because he is employed directly by the institution or is affiliated with them in some form of consultative or trainee capacity.

In general, these clients belong to the lower-class (Hollingshead and Redlich 1958; Goffman 1961). They end up in such institutions by various routes. Some are taken there by force and threat; some are taken by misrepresentation; others go because of family pressure; and some go voluntarily. Some juveniles in detention homes have violated the law.

In each case, the client's condition is defined by the institution. A physician labels the client as "mentally sick" or "ill." Once labeled, the client loses his autonomy and individuality, and his next of kin becomes responsible for him. In any institution, a dehumanizing process sets in. The client becomes a patient, ward, or inmate. His identity as a human being begins to erode, and certain rights are denied. For example, an institutionalized person cannot vote, have a bank account or drivers license, transact business, and so on (Goffman 1961; Szasz 1962).

Institutions expect their therapists to see these people in psychotherapy. Under such circumstances, a therapist must ask himself two questions. First, in such institutions, "whose agent is the therapist?" Is he the agent of the client or of the institution that has hired him and pays his salary (Szasz 1965, 1967)? Second, can the same principles and techniques of therapy that are applied to volunteer clients be applied to those clients who are incarcerated and whose basic rights have been taken from them?

In such institutional settings the social role of a therapist is different from his role in an outpatient setting or in private practice. Generally, it contradicts the social role of the patient, for there is an implicit conflict between the powerlessness of the patient and the legal-coercive power of the institution for which the therapist is an agent.

Some believe that this contradiction is not important for the therapist. A therapist is there to help the client and not to get involved in the social and political operations of the institution. The helpful intentions of the therapist, they believe, resolve the contradiction. However, anyone who has worked in such settings quickly learns that sooner or later (usually sooner) he has to side either with the client or with the institution. The choice is difficult to avoid because the conflict between the powerlessness of the patients and the (legal) coercive power of the institutions over its inmates soon begins to manifest itself in various ways (Szasz 1962; Berman and Segal 1982).

A therapist must resolve this issue. He cannot side with both the institution and the client. He may, however, act as an agent of the institution and of the patient at the same time. How would the therapist play a double role? On the one hand he would have to protect the interests of the institution that hired him, and therefore act against the interests of the client. On the other hand, he would have to side with the patient in the name of professionalism and the patient's welfare for which he is supposedly working (Szasz 1967). It is not easy for any therapist to resolve this contradiction. In the author's view, the best a therapist can do in such a situation is to explain clearly his position to the inmate—that in certain matters and up to a point the therapist will act as the patient's agent; beyond that point he will act as the agent of the institution. Obviously the social role of the therapist is crucial. If it is not clear, then the therapist may misrepresent his position and purpose either to the client or to the institution. Even in outpatient settings, the therapist's role must be clear to avoid conflicts and contradictions.

For example, a therapist may be working in an outpatient clinic which seems to have no affiliation with any other institution or agency. However, a judge in a juvenile court may give a suspended sentence to a youth, contingent upon his seeking therapy in an outpatient clinic. In this situation, the client is likely to view the therapist as an extension of the court system that has indirect power over him. The client will remain guarded and suspicious of the therapist unless the therapist clarifies his role to the client.

Little has been mentioned in the literature about whether the principles and techniques that apply to an outpatient can be applied to an institutionalized person. Usually the literature assumes that they can. The author cannot accept that because the assumptions of an institution and of psychotherapy are fundamentally antagonistic to each other. Psychotherapy is based upon the assumption that an individual is an active agent in generating his conflicts, and that he should also be active in resolving the conflicts. In an institution he is a coerced inmate and may not be able to activate the resolution of his troubles. For a psychotherapy client to change, he must enact his newly acquired behavior in society. In institutional settings, little opportunity exists for testing such behavior. Furthermore, institutions dehumanize patients, while the assumption of psychotherapy is that the client should develop autonomy as a human being. Any expression of autonomy in an institutional setting is taken as evidence of a patient's uncooperativeness toward the institution, and hence a further manifestation of his mental illness.

Fads, Fashions, and Social Prestige   Some people go to a therapist because it is in fashion. In the social circle of such clients it is prestigious to be in therapy. A more modern version of this phenomenon is the vogue of encounter groups, marathon groups, sensitivity groups, self-actualizing groups, and so on.

The therapy faddists do not suffer from serious personal troubles or anguish. They seek self-growth or actualization of their potential. These are not the main motives for the disturbed to seek therapy.

Those who seek therapy because of the social prestige usually come from an educated and well-to-do socioeconomic background. They do not go to therapy to eliminate their conflicts or to change their lives but to discover themselves. Their motivation to seek therapy is heavily influenced by their peers and the mores of their subculture, rather than by personal turmoil.

The task of a therapist with such clients is also different. His task is not to help reduce their conflicts, to resolve their dilemmas, or to clarify their confusions, but rather to facilitate self-discovery and to help them realize their potential. With such clients, the therapist acts as a mentor to help the client find self-enlightenment.

Male versus Female Clients

By now it is well known that more middle-class female adults go to therapy than male adults in an outpatient setting. Figures on the proportion of female to male outpatients vary, but they are approximately 65 percent female vs. 35 percent male, or roughly two to one (Veroff 1981).

The clientele of child guidance clinics, however, consists of a higher proportion of boys than girls. Most of the studies suggest a ratio of about two boys to one girl—a reversal of the ratio in the adult clinics (Gilbert 1957; Lessing and Shilling 1966; Ramsey-Klee and Eiduson 1969; Gove and Herb 1974; Marmor 1975). Many reasons may account for it.

First, young boys may find it difficult to acquire and maintain appropriate sexual role behavior; both at home and in school, young boys are enmeshed in a world dominated by females (Gove and Herb, 1974). Also, the parents, especially mothers, seem to show more annoyance with and less acceptance of so-called deviant behavior in boys than in girls. Such behavior includes a lack of persistence, distractibility, and hyperactivity (Shepard, Oppenheim and Mitchell 1966; Battle and

Lacey 1972). Similarly, in schools, disruption by boys rather than girls is more likely to elicit a reprimand (Serbian and O'Leary 1975).

Some authors have suggested aggressive behavior as another category of behavioral problem in the young child. Aggression in girls is more likely to assume a prosocial mode, whereas in boys aggression is more likely to be destructive (Feshbach 1970) and is therefore less acceptable by adults.

Hence for all these reasons (and many others) the females—mothers and teachers—are more likely to view the same disturbance as more pathological in males than in females. And since they are the primary source of referral and evaluation in epidemiological studies, there is the resultant excess of males with adjustment problems. (Eme 1980) Parents, especially mothers, may view male children, in contrast to female children, as unmanageable by their parents, and therefore take them to the child guidance clinic.

The reversal of the male-female proportion between child guidance clinics and adult outpatient clinics suggests that as children grow into adolescence and adulthood, social requirements, role expectations, and the demands of the contradictory social cultural forces become more difficult for the female to fulfill and resolve for a number of reasons.* First, there is a sudden narrowing of the female sexual role in adolescence and postadolescence because the female is restricted from engaging in activities that are deemed too masculine. For example, females who were once rewarded for academic success find, in adolescence, that they should not surpass men. Consequently, they come to fear success (Gove and Herb 1973), and they become more attuned to the negative consequences of academic and occupational success (Hoffman 1977). As the female adolescent starts to move into adult roles, she becomes aware that males are favored in society and starts experiencing the stress associated with the adult sex role (Peskin 1972; Gove and Herb 1973). Both of these factors engender feelings of diffidence and anxiety.

Second, females begin to perceive their roles as depending upon the actions of others, and therefore they experience uncertainty about their future. For a majority of females, the future adult role they

---

*Marmor's survey (1975) shows that ". . . beginning at age 15 there is a preponderance of females, a reflection perhaps of increasing, conflict-laden sexual pressures to which girls become subject at this age."

can most easily identify is that of wife and mother (Douvan and Adelson 1966; Conger 1977). The male role seems to be more tied up with an occupation or profession. Unlike an occupation, marriage is less a matter of simple individual choice; it is dependent upon actions of others and lies in some unspecified future time. Consequently, the female adolescent's adaptation is more difficult because she faces a more ambiguous task in adapting her present life and her self-concept to the future. Furthermore, with the traditional feminine role in a state of flux and transition, the assumption of future feminine identity is becoming even more ambiguous. Such sociocultural forces can generate a vague anxiety and a lack of self-assuredness with regard to one's personal identity.

Third, the physical changes of puberty cause more concern for the female than the male. Many females report shame and anxiety over menstruation. The female adolescent's concern about her sexuality is further exacerbated by the fact that only the female has to face the possibility of an unwanted pregnancy. This possibility, a primary worry for parents of girls, is communicated to them (Hoffman 1977).

The cultural emphasis on physical attractiveness is a further cause of concern. The overriding importance of appearance, which often outweighs all other concerns in adolescents, becomes a source of concern and anxiety. Female popularity is more closely related to physical attractiveness, and it causes them more concern than it does males (Berscheid and Walster 1975).

Fourth, the female adolescent begins to discover a double moral standard by which male and female behavior is judged. For example, after a quarrel with his wife, if a man goes out and picks up a woman from a bar and spends the night with her, his behavior might be "understandable" or condoned. If, however, the wife behaves in the same way, she will earn a label of impulsive "nymphomania." The double moral standard shuts many cultural doors and outlets for a female which remain open to a male.

Fifth, the cultural role and image of a female is that of a dependent and passive individual who needs assistance and help and for whom it is acceptable to seek help. Men are expected to be independent, aggressive, and outgoing individuals who do not or should not need any help.*

---

*Because of the feminist movement, the role of women in Western societies has changed. Many housewives feel unfulfilled in their role and want to find a job.

Most of the mental health facilities are available during the hours that are relatively more convenient for people not employed full time. For these and other reasons, many more women than men apply for therapy.

Ethnicity and Social Class

In psychotherapeutic literature and practice, the issue of ethnicity and social class is not clearly delineated. There are many reasons for it. First, in the United States a high percentage of ethnic minorities belong to the lower class. For this reason, some studies have simply assumed an equivalence of the two, that is white groups are high status, nonwhite groups low status (Kleiner et al. 1960).

Other studies, however, ignore class differences within the minority or ethnic groups. Such studies may compare the symptomatology of the clients of different groups—whites, blacks, orientals—ignoring or overlooking the socioeconomic status of the clients (Fitzgibbons, Culter and Cohen 1971). Thus, two separate but interacting variables have been generally confounded.

A second factor contributing to the lack of clarity in the issue of minorities and socioeconomic class is the source of data and how the data are obtained. Generally, data gathered on the basis of pencil and paper tests, questionnaires, surveys, and analogue studies tend to blur the differences between ethnic groups and/or class (Khaton and Carriera 1972; Wolkon, Moriwaki and Williams 1973; Smith 1974; Abramowitz and Dokecki 1977). A comparison of the analogue interviews with real therapy behavior (of the same therapist) shows that analogues were poor predictors of the real therapy behavior (Kushner et al. 1979). Studies done in real life situations generally tend to show differences.*

Jones (1978) has identified a third contributory factor:

In many studies therapy consists of a single, initial interview. . . . The fact that many critical changes occur between the first therapy session and subsequent

---

Some women, therefore, go to therapy complaining that their husbands do not allow them to work.

  *The Winston et al. study (1972) is an exception to this finding. In this study, white therapists treated both black and white patients in an inpatient setting. They found that black patients showed greater improvement than the white patients. It is noteworthy that most of the nursing staff on the ward was black. The effect of the interaction between the black staff and the black patient population is not controlled for in this study.

hours bears repetition since it raises serious questions about the studies, particularly investigations of the race in therapy that derive their data from the first hour or initial interview. Such studies are based upon a biased and narrow sample of events occuring in psychotherapy and their results cannot be generalized beyond the first encounter.

Interpretation of data is a fourth source of confusion. Authors use arbitrary criteria for determining success and/or failure in therapy, which makes it difficult to compare different studies and arrive at a general conclusion. For instance, in some studies if a client stays in therapy beyond the third session, therapy is counted as successful. If, however, the sixth session is used as the point to determine success or failure for the same set of data, then the picture changes significantly. Or, if the therapist encourages the client not to return or to go somewhere else, the case is not counted as a dropout in some studies, whereas in other studies it is (Fiester et al. 1974; Pettit et al. 1974; Craig and Huffine 1976; see also Chapter 6).

The final source of confusion is the way the concept of socioeconomic class is used in research studies. Generally, investigators have used Hollingshead's Index of Social Position (based upon area of residence, occupation, and education) to classify the clients in five classes. Classes IV and V are usually lumped together as lower class. Of the Class IV membership, half are semiskilled, a third skilled, and about a tenth are white-collar employees with less than high-school education. Skilled and semiskilled workers (blue-collar workers) belong to a union and are organized around their jobs. In contrast, members of Class V are usually unskilled or semiskilled workers who are nonunionized and have a grade-school education or less. They occupy the lowest occupational steps. Usually they are migrant workers, dishwashers, household workers, and so on. Class V consists mostly of ethnic minorities. Indeed, the socioeconomic distance between Class III (the lower middle class) and Class IV is about the same as between Class IV and V. Lumping Classes IV and V together creates an inaccurate picture of the lower class (Miller and Mishler 1964; Schubert and Miller 1980).

In this work, an attempt is made to sort out the interaction between the members of ethnic minorities and the therapists, and in the next section, between the members of various socioeconomic classes and the therapist.

Psychotherapy with Ethnic Clients It is generally recognized that minorities underutilize existing mental health facilities and services even when cost may not be a factor (Gordon 1965; Karno and Edgerton 1969; Torrey 1970; Mayo 1974; Padilla, Ruiz, and Alverez 1975; Sue and McKinney 1975). There are many reasons for minorities' underutilization of services. First are stereotypes held by practicing psychotherapists toward minority-group patients (Mexican-Americans, blacks, Japanese, Chinese, Jews, and others). Studies suggest that negative attitudes held by therapists toward minorities are the same, although less intense, as those found among the general public. These prejudices motivate therapists to establish and maintain social distance between themselves and the minority group patients (Bloombaum, Yamamoto, and Evans 1968; Crosby, Bromley, and Saxe 1980) and make it difficult to establish an intimate interpersonal relationship, which is basic to any form of psychotherapy (Padilla and Ruiz 1973).

Second, the institutional structure of the mental health services and treatment offered to the minority groups is such that it discourages them from exploring it further. As one observer states, "The White institution's lack of sensitivity and understanding of the Black person's life styles and coping mechanisms renders it ineffective in treating Black patients" (Fishman 1969).

Findings suggest that compared to Caucasian patients, minority-group patients (especially men) seen at outpatient clinics are diagnosed as more seriously ill, are discharged quicker, or are less frequently recommended for continued sessions (Jackson 1983). They are most often seen for minimal supportive psychotherapy or seen in emergency rooms, rather than in individual or group long-term therapy; and they are referred more often than white patients to ataractic medication (Gross, Herbert, Knatterud, and Donner 1969; Padilla, Ruiz, and Alverez 1975; Cole and Pilisuk 1976; Sue 1976). For these reasons, the ethnic clients drop out of therapy earlier than white clients (Yamamoto et al. 1967; Dodd 1970; Sue, McKinney, Allen, and Hall 1974; Sue and McKinney 1975; Sue 1977).*

Generally, psychiatrists or therapists seem to refer to therapy those persons who are most like themselves, that is, white rather than

---

*Tischler, Henisz, and Myers's (1975) report that "these findings suggest a diminished importance of social class and ethnicity as biases or barriers to the allocation of mental health services in the community" is one of the few exceptions to the conclusions mentioned above.

nonwhite, those in the upper rather than in lower-income range (Rosenthal and Frank 1958; Lowinger and Dobie 1968), and those with "fewest environmental (reality based) difficulties" (Cole and Pilisuk 1976). Third, the minority clients perceive the Anglo therapists as cold and insincere (Kline 1969) and feel alienated from and poorly understood by them (Warren et al. 1973).

Fourth, the cultural differences between the Anglo therapists and their ethnic minority clients, the divergent interpretation of the deviant behavior or mental illness, and the differences in attitudes toward mental illness are wide enough between the two groups that neither of them feels comfortable with each other. At best, these differences are likely to lead to mutual disappointment (Levine and Padilla 1980).

Reviews of the literature on black and white therapist-client relationships conclude that more positive relationships result when client and therapist are of the same group (black or white) (Sattler 1970; Siegel 1974). Gardner (1972) states

The studies reviewed . . . offer support for the clinical observation that biracial dyads may have greater difficulty in establishing an effective therapeutic alliance than similar race dyads. A general finding of these studies was that clients of a different race than their therapist tend to explore themselves least in an initial interview and develop less rapport with their therapist.

Sue and McKinney (1975) and Sue (1976) who worked mostly with Asian-Americans, Roll, Millen, and Martinez (1980) who worked with Chicanos, and Warren et al. (1973) who worked with blacks, state that cultural background of the client is an extremely important factor in psychotherapy. Sue (1977) goes so far as to state that "the persistent relationship between ethnicity and dropping out, despite controlling for the other eleven variables, indicates that ethnicity is an important correlate above and beyond the variables examined."

These general conclusions seem to be supported by other studies: that clients show a preference for counselors of the same ethnic background (Grantham 1973; Harrison 1975); that black clients report that they would more readily return to see black counselors than white counselors after an initial interview (Banks, Berenson, and Carkhuff 1967); that "race is related to understanding in counseling. Black counselors understand black counselees best" (Bryson and Cody 1973). Furthermore, clients of background, either black or white American, similar to the therapist's engage in greater self-exploration (Carkhuff and Pierce 1967; Banks 1972). Some authors state that "there is a need within the treatment sessions to acknowledge and discuss the social and political issues of racism. . . . Racism has a pervasive influence on the patients and how they view themselves" (Jones, Gray, and Jospitre 1982).

Although these findings seem to present convincing evidence, they are somewhat limited. Additional factors appear to be important in successful therapy with minorities. Gardner (1972) found that both the background and the experience of the therapist are the major factors that determine maximum counselor effectiveness with black students. Cimbolic (1972) found that experience is more important than skin color, that "black clients did not show a preference for the counselors as a function of race, but they showed a preference as a function of the counselors' experience levels."

Beside the background (black or white American) and the experience of the therapist, another variable emerges as important in successful therapy with minorities. In a study by Jones (1978), white and black therapists worked with black middle-class female clients. The success rates of black and white therapists with black clients were the same, although during the course of therapy, the topics discussed and the feelings that emerged differed according to whether the therapist was black or white. One reason for the similar results, he states, could be that the "white therapists in this study were a relatively select (not random) sample—they are especially distinct from their fellow therapists in their willingness to confront squarely the racial issues in their professional work." His findings include the following results.

The average scores for therapists' replies on the outcome questionnaire, which had been completed for each client, were found to be almost identical for each racial matching. Similarly, there were no significant differences in mean questionnaire scores on client's ratings of impression of therapy after ten hours. Finally, there were no differences in the client drop-out rate.*

Working with long-term lower-class blacks in the ghetto setting, Lerner (1972) and Lerner and Fiske (1973) found that the success rates

---

*Vail (1978) randomly assigned lower-class black clients (male and female) to ten therapists who were black or white, male or female. Fifty percent of the clients dropped out in the first three sessions. Among those who stayed, he found no significant relationship between the race of the therapist and continuation in therapy. Jones (1982) also states that "therapist-patient racial match has little influence on the outcome in longer-term therapy."

of black and white therapists were similar. In this study, the white therapists had volunteered to work in the ghetto and were open about their racial attitudes. These authors conclude that the reason for the similar rate of success for black and white therapists working with black clients was the therapist's openness to his own racial attitudes, his willingness and ability to examine himself on this issue, or the democratic values of the therapist and his willingness to work with lower-class and disturbed clients.

A study of the published reports on the therapeutic process of Anglo therapists working with ethnic minorities leads one to surmise that the counter-transference problems of the Anglo therapist usually begin to increase as therapy progresses, because of both the therapist and the client. The ethnic difference leads to divergence in interpretation of the same material by the therapist and the client; the therapist is then likely to become obtrusive or defensive. (See Chapter 9.) There may be more suspiciousness and guardedness among the ethnic minority clients toward the Anglo therapist (Rosen and Frank 1962; Sager, Brayboy, and Waxenberg 1972). The greater potential for the development of counter-transference between the Anglo therapist and the ethnic client has been mentioned by many writers (Fanon 1967; Block 1968; Vontress 1971; Jones and Seagull 1977). Turner and Armstrong's survey (1981) shows that "white therapists, however, reported higher level of subjective distress around race, during all phases of treatment: they felt unduly over-solicitious, less able to help black clients feel better about themselves, and less comfortable in confronting and working through a client's negative attitudes about therapy."

For these reasons, some have attempted to use a more "appropriate" model for the minority groups. Friedman (1966), for example, says,

I did pretty much forget (as much as possible) Freud, Sullivan, Rogers, Jung, et al., in some important aspects of my work with [a black client].

Instead, I used the creative documents of James Baldwin to help myself and her to better understand certain themes of the life history which she presented. . . . Baldwin points out that the Negro often reacts in terms of or against a stereotype promulgated by the dominant society, filtered through family and peers, and finally internalized by the Negro himself . . . [this in turn] . . . leads to a non-identification with one's own race, a hatred of that race, and eventually of oneself. . . . Lowered self-esteem, based upon this non-identification with other Negroes and a resulting sense of isolation and double alienation is another common result of the nigger phobia.

Karno and Morales (1971), Philippus (1971), Abad, Ramos, and Boyce (1974), Boulette (1975), and Heiman, Burruel, and Chavez (1975) have attempted to modify their approaches in working with the Chicano and Spanish-speaking communities. Besides using nontraditional approaches—including no waiting list, nonadherence to fifty-minute sessions, serving coffee—they found that the use of bilingual receptionists and therapists was a useful tool for success. Sue (1977) also recommends the hiring of ethnic specialists to serve as a bridge between the ethnic group and the institution. Some have suggested that to be effective with ethnic clients, mental health services should be established in ethnic neighborhoods (Levine and Padilla 1980). Sue and McKinney's 1975 study shows that

an Asian American counseling and referral service was recently started in Seattle, . . . this agency has in one year seen nearly the same number of Asian patients as did the seventeen community mental health facilities over a period of three years. The greater responsiveness of Asians to this agency appears to be due to widespread publicity, the use of bilingual therapists, and the ability of the therapist to understand the needs and lifestyle of Asians in the community.

Clearly, the process of therapy in mixed dyads is quite complex. Whether a therapist is a black or white American is not the sole determining factor in successful therapy, although it is an important factor. At least three other factors seem to emerge as significant in making therapy successful in mixed dyads: the experience of the therapist, the openness and examination by the therapist of his own prejudicial attitudes and positions, and the milieu or atmosphere of the setting where therapy is conducted. In a setting where the minority client is made to feel welcome and equal, the likelihood of success seems to increase.

Social Class and Psychotherapy   The weight of the existing evidence seems to show that "in diverse locales and settings, both inpatient and outpatient, there appears to be a consistent relationship between the type of treatment (psychotherapy versus physical treatment) and social class, with psychotherapy going to those of higher status" (Meltzoff and Kornreich 1970). After having reviewed the studies in this area, others have arrived at a similar conclusion.

The research literature indicates that persons from lower socioeconomic class backgrounds are less frequently accepted for treatment, are more likely to be assigned to inexperienced therapists and continue in therapy for a briefer period of time than their middle-class counterpart. All of this is undoubtedly related to the fact that therapists prefer clients who are intelligent, verbal, educated, and introspective. They consider lower-class clients to be undesirable or lacking in requisite attributes of candidates for psychotherapy (Jones 1978).

Freud (1924) was vaguely aware of the class nature of psychoanalysis (psychotherapy). Twice he touched upon this issue. In 1904, while describing "the conditions under which this method (psychoanalysis) is indicated or contraindicated," he said that "those patients who do not possess a reasonable degree of education and a fairly reliable character should be refused [therapy]. . . . It is gratifying that precisely the most valuable and highly developed persons are best suited for these curative measures. . . ." He discussed the limitation of psychoanalytic psychotherapy again in 1919. He stated that "the necessity of our own existence limits our work to the well-to-do classes. . . . We shall probably discover that the poor are even less ready to part with their neurosis than the rich, because the hard life that awaits them when they recover has no attraction, and illness in them gives them more claim to the help of others."

However, the theme of class bias of psychotherapy has not been explicitly dealt with by the psychoanalysts and psychotherapists who came after Freud. Over the years, therapists have begun to maintain that psychoanalysis and/or psychotherapy is independent of the social class and is also culture (ethnicity) free (Baum and Felzer 1964; Fierman 1965; Weiner 1975), since it deals with the unconscious conflicts of the individual. Studies during the past two decades, however, suggest that this assumption does not correspond to the findings.

There appear to be several reasons for therapists' difficulties with lower-class clients. First, therapists belong to the middle or upper middle class (Henry, Sims, and Spray 1971). Their *weltanschauung* is molded by their socioeconomic background and their educational achievements. Thus, therapists are usually not receptive to lower-class clients. "Generally, the lower socioeconomic patient with his poor motivation, lower intelligence, lack of education, chronicity of problem, etc., does not readily participate in the 'talking' process. This arouses resistance and rejection on the therapist's part which manifests itself in different ways" (Baum and Felzer 1964). In addition, therapists wittingly or unwittingly disapprove of the behavior of lower-class clients—for example, their crude language and apathetic response to treatment (Affleck and Garfield 1961).

Therapists also tend to "feel pessimistic, annoyed, bored, remote or anxious with the least privileged patient, and to like or feel liked by or become interested in the more privileged one" (Brody 1958). Such attitudes and outlooks tend to inhibit communication with lower-class clients, owing to lack of empathy or rapport (Schaffer and Myers 1954; Baum, Felzer, and D'Zmura 1966).

Therapists frequently complain that lower-class clients lack motivation for psychotherapy and do not possess "psychological mindedness" to be accepted for psychotherapy.* While it may be partially true that the lower class client does not have the same degree of motivation as a middle-class client, it is noteworthy that when therapists attribute lack of motivation to lower-class clients, they implicitly use a complex set of factors to arrive at that assessment. These factors appear to be biased in favor of the middle class. Generally, "education, occupational level, awareness of psychological difficulties, type of treatment expected (by the client viz. physical or psychological) and liking for the patient are significantly correlated with therapist ratings of motivation to get into therapy" (Raskin 1961).

Furthermore, when a therapist assesses the client's suitability for insight psychotherapy (in terms of the client's psychological mindedness), "he attends primarily to linguistic-symbolic or semiotic behavior of the prospective client—psychological mindedness seems to be a hypothetical construct reifying some of the language spoken by a person using the elaborate code or dialect" (Meltzer 1978). Meltzer's study shows that the higher the client's social class, the more likely he is to be judged suitable for insight psychotherapy by the therapist. Therapists were not aware of the fact that they made their assessments on the basis of the language used by the client. In other words, the criteria for judging the motivation for therapy and the suitability for therapy has a built-in class bias.

Lower-class clients are diagnosed as psychotic more frequently than middle-class clients, who are generally diagnosed as neurotic with better prognosis (Lee and Temerlin 1970). Lower-class clients are more likely to be dropped as failures (Myers and Roberts 1959), and

---

*Rosenbaum and Horowitz's study (1983) shows that motivation is neither a static nor a unidimensional construct. A factor analysis of the measure used in their study of patient motivation for psychotherapy revealed four factors: "Active Engagement, Psychological Mindedness, Incentive-Mediated Willingness to Sacrifice, and Positive Valuation of Therapy." See also Krause (1967), Sifneos (1968), and Keithley et al. (1980) on construct of motivation in therapy.

frequently the therapist perceives lower-class clients as "untreatable" (Heine and Trosman 1960). The therapist then avoids accepting the lower-class client in psychotherapy even when economics of treatment are inconsequential (Schaffer and Myer 1954; Brill and Storrow 1960; McMahon 1964; Adams and McDonald 1968). While in therapy, the middle- or upper-class client tends to stay longer than his lower-class counterpart (Auld and Myers 1954; Imber, Nash, and Stone 1955).

Contrary to these findings, at least two recent studies found that the

duration of psychiatric treatment measured by number of medication clinic visits, individual psychotherapy sessions and group psychotherapy sessions . . . was equivalent across income groups. . . . The poor were not shunted off into medication clinics. Individual psychotherapy proved to be the modal treatment for all income groups rather than the preserve of the more affluent (Edwards, Greene, Abramowitz, and Davidson 1979).

Stern (1977) also reported a lack of relationship between patient education and type of treatment offered.

For the most part, however, in institutional and/or outpatient settings, lower-class clients are less frequently assigned to individual therapy than upper-class clients (Schaffer and Myers 1954; Hollingshead and Redlich 1958; Yamamoto and Goin 1966; Myers and Bean 1968). Such a bias is not confined to any single diagnostic category. Working with outpatient and hospitalized schizophrenic patients, Schmidt, Smart, and Moss (1968) report that the higher the social class of the client, the greater the likelihood that individual psychotherapy will be recommended; and the lower the social class, the greater the likelihood of recommendation for drugs or physical therapy. Indeed, there appears to be a significant relationship between educational level, occupation, and assignment to psychotherapy (Rosenthal and Frank 1958; Sullivan, Miller, and Smelser 1958). Other studies support the finding that lower-class clients of all diagnostic categories are most likely to be assigned to some form of somatic treatment or inpatient treatment, or referred elsewhere (Hollingshead and Redlich 1958; Bailey, Warshaw, and Eichler 1960; Yamamoto and Goin 1966; Lubin, Hornstra, Lewis, and Bechtel 1973).

The attrition rate for low-income clients in individual therapy was found to be significantly higher than for the middle and upper classes (Kamin and Caughlan 1963; Terestman, Miller, and Weber 1974). Patients with low socioeconomic status terminate therapy prematurely significantly more often than the patients from higher socioeconomic status levels (Dengrove and Kutash 1950; Winder and Hersko 1955; Sullivan, Miller, and Smelser 1958; Stern et al. 1975).

Some authors hypothesize that the poor rate of success of psychotherapy with lower-class clients may be due to their unrealistic beliefs about what the therapist will do and how long treatment will take, indicating that the clients are not attuned to the realities of traditional psychotherapy (Lorion 1974; Heitler 1973). Levitt (1966) sums up these misconceptions by suggesting that the expectations of a certain group of clients (mostly lower class) are more appropriate for a general medical practitioner. The patient expects that the treatment will take from five to ten hours, that he will experience a significant relief of symptoms in a few hours, and that the therapist will be directive and actively probing, will find out what is wrong with him, and will offer remedies. The patient sees himself as relatively passive. All of the patient's expectations clash with those of the therapist.

Because of such findings, attempts have been made to bridge the attitudinal gap between the middle-class therapist and the lower-class client. Four suggestions have been put forth to this end. First, because events that result in a negative outcome occur early in therapy, it is recommended that the initial stages of therapy should be considered carefully. Early sessions of therapy were used by social workers to help applicants formulate problems and treatment goals and to explain the nature of therapy and the role of the participant (Albronda, Dean, and Starkweather 1964). Others have tried to prepare lower-class clients for short-term individual therapy through "role induction interviews" designed to help clients develop accurate therapy expectations and to teach them to participate productively in therapy (Hoehn-Sarik et al. 1964; Nash et al. 1965). Under both of these conditions, according to the authors, a significant improvement in the duration and outcome of therapy was noted.

To enhance the chances of success in therapy with lower-class clients, variations in these techniques have also been used in group therapy. Strupp and Bloxom (1973) used a role induction film addressed specifically to lower-class patients who were assigned to group therapy. Heitler (1973) used "anticipatory socialization interviews" geared to fostering realistic expectations about group therapy. Both of these studies report quantitative and qualitative differences in prepared patients.

The second approach recognizes the general unreceptive attitude of the middle-class therapist toward lower-class clients. This approach attempts to train the therapist to recognize and deal with his own attitudes. It is believed that an awareness and an open discussion of the negative and resistant attitude of the therapist would facilitate therapeutic relationships and hold lower-class clients longer in therapy than otherwise. The authors have reported success with this method (Miller and Mishler 1964; Frank 1961; Bernard 1965).

The third approach suggests that certain therapeutic methods and techniques lead to a more successful treatment for the blue-collar workers. These methods include a more directive approach, informality and an easy rapport, establishing contact on a nonverbal level, flexibility in the length of session, and so on (Gould 1967).

The fourth approach emphasizes the personality characteristics of the therapist as important variables in bridging the gap. Therapist's skills (Terestman et al. 1974; Siassi and Messer 1976) and a broad clinical experience (Baum et al. 1966) have been mentioned as two significant variables for success with the lower class. Studies on the middle-class therapist working with lower-class clients in a ghetto setting conclude that the most important variable in success was in the democratic or nonauthoritarian values of the therapist (Lerner 1972; Lerner and Fiske 1973).

Ideology of Psychotherapy

Despite the successes reported by the role induction interview and other methods with lower-class clients, enough direct and indirect evidence suggests that the acceptance of middle-class orientation and ideology is a necessary condition for going to and being accepted into psychotherapy (Goldstein 1973; Terestman, Miller, and Weber 1974). When the lower socioeconomic level clients had a steady job, could afford to pay for therapy (on a sliding scale), could state their preference for the kind of therapist they wanted to work with in therapy, and came for psychotherapy rather than for drugs, their success rate was about the same as for any other group (Pettit et al. 1974). In other words, the more the lower-class client embraces a middle-class ideology, the better his chances of success. It is, therefore, not entirely coincidental that the characteristics regarded as implying a good prognosis for psychotherapy also tend to be the cardinal virtues of the middle class (Lowe 1969).

Studies directly comparing middle- and lower-class clients, however, do not support the findings that role induction, a pretherapy training of lower-class clients, shows much enduring success. Goldstein (1971) found that the methods and techniques more useful in enhancing "therapeutic attraction" for middle-class clients were not successful for lower-class clients. He states,

The results of this research program were remarkably consistent. Almost every procedure worked successfully to increase the attraction of YAVIS (young, attractive, verbal, intelligent, successful; i.e., the middle class) patients to their therapist; almost every procedure failed to do so with non-YAVIS (lower-class) patients. . . . Our research program may be viewed as but one more example of the manner in which the technology of contemporary psychotherapy is a middle-class technology. Two of our extended extrapolations (to increase the therapeutic attractiveness for the lower-class patient) that were partially successful did involve hospitalized patients who in many ways were more YAVIS-like than non-YAVIS. (Goldstein 1973)

The moral-valuative assumptions of psychotherapy are essentially middle class in nature. They are: adjustment and conformity, control of events and problem solving, value of work, control of emotions, planning ahead, striving and achievement, thrift and accumulation of wealth (Davis, 1938; Gursslin, Hunt, and Roach 1959; see also Chapter 3).

Additionally, the ideological thrust of the publicity and the image of the mental health movement does not support the lower-class outlook and ideology. Rather,

The content analysis of the mental health pamphlets addressed to the general public indicate certain basic parallels between the mental health content and the middle-class orientation on one hand, and a disjunction between this content and the lower-class orientation on the other. The middle-class prototype and the mentally healthy are in many respects equivalent; and the mental health movement contributes to the maintenance and persistence of the middle-class socio-cultural structure by providing authoritative and specific support to the middle-class values and orientation (Gursslin, Hunt, and Roach 1959).

It should be noted that the ideology of psychotherapy is individualistic in nature; it deals with the individual—the self-cultivation and self-expression of the individual; it deals with personal ego. It is not a collectivist ideology in that it does not deal with social and/or shared experiences; it does not encourage the individual to subordinate his needs or interests to those of others, to someone or to some cause or tradition outside himself (Hinton 1975; Lasch 1979). Rather, it teaches its clients to leave the problems and troubles of other people alone by saying, "It is his problem." It does not focus upon social conflicts and contradictions which generate individual conflicts. Indeed, it takes social contradictions and conditions as given and good, which should be accepted as they are. Any questioning of the social order or a critical discussion thereof is itself taken as evidence of a need for therapy, or as a defense against one's personal problems.

A growing analysis of class and ethnic aspects of psychotherapy has led some radical therapists within the field to advocate that psychotherapy is nontherapeutic, that it is a device to adjust the person to the status quo, and that one should cease practicing psychotherapy and even refrain from referring people for psychotherapy. They maintain that therapy should mean a change of the social institutions and the social structure, for these institutions generate psychological conflicts in the individual. They believe that only radical therapy can be beneficial to people (Agel 1971; Brown 1971).

The traditionalists, on the other hand, have either ignored or denied all such criticisms of the enterprise of psychotherapy. They have pointed to their own therapeutic successes with "sick" people, and to various studies, as evidence of the beneficial nature of psychotherapy regardless of the class and ethnic background of the client.

As this discussion has attempted to show, the enterprise of psychotherapy has definite limitations. Its effectiveness can be defined by certain social boundaries. Owing to its underlying assumptions and its very ideology, it applies far more readily to the middle class than to the lower classes. According to a 1973 American Psychiatric Association report, a typical patient is female (62 percent of all such patients), white (97 percent), middle-class, and neurotic (Gross 1978). Thus, the enterprise of psychotherapy has been successful in helping to resolve the troubles and turmoils of the middle class. It has also been successful in helping members of this class adjust to the given society. It has provided them with acceptable explanations of their personal troubles and even the troubles of society which may be bothersome to the members of this class (Sharma 1977). Thus, it has provided an important service to the members of its own class, and has served them well.

Summary

Generally, a therapist works with four kinds of clients: those who seek therapy voluntarily; those who go under duress and coercion; the institutionalized clients; and those who seek therapy for personal growth rather than to resolve personal conflicts. The role relationship of a therapist is different with clients in each category and should be clearly understood by the therapist.

Before a client goes to a therapist, he goes through a series of steps. He has to formulate his troubles in a certain way for the process of psychotherapy; he reads about his troubles, discusses them with others, and frequently tries to somatize them. Only when such efforts fail to resolve his conflicts does a person go to a therapist.

Problems of minorities and socioeconomic class are important in psychotherapy. Clients whose ethnic background or socioeconomic class differ significantly from the therapist's are likely to present attitudes and behavior with which a therapist may not be familiar. Thus the therapist has difficulty in empathizing and feeling comfortable with them. These clients tend to drop out of therapy sooner than the white, middle-class clients.

Contrary to prevailing belief, psychotherapy has an ideology. It presents a *weltanschauung* to the client. The ideology of psychotherapy is individualistic in nature; it encourages the cultivation of self and preaches a middle-class value structure. Within this ideological framework, psychotherapy is a useful institution in society.

References

Abad, V., J. Ramos, and E. Boyce. 1974. A model for delivery of mental health services to Spanish-speaking minorities. *American Journal of Orthopsychiatry* 44:584–95.

Abramowitz, C. B., and P. R. Dokecki. 1977. The politics of clinical judgment: Early empirical returns. *Psychological Bulletin*, 84:460–76.

Adams, P. L., and N. F. McDonald. 1968. Clinical cooling out of the poor people. *American Journal of Orthopsychiatry* 38:457–63.

Affleck, C., and S. L. Garfield. 1961. Predictive judgments of therapists and duration of stay in psychotherapy. *Journal of Clinical Psychology* 17:134–37.

Agel, J. 1971. *The radical therapist*. New York: Ballantine Books.

Albronda, H. F., R. L. Dean, and J. A. Starkweather. 1964. Social class and psychotherapy. *Archives of General Psychiatry* 10:276–83.

Auld, F., and J. Myers. 1954. Contributions to a theory for selecting psychotherapy patients. *Journal of Clinical Psychology* 10:56–60.

Bailey, M. A., L. Warshaw, and R. M. Eichler. 1960. Patients screened and criteria used for selecting psychotherapy cases in a mental hygiene clinic. *Journal of Nervous and Mental Disease* 130:72–77.

Banks, W. M. 1972. The differential effects of race and social class in helping. *Journal of Clinical Psychology* 28:90–92.

Banks, W. M., B. F. Berenson, and R. R. Carkhuff. 1967. The effects of counselor race and training upon counseling process with negro clients in initial interviews. *Journal of Clinical Psychology* 23:70–72.

Battle, E., and B. A. Lacey. 1972. Context for hyperactivity in children over time. *Child Development* 43:757–72.

Baum, O., and S. Felzer. 1964. Activity in initial interviews with lower social class patients. *Archives of General Psychiatry* 10:345–53.

Baum, O. E., S. B. Felzer, T. L. D'Zmura, and E. Schumaker. 1966. Psychotherapy, drop-outs and lower socio-economic patients. *American Journal of Orthopsychiatry* 36:629–35.

Begley, E. C., and L. R. Lieberman. 1970. Patients' expectations of therapists' techniques. *Journal of Clinical Psychology* 26:113–16.

Berman, E., and R. Segal. 1982. The captive client: Dilemmas of psychotherapy in the psychiatric hospital. *Psychotherapy: Theory, Research and Practice* 19:31–42.

Bernard, V. W. 1965. Some principles of dynamic psychiatry in relation to poverty. *American Journal of Psychiatry* 122:254–67.

Berscheid, E., and E. Walster. 1975. Physical attractiveness. In L. Berkowitz, ed., *Advances in experimental social psychology*, vol. 8. New York: Academic Press. 1975.

Bloch, J. B. 1968. The white worker and the negro client in psychotherapy. *Social work* 13(2):36–42.

Bloombaum, M., J. Yamamoto, and R. Evans. 1968. Cultural stereotypes among psychotherapists. *Journal of Consulting and Clinical Psychology* 32:99.

Boulette, T. R. 1975. Group therapy with low income Mexican Americans. *Social Work* 20:403–4.

Brill, N., and H. Storrow. 1960. Social class and psychiatric treatment. *Archives of General Psychiatry* 3:340–44.

Brody, E. B. 1968. Status and role influence on initial interview behavior in psychiatric patients. In S. Lessee, ed., *An evaluation of the results of psychotherapies*, Springfield: Thomas. 269–79.

Brown, P., ed. 1971. *Radical psychology*. New York: Harper and Row.

Bryson, S., and J. Cody. 1973. Relationship of race and level of understanding between counselor and client. *Journal of Counseling Psychology* 6:495–98.

Carkhuff, R. R., and R. M. Pierce. 1967. The differential effects of therapist's race and class upon patient's depth of self exploration in initial clinical interviews. *Journal of Consulting Psychology* 31:632–34.

Cimbolic, R. 1972. Counselor race and experience effects on black clients. *Journal of Consulting and Clinical Psychology* 40:328–32.

Clausen, J. 1981. Stigma and mental disorders: Phenomenon and terminology. *Psychiatry* 44:287–97.

Cole, J., and M. Pilisuk. 1976. Differences in the provision of the mental health services by race. *American Journal of Orthopsychiatry* 46:510–25.

Conger, J. 1977. *Adolescence and youth*. New York: Harper and Row.

Craig, T. J., and C. L. Huffine. 1976. Correlates of patient attendance in an inner city mental health center. *American Journal of Psychiatry* 133(1):61–65.

Crosby, F., S. Bromley, and L. Saxe. 1980. Recent unobtrusive studies of black and white discrimination and prejudice: A literature review. *Psychological Bulletin* 88: 546–63.

Cummings, N. A. 1977. The anatomy of psychotherapy under national health insurance. *American Psychologist* 9:711–18.

Davis, K. 1938. Mental hygiene and the class structure. *Psychiatry* 1:55–65.

Dengrove, E., and S. B. Kutash. 1950. Why patients discontinue treatment in a mental hygiene clinic. *American Journal of Psychotherapy* 4:457–72.

Derogatis, L. R., L. Covi, R. S. Lipman, D. M. Davis, and K. Rickeles. 1971. Social class and race as mediator variables in neurotic symptomatology. *Archives of General Psychiatry* 25:31–40.

Derogatis, L. R., H. Yeuzeroff, and B. Wittlesberger. 1975. Social class, psychological disorder, and the nature of the psychopathological indicator. *Journal of Consulting and Clinical Psychology* 43:183–91.

Dodd, J. 1970. A retrospective analysis of variables related to duration of treatment in a university psychiatric clinic. *The Journal of Mental and Nervous Disease* 151:75–84.

Douvan, E., and J. Adelson. 1966. *The adolescent experience*. New York: Wiley.

Edwards, D. W., L. R. Greene, S. I. Abramowitz, and C. V. Davidson. 1979. National health insurance, psychotherapy, and the poor. *American Psychologist* 5:411–19.

Eme, R. F. 1980. Sex differences in childhood psychopathology: A review. *Psychological Bulletin* 3:574–95.

Enright, J. 1975. One step forward: Situational techniques for altering motivation for therapy. *Psychotherapy: Theory, Research and Practice* 4:344–48.

Fanon, F. 1967. *Black skin, white masks*. New York: Grove Press.

Feshbach, S. 1970. Aggression. In P. Mussen, ed., *Carmichael's manual of child psychology*, vol. 2. New York: Wiley.

Fierman, L. B. 1965. Myths in the practice of psychotherapy. *Archives of General Psychiatry* 12:408–14.

Fiester, A. R., A. R. Mahrer, L. M. Giambra, and D. W. Ormiston. 1974. Shaping a clinical population: The drop-out problem reconsidered. *Community Mental Health Journal* 10:173–79.

Fishman, J. 1969. Poverty, race and violence. *American Journal of Psychotherapy* 23(4):599–607.

Fitzgibbons, D. J., R. Cutler, and J. Cohen. 1971. Patients' self-perceived treatment needs and their relationship to background variables. *Journal of Consulting and Clinical Psychology* 39:253–58.

Framo, J. L. 1978. The friendly divorce. *Psychology Today* (February): 77–79, 100–102.

Frank, J. D. 1961. *Persuasion and healing: A comparative study of psychotherapy*. New York: Schoeken Books.

Frank, J. D., L. H. Gliedman, S. D. Imber, B. H. Nash, and P. R. Stone. 1957. Why patients leave psychotherapy. *Archives of Neurological Psychiatry* 77:283–99.

Freud, S. 1924. On psychotherapy. In *Collected Papers*, vol. 1, 257–59. London: Hogarth Press.

———. 1924. Turnings in the ways of psychoanalytic psychotherapy. In *Collected Papers*, vol. 2, 401–2. London: Hogarth Press.

Friedman, M. 1966. James Baldwin and psychotherapy. *Psychotherapy: Theory, Research and Practice* 3:177–83.

Gardner, W. E. 1972. The differential effects of race, education and experience in helping. *Journal of Clinical Psychology* 28:87–89.

Gendlin, E. T. 1961. Initiating psychotherapy with unmotivated patients. *Psychiatric Quarterly* 35:135–39.

Gilbert, G. 1957. A survey of referral problems in metropolitan child guidance centers. *Journal of Clinical Psychology* 13:37–42.

Goffman, E. 1961. *Asylums*. Garden City: Anchor Books.

Goldstein, A. 1973. *Structured learning therapy*. New York: Academic Press, 24.

———. 1971. *Therapeutic attraction*. New York: Pergamon Press.

Gordon, S. 1965. Are we seeing the right patients? Guild guidance intake: The sacred cow. *American Journal of Orthopsychiatry* 35:131–37.

Gould, R. E. 1967. Dr. Strangeclass: Or how I stopped worrying about the theory and began treating the blue collar worker. *American Journal of Orthopsychiatry* 37:78–86.

Gove, W. R., and T. Herb. 1974. Stress and mental illness among the young: A comparison of the sexes. *Social Forces* 53:256–63.

Gove, W. R., and J. F. Tudor. 1973. Sex roles and mental illness. *American Journal of Sociology* 4:872–35.

Grantham, R. J. 1973. Effects of counselor's sex, race, and language style on black students in initial interviews. *Journal of Counseling Psychology* 6:553–59.

Griffith, M. S. 1977. The influence of race on the therapeutic relationship. 1:27–40.

Gross, H. S., M. R. Herbert, G. Knatterud, and L. Donner. 1969. The effect of race and sex on the variation of diagnosis and disposition in a psychiatric emergency room. *The Journal of Nervous and Mental Disease* 148:638–42.

Gross, M. L. 1978. *The psychological society*. New York: Random House.

Gurin, G., J. Veroff, and S. Feld. 1960. *Americans view their mental health*. New York: Basic Books.

Gursslin, O. R., R. G. Hunt, and J. L. Roach. 1959–60. Social class and the mental health movement. *Social Problems* 3(Winter):210–18.

Harrison, D. K. 1975. Race as a counselor—Client variable in counseling and psychotherapy: A review of the research. *The Counseling Psychologist* 5:124–33.

Heiman, E., C. Burruel, and N. Chavez. 1975. Factors determining effective outpatient treatment for Mexican Americans. *Hospital and Community Psychiatry* 26:515–17.

Heine, R. W., and H. Trasman. 1960. Initial expectations of the doctor-patient interaction as a factor in continuance in psychotherapy. *Psychiatry* 23:275–78.

Heitler, J. B. 1973. Preparation of lower-class patients for expressive group psychotherapy. *Journal of Consulting and Clinical Psychology* 41:251–60.

Henry, W. E., J. H. Sims, and S. L. Spray. 1971. *The fifth profession*. San Francisco: Jossey-Bass.

Hinton, W. 1975. Interview with Chou-en Lai. *New China* 2(Summer):75–77.

Hoehn-Sarik, R., J. D. Frank, S. S. Imber, E. H. Nash, A. R. Stone, and C. L. Battle. 1964. Systematic preparation of patients for psychotherapy. *Journal of Psychiatric Research* 2:267–81.

Hoffman, L. W. 1977. Changes in family roles, socialization and sex differences. *American Psychologist* 32:644–57.

Hollingshead, A. B., and F. C. Redlich. 1958. *Social class a mental illness*. New York: John Wiley and Sons.

Howard, K. I., and D. E. Orlinsky. 1972. Psychotherapeutic process. In P. Mussen and M. Rosenzweig eds., *Annual Review of Psychology*. Palo Alto: Annual Reviews Inc., 623.

Imber, S. D., E. H. Nash, and A. R. Stone. 1955. Social class and duration of psychotherapy. *Journal of Clinical Psychology* 11:281–84.

Jackson, A. M. 1973. Psychotherapy: Factors associated with the race of the therapist. *Psychotherapy: Theory, Research and Practice* 10:273–77.

Jackson, A. M. 1983. Treatment issues for black patients. *Psychotherapy: Theory, Research and Practice* 20:143–52.

Jones, A., and A. Seagull. 1977. Dimensions of the relationship between the black client and the white therapist. *American Psychologist* 12:850–55.

Jones, B. E., B. Gray, and J. Jospitre. 1982. Survey of psychotherapy with black men. *American Journal of Psychiatry* 139:1174–77.

Jones, E. E. 1978. Effects of race on psychotherapy process and outcome: An exploratory investigation. *Psychotherapy: Theory, Research and Practice* 3:226–36.

Jones, E. E. 1982. Psychotherapists' impressions of treatment outcome as a function of race. *Journal of Clinical Psychology* 38:722–31.

Kadushin, C. 1969. *Why people go to psychiatrists*. New York: Atherton Press.

Kamin, I., and J. Caughlan. 1963. Subjective experiences of outpatient psychotherapy. *American Journal of Psychotherapy* 17:660–68.

Karno, M., and R. Edgerton. 1969. Perception of mental illness in a Mexican American community. *Archives of General Psychiatry* 20:233–38.

Karno, M., and A. A. Morales. 1971. Community mental health services in a metropolis. *Comprehensive Psychiatry* 12:115–21.

Keithley, L., S. Samples, and H. Strupp. 1980. Patient motivation as a predictor of process and outcome in psychotherapy. *Psychotherapy and Psychosomatics* 33:87–97.

Khaton, O. M., and R. P. Carriera. 1972. An attitude study of minority group adolescents toward mental health. *Journal of Youth and Adolescence* 1:131–40.

Kleiner, R. J., J. Tuckman, and M. Lavell. 1960. Mental disorders and status based on race. *Psychiatry* 23:271–74.

Kline, L. Y. 1969. Some factors in the psychiatric treatment of Spanish Americans. *American Journal of Psychiatry* 126:1664–81.

Krause, M. S. 1967. Behavioral index of motivation for treatment. *Journal of Counseling Psychology* 14(5):426–35.

Kulka, R., J. Veroff, and L. Douvan. 1979. Social class and the use of professional help for personal problems: 1957 and 1976. *Journal of Health and Social Behavior* 20:2–17.

Kushner, K., E. Bordin, and E. Ryan. 1979. Comparison of Strupp & Jenkins audiovisual therapy analogues and real psychotherapy interviews. *Journal of Consulting and Clinical Psychology* 47:765–67.

Lasch, C. 1979. *The culture of narcissism*. New York: W. W. Norton and Company, 13.

Lee, S. D., and M. K. Temerlin. 1970. Social class, diagnosis and prognosis for psychotherapy. *Psychotherapy: Theory, Research and Practice* 3:181–85.

Lerner, B. *Therapy in the ghetto*. 1972. Baltimore: Johns Hopkins University Press.

Lerner, B., and D. E. Fiske. 1973. Client attributes and the eye of the beholder. *Journal of Consulting and Clinical Psychology* 40:272–77.

Lessing, E. E., and F. H. Schilling. 1966. Relationship between treatment selection variables and treatment outcome in a child guidance clinic: An application of data processing methods. *Journal of American Academy of Child Psychiatry* 5:313–48.

Levine, E. S., and A. S. Padilla. 1980. *Crossing cultures in therapy*. Monterey: Brooks/Cole Publishing Company.

Levitt, E. 1966. Psychotherapy research and the expectation-reality discrepancy. *Psychotherapy: Theory, Research and Practice* 3:163–66.

Lorion, R. P. 1973. Socioeconomic status and traditional treatment approaches reconsidered. *Psychological Bulletin* 79:263–73.

Lowe, C. M. 1969. *Value orientation in counseling and psychotherapy*. Cranston: Carrol Press.

Lowinger, R., and S. Dobie. 1968. Attitudes of psychiatrist about patient. *Comprehensive Psychiatry*, 9:627–32.

Lubin, B., R. K. Hornstra, R. V. Lewis, and B. Bechtel. 1973. Correlates of initial treatment assignment in a community mental health center. *Archives of General Psychiatry* 29:497–500.

Marmor, J. 1975. Psychiatrists and their patients. Joint Information Services of the American Psychiatric Association and the National Association for Mental Health. Washington, D.C., 116.

Mayo, J. A. 1974. The significance of socio-cultural variables in the psychiatric treatment of black outpatients. *Comprehensive Psychiatry* 6:471–82.

McMahon, J. T. 1964. Working class psychiatric patient. In F. Reissman, J. Cohen, and A. Pearl, eds. *Mental health of the poor*, 283–303. New York: Free Press.

McSweeny, A. M. 1977. Including psychotherapy in national health insurance. *American Psychologist* 9:722–30.

Meltzoff, J., and M. Kornreich. 1970. *Research in psychotherapy*. 244. New York: Atherton Press.

Meltzer, J. D. 1978. A semiotic approach to suitability for psychotherapy. *Psychiatry* 4:360–77.

Miller, S. M., and E. G. Mishler. 1964. Social class, mental illness and American psychiatry: An expository review. In R. Riessman, J. Cohen, and A. Pearl, eds., *Mental health of the poor*, 16–37. New York: Free Press.

Moore, R. A., E. P. Benedek, and J. G. Wallace. 1963. Social class, schizophrenia and the psychiatrist. *American Journal of Psychiatry* 120:217–20.

Myers, J. K., and L. L. Bean. 1968. *A decade later*. New York: John Wiley.

Myers, J. K., and B. H. Roberts. 1959. *Family and class dynamics in mental illness*. New York: John Wiley, 223.

Nash, E. H., R. Hoehn-Sarik, C. C. Battle, A. R. Stone, S. D. Imber, and J. D. Frank. 1965. Systematic preparation of patients for short-term psychotherapy. II. Relation to characteristics of patient, therapist, and the psychotherapeutic process. *Journal of Nervous and Mental Disease* 140:374–83.

Olbrisch, M. D. 1977. Psychotherapeutic intervention in physical health. *American Psychologist* 9:761–77.

Padilla, A. M., and R. A. Ruiz. 1973. *Latino mental health: A review of the literature*. Washington, D.C.: U.S. Government Printing Office.

Padilla, A. M., R. A. Ruiz, and R. Alverez. 1975. Community mental health services for the Spanish/speaking surnamed population. *American Psychologist* 9:892–905.

Peskin, H. 1972. Multiple prediction of adult psychological health from preadolescent and adolescent behavior. *Journal of Consulting and Clinical Psychology* 38:155–60.

Pettit, I. B., T. F. Pettit, and J. Welkowitz. 1974. Relationship between values, social class and duration of psychotherapy. *Journal of Consulting and Clinical Psychology* 42:482–90.

Philippus, M. J. 1971. Successful and unsuccessful approaches to mental health services for an Hispano-American population. *Journal of Public Health* 61:820–30.

Rabkin, J. 1972. Opinions about mental illness: A review of the literature. *Psychological Bulletin* 77:153–71.

Raimy, V. *Misunderstandings of the self*. 1975. San Francisco: Jossey-Bass.

Ramsey-Klee, D. M., and B. T. Eiduson. 1969. A comparative study of two child guidance clinic populations. *Journal of American Academy of Child Psychiatry* 8:493–516.

Raskin, A. 1961. Factors therapists associate with motivation to enter psychotherapy. *Journal of Clinical Psychology* 17:62–65.

Redlich, F. C., A. B. Hollingshead, and E. Bellis. 1955. Social class differences in attitude toward psychiatry. *American Journal of Orthopsychiatry* 25:60–70.

Robinson, A. H., F. C. Redlich, and J. Myers. 1954. Social structure and psychiatric treatment. *American Journal of Orthopsychiatry* 24:307–16.

Roll, S., L. Millen, and R. Martinez. 1980. Common errors in psychotherapy with Chicanos: Extrapolation from research and clinical experience. Psychotherapy: *Theory, Research and Practice* 17:158–68.

Rosen, H., and J. D. Frank. 1962. Negroes in psychotherapy. *American Journal of Psychiatry* 119:456–60.

Rosen, J. C., and A. N. Wiens. 1979. Changes in medical problems and use of medical services following psychological intervention. *American Psychologist* 5:420–31.

Rosenbaum, R., and M. Horowitz. 1983. Motivation for psychotherapy: A factorial and conceptual analysis. *Psychotherapy: Theory, Research and Practice* 20:346–54.

Rosenthal, D., and J. D. Frank. 1958. The fate of psychiatric clinic outpatients assigned to psychotherapy. *Journal of Nervous and Mental Disease* 127:330–43.

Ryan, W., ed. 1969. *Distress in the city*. Cleveland: The Press of Case-Western Reserve University, 17–18, 175.

Sager, C., T. Brayboy, and B. Waxenberg. 1972. Black patient–white therapist. *American Journal of Orthopsychiatry* 42:415–23.

Sarbin, T. R., and J. D. Mancuso. 1970. Failure of a moral enterprise: Attitudes of the public toward mental illness. *Journal of Consulting and Clinical Psychology* 35:159–73.

Sattler, J. M. 1970. Racial experimental effects. In experimentation, testing, interviewing and psychotherapy. *Psychological Bulletin* 73:137–60.

Schaffer, L., and J. K. Myers. 1954. Psychotherapy and social stratification. *Psychiatry* 17:83–93.

Scheff, T. F. 1966. *Being mentally ill*. Chicago: Aldine.

Schmidt, W., R. G. Smart, and M. K. Moss. 1968. *Social class and treatment of alcoholism*. Toronto: University of Toronto Press.

Schofield, W. 1964. *Psychotherapy, the purchase of friendship*. Englewood Cliffs, N.J.: Prentice Hall.

Schonfield, J., A. R. Stone, R. Hoehn-Sarik, S. R. Imber, and S. K. Pande. 1969. Patient-therapist convergence and measure of improvement in short-term psychotherapy. *Psychotherapy: Theory, Research and Practice* 6:267–72.

Schubert, D. S., and S. I. Miller. 1980. Differences between the lower social classes: Some new trends. *American Journal of Orthopsychiatry* 50:712–17.

Serbian, L., and D. O'Leary. 1975. How nursery schools teach girls to shut up. *Psychology Today* (December):57–58.

Sharma, S. L. 1970. An historical background of the development of nosology in psychiatry and psychology. *American Psychologist* 25:248–53.

———. 1977. *Psychology and ideology*. Paper presented at meeting of the American Psychological Association, San Francisco.

Shepard, M., B. Oppenheim, and S. Mitchell. 1966. Childhood behavior disorders and the child guidance clinic: An epidemiological study. *Journal of Child Psychology and Psychiatry* 7:39–52.

Siassi, I., and S. B. Messer. 1976. Psychotherapy with patients from lower socio-economic groups. *American Journal of Psychotherapy* 30:29–40.

Siegel, J. M. 1974. A brief overview of the effect of race in clinical services interaction. *American Journal of Orthopsychiatry* 44:555–62.

Sifneos, P. 1968. The motivational process: A selection for prognostic criteria for psychotherapy of short duration. *Psychiatric Quarterly* 42:271–80.

Smith, M. L. 1974. Influence of client sex and ethnic group on counselor judgment. *Journal of Counseling Psychology* 21:516–21.

Srole, L., T. S. Langer, S. T. Michael, M. K. Opler, and T. A. Rennie. 1962. *Mental health in the metropolis*, vol. 1. New York: McGraw-Hill.

Steiper, R. S., and D. N. Weiner. 1965. *Dimensions of psychotherapy*. Chicago: Aldine.

Stern, M. S. 1977. Social class and psychiatric treatment of adults in mental health centers. *Journal of Health and Social Behavior* 18:317–25.

Stern, S. L., S. F. Moore, and J. S. Gross. 1975. Confounding of personality and social class characteristics in research on premature termination. *Journal of Consulting and Clinical Psychology* 43:341–44.

Strupp, H., R. Fox, and K. Lessler. 1969. *Patients view their psychotherapy*. Baltimore: Johns Hopkins Press.

Strupp, H. H., and A. L. Bloxom. 1973. Preparing lower-class patients for group psychotherapy. *Journal of Consulting and Clinical Psychology* 41:373–84.

Sue, S. 1976. Clients' demographic characteristics and therapeutic treatment: Differences that make a difference. *Journal of Consulting and Clinical Psychology* 44:864.

―――. 1977. Community mental health services to minority groups. *American Psychologist* 32:616–24.

Sue, S., and H. McKinney. 1975. Asian Americans in the community mental health care system. *American Journal of Orthopsychiatry* 45:111–18.

Sue, S., H. McKinney, D. Allen, and J. Hall. 1974. Delivery of community mental health services to black and white clients. *Journal of Consulting and Clinical Psychology* 42:794–801.

Sullivan, P. L., C. Miller, and W. Smelser. 1958. Factors in length of stay and progress in psychotherapy. *Journal of Consulting Psychology* 22:1–9.

Swanson, M. G., and A. M. Woolson. 1973. Psychotherapy with the unmotivated patient. *Psychotherapy* 2:175–83.

Szasz, T. S. 1965. *The ethics of psychoanalysis*. New York: Basic Books.

―――. 1972. *Law, liberty and psychiatry*. New York: Macmillan.

―――. 1961. *The myth of mental illness*. New York: Hoeber, Harper.

―――. 1967. The psychiatrist as double agent. *Transaction* (October):16–24.

Tennov, D. 1976. *Psychotherapy: The hazardous cure*. Garden City: Anchor Books.

Terestman, N., D. Miller, and J. J. Weber. 1974. Blue collar patients at a psycho-analytic clinic. *American Journal of Psychiatry* 131:261–66.

Tischler, G., J. Henisz, and J. Myers. 1975. Utilization of mental health services. *Archives of General Psychiatry* 32:416–18.

Torrey, E. 1970. Irrelevance of traditional mental health services for urban Mexican Americans. In *Current population reports* (series 213), Washington, D.C.: U.S. Government. 20.

Turner, S., and S. Armstrong. 1981. Cross-racial psychotherapy: What the therapists say. *Psychotherapy: Theory, Research and Practice* 18:375–78.

Vail, A. 1978. Factors influencing lower-class black patients remaining in therapy. *Journal of Consulting and Clinical Psychology* 46:341.

Veroff, J. 1981. The dynamics of help seeking in men and women: A national survey study. *Psychiatry* 44:189–201.

Vontress, C. E. 1971. Racial differences: Impediments to rapport. *Journal of Counseling Psychology* 18:7–13.

Warren, R. C., A. M. Jackson, J. Nugaria, and G. K. Farley. 1973. Differential attitudes of black and white patients toward treatment in a child guidance clinic. *American Journal of Orthopsychiatry* 3:384–93.

Weiner, I. B. 1975. *Principles of psychotherapy*. New York: John Wiley.

Wheelis, A. 1958. The quest for identity. New York: W. W. Norton.

Why blue-collar workers avoid psychiatric help. 1976. *Psychology Today* (October):34–35.

Winder, A. E., and M. Hersko. 1955. The effect of social class on the length and type of psychotherapy in a veteran administration hygiene clinic. *Journal of Clinical Psychology* 11:77–79.

Winston, D., H. Pardes, and D. Papernick. 1972. Inpatient treatment of blacks and whites. *Archives of General Psychiatry* 26:405–9.

Wolkon, G., S. Moriwaki, and K. Williams. 1973. Race and social class as a factor in the orientation toward psychotherapy. *Journal of Consulting Psychology* 20:312–16.

Yamamoto, J., and M. K. Goin. 1966. Social class factors relevant for psychiatric treatment. *Journal of Nervous and Mental Disease* 142:332–39.

Yamamoto, J., A. James, M. Bloombaum, and J. Hattem. 1967. Racial factors in patient selection. *American Journal of Psychiatry* 124:630–36.

Yamamoto, J., Q. C. James, and N. Palley. 1968. Cultural problems in psychiatric therapy. *Archives of General Psychiatry* 19:45–49.

2

The Medical or Illness Model and Its Relation to Psychotherapy

It is extremely important for a student and practitioner of psychotherapy to understand the concept of the medical or illness model of psychotherapy for several reasons. First, the medical (illness) model is widely accepted as an explanation of emotional disturbances. Second, it is extensively used as a model for therapy. Third, the underlying assumptions of the model used determine the course of therapy and the role of the therapist.

Basic to the medical or illness model is the issue of whether the mental and emotional disturbances (mental illness) are illnesses like physical illness whose origin and etiology are organic in nature. Or are they different in nature and structure since they involve the interpersonal conflicts and moral and ethical dilemmas of the individual? If mental illness is like physical illness, then biophysiochemical treatments are more appropriate for it; if it is not, then nonphysiochemical and nonsomatic methods are relatively more suited for its handling.

In their work with clients, psychotherapists used various models

—including the behavioral model, game model, transactional model, contractual model, and psychoanalytic (or hydraulic) model. (See Chapter 4.) Yet the medical model supercedes all the other models, or rather could be superimposed upon any of them. For instance, a therapist using a behavioral model or psychoanalytic (hydraulic) model may believe that the clients he is working with suffer from mental illness or mental disease, while the therapy he is conducting is some form of treatment, in a medical sense. Hence he would not hesitate to recommend the use of pills, shock therapy, and involuntary hospitalization. The same holds true for therapists using other models.

This chapter traces the historical development of the medical model concept. It attempts to show how and for what reasons psychotherapy came to be a medical specialty. What happens to a therapist if he conceptualizes psychotherapy within the framework of the medical model? Finally, is there a more appropriate conceptual model for psychotherapy?

In his long career, Freud frequently struggled with the issue of whether disturbed and conflicted people were "sick" or "ill" in a medical (physical) sense or not. Szasz summarizes Freud's struggle succinctly.

In 1914, Freud asserts: "All our provisional ideas in psychology will presumably someday be based on an organic substructure. This makes it probable that it is special substances and chemical processes which perform the operations of . . . special psychical forces." In 1930 he declares: "The hope of the future lies in organic chemistry or access to it through endocrinology. This future is still far distant, but one should study analytically every case of psychosis because this knowledge will one day guide the chemical therapy." And in 1939 in *An Outline of Psychoanalysis* he reiterates this view and extends it to encompass all mental diseases: "The future may teach us to exercise a direct influence, by means of particular chemical substances, on the amounts of energy and their distribution in the neural apparatus. It may be that there are still undreamt-of possibilities of therapy. But for the moment we have nothing better at our disposal than the technique of psychoanalysis." These excerpts show us Freud as the cryptobiologist and the secret believer in the chemical treatment of mental diseases.

There was, however, another side to Freud, a side that looked upon psychoanalysis not as a poor substitute for a future chemical miracle cure, but as a valuable discovery for probing the unconscious and as an invaluable therapy for the neuroses. For example, in 1919, Freud writes that the analyst's task is "to bring to the patient's knowledge the unconscious, repressed impulses existing in him." In 1928, he repeats his "wish to protect analysis from the doctors (and the priests)." And in 1927, in his essay on lay (nonmedical) analysis, he declares, "I have assumed that psychoanalysis is not a specialized branch of medicine. I cannot see how it is possible to dispute this." But if psychoanalysis is not a branch of medicine, what is it a branch of? This is Freud's answer: "The words, secular pastoral worker, might well serve as a general formula for describing the function of the analyst. . . . We do not seek to bring [the patient] relief by receiving him into the Catholic, Protestant, or Socialist community. We seek rather to enrich him from his own internal sources. . . . Such activity as this is pastoral work in the best sense of the word." (Szasz 1978)*

Freud was unable to resolve this dilemma. He never completely gave up the illness model. Yet, at the same time, he was able to raise some fundamental questions with regard to the medical or illness model of psychotherapy.

The credit for introducing the concept of the medical or illness model into the lexicon of psychiatry and psychology goes to Szasz (1961, 1976). He laid down the historical development of this concept and explained how psychotherapy, a nonmedical operation, came to be defined as a medical specialty under the control of medicine. The most crucial aspect in understanding the concept of the medical model may be its historical development. The term is not a scientific concept, as is often implied (McKeachie 1967; Siegler and Osmond 1974), but rather a sociohistorical one. Several recent books demonstrate vividly this point (Szasz 1961; Dain 1964; Foucault 1965; Grob 1966; Silverman 1983).

At the risk of oversimplifying a major sociohistorical development, one might describe it as fallout from the scientific era. The advent of the scientific and industrial revolution, combined with the advances made in physical medicine during the eighteenth and nineteenth centuries, brought many new discoveries. Previously incurable physical diseases were conquered. Hence, the idea arose that such new developments could also be used to handle emotional distresses and personal troubles. The disturbed and deviant were taken to, and increasingly sought the services of, a physician, whereas previously clerical help had been requested.

The clerics customarily labeled these people possessed or under

---

*Sulloway (1979) apparently agrees with Szasz's assessment of Freud's position. In the introduction to his book he states, ". . . This is an intellectual biography with a particular thesis. A central message is that Freud, through the years, has become a crypto-, or covert, biologist, and that psychoanalysis has become, accordingly, a crypto-biology."

the influence of Satan, and they were badly treated. The expectation was that the new scientific knowledge would be more effective than theology in controlling such deviances (Dain 1964) and that the emotionally disturbed would be treated more humanely. In a doctor-patient relationship the patient is entitled to be treated with kindness and care, not to be held accountable for his disability, and to be excused from certain social responsibilities (Leifer 1970). Thus, toward the end of the eighteenth and the beginning of the nineteenth centuries, the control and management of the deviant and the disturbed passed on from the clerical-theological to the physiomedical realm.

It should be noted that this shift in control and management was a social-humanitarian step and not a scientific step. This shift was not based upon any specific discovery nor upon any new findings pertaining to the emotional and mental disturbances. Nor was there any new information or logic added to the understanding of the disturbed. Basically, the reclassification of the deviants and the emotionally disturbed consisted of giving a different name or label to the same or similar behavior that was handled by the clerics. For example, if a person said that he talked to God, the cleric might have called him a person who either has developed scruples or is possessed by Satan. The physician gave him a new name and called him a paranoid.

This change of names or labels for the same behavior did not mean that any new knowledge was added to the understanding of such behavior. However, the new labeling created an illusion of science about the handling of the deviants and the disturbed. Later on, this new labeling was to create confusion in the fields of psychiatry and psychotherapy, since it assumed a direct, albeit implicit, relationship between the new label, the origins of the disease so labeled, and the treatment for it.

When a disturbed and deviant individual was taken to a physician, the physician declared him sick or ill. But since nothing could be found physically wrong (Grob 1970), the question of where he could be sick arose. The natural answer was that he was sick in his head or mind. He was so declared because his thoughts and actions were peculiar or different from those of people around him (Szasz 1961, 1976). Such people were labeled mentally sick, and the term *mental illness* was born.*

---

*Some have attributed the first use of the term *mental illness* to Teresa of Avila in the sixteenth century. "A group of nuns were exhibiting conduct which at a

Why did the physician use the term *mental illness*? The answer seems to be twofold. First, it was to avoid the maltreatment of those who were disturbed and troubled. Second, he used the term in a metaphoric sense, as a presentation of facts about the person's behavior using the idiomatic language of the body (Leifer 1970) to explain the deviant behavior that had no signs of physical dysfunction.* What the physician meant when he used such an expression was that the person thinks, talks, and acts as if he is sick or ill. In this context, the phrase *as if* denotes the metaphoric quality of illness since no concrete evidence of illness was found.

However, partly because the passage of time diluted the original metaphoric use of the term *mental illness*, partly because physicians began to manage and handle the disturbed and the deviants, and partly because of the advent of Galenic medicine, a causal approach to human conduct came into fashion (Waldman 1971). Disturbed and deviant behavior was thereupon construed as an outcome of internal pathology (Esterson 1982). The metaphoric quality of the expression was lost, and the metaphor was converted into a myth wherein human conduct came to be explained in physical terms (Waldman 1971). It can thus be seen that the relationship between medicine and the treatment of mental and emotional disturbances and deviances (or psychiatry) is a historical one rather than a logical or scientific one (Leifer 1970).

Mental illness then became a rubric or context for medical classification. Mental illness was classified as a disease entity. Mild emotional disturbances were declared neuroses, to indicate that the person was suffering from a disease of the nerves. The more serious disturbances were labeled psychosis, or disease of the psyche (Szasz 1959). Because mental illness was now being classified as a disease entity, the language and concept of physical disease were then introduced into the field of psychiatry and psychology, with words like *treatment, patient, disease, symptoms, cure, diagnosis, prognosis, remission, acute, chronic*, and so on. The language of medicine became the language of psychiatry and psychotherapy (Leifer 1970). With the

---

later date would have been called hysteria. By declaring these women to be infirm or ill, Teresa was able to fend off the Inquisition" (Sarbin 1967).

*A similar metaphor is "war on poverty." The metaphorical use of the expression is self-evident. Nobody believes that to fight poverty, tanks and an army should be sent. However, if the metaphorical quality of the expression is lost, then one may take the expression literally or as a fact and may send the army to fight poverty. (Borrowed from a lecture by Thomas Szasz)

introduction of medical language, the claim was laid that medical diseases and emotional diseases and medical and mental patients were similar (Leifer 1970). Thus, a similarity of language became a similarity of fact.

Numerous private and public organizations spend much money, time, and energy to convince the general public that the person with mental illness is sick, as is a person with any other disease, and that mental illness is a major health problem that claims as many as one person in ten as its victim and fills every other hospital bed with those who suffer from its effects. A general acceptance of these claims by the professionals in the field and by the educated strata of the society is an important factor in the success of the medical view of psychiatry (Leifer 1970; Sarbin and Mancuso 1970).

This physiomedicobiological conception of interpersonal conflicts and emotional turmoil is the medical or illness model of mental illness (Leifer 1982).*

An illness model assumes an organic or biochemical causation of emotional-interpersonal disturbance and recommends physiochemical methods for "curing" emotional disturbances. It uses medical language to describe and explain the emotional interpersonal disturbance, creates institutions for such people called hospitals, and bestows authority and power in the hands of those who can administer biochemical treatment. It also prescribes the role relations between therapist and client.

Disease, the Medical Model, and Psychotherapy

When emotional disturbances are viewed as illness or disease, it becomes necessary, as with physical diseases, to classify them (Robbins 1966). As Table 1 shows, a physical disease is fundamentally different from an emotional disturbance. It has a causative agent; it produces physiological or histopathological changes in the body that can

---

*A somewhat different but incomplete analysis of the medical model and its implications is presented by Sarason and Ganzer (1968) and by Blaney (1975). A linguistic analysis of the medical model is presented by Begelman (1971). Reasons for accepting the medical model are presented by Ausubel (1961), and Siegler and Osmond (1974), while Ellis (1967) attempts to present arguments both for and against the medical model, albeit unclearly. Gorenstein (1984) attempts to bring a rapprochment between the medical model and the nonmedical model(s), but from the author's standpoint, he becomes muddled and hence falls short of it.

TABLE 1
Differences Between Physical Illness
and Emotional Disturbance

PHYSICAL ILLNESS	EMOTIONAL DISTURBANCES
1. Causative agent (bacteria, virus, etc.).	1. Series of interpersonal interactions
2. Physiochemical, histological, or structural change.	2. No physiochemical or structural changes.
3. Objective, verifiable standard.	3. No objective, verifiable standard.
4. Happens to a person; is experienced passively.	4. Individual is an active participant.
5. Independent of the culture.	5. Defined by the culture and society.
6. Closed system.	6. Open system.

be described as symptomatic of illness. Such physiological changes can be observed and verified in terms of a normative standard. Physical illness is experienced by the individual without his willing participation in the process. The individual does not willingly bring the disease upon himself. The form it takes is universal and independent of the individual or of the society in which he lives (Szasz 1961). Cancer, for example, is generally diagnosed and treated in the same manner in practically every society.

An emotional or mental disturbance, in contrast, involves the whole person acting in a social role. It has no physiochemical or histopathological basis. Any physiological changes are a consequence of emotional conflicts and turmoil. In an emotional disturbance, the individual is considered to be an active participant, who at least partially brings the troubles upon himself. It is a "doing" of the individual. It is necessarily defined by the social and cultural conditions in which the individual lives and can be understood essentially in this context.

When an equivalent structure between the two is assumed, with physical illness and emotional disturbance presumed similar in nature, the essential differences are ignored. The classification and diagnosis of mental illness as a disease entity, independent of the person and his social role, became intrinsic to psychiatric thought.

A physical disease is a closed system, which follows a preestablished pattern of unfolding. Personal distress and emotional disturbance, however, are essentially open systems that do not follow a predetermined sequence (Marzolf 1947). When emotional disturbances were viewed as disease entities, however, it became necessary to chart the unfolding of mental illnesses. Patients institutionalized and incarcerated in mental hospitals were observed for long periods of time to study the growth and development of mental illness in order to develop a nosological system so that symptom clusters could be correlated for diagnosis (Zilboorg 1941). The early patients constituted the population sample on which the current diagnostic system is based (Szasz 1959). A closed system of physical disease was thus used as a model for mental illness within the physically closed environs of a state mental hospital, and a pseudo-equivalence of physical and mental illness was established (Sharma 1970).

Table 1 shows that in psychiatry the terms *disease* or *illness* are used for social conditions and interpersonal troubles, while in medicine, they refer to undesirable body states (Leifer 1970). For this reason, namely that psychiatry and psychotherapy deal with social and interpersonal and not with physiochemical disturbances, the psychiatrist feels expertly qualified to discuss just about every social issue, from marriage, child molestation, and poverty to art, drama, marijuana smoking, and delinquency. No other medical group feels qualified to discuss the social issues (Leifer 1970; Halleck 1971).

Another fundamental but grossly neglected difference between physical disease and mental illness is that in medicine one can have more than one disease or illness at the same time. In psychiatry, however, one cannot. One is either a neurotic, a psychotic, a depressive, or a schizophrenic. In physical medicine the disease refers to the malfunctioning of an organ, a body part or its subsystem, and more than one organ can malfunction at one time. In psychiatry, however, the term *illness* refers to one's social role and social being, or to one's personal identity. Since an individual can have only one identity at a time, he can have only one mental illness at a time. Thus, one cannot be a neurotic and a psychotic at the same time anymore than one can be American and Turkish at the same time, since each of these refers to the national identity of the person. In other words, medical illness refers to what one has, while mental illness refers to what one is (Waldman 1971).

The language used in the field of psychiatry and psychotherapy clearly suggests that the disorder encompasses the identity of the individual and not anything apart from one's being. For example, the common expression is not that one has depression, schizophrenia, or alcoholism, but that one is schizophrenic, alcoholic, or depressive, all reflecting upon the way of being or the identity of the individual.

The Sick Role

To conceptualize emotional disturbance as, or to equate mental illness with a physical illness is to make a category mistake (Ryle 1949). What is labeled as mental illness is the social behavior of the individual, which is classified and judged to be disturbed. Classification of social behavior necessarily involves valuative assumptions on the part of the classifier (Sharma 1970).

Item 1 of Table 2 shows that to be labeled physically sick, an observable physical condition—for example, high temperature—must be present and the patient must assume a sick role, for example, by staying in bed. Item 2 shows that one may have an observable physical condition (high temperature) but may not assume a sick role. Under these conditions he will be classified as "superstitious" (or a Christian Scientist). One may not have an observable physical condition but still assume a sick role; in that case he will be labeled as a malingerer, a hypochrondriac, or as mentally ill. The label of mental illness (Item 3) is applied to what is essentially a social role without an

TABLE 2
Logical Fallacies in the Nosology of Mental Illness

ITEM	OBSERVABLE PHYSICAL CONDITION	SICK ROLE	LABEL
1	yes	Assumes	Sick (physically)
2	yes	Does not assume	Superstitious or Christian Scientist
3	no	Assumes	Mentally ill or hypochondriac
4	no	Does not assume	Well

Note: Borrowed from a lecture by Thomas Szasz

observable physical condition. To equate mental illness with physical illness is to ascribe an observable physical condition to mental illness, which, per se, does not exist. Ryle (1949) calls this a "category error," that is, the representation of the facts of mental life as if they belong to one (physical) logical type or category (or range of types or categories) when they actually belong to another. As this work shows, this form of category error in conceptualization does affect the course of therapy and the kind of relationship a therapist will be able to develop with his clients.

Vested Interest of Psychotherapy and Psychiatry

When the field deals with social-interpersonal conflicts and moral dilemmas of an individual living in a society, why is medical and not ordinary language used to describe and explain one's behavior and conduct? Why has it become the task of medicine to address itself to these issues, whereas nonmedical professionals are either barred from or assigned to a subordinate role in this field? It primarily has to do with political economy. Several social and personal gains can be derived from declaring mental illness medical-like and by using medical language (Leifer 1970).

First, by using the medical rhetoric, one can obfuscate the real issues. By presenting the social-interpersonal issues as medical issues, one can lay claim to objectivity. In other words, one can claim one's opinion to be free of value judgments and without social influence and coercion. After all, medical statements about a person's illness and health are supposed to be based upon the scientific findings which are free of value judgments.

Second, the use of such language creates the illusion of science providing a lever for social control of behavior which may be unacceptable to the dominant class of the society. For example, in the name of mental health a majority of psychiatrists denounce the use of marijuana, the freedom of abortions, and other radical sociopolitical issues. If a therapist or psychiatrist said he was presenting his own opinion about abortion or marijuana he would be looked upon as an advocate of the status quo. He would lose his credibility as an unbiased observer and be considered a partisan propagandist or ideologue.

Third, the power to institute social control not only sets the psychiatrists apart from the public at large, because they have more power and status, but also provides them with great financial rewards. Until recently, a psychiatrist had the social power to decide who could have an abortion and who could not. He could do so because he was given the social-legal authority to judge for whom abortion (or pregnancy) would engender mental illness. For this and other such decisions, a psychiatrist collects handsome fees from the parties concerned. It is well known that the average income of a medical specialist, including a psychiatrist, is five to seven times higher than the income of an average American (Ehrenreich 1978).

Relationship of the Illness Model to Psychotherapy: The Contradictions

In recent years the appropriateness of the medical model to explain and to conceptualize mental illness and psychotherapy has been seriously questioned (Szasz 1961, 1978; Adams 1964; Albee 1966; Braginsky 1969). Yet the model is still applied to psychotherapy. The question of what happens when a therapist uses the medical model, or how well the medical model "fits" the psychotherapeutic model, should then be raised. To understand this, let us examine what a therapist does in a therapy session.

A therapist meets regularly with his client in an office. He listens to the client talk about his life, his fears, troubles, wishes, dilemmas. This dialogue is used by the therapist in several ways for the clarification of the clients' confusions and dilemmas, for persuasion, for convincing the client to give up certain behavior, and for examining his values and ethical system (Breggin 1971; Frank 1973). In these sessions the therapist uses no other instrument than conversation (unless one believes in the medical model and dispenses pills and shock treatments). In other words, a therapist talks with his clients (Szasz 1978).

It should be noted that the conflicts and concerns which the client discusses in therapy have little to do with illness or sickness. Content analyses of psychotherapy sessions show that the topics most frequently discussed by female outpatient clients are relations with the opposite sex, hopes or fears about the future, work, career, or education, and their mothers (Howard et al. 1969). Other studies show that patients' modal concerns in therapy are personal identity, self-disclosure, responsibilities, loneliness, loving, and anger (Orlinsky et al. 1970). To fit the conducting of psychotherapy within the framework of an illness model creates various contradictions for the therapist, which he will have to resolve or ignore.

First, a therapist who follows the medical model will have to convince the client that he is sick much like an individual is physically ill. If the client is already convinced (through exposure to media, friends, and so forth), then the therapist is the expert about the illness or the disease from which the client is suffering, and the client is ignorant about it. In order to continue treatment, the client must defer to the expertise and the superior knowledge of the therapist and attempt to follow his suggestions and advice. Yet in this situation, the "disease" is nothing other than the client's social relations and his life, about which the therapist knows little (at least in the beginning of therapy) and the client knows more. Thus, the first contradiction for the medical model therapist is that he has to treat as a disease or illness the lifestyle of another person, which he cannot know without the client's telling him. Yet the therapist has to tell the client what will cure his illness.

A medical model therapist can resolve this contradiction in two ways. First, he can pontificate and moralize to the client about his lifestyle according to the therapist's moral judgment. Second, he can dispense some form of medicine, pills, or shock therapy. The contradiction of "knowing little" accompanies the contradiction of "directing all."

As mentioned before, physical illness is passively experienced by an individual. It happens to the person. He does not actively seek to bring the disease upon himself. In contrast, mental illness or emotional disturbance is a "doing" in which the person is an active agent. A medical model therapist believes that mental illness, like physical illness, happens to the person. Hence, the therapist will have to formulate the goals of the "treatment" without the active participation of the client.

Yet psychotherapy is based upon the premise that the client, at least partially, is an active participant in bringing upon himself the troubles and problems he is complaining about. This is amply demonstrated by the expressions or enjoinments, almost universally used by the therapist toward clients, "Do what you feel is best for you," or "Do what you feel most comfortable with." Hence, the second contradiction is: The therapist expects the client's passive acceptance of what the therapist says or does, while he also hopes and expects that the client will actively seek to change his life. This contradiction can be resolved by the therapist by taking a vascillating position in therapy, by sometimes encouraging and exhorting the client to be dependent (upon the therapist) while at the other times asking him to be autonomous and independent.

A third contradiction the medical model therapist encounters can be called "imposed value neutrality." Espousing the medical model, the therapist will have to believe in mental health as the counterpart of mental illness.* But there are no objective criteria of mental health, other than the beliefs, values, and ethics of the middle class (Jahoda 1958). Thus, in the name of mental health, the therapist will wittingly or unwittingly enforce his own ethics and morality, as well as those of the society, upon the client.

Yet the therapist may believe that his treatment is value free, like the medical treatment, while in his therapy sessions he implicitly (and sometimes not so implicitly) enforces his own ethics and values. He can resolve this contradiction by denying that he is enforcing his values and those of the society, and claim he is only treating illness. (See also Rabkin 1977.)

To follow the medical model of mental illness, one has to believe in it. One must accept and recommend various forms of physical treatments, such as shock therapy, insulin therapy, pills, lobotomy, hospitalization, or any other physical intervention, to the client as one of the fundamental forms of treatment for emotional disturbance. Therefore, the fourth contradiction for such a therapist is how to resolve the emotional, interpersonal, and ethical dilemmas by the physical methods of pills, shock, and so on. The therapist can resolve this contradiction by believing that such models do help resolve the ethical-moral conflicts and dilemmas of life, despite strong evidence to the contrary.

This contradiction is vividly demonstrated when a medical model therapist treats an ethnic client. Since the sociocultural differences between the two are great, an Anglo therapist has difficulty grasping the full context, meaning, ramifications, and importance of the conflicts of the ethnic client. Believing that the client is suffering from an illness, it is simple for a medical therapist to dispense pills and other forms of somatic treatment to cure the illness. Pills and somatic

---

*Reader should be made aware of the fact that dozens of books and articles have attempted to define mental illness and mental health. To this author's knowledge, none has been successful in formulating a satisfactory definition.

treatments, then, become one of the basic methods for solving the life problems of the ethnic clients. (See Chapter 1.)

Thus, it is difficult to see how an open and authentic encounter can occur between a therapist who espouses the medical model and his clients. The therapist will treat the client as someone who knows little about himself. This assumes the therapist has more knowledge and authority about the client's life than the client himself. Furthermore, the therapist must be directive with the client, since he has higher social status and authority.

Other Models of Psychotherapy

In the history of the management of the disturbed and the deviant, numerous conceptual models have been used (Bockoven 1963; Foucault 1965; Szasz 1970). A few of these include the theological model, the criminal model, the moral (or sin) model, the medical or illness model, the witchcraft model, and so on. Each model creates its own definition of deviance, sets criteria for judging the disturbed and the deviant, establishes methods and procedures for handling them, and creates social institutions to manage them.

A therapist can choose to work within the framework of any of these models. However, his task is made easy and effective if his chosen model is commensurate with what he does in practice. It is this author's contention that a social-educational model is the most congruent with the operations of a psychotherapist.

Social-Educational Model

In a study of the outcome of psychotherapy for clients, Strupp et al. (1969) found that patients view psychotherapy as an educational or re-educational process. Within the framework of a social-educational model, the therapist utilizes his knowledge and the interpersonal relationship between himself and the client to institute changes in the client's life. In this relationship the major responsibility for change falls upon the client. To see this as necessary one has only to look at what is to be changed—the client's life-style, his conflictual relationships, his upsets, and his ungratifying behavior pattern.

For the client to resolve his conflicts and dilemmas, he has to want to change his outlook; he must be willing to modify himself through self-understanding, learning, and education. The process of changing oneself involves a struggle, a questioning of one's values, aspirations, life goals, and outlook on life. This can hardly be achieved unless the client examines his life openly and honestly. A client cannot be open and honest in the therapeutic situation and with the therapist unless he is assured that the therapist will not attempt to influence the course of the client's life in an arbitrary and authoritarian way (Leifer 1970).

The education and learning that go on in therapy are not about abstract issues, but rather about the client himself, which in turn, assist the client to modify his outlook and his relationships. This learning and education proceed on many levels. First is a personal level. Since a client generally comes to therapy for personal troubles and conflicts, he has to learn to recognize the mode of operation or life-style he is currently pursuing, which is generating difficulties and conflicts for him.

Although not always necessary, a discussion of the client's personal background could lead to an awareness of the sources of conflicting values and attitudes. These conflicting values may have become part of the client's life-style and may be a source of his troubles (Leifer 1970). The client also learns how his relationships with "significant others" have taught him how to behave or in what way his behavior is generating conflict. In short, he learns how his personality has been molded and what he might have to do to change it.

Generally, the client is at least vaguely aware of the conflicting motives and values, contradictory attitudes and behaviors. This awareness has to be brought out in the open so that an open acceptance of and a relearning on a more conscious level can occur, and the client can accept full responsibility for his behavior. Thus, the choice and direction of his life can be more under his own control.

A more general kind of education and learning for the client is the culture and society in which he grew up and in which he now lives. The client's culture may itself have social contradictions built into it. In the process of coping with such a culture, one incorporates its contradictions, which then become a source of the client's dilemmas. For instance, for a young unmarried female it is a source of status and prestige to be asked out frequently and to be popular. She has to learn the behavior and attitudes appropriate for such a role. After she gets married, all such attitudes have to be discarded rather suddenly; new monogamous and housewifely behavior has to be acquired.

Social contradictions may and do assume various invidious

forms often not easily discernible as contradictions. Their effects upon a client's life are usually very subtle and insidious. For example, in the present American culture, the institution of marriage is morally sanctioned while a bachelor's life is glorified and eroticized. People begin to feel that they should be able to enjoy both aspects of life—married and single. Such contradictory cultural pressures and images induce conflicts. Some see a resolution to this contradiction in living in an "open marriage" (O'Neill 1972). Clients begin to subscribe to such contradictory resolutions and become conflicted about their roles in interpersonal relationships.

One of the functions of the therapist is to help the client learn about the social contradictions, to make them explicit for the client, and to show him how they may be causing difficulties for him with the hope that the client will be able to choose one or the other aspect of the contradiction or attempt to resolve it at the next higher stage. Thus, it is also the task of the therapist to help educate the client in grasping the relationship between the individual's conflicts and the structural contradictions of society.

Generally, until the client's personal troubles and torments are reduced, it is difficult for him to see the relationship between individual conflicts and social contradictions simply because his own torments are too pressing and burdensome to provide him a distance from which to judge the social conflicts.

A student in my psychotherapy class insisted that most of women's conflicts and troubles for which they seek therapy have their roots in the contradictions and conflictual values of the society. She maintained that the individual conflicts of the female clients could be resolved by explaining and discussing the social, economic, and moral contradictions in which most of the American middle-class women find themselves. To demonstrate this, she launched an experiment by advertising in the university newspaper for such a therapy group. Eleven female subjects responded. From the first session on, they all began to talk of their personal troubles and conflicts. The student-therapist persistently tried to tell them that all these troubles and torments were derived from the contradictions of the society itself, rather than from their personal biographies. Soon (within four sessions), nine of them quit coming, complaining that they were unable to see what the therapist was trying to accomplish. Only two stayed on and ultimately were able to relate their own personal conflicts to the contradictions of the society.

Power and Therapy

As an educator, one should have little (or no) power over the client. (See Chapter 5.) It is true that in the context of psychotherapy, a therapist generally has higher status and more social power than the client—power to persuade and influence—as well as legal power. It also seems true that the clients are willing to surrender their power and autonomy to the therapist. The temptation for the therapist to take over the client's autonomy, especially when it is being offered, is all the greater. The therapist should refrain from using such power to force the client to live a certain way or to believe in certain values.

The aim of the educator is not to mold his client's behavior into specific moral and ethical standards. A social educator should, therefore, have no need to exercise social power over his clients (Leifer 1970). A therapist should constantly try to reduce his social power over clients, for a power relationship inhibits an open and equal exchange between the parties; it curbs the development of autonomy in the client, and it is contradictory to the ideology of egalitarianism.

In psychotherapy, the therapist advertently or inadvertently assumes the role of an educator or preacher rather than that of a physician-healer. In many ways the client also views him as a priest or a guru. It is no wonder that clients frequently quote their therapist as an authority on matters of guidance and self-enlightenment. Viewed in this light, the somewhat sarcastic remark that a psychotherapist is nothing but a modern-day priest or shaman has some validity. Like the priest or shaman of previous societies, the modern therapist has the role of clarifying the client's inner confusions, value conflicts, and social contradictions. This process can best be achieved if a therapist eschews the medical model, since it is incongruent with the therapist's role.

Summary

The biomedical conception of interpersonal conflicts and emotional disturbances within the framework of illness and health is defined as the medical model of mental illness. It is important to understand this model because it is widely accepted as an explanation of emotional disturbance. It is extensively used as a model for therapy, and ultimately the underlying assumptions of the model determine the course of therapy and the role of therapist.

The development of the medical model is a historical phenomenon. During the late eighteenth century and the early nineteenth century, as the control of the deviant and the disturbed passed from a clerical-theological realm to a medical realm, emotional disturbances also came to be viewed and classified as illness like physical illness. From then on, mental and emotional disturbances were classified as diseases and an elaborate diagnostic system was introduced.

However, a physical disease has certain fundamental differences from emotional disturbances. It has a causative agent; it produces physiochemical or histopathological changes that can be described as symptomatic of illness. Such changes can be observed and verified in terms of normative standards: physical illness happens to an individual, and the individual does not actively bring it upon himself. The form it takes is universal or independent of the individual. An emotional or mental disturbance, in contrast, involves the whole person acting in a social role. It has no physiochemical or histopathological basis. In an emotional disturbance the individual is considered an active participant, who at least partially brings the troubles upon himself. It is necessarily defined by the social and cultural conditions in which the individual lives and can be understood essentially in this context. When an equivalence is assumed between physical and emotional disease, then the essential differences are ignored. Thus, in medicine the term *disease* refers to undesirable bodily states, while in psychiatry it refers to social conditions and interpersonal troubles.

If a therapist uses the medical model to conduct psychotherapy, he is faced with various contradictions during the course of therapy, for the underlying assumptions of the medical model and those of psychotherapy are not in accord with each other. A more appropriate model for psychotherapy is the social-educational model. In this model a therapist attempts to educate the client about the history and reasons of his conflicts, his conflicting ethics and values, and the structure of his interpersonal dilemmas. The education and learning that go on in therapy are not about abstract issues, but rather about the client and his life. Such self-education assists the client to question and modify his values and outlook on life. Contrary to the medical model, in a social-educational model, a therapist should have no power over the client since a power relationship curbs the development or the autonomy of the client, inhibits an open and free exchange between the two parties, and is antithetical to the ideology of egalitarianism.

References

Adams, H. B. 1964. Mental illness or interpersonal behavior? *American Psychologist* 19:191–97.

Albee, G. 1966. Dark at the top of the agenda. *Clinical Psychologist Newsletter* 1:7–9.

Ausubel, D. 1961. Personality Disorder is a Disease. *American Psychologist* 16:69–74.

Begelman, D. A. 1971. Misnaming, metaphors, the medical model and some muddles. *Psychiatry* 34:38–58.

Blaney, P. H. 1975. Implications of the medical model and its alternatives. *American Journal of Psychiatry* 132:911–14.

Bockoven, J. S. 1963. *Moral treatment in American psychiatry*. New York: Springer Publishing Company.

Braginsky, B. M., and D. D. Bragwsky. 1969. *Methods of madness*. New York: Holt, Rinehart and Winston.

Breggin, P. 1971. Psychotherapy as applied ethics. *Psychiatry* 34:59–73.

Brown, S. 1980. Coping skills training: An evaluation of psychoeducational programs in a community mental health setting. *Journal of Counseling Psychology* 27:340–45.

Dain, N. 1964. *Concepts of insanity in the United States*. New Brunswick: Rutgers University Press.

Ehrenreich, J. 1978. The cultural crisis of modern medicine. New York: Monthly Review Press, 57–59.

Ellis, A. 1967. Should some people be labeled mentally ill. *Journal of Consulting Psychology* 31:435–46.

Esterson, A. 1982. The Helping Profession. *Meta-medicine*. Reidel Publishing, Dordrecht, Netherlands, 325–37.

Foucault, M. 1965. *Madness and civilization*. New York: Pantheon Books.

Frank, J. D. 1973. *Persuasion and healing* (rev. ed.). Baltimore: Johns Hopkins University Press.

Gorenstein, E. 1984. Debating mental illness: Implications for science, medicine and social policy. *American Psychologist* 39:50–56.

Grob, G. N. 1966. *State and the mentally ill*. Chapel Hill: University of North Carolina Press.

———. 1970. Social origins of American psychiatry. In S. L. Sharma ed., *The medical model of mental illness*. Woodland, Calif.: Magestic Publishing Co.

Halleck, S. L. 1971. *The politics of therapy*. New York: Science House.

Howard, K. I., D. E. Orlinsky, and J. A. Hill. 1969. Content of dialogue in psychotherapy. *Journal of Counseling Psychology* 16:396–404.

Jahoda, M. 1958. *Current concepts of positive mental health*. New York: Basic Books.

Leifer, R. 1970. *In the name of mental health*. New York: Science Books, 18–38, 172–85.

Leifer, R. 1982. Psychotherapy, language and freedom. *Meta-Medicine*. Reidel Publishing, Dordrecht, Netherlands, 397–417.

Marzolf, S. S. 1947. The disease concept in psychology. *Psychological Review* 54:211–21.

McKeachic, W. M. 1967. On multiple models. *Clinical Psychologist Newsletter* 3:108–10.

O'Neill, N., and G. O'Neill. 1972. *Open marriage*. New York: M. Evans and Co.

Orlinsky, D. E., K. I. Howard, and J. A. Hill. 1970. The patient's concerns in psychotherapy. *Journal of Clinical Psychology* 26:104–11.

Rabkin, J. G. 1977. Therapist's attitudes toward mental illness and health. In A. S. Gurman and A. M. Razin eds., *Effective Psychotherapy*. New York: Pergamon Press, 162–88.

Robbins, L. L. 1966. A historical review of classification of behavior disorders and one current perspective. In L. Eron ed., *The classification of behavior disorders*. Chicago: Aldine.

Ryle, G. 1949. *The concept of mind*. New York: Barnes & Noble.

Sarbin, T. R. 1967. On the futility of the proposition that some people be labeled as mentally ill. *Journal of Consulting Psychology* 32:447–53.

Sarbin, T. R. 1967. On the futility of the proposition that some people be labeled as mentally ill. *Journal of Consulting Psychology* 32:447–53.

Sarbin, T. R., and J. C. Mancuso. 1970. Failure of a moral enterprise: Attitude

Sarason, I. G., and V. Ganzer. 1968. Concerning the medical model. *American Psychologist* 23:507–10.

Sharma, S. L. 1970. A historical background of the development of nosology in psychiatry and psychology. *American Psychologist* 3:248–53.

Siegler, M., and H. Osmond. 1974. *Models of madness, models of medicine*. New York: Harper and Row.

Silverman, I. 1983. *Pure types are rare*. New York: Praeger Publishers.

Strupp, H., R. Fox, and K. Lessler. 1969. *Patients view their psychotherapy*. Baltimore: Johns Hopkins Press, 14.

Sulloway, F. J. 1979. *Freud: Biologist of the mind*. New York: Basic Books, 3.

Szasz, T. S. 1959. The classification of mental illness: A situational analysis of Psychiatric operations. *Psychiatric Quarterly* 33:77–101.

———. 1965. *The ethics of psychoanalysis*. New York: Basic Books.

———. 1970. *The manufacture of madness*. New York: Harper and Row.

———. 1961. *The myth of mental illness*. New York: Hoeber Harper.

———. 1978. *The myth of psychotherapy*. Garden City: Doubleday-Anchor-Press, 179–80.

———. 1976. *Schizophrenia*. New York: Basic Books.

Waldman, R. 1971. *Humanistic psychiatry*. New Brunswick: Rutgers University Press.

Zilboorg, G. 1941. *A history of medical psychology*. New York: W. W. Norton.

3

Values and Ethics in Psychotherapy: The Embedded Assumptions of Therapy

If we do not view emotional disturbance as disease or illness in a medical sense, or within the framework of the medical model, then the problems of psychotherapy become the problems of interpersonal relations and of value conflicts and ethical dilemmas that a client faces in his life.* Recently many authors have begun to acknowledge this. Hobbs (1964), for instance, says that "mental illness is not the private organic misery of an individual but a social, ethical and moral problem." Szasz (1965) and Leifer (1970) are perhaps the most forceful and clear exponents of this viewpoint. Szasz (1965) maintains that a far more realistic and accurate term for the troubles and conflicts for

---

*Many authors, however, have attempted to remove psychotherapy from the matrix of values and ethics. Heinz Hartman (1960), perhaps the most outstanding spokesman of this group, attempted to present "analytic therapy (as) a kind of technology." Freud (1949) toyed with such a concept of psychoanalysis. He said, "Psychoanalysis neither has, nor can have, a philosophical standpoint. In reality psychoanalysis is a method of investigation, an impartial instrument like, say, infinitesimal calculus." However, the bulk of his writings does not support such a position.

which a client goes to therapy is not *symptoms*, or some form of *illness*, but rather *problems*—the moral, ethical, and value conflicts that should be called "problems of living." Problems of living involve discontent, confusions, doubts, indecisions, interpersonal conflicts, anguish, conflicts of choice, and so on.

Regardless of how a therapist conceptualizes a client's conflicts and anguish (the so-called symptoms), the issues of values, morality, and ethics form the foundation of psychotherapy; they are the basis on which all psychotherapy is conducted. As Rollo May (1953) observes, "Value judgements and ethical standards are inextricably interwoven with the process and the goals of therapy." Watson observes that "an amoral therapy is a contradiction in terms" (1958).

With regard to the process of psychotherapy, London (1964) states that

much of the material with which he (the therapist) deals is neither understandable nor usable outside the context of a system of human values. This fact is unfortunate and embarrassing to one who would like to see himself as an impartial scientist and unprejudiced helper. It is a fact, nonetheless, and one which, for both technical and theoretical reasons, may be painfully important to students of human behavior in general and to psychotherapists in particular. Moral considerations may dictate, in large part, how the therapist defines his client's needs, how he operates in the therapeutic situation, how he defines "treatment," and "cure," and even "reality."

Definition of Values and Ethics

The concept of values has been defined variously by different authors. Some writers, for instance, have differentiated among three types of values (Parson and Shils 1952; Morris 1956). Others distinguish between two types of values (Margenau 1959; Rokeach 1973). Still others do not make such distinctions.

For Morris (1956), the three types of values are object values, characterized by what is actually preferable; operative values, referring to goal-directed behavior and to actual behavioral choices among objects; and conceived values, involving more abstract preferences for a "symbolically indicated object." Parson and Shils (1952) categorize values in accordance with truth, taste, and morals.

Margenau (1959) and Rokeach (1973) differentiate between two kinds of values. Margenau distinguishes between factual values and normative values. Factual values are "observable preferences, appraisals and desires of concrete people at a given time . . . [they] are neither right nor wrong but are facts of observations; they vary from place to place and from time to time; their claim is only with respect to prevalence and persistence." The "factual value has a fixed abode. It resides in the determinate specificity of human action, of stated preferences, of opinion polls, and can be discovered by means both known and generally agreed upon." Normative values, on the other hand,

are those which point to and receive their value from a command or a directive to which a person is committed. . . . If a person is committed to the maxim, "Thou shall not kill," then life has or is a value. Life has no value for a person committed to the destruction of it. The same holds true for honesty, friendship, love of mankind, etc. Removal of commitment or the reversal of command destroys or changes the sign of a value."

Rokeach (1973) also differentiates between two kinds of values— instrumental values, which refer to modes of conduct such as honesty and courage; and terminal values, which refer to end states such as freedom and equality. Rokeach defines value as

an enduring belief that a specific mode of conduct or end state of existence is personally or socially preferable to an opposite or converse mode of conduct or end state of existence. A value system is an enduring organization of beliefs concerning preferable modes of conduct or end states of existence along a continuum of relative importance.

Feather (1975) notes that "according to Rokeach, an important function that values serve is to provide standards that guide our behavior in various ways. For instance, values may influence our attitudes and our commitment to particular ideologies, religious or political."

Other authors, however, do not make such a distinction. They view all values as belonging to the same category although they may be hierarchically organized. Wolf and Schwartz (1967) state,

A value is that which is good. The word good is synonymous with values. By good is meant ethical. So when we say values, we are speaking about what we believe is good. In psychological terms, values are long range attitudes, convictions, wishes, hopes, dreams and faith. They are what we hold near and dear and good. These are values; the principles we live and die for, so to speak.

Raths, Hamrin, and Simon (1966) state,

People grow and learn through experiences . . . [and] out of experiences may come certain general guides to behavior. These guides tend to give direction to life and may be called values. Moreover, because values are a part of everyday living, they operate in very complex circumstances which usually involve more than simple extremes of right or wrong, good or bad, true or false. The conditions under which behavior is guided, in which values operate, typically involve conflicting demands, a weighing, a balancing, and finally an action that reflects a multitude of forces. Thus values seldom function in a pure and abstract form. Complicated judgements are involved and true values are ultimately reflected in the outcome of life as it is finally lived.

For our purposes we shall not make a distinction between various types of values; rather, like Ehrlich and Weiner (1961), we shall pull out the common threads that run through most of the definitions and define values as enduring personal preferences, which are either explicitly or implicitly considered "good" by the holder of those preferences. They are a part of a person's personality which influence choice and conduct. Values are abstractions inferred from patterns of specific individual behaviors.

The concept of ethics has also been defined in various ways. Some authors, such as Wolf and Schwartz (1967), equate values and ethics, or rather use the two terms interchangeably. Others define ethics abstractly as a philosophical discipline concerned with human conduct and moral decision making. It is concerned with principles that ought to govern human conduct. (Brandt 1959; Van Hoose and Kottler 1977).

Johnson (1974) states,

Ethics is the Science of Conduct . . . which concerns itself with norms or standards, in contrast to descriptive sciences, which concern themselves with describing empirical facts . . . the ethicist is concerned with only that kind of behavior, which he calls conduct, where one makes a voluntary choice between alternate courses of action. . . . Ethics . . . is a term that refers not directly to practice but rather to theory.

For our purposes, we shall define ethics as a loosely integrated system of values (or valuative judgments) by which one guides and judges one's conduct.

Values, Ethics, and the Client's Symptoms

It is true that "clients seldom describe their need for therapy in terms of problems involving values, just as therapists seldom describe themselves as moralists" (Lowe 1969). Similarly, no major system or school of psychotherapy views its primary purpose as that of changing clients' values.

London (1964) and Daubner and Daubner (1970) believe that many therapists strive to deny the influence of values, ethics, and morality upon the process of psychotherapy. According to London, many therapists argue that

moral concerns are simply manifestations of "resistances" and that the underlying dynamics of the client's situation never relates to moral problems . . . [and that the therapist] must formally remove himself from the discussion by telling the client that the therapy session can be helpful for discussion of "personal, emotional problems, not moral ones."

Thus the issues of ethics and values have been relegated to a secondary place in the framework of psychotherapy.

It is not unusual for therapist and client to collude in the agreement that the troubles and conflicts for which the client comes to therapy are "symptoms" (in a medical sense). The terms which are then used to describe the changes sought in the client's life reflect such a belief system with regard to the client's conflicts—for example, curing the patient's illness; alleviating symptoms; reducing anxiety; solving an identity crisis, and so on.

All such "presenting symptoms" and attempts at symptom alleviation, at least on the surface, appear to be morally neutral (Lowe 1969). Yet a cursory exploration of any of the presenting symptoms makes it clear that each of the symptoms pertains to some valuative conflict or ethical dilemma with which a client is struggling.

Generally, when a client is asked to describe the nature of his presenting symptoms, it becomes apparent that they have a submerged value conflict, or that the client's description pertains to some form of value and ethical conflict. What is labeled as symptom by the psychiatrist is usually described by the client as a behavior that the client cannot help doing. The patient experiences psychiatric symptoms as more or less involuntary occurrences (Szasz 1965). In fact, the very description of one's behavior as showing psychiatric symptoms means a loss of freedom. As Szasz (1965) states,

Phenomenologically, psychiatric symptoms are endlessly diverse . . . the common element in these and other so-called psychiatric symptoms is the expression of loss of control or freedom. Each symptom is experienced or defined by the patient as something he must do. The alcoholic, for example, asserts that he cannot stop drinking; the habitually tardy person, that he cannot help being late; the volatile person, that he cannot control his temper; the hallucinating person, that he cannot shut out "voice" and "visions"; the depressed person, that he cannot experience pleasure or self-esteem; and so forth.

A different set of ethical and value conflicts is submerged under other presenting symptoms. For instance, when the symptom is identity crisis, the client implicitly complains that he has not been able to consolidate a value system and ideological orientation and find a role for himself within the given historical and sociocultural system that will give meaning and direction to his existence. Or when the symptom for a female client is fear of open space, it could mean a conflict between her (erotic) wishes and moral values.

Similarly, when a client presents multiple symptoms, he may be beseiged by more than one set of interlocking value and ethical conflicts. If such symptoms are taken at their face value—that is, as manifestations of an underlying disease—and not interpreted or retranslated as ethical conflicts, then the therapist will not be successful in dealing directly with the client's conflicts. The reason is that the moral and ethical conflicts will remain hidden behind the screen of symptoms and illness. Hence, as a general rule, the task of a therapist is to reconvert or retranslate the so-called symptoms into moral and ethical conflicts.

One recent author who discusses the role of values in psychotherapy makes an implicit distinction between the so-called symptoms of the patient and the value system of the patient. He states, "For the most part, new patients approach the therapist seeking a relief of symptoms. This inquiry may extend to a deep dissatisfaction with their current mode of life but rarely does the inquiry extend to a desire to alter their 'basic belief' or value system" (Graham 1980). In contrast, this author views the presenting symptoms as a denouement of the ethical and moral conflicts of the client. That is, symptoms are a manifestation of value conflicts, rather than something apart from them.

Theories of Psychotherapy and Their Ethical Presuppositions

Theories and techniques of psychotherapy are based upon certain ethical and valuative presuppositions. Such presuppositions set the tone for the course of psychotherapy. For example, client-centered therapy is based upon the assumption that each person is a person of worth in himself and therefore to be respected as such. Furthermore, each individual has the right of self-direction, the right to choose or select his own values and goals and to make his own decisions. It views man as basically "cooperative, constructive and trustworthy when he is free from defensiveness. . . . Anti-social emotions (jealousy, hostility, etc.) exist and are evident in therapy but these are not spontaneous impulses that must be controlled, rather they are reactions to frustration of more basic impulses—love, belonging, security, etc." (Patterson 1973).

Psychoanalytic theory and therapy are based on the valuative system that a man, by nature, is dominated by destructiveness, narcissism, and defensiveness, and is in constant conflict with the society. Further, it is only through "rationality," in contrast to supernatural beliefs, belief in religion, belief in the occult, and so on, that one can solve his troubles and conflicts.

The values and ethical underpinnings of reality therapy are that emotional disturbances and behavioral deviance arise because one does not accept and incorporate the value system and the moral standards of the given "social reality" and the social institutions.

In addition, theories of psychotherapy have an implicit or explicit concept of normality (or a healthy personality, a mature or well-functioning personality). Such a concept of "normal," "healthy," or "well-adjusted" is a value or an ethical presupposition. Directly or indirectly, a therapist encourages the client to attain a certain normality. Frequently, such a concept of normality is the therapist's overriding vision of success in therapy.

Values and the Client-Therapist Interaction

Most clients come to therapy with vague emotional problems, anxieties about their attitudes and relationships, and general dissatisfaction with their lives. In therapy, a great amount of time is spent by the clients in talking about their interpersonal conflicts and their difficulties with developing a satisfactory life-style. They would like to construct different attitudes enabling them to integrate experiences and relationships in a more meaningful and satisfactory manner. In other words, they would like to have a different outlook and value orientation (Lowe 1969). In view of this, Pratt (1955) contends that "psychotherapy involves a systematic and conscious modification of patient's values by means of the application of the method of science, literature and religion." Hence the process of psychotherapy itself, at least partly, consists of reorientation of values and ethics.

Psychotherapy also involves persuasion (Szasz 1978). In a therapeutic relationship a therapist has no pills, no medicine, and no instrument but himself and his conversation, which he uses as instruments to persuade a client to change his values and ethical posture. "Every psychotherapist, willy-nilly, cures with what he himself is, as well as his studied arts" (Watson 1958). Since a therapist himself has a value orientation and believes in what is good and right, he attempts to shape the client in a certain image which inevitably reflects some of the therapist's values and ethics.

An interaction between two people which occurs in the nexus of values and ethics is likely to influence and change the values of the client and also of the therapist*. Many studies support this proposition. Harway (1959) found that "the goals that a therapist sets for the patient are related to the therapist's personality structure [and] in setting goals for his patient the therapist is more concerned with what the patient should be like than with what he should not be like." Thus the therapist seems to support and encourage the client to become like him, and by implication, wishes the client to incorporate his values and ethics.

Rosenthal (1955) found that improvement in psychotherapy was significantly but not highly associated with changes in the direction of the therapist's moral values. He observed that patients who were unimproved or worse actually tended to move away from the therapist's values. Palmore et al. (1959) found "an increasing similarity between the patients' and the therapists' verbal behavior along the following dimensions: Primary System Reference, Evaluative Propositions and Affective Propositions. It was found that as therapy proceeds the patients and the therapist behaved more similarly. . . ."

Welkowitz et al. (1967) found

The value similarity between therapists and their own patients is greater than the value similarity between therapists and random not-own patients. . . . The value similarity tends to increase as a function of the length of time in therapy. [Furthermore] . . . the "improved" patient is moving closer to his own therapist's values than is the "unimproved" patient. . . .

Schonfield et al.'s (1969) findings show that "patients rated themselves as most improved where the convergence score of therapist and pa-

---

*The therapist also changes his perceptions and values during his interaction with his clients; however, the therapist changes less than the client and his perceptions and values appear to be more stable than that of the client (Van DerVeen 1965; Pande and Gart 1968).

tient were greatest (i.e., where they had come closer to agreement regarding appropriate therapy behavior)." Pentony (1966) also found that "the observed trends are in the direction of making the client group resemble the staff group more closely as therapy proceeds."

Using clients at a university counseling clinic, Cook (1966) studied the value similarity between the clients and therapists and the degree of change. He found that a medium degree of value similarity between client and counselor (rather than either high or low similarity) appeared to bring about a more positive evaluation of the client's education, and future (two of the four dimensions tested).

A number of studies, however, tend to cast doubt on these findings. Cartwright and Lerner (1963) found that after therapy the self-description of the improved patient moves away from the therapist's pretherapy description. The unimproved patient's self-description remains more like his therapist's pretherapy description of him. Therapists of the improved cases change their conceptions of the patients in ways that bring them closer to the patients' views, rather than the patients changing their views to match the therapists'.

Farson (1961) found that after therapy, the client's self-description does not resemble his own therapist's, but that of the therapists in general. Nawas and Landfield (1963) found that improved clients tend to increase their preference for their own personality traits and values whereas the least improved tend to internalize those of the therapist.

Landfield and Nawas (1964) found that improved clients may be influenced positively by the therapist's ideals where internalization of the therapist's ideals can be accomplished within the client's own personal frame of reference and language system.

The differences in the findings of these four studies and other studies could be explained on the following grounds. Some of these studies used clients in short-term therapy, while most of the other studies used clients in long-term therapy. Such a difference perhaps did not allow enough time for the clients to incorporate some of the values of the therapist. Studies suggest that a certain minimum length of time "has to be spent by the therapist teaching his patients appropriate therapy behaviors" (Schonfield et al. 1969).

Second, the instruments used to measure values (Role Construct Repertory Test, used by Nawas and Landfield and Landfield and Nawas, the modified version of Q sort used by Farson, and the therapist's self-description and client's description by Cartwright and Lerner) differed from those used in other studies. The instruments used in these studies represent more a measure of personality traits or empathic ability than value preferences.

After weighing the existing evidence, our conclusion is that in long-term therapy (ten months or more) the client's values begin to converge toward those of the therapist. The longer a client stays in therapy, the more the values change in accordance with those of the therapist (Pentony 1966).

The therapist's values are revealed to the client through various methods and devices—his approval and disapproval of the client's behaviors; the manner of his intervention, which accurately reflects his values; and the importance he attaches to certain behaviors and issues in the client's life (Parloff et al. 1961). The client then begins to sense which of the values should be changed and in what direction. The old moral injunctions and values are seen in a new light, that is, in an ethical and moral framework, which is at least partially provided by the therapist and which ideally gives the client a greater inner freedom (Breggin 1971).

Professional Ethics of the Therapist

Generally, therapists belong to some professional organization, which probably has an ethical code to which the members are expected to subscribe. Not only does a therapist learn to conduct himself in a professionally ethical way, he accepts the given ethics as his own (Lowe 1969). The therapist formulates the goals of therapy in the light of this ethical system and tries to convey such goals to the client. He formulates the goals of therapy to change the conduct of the client by this ethical system (Margolis 1966). As one philosopher observes,

The counselor usually works from a value frame of reference in which he makes normative value judgements by appealing to the first principles of his system. Given a system such as American Personnel and Guidance Association's Ethical Standards . . . or Ethical Standards of Psychoanalysis . . . the task is that of applying the principles to particular cases (Golightly 1971).

Let us suppose that there is little agreement between the therapist and the client about values, ethics, and outlook on life. The result is inevitably a clash between the therapist and the client. Or the therapist may distort his perception of the client's life because he uses different moral standards to evaluate behavior (Lowe 1969). Indeed, the therapist shows preference for, and prejudice against, those who have not quite accepted his value and ethical system. The more that the therapist and client differ, the more difficult they find it to agree upon the goals of therapy (Lowe 1969).

Psychotherapists and the Values and Ethics of the Middle Class

By virtue of the fact that they live in society, therapists have a class affiliation. Studies suggest that their affiliation is usually middle and upper-middle class (Henry et al. 1971). Since therapists formulate the principles of psychotherapy, one may assume that the principles are not value-free and that they reflect an underlying class ideology. A close examination of this ideology reveals that the principles of psychotherapy are submerged in a matrix of middle-class values, in which the given society and the arrangements of its institutions are generally accepted as legitimate and good. Questioning of the social and institutional arrangements is in itself interpreted as deviant, or perhaps as evidence of mental disturbance or social malcontentedness requiring psychotherapy. This middle-class ideology is based on strong values in the following specific areas: work, time, money, property and material possessions, achievement or achievement motive, emotional control, and conformity and adjustment.*

IDEOLOGY OF WORK. Work is a quasi-religious duty; it is a calling of God, therefore the expression developed, "To work religiously" (Albee 1977). Work has a redemptive quality; one can redeem oneself through hard work. Work is also a virtue. To work hard, to strive, is a virtue. Its opposite, idleness, is a form of sin, and the idle person is an abode of the devil. Those who do not work hard are indolent. In fact, there is a prevalent belief that people are poor because they do not work hard; that is, poverty is punishment for the sin of not working hard. Many theories of psychology and sociology are based upon this ideological precept. A mentally healthy person places a great emphasis on the importance of a vocation (Gursslin et al. 1959–60).

IDEOLOGY OF TIME. Time is a valuable commodity. It should be

---

*Some studies suggest that there is a significant contrast between the values of mental health professionals and those of a large portion of the clients. This contrast of values is noteworthy in the religious aspects of life (Bergin 1980). While most therapists profess agnosticism, the clients believe in some form of God or gnosticism. See also Nix (1978), and Bergin (1983).

saved and not wasted or used frivolously. To make the best of it, it should be used in a precise and punctual manner. Time is money, for it is through the dimension of time that "value"—money-producing work—is accomplished. All professionals charge according to the time spent, and no professional would spend his time on anything without being paid for it. The expression "time is money" can be seen in its concrete, operational form in our field.

IDEOLOGY OF MONEY. Money is an ultimate value in our society for it represents prosperity. It can buy power, fame, pleasure, and even immortality. Profit is the most powerful ideological goal in capitalistic society. Money should be saved, used prudently, and reinvested so that it can regenerate itself and provide dividends. In fact, money should work for the individual, not the reverse.

IDEOLOGY OF PROPERTY AND MATERIAL POSSESSIONS. Material possessions are a measure of personal worth. Material possessions serve as an extension of one's ego or self. Since the effort to acquire material goods or possessions takes up a major part of an individual's lifework, one often becomes more attached to material possessions than to human relations. The common expression, "What do you have to show for it?" (What material possessions do you have to show for your work?) succinctly sums up this ideological position.

IDEOLOGY OF ACHIEVEMENT OR ACHIEVEMENT MOTIVE. The drive for achievement and competition is the hallmark of the middle class. If an individual does not seem to strive for success, he or she is considered deficient in some basic personality trait.

IDEOLOGY OF EMOTIONAL CONTROL. Affect-emotion and reason-rationality are viewed as opposite ends of a spectrum. One can be either emotional or rational, but not both. Emotions are not to be trusted; only rationality can be trusted. Lack of control of emotions is equated with irrationality. To be successful, one must control his emotions or direct them toward approved or harmless outlets. The possibility of being emotional about "rational issues" is not seriously accepted.

IDEOLOGY OF CONFORMITY AND ADJUSTMENT. Since the middle-class ideology accepts the given society and its institutional arrangements as legitimate and good, it urges its members to conform to these institutions. Friction in either interpersonal or institutional relationships is viewed as a sign of mental disturbance (mental illness). As a corollary, it is believed that if one is "mentally healthy" one should be able to get along with others, including the institution where one works. Thus, there is a social premium on and reward for conformity and adjustment, as opposed to questioning and changing (Gursslin et al. 1959–60).

This ideology may not always be stated in affirmative terms. More frequently it is stated negatively. For example, if one ceased to work, he would be labeled indolent and stigmatized as "living on hand-outs." Spending money recklessly is viewed with suspicion. Lack of respect for one's own or others' property is condemned as some form of aberration. Violation of this ideology comes close to the description and criteria of mental illness (Gursslin 1959–60). "In fact, if one were to examine the case histories of mentally ill persons, it would be an easy task to identify the conventions and morals from which they have deviated upon which the label of mental illness was based" (Leifer 1970).

Directly or indirectly, this middle-class ideology bears upon the behavior expected of the client in therapy, upon the interpretations a therapist makes during the course of therapy, and upon the overall direction of therapy. Frequently, the therapist subtly sets up the contingencies of reinforcements for the client to accept such an ideology.

Structural Interaction of Therapy and Its Ethics

There are certain built-in behavioral and ideological requirements in the structural situation of therapy over and above those discussed. In psychotherapy literature, these requirements have been accorded a quasi-ethical status. Generally, therapists also accept them as ethical guidelines of the therapeutic situation. These requirements are as follows.* (1) The client should be accepted as he is.** (2) The therapist should have certain expectations of the client. He should expect the client's vigorous involvement in the situation and his openness and honesty with himself and with the therapist. (3) The therapist should not interfere in the therapeutic situation because of his own

---

*These points were brought to my attention many years ago by Dr. Louis Paul of the Southern California Psychoanalytic Association, Los Angeles.

**The validity of this tenet can be questioned: If a client is accepted as he is, then why should he change? A better formulation of this tenet is: a client is not to be rejected for his beliefs and behaviors which may differ from those of the therapist.

moral and ethical biases, and the client should have an opportunity to develop his own value system. (4) The therapist should not hold the client responsible for his feelings (the client can't help but have feelings), but only for what he does with them and how he manages them. The therapist does expect the client, as an adult, to be able to identify his feelings and emotions. (5) Because the client incurs or brings upon himself, either knowingly or unknowingly, the situation of which he complains, he should bear the consequences of his actions. (6) The therapist must inhibit physical destruction—the client's cruelty, harm, vengeance, and hatefulness against himself and others. (7) The therapist is not to obtain the gratification of his desires and wishes, or the resolution of his own conflicts either through the client or the therapeutic situation. He should do so outside the therapeutic setting.* It is true that a certain narcissistic and professional gratification and pride accompany the client's progress and growth, but a distinction should be made between personal gratification and a professional one. Professional gratification is the reward for a therapist's work and acumen. (8) The therapist should not endorse self-deception or magical beliefs. Since psychotherapy has an empirical foundation and strives to be a scientific endeavor, acceptance of magical powers is contrary to its basic assumptions. (9) The client and the therapist are not to intrude into each other's stated boundaries.

These quasi-ethical presuppositions are more or less accepted by the therapist; they become part of the structure of psychotherapy, and in successful therapy the client begins to accept them and to conduct himself accordingly.

The Role of the Therapist

In classical analysis and in certain schools of therapy, the therapist is encouraged to avoid imposing his values and ethics upon the client. It is maintained that this may be achieved by the therapist undergoing personal analysis or therapy. In analysis, a therapist would become aware of his ethics, morality, and values and thus would be better able to discern and control the imposition of them upon the

---

*This contradicts what has been said in the chapter on counter-transference (Chapter 9). Nevertheless, such behavior remains the ethical desideratum of the therapeutic profession.

client. Contrary to this assumption, however, the existing empirical studies suggest that the influence of a therapist's values and ethics upon the client cannot be avoided during the course of therapy, regardless of the therapist's analysis. The question arises, then, as to whether a therapist should avoid discussing his values because he may influence the client or impose them on the client. This question has presented perplexing dilemmas for therapists. Two things seem persuasive to the author.

First, a therapist should recognize and accept his own values and ethics. This may help him consciously to exclude some of them from the therapeutic encounter (Green 1946; Ginsburg 1950; Ginsburg and Herma 1953). Personal analysis may be helpful in such a clarification process. If a therapist's values are not clear to him and if he is not willing or able to encounter them squarely, there is greater likelihood that he will impose them upon the client in the cause of "mental health," "adjustment," "maturity," or even the "principles of psychotherapy."

A therapist should not resist expressing his values and ethics when asked to by the client. However, he should make clear that they are his own values and leave the client free to accept or reject them.

Second, the therapist should be aware that he cannot conduct an ethics-free psychotherapy. In one form or another, both the client and the therapist seek some form of value and ethical reorientation. It appears, therefore, that the best the therapist can strive for is a minimal imposition of his values upon the client. Ideally, then, the client's values could prevail.

A general orientation to therapy, which may help a beginning therapist minimize imposing his morality upon the client, requires that the therapist pay attention to the client's description and view of his conflicts. The client's difficulties are a result of his value conflicts. This approach should objectify for the therapist the client's moral dilemmas and thus help him suspend his own values and let those of the client emerge.

Summary

Both the client and the therapist bring certain values and ethical considerations to the process of psychotherapy. A majority of clients go to psychotherapy because of ethical and moral conflicts which create confusion. They seek reorientation and clarifications of their values in therapy.

The therapist's values enter into therapy in more than one way. The theories of psychotherapy that a therapist follows are based upon certain ethical presuppositions about the nature of human conflicts. The professional role of the therapist demands a certain ethical behavior; the structural requirements of therapy require a certain ethical belief on the part of the therapist. Finally, the therapist brings certain middle-class values to therapy. All of these forces influence the therapist's behavior, expectations, and formulations. In short, little in psychotherapy is value- or morality-free.

Directly or indirectly, a therapist influences the values of the client. It is not easy for the therapist to keep his morality out of therapy and to let the client's values emerge. The best a therapist can strive for is to minimize his influence, and to do so, he must be clear about his own values and about the mechanisms and the method by which he may impose them upon the client. Only when he is able to do this will the values of the client have a chance to emerge and the client have the opportunity to sort them out.

References

Albee, G. 1977. Protestant ethics, sex and capitalism. *American Psychologist* 32:150–61.

Bergin, A. E. 1980. Psychotherapy and religious values. *Journal of Consulting and Clinical Psychology* 48:95–105.

———. 1983. Religiosity and mental health: A critical re-evaluation and meta-analysis. *Professional Psychology: Research and Practice* 16:170–84.

Brandt, R. B. 1959. *Ethical theory*. Englewood Cliffs, N.J.: Prentice Hall, 2.

Breggin, P. R. 1971. Psychotherapy as applied ethics. *Psychiatry* 34:59–73.

Cartwright, R. D., and B. Lerner. 1963. Empathy, need to change, and improvement with psychotherapy. *Journal of Consulting Psychology* 27:138–44.

Cook, T. E. 1966. The influence of client-counselor value similarity on change in meaning during brief counseling. *Journal of Counseling Psychology* 1:77–81.

Daubner, E. V., and E. S. Daubner. 1970. Ethics and counseling decisions. *Personnel and Guidance Journal* 48:433–42.

Ehrlich, D., and D. N. Wiener. 1961. The measurement of values in psychotherapeutic settings. *The Journal of General Psychology* 64:359–72.

Farson, R. E. 1961. Introjection in the psychotherapeutic relationship. *Journal of Counseling Psychology* 8:337–43.

Feather, N. T. 1975. *Values in education and society*. New York: Free Press, 8.

Freud, S. 1928, 1949. *The future of an illusion*. New York: Liveright Publishing Corporation, 64.

Ginsburg, S. W. 1950. Values and the psychiatrist. *American Journal of Orthopsychiatry* 20:466–78.

Ginsburg, S. W., and J. Herma. 1953. Values and their relationship to psychiatric principles and practice. *American Journal of Psychotherapy* 7:546–73.

Golightly, C. L. 1971. A philosopher's view of values and ethics. *Personnel and Guidance Journal* 50:289–94.

Graham, S. R. 1980. Desire, belief and grace: A psychotherapeutic paradigm. *Psychotherapy: Theory, Research and Practice* 17:370–71.

Green, A. W. 1946. Social values and psychotherapy. *Journal of Personality* 14:199–228.

Gursslin, O. R., R. G. Hunt, and J. L. Roach. 1959–60. Social class and the mental health movement. *Social Problems* 3 (Winter): 210–18.

Hartman, H. 1960. *Psychoanalysis and moral values*. New York: International University Press, 20–21.

Harway, N. 1959. Some factors in psychotherapists' perception of their patients. *Journal of Consulting Psychology* 23:379–86.

Henry, W. E., J. H. Sims, and S. L. Spray. 1971. *The fifth profession*. San Francisco: Jossey-Bass.

Hobbs, N. 1964. Mental health's third revolution. *Journal of Orthopsychiatry* 34:822–33.

Johnson, O. A. 1974. *Ethics*. New York: Holt, Rinehart and Winston, 1–2.

Landfield, A. W., and M. M. Nawas. 1964. Psychotherapeutic movement as a function of communication and adoption of therapist's values. *Journal of Counseling Psychology* 11:336–41.

Leifer, R. 1970. *In the name of mental health*. New York: Science House, 114.

London, P. 1964. *The modes and morals of psychotherapy*. New York: Holt, Rinehart and Winston, 5, 7–8.

Lowe, C. M. 1969. *Value orientations in counseling and psychotherapy*. San Francisco: Chandler Publishing Co., 36–37, 39, 46, 273.

Margenau, H. 1959. The scientific basis of value theory. In A. H. Maslow, ed., *New knowledge in human values*, 38, 42, 51. New York: Harper and Row.

Margolis, J. 1966. *Psychotherapy and morality*. New York: Random House, 19–21.

May, R. 1953. Historical and philosophical presuppositions for understanding therapy. In O. H. Mowrer, ed., *Psychotherapy: Theory and research*, 40. New York: Roland Press.

Morris, C. 1956. *Varieties of human values*. Chicago: University of Chicago Press.

Nawas, M. M., and A. W. Landfield. 1963. Improvement in psychotherapy and adoption of the therapist's meaning system. *Psychological Reports* 13:97–98.

Nix, V. C. 1978. A study of religious values and psychotherapists. (Ph.D. diss., New York University), *Dissertation Abstract International* 39:1965-B.

Palmore, E., H. L. Lennard, and H. Hendin. 1959. Similarities of therapist and patient verbal behavior in psychotherapy. *Sociometry* 22:12–22.

Pande, S. K., and J. J. Gart. 1968. A method to quantify reciprocal influences between therapist and patient in psychotherapy. In J. M. Shlien, ed., *Research in Psychotherapy*, 395–415. Washington, D.C.: American Psychological Association.

Parloff, M. B., N. Goldstein, and B. Iflund. 1960. Communication of values and therapeutic change. *Archives of General Psychiatry* 2:300–304.

Parson, T., and E. A. Shils, eds. 1952. *Towards a general theory of action*. Cambridge, Mass.: Harvard University Press, 59–60.

Patterson, C. H. 1973. *Theories of counseling and psychotherapy*. New York: Harper and Row, 380.

Pentony, P. 1966. Value change in psychotherapy. *Human Relations* 19:39–46.

Pratt, D. 1955. Values—their dynamics in behavior and psychotherapy. *Journal of Pastoral Care* 9:189–202.

Raths, L., M. Harmin, and S. Simon. 1966. *Values and teaching*. Columbus, Ohio: Merrill, 26.

Rokeach, M. 1973. *The nature of human values*. New York: Free Press, 5.

Rosenthal, D. 1955. Changes in some moral values following psychotherapy. *Journal of Consulting Psychology* 19:431–37.

Schonfield, J., A. R. Stone, R. Hoehn-Saric, S. Imber, and S. Pande. 1969. Patient-therapist convergence and measure of improvement in short-term psychotherapy. *Psychotherapy: Theory, research and practice* 6:267–72.

Szasz, T. 1965. *The ethics of psychoanalysis*. New York: Basic Books, 14–15.

———. 1978. *The myth of psychotherapy*. Garden City, N.Y.: Anchor Press/Doubleday.

Van DerVeen, F. 1965. Effects of the therapist and the patient on each other's therapeutic behavior. *Journal of Consulting Psychology* 29:19–26.

Van Hoose, W. H., and J. A. Kottler. 1977. *Ethical and legal issues in counseling and psychotherapy*. San Francisco: Jossey-Bass Publishers, 6–7.

Watson, G. 1958. Moral issues in psychotherapy. *American Psychologist* 13:574–76.

Welkowitz, J., J. Cohe, and D. Ortmeyer. 1967. Value system similarity: Investigation of patient-therapist dyad. *Journal of Consulting Psychology* 1:48–55.

Wolf, A., and E. K. Schwartz. 1967. Psychoanalysis in groups: The role of values. In O. H. Mowrer, ed., *Morality and mental health*. Chicago, Ill.: Rand McNally and Company, 104–18.

4

Social Context and Conceptual Structure of Psychotherapy

Little attention has been paid, in either the literature or practice of psychotherapy, to the social context and the conceptual structure of psychotherapy. It is important to understand both of these because they have a direct influence upon the interaction between therapist and client during the course of psychotherapy.

Various authors have wrestled with the effects of the social context and conceptual structure on the process of therapy. Some have attempted to protect psychotherapy from its social and political context by developing certain kinds of models; others have attempted to create models of psychotherapy wherein sociopolitical influences become an integral part of the therapeutic process; still others have tried to create models that will be "neutral" with regard to the sociopolitical and intellectual climate; and some have taken the sociopolitical conditions as merely a backdrop against which psychotherapy is conducted.

Halmos (1966) summarizes the historical background and the rationale for the development of a conceptual structure of psychotherapy which endeavors to divest itself of the social and political influences. He observes that people turned to psychotherapy toward the end of the nineteenth century out of disappointment with the sociopolitical solutions to human problems. Such an individual, termed by Halmos as a "post-political man," turned to psychotherapy rather than politics in search of a more satisfactory life and was influenced by seven factors, most of them sociopolitical in nature: the complexity of social life; the deception of political ideological doctrines; the discovery that compassion for one's fellow beings can be expressed by tending to his personal problems in the newly invented role of secular counselor; the belief that political action is wasteful of human sympathy; the belief that one cannot care for persons and impersonal causes at the same time; the notion that politics are stereotyped, in that tactical considerations dictate their being addressed to the lowest common denominator; the concern with the loneliness of man in mass society and with personal relationships.

To fulfill the needs of such an individual, schools and systems of psychotherapy emerged during the early twentieth century which would minimize the effects of sociopolitical forces upon the individual. Psychoanalysis is a case in point: It attempted to depoliticize psychotherapy by declaring it a method for treatment of the illness of mind, much like treatments for physical illness, which are free of social and political influences.

During the sociopolitical turbulence of the 1960s, therapists advocated the opposite, that "psychiatrists should develop a philosophical orientation that could direct them in their participation in social change—and they should develop a dual role of helpers and social reformers" (Halleck 1971). Some therapists added another dimension to this approach. They believed the function of psychotherapy was to change the existing social institutions and even the social order. According to them, it is the social institutions that generate psychological disturbances (neuroses) through oppression, exploitation, and alienation. They called themselves Radical Therapists and advocated a quasi-revolutionary model of therapy. This form of therapy would be linked to the changes in the institutions of the society, including the psychiatric institutions and its practices (Agel 1971; Brown 1971; Hurvitz 1977).

With the evolution of the women's liberation movement during the same period, theories and practices of psychotherapy came under scrutiny and criticism. The women's movement saw the institutions of psychiatry and psychotherapy and their theories and practices as male ideological weapons perpetuating the inferiority and suppression of women. The movement also emphasized the changes in the existing social institutions and psychiatric theories in the direction of feminine egalitarianism.

Thus, the decades of the 1960s and 1970s witnessed many novel and challenging approaches to psychotherapy. At the same time, explanations of human behavior and human conflicts abounded, ranging from biochemical causes and vitamin deficiency, to lack of orgasmic release, to an inability to scream. Diverse approaches to psychotherapy began to emerge. As one observer put it, "While earlier psychoanalysis was the dominant mode of psychotherapy, today there are 130 schools of therapy competing for recognition" (Parloff 1976). Many began to wonder whether each (or a number) of the schools and systems may not have some truth in them. Hence, many began to develop an approach to therapy that incorporated different aspects of various schools and systems. An eclectic approach to psychotherapy became popular and began to represent the mainstream of therapeutic practice (Garfield and Kurtz 1976).

Schools and systems of psychotherapy thus seem to develop within a sociohistorical and intellectual context and reflect some of the values of the period from which they emerge. Each school (system) of therapy explicitly or implicitly sets forth an image of man, the nature of human conflicts, the standards of normality and abnormality, and the guidelines and methods of resolving conflicts. Out of these theories, each school formulates a model of psychotherapy which is usually embedded in, but perhaps not identical with, the underlying theory or system.

Psychoanalysis, for example, has a complex theoretical system of personality development, psychopathology, and psychotherapy but uses a hydraulic model. Radical therapy uses a quasi-revolutionary model of therapy.* Client-centered (Rogerian) therapy uses a nondirective model, and so on. Although therapists subscribe to various theories or systems, it is generally the model, embedded in that system, that guides him in his daily work with his clients.

---

*It is interesting to note that in the People's Republic of China the image of man and psychotherapeutic and psychiatric practice is much influenced by Mao Tse Tung thought. The model of psychotherapy and the method of resolving conflicts which emerged out of such a thought system could be roughly labeled as a Politico-Revolutionary Model (*Science for the People* 1974; Munro 1977; Ho 1978).

An examination of the process of psychotherapy suggests that there are four separate but interacting aspects which form the social context and conceptual structure. They are: the conceptual model of therapy used by the therapist; the therapist's social position; the client's socioeconomic, cultural, and psychological status when he comes to therapy; and the setting of therapy. Each aspect influences the therapeutic process and the role of the therapist during the course of therapy.

The Conceptual Model of the Therapist

The therapist's conceptual model of psychotherapy (and its counterpart, psychopathology) predetermines the moves he makes during the course of therapy (Norcross and Prochaska 1983a). Numerous systems of therapy are mentioned in the literature. For this discussion, we have chosen some of the major systems used by the majority of therapists (Garfield and Kurtz 1976) to demonstrate the ways in which the conceptual model affects the therapist's approach to therapy.*

The major systems of psychotherapy are psychoanalytic therapy—the hydraulic model (Fenichel 1946; Freud 1950; Menninger and Holzman 1973); rational emotive therapy—the rational model (Ellis 1962; Raimy 1975); transactional analysis—the game model (Berne 1961, 1964; Harris 1969); client-centered or Rogerian therapy—the nondirective model (Rogers 1942); radical therapy—the quasi-revolutionary model (Agyl 1971; Brown 1971); and reality therapy or task-oriented therapies—the reality model (Glasser 1967).

Psychoanalytic Therapy—The Hydraulic Model Psychoanalysts and psychoanalytically oriented therapists operate from a hydraulic model of psychotherapy. Just as water compressed in a cylinder exerts pressure to emerge, the thoughts and feelings repressed in a human (unconscious) mind exert pressure to emerge and to gain expression and gratification. They have been restrained by a psychical force called repression (and other similar mechanisms). Certain

---

*I have omitted discussion of the medical model in this section because it is derived from a physiobiochemical theory of physical illness. Here, only models derived from psychological theory are discussed. The medical model is discussed in Chapter 2.

thoughts and feelings are in the unconscious because they are painful and/or unacceptable to the individual. The process of repression starts in early childhood and continues throughout one's life unless it is allowed direct expression and gratification. When not allowed direct expression, buried thoughts and feelings emerge in the form of various symptoms. Thus the individual will substitute symptoms unless the feelings are allowed a direct expression (Brenner 1973). A therapist's task, therefore, is to lift the repression and allow direct expression under the control of the ego.

Rational Emotive Therapy—The Rational Model   The conceptual model for therapy of this school is inculcation of rationality in the client (Ellis 1962). On the other hand, the model for psychopathology is the client's irrationality or the client's faulty cognitions or misconceptions—particularly of himself and his relations with others (Raimy 1975). Ellis believes that eleven irrational, superstitious, or senseless ideas characterize neurotic clients.* Following a similar conceptual model, Raimy holds that different kinds of clients—depressive, obsessive, or hysterical ones—also have misconceptions of self. For instance, a depressive believes that he is, has been, and will remain hopeless, helpless, worthless, a creature of guilt and that he shall never recover from whatever ails him. These kinds of misconceptions are the cause of neurosis. Within this conceptual model, the therapist's task is to get rid of illogical, irrational ideas and attitudes and to substitute logical, rational ones. The therapist must "locate the misconceptions and root them out" (Raimy 1975).

Transactional Analysis—The Game Model   Therapists who use the game model of therapy make analogies between psychotherapy and certain types of games—baseball, chess, children's games,

---

*Ellis's eleven irrational ideas are: (1) It is essential that one be loved or approved by virtually everyone in his community. (2) One must be perfectly competent to consider oneself worthwhile. (3) Some people are bad or villainous and therefore should be blamed or punished. (4) It is a terrible catastrophe when things are not as one wants them to be. (5) Unhappiness is caused by outside circumstances, and the individual has no control over them. (6) Dangerous or fearsome things are causes for great concern, and their possibility must be dwelt upon. (7) It is easier to avoid certain difficulties and self-responsibilities than to face them. (8) One should be dependent on others and have someone stronger on whom to rely. (9) Past experiences and events determine present behavior; the influence of the past cannot be eradicated. (10) One should take other people's problems and disturbances seriously. (11) There is always a right or perfect solution to every problem, and it must be found or the results will be catastrophic.

and so on. The game model is likely to guide the therapist in two ways during the course of therapy. First, if he uses chess or baseball as his model, then he is likely to interpret the client's behavior as tactics, "decoys," or "maneuvers." The client is likely to be viewed as the adversary or opponent, as he would be in a game; the aim is to checkmate or defeat him.

The use of such a game model of therapy allows the therapist to speak of the client as being manipulative or attempting to outmaneuver the therapist (Bursten 1973; MacKenzie et al. 1978). The therapist will also try to outwit the client, or as Haley (1963) phrases it, try one-upmanship. The therapist, however, generally does not interpret his own moves as manipulative. Or if he does, he would consider them for the benefit of the client. Thus the therapist views the client's behavior, not his own, within the framework of a game model. Usually, however, the behavior of the client toward the therapist does not differ much from his behavior outside the therapy situation, with his friends, spouse, and acquaintances. A therapist's interpretation of a client's behavior in therapy as manipulative or strategic, then, is predetermined by the model.

The word *game* in psychotherapy should, of course, be used metaphorically; in this sense, it is innocuous. However, therapists often forget the metaphoric basis of the game model. They conceive of the client's attempts to make decisions concerning his life as moves in a game, as frivolous, not serious, repeatable, make-believe. In his writing, Berne clearly implied that he had dropped the metaphorical sense of the games. For a therapist, then, the client's words and actions represent a game that the client is playing, either with the therapist or in his life.

A client's decisions, like those of any individual, are hardly ever frivolous; they are serious and irretrievable. Each move of the client commits him to a different state of being from which he cannot retreat. Unlike a game, life cannot be replayed. Therapists who use the game model in psychotherapy or psychopathology interpret the client's behavior in a predetermined manner.

Client-Centered Therapy—The Nondirective Model   The proponent of the client-centered or Rogerian school of therapy holds that the individual is basically good and has the capacity to realize his potential. He is thwarted by threatening external conditions. If a therapist provides the client with a nonthreatening, warm, and accepting environment and does not try to intervene or impose his own values, the client is likely to discover and attain his goals. In this system, the therapist is likely to use a nondirective model with a minimal amount of intervention, direction, and evaluation.

Radical Therapy—The Quasi-Revolutionary Model Therapists who espouse the system of radical therapy are likely to use a quasi-revolutionary model. They believe that the institutions of the society and prevailing contradictory values systems are likely to generate oppression, mystification, and alienation for the individual. The social condition and institutional arrangements are the source of the individual's psychological disturbance (neurosis). Hence, the client's troubles and conflicts emanate fundamentally from the external institutions, agencies, and their representatives. It is society that requires change, the individual less so. Hence, the therapist's task is to help the client see the sources of his troubles and change them by suggesting and encouraging him to participate actively in the act of altering such institutions.

Reality Therapy and the Task-Oriented Behavior Therapies— The Reality Model Therapists who subscribe to reality therapy maintain that the source of a client's conflict is that the client has not accepted reality; that is, he has not adhered to the rules, laws, and dictums of society (the reality of society). The client has not been successful in incorporating the values of society and its institutions and therefore is in conflict with them. The therapist using the reality model tries to convince the client to incorporate the values of the society, which will help him develop a sense of social reality and show him the consequences of his behavior, if it goes against the social reality.

Conceptual Models, Focusing, and Interpretations in Psychotherapy

How do the conceptual models of therapy affect the course of therapy? What effects do they have? First, it should be noted that whatever the client presents during the course of therapy can be focused upon and interpreted by the therapist in a variety of ways. For instance, the client's conflicts can be viewed as (1) interactions between him and the significant figures in his past, (2) irrational thoughts or erroneous belief systems, (3) interactions between him and the therapist, (4) contradictory emotions, (5) the oppression of social institutions and contradiction of social values and ideology, and (6) as inter-action between him and the external world.

The therapist usually selects certain aspects of the conflicts pre-sented by the client during a session, and focuses upon and interprets them. Focusing and interpreting are done within the framework of the therapist's conceptual model of therapy and are thus dependent upon that model.

For schematic purposes, Table 3 shows that the major thrust of the therapist's formulation of the client's troubles is likely to rest upon the conceptual model. Similarly, by focusing upon certain as-pects of the client's conflicts, the therapist is likely to underplay or sometimes even ignore some of the other aspects.

If a therapist follows the psychoanalytic system of therapy, or the hydraulic model, then as therapy unfolds, he is more likely to focus upon the genetic background of the client's conflicts, upon the past interaction between the client and his parents and his feelings associ-ated with them. The therapist is likely to ignore or underplay the role of the client's current conflicts and the social factors involved.

If the therapist uses transactional analysis or the game model, he is likely to focus upon the interaction between the therapist and the client (the client's feelings, reactions, and sensations in the present) and is likely to interpret the client's life moves as a game following a script or hidden agenda. The therapist is likely to underplay the effect of the client's past and the role of social forces in stimulating the cli-ent's conflicts.

If the therapist's model is rational emotive, then he is likely to focus upon the client's irrational beliefs or misconceptions. The cli-ent's current struggles and the social contradictions and social forces that may be bothersome for him are likely to take a secondary place.

If the therapist uses client-centered therapy—the nondirective model—then the focus of the therapist will be upon the emotional state of the client. The therapist is less likely to focus upon other as-pects of the client's life. He may not attach much importance to the client's past or future or to the social forces that may be instrumental in triggering his conflicts.

The school of radical therapy, the quasi-revolutionary model, is likely to focus upon the social institutions and contradictions of social values which generate conflicts. The individual's psychological strug-gles recede into the background.

TABLE 3

THEORY OF THERAPY	MODEL	FOCUS OR INTERPRETATION OF CLIENT'S CONFLICTS AS:	FACTORS UNDERPLAYED OR IGNORED	AUTHORS
Psychoanalysis and Psychoanalytically Oriented Therapy	Hydraulic	Interaction between the client and his past	External and social conflicts	Freud and others
Rational Emotive Therapy	Rational	Irrational or erroneous beliefs of the client corollary-logic and rationality	Social forces and social behavior of the client	Ellis Raimey
Transactional Analysis Gestalt Therapy	Game	Present interaction between the client and the therapist	Effect of the past upon present Social forces	Perls Berne
Client-Centered Therapy	Nondirective	Emotional states of the client	External world	Rogers
Radical Therapy	Quasi-Revolutionary	Interaction between the client and the institutions of society	Inner struggles of the client	Agel Brown
Reality Therapy Task-Oriented Therapy Behavior Modification	Reality	Interaction between the client and the external world Acceptance of reality	Client's feelings and inner struggles	Glasser Wolpe, et al. Eysenck Krassner

If a therapist subscribes to the school of reality therapy, or task-oriented therapy, the reality model, then he is likely to focus upon the interaction between the client and the external world. The emotional-mental conflicts become secondary for the purpose of therapy.

The conceptual model used by the therapist sets the limits of his modus operandi. None of the conceptual models that the therapist brings to therapy are comprehensive or adequate enough to encompass the conflicts and turmoils in the lives of the clients (Garfield and Kurtz 1977). At best, each conceptual model covers only a certain dimension of the client's troubles. It is possible, however, that occasionally a therapist may see a client whose troubles are circumscribed (certain kinds of phobias, for example), and hence the client may respond to therapy conducted within a particular conceptual framework.

Because the framework of each model is not broad enough, sooner or later the therapist must expand his model and incorporate other conceptual models. Most therapists, therefore, try to incorporate aspects of different models or therapies which they believe allow them efficiently to meet the needs of the clients (Garfield 1982). For this reason, a majority of therapists, particularly the experienced ones, begin to develop and identify themselves with an eclectic approach, in contrast to a particular theoretical orientation (Garfield 1982; Smith 1982). Within the framework of eclectic orientation most therapists strive to achieve "synthetic eclecticism (integrating a diversity of contemporary theories), and technical eclecticism (use of a variety of techniques within a preferred theory" (Norcross and Prochaska 1982).

Owing to such developments in the professional career of a therapist, therapists of diverse backgrounds and theoretical persuasion become similar, particularly in their characterization of the ideal therapeutic relationship and behavior in therapy (Fiedler 1950; Sundburg and Barker 1962; Cartwright 1966; Frey and Raming 1977).* Inexperienced therapists of a particular school probably adhere more than the experienced therapists to what they consider to be the technique of their school, and, within any one school, they would be more similar to one another than to experienced therapists (Fey 1958; Strupp 1960; Norcross and Prochaska 1983).

---

*Somewhat contrary to these authors, Wogan and Norcross (1985), on the basis of their study, state that "the effect of theoretical orientation far outweighed the effect of clinical experience."

Some authors (Patterson 1967; Garfield 1980) have suggested other reasons for the resemblances between therapists of different orientations and theoretical persuasions. These reasons have frequently been considered "nonspecific elements" of psychotherapy since presumably they are not related to the specific nature of the disturbance present in the client. Although they may be considered a necessary condition for therapy, they are not considered a sufficient condition for the progress of therapy. Garfield (1980) maintains that "despite many apparent differences in theoretical orientation and procedures, many of the divergent schools of psychotherapy rely on essentially common factors for securing some of the changes that are believed to occur in their respective psychotherapeutic endeavors."

The more obvious similarities are listed below. (1) Most psychotherapies begin when an individual experiences a degree of discomfort or difficulty which finally motivates him to consult a therapist. (2) Most approaches regard humans as capable of changing, or at least of being changed. (3) Most therapies involve a therapist who has been designated as such and who is perceived generally as a socially sanctioned healer. (4) The fact that the patient is doing something constructive about his difficulties and has engaged the services of an expert who appears to understand his problems may give the patient hope that his situation will change for the better. Therapists schedule regular appointments, and the client has the assurance that he will see his therapist at a fixed time and can look forward to such meetings. There is thus a promise of continued support and help. (5) Most psychotherapies utilize a verbal means of communication and interaction between the therapist and the client. (6) In all therapies a client is afforded an opportunity to tell the therapist about his problems, to confide personal matters, and generally to unburden himself of those things which have been troubling and perplexing him. (7) The therapist, in most instances, will manifest an attentive interest in, empathy with, and understanding of the client. (8) Another common characteristic of widely differing approaches is the fact that each therapist has confidence in the theory and method he uses (Patterson 1967). (9) Most approaches seem to include a relationship which, on the part of the therapist, is characterized by a belief in the ability of the client to change and an expectation that he will do so. In most therapies, the therapist has the opportunity to observe and react to the characteristic behavior of the client. The client may also receive assurance and support from the therapist directly or indirectly, which encourage him to try out new behavior.

The Therapist's Social Position

It is naive to believe that the therapist's actions during the course of therapy are not influenced by his social position. A number of factors combine to make the therapist's social position superior to that of the client. First, psychotherapists as a group belong to a higher socioeconomic class than the clients they see (Henry et al. 1971). This is particularly true for the medical psychotherapist. As a group, therapists have more education, social prestige, and income than their clients (Henry et al. 1971). Furthermore, the therapist has been given a mandate by society to interpret the behavior of the client with regard to its social appropriateness and to define "reality" for him (Lowe 1969; Halleck 1971). This puts them in a superior and sociolegal position vis-à-vis the client in the context of the existing social structure.

There are other reasons for the therapist's superior position. The patients are usually referred to him by people who point out what a capable authority he is and how much the patient needs help. Furthermore, the patient must be willing to pay money even to talk to the therapist, and the therapist can either treat him or dismiss him, and so controls whether or not there is going to be a relationship. Not only the therapist's prestige is emphasized in the initial meeting but also the patient's inadequacy. The patient is at a disadvantage, since he must emphasize the difficulties in his life to a person who apparently has none (Haley 1963).

Haley (1963) maintains that the physical setting also emphasizes the client's inferiority. The therapist sits behind a desk, a symbol of authority, while the client sits in a chair, a position of a supplicant. During the therapy sessions, it is the therapist who defines what kind of relationship they will have and maintains the control of the relationship. Indeed, some traditional therapists have recommended, and the belief is widespread, that the therapist must necessarily assume a somewhat authoritative role at the beginning of therapy, whether he likes it or not (Singer 1965; Chessick 1974). Others have said, "The fact that a therapist must be in a superior position and take charge in therapy is obvious when one considers how impossible the situation would be if he did not" (Haley 1963).

Thus, because of the social situation, the therapist brings into the psychotherapeutic context a superior and authoritative social position. He should have some control (or at least some say) over the client's behavior and some control in setting up certain kinds of relationships in the therapeutic process, which are generally arranged on the therapist's terms. The therapist expects that such control or prestige should be accorded to him by the client. Since he is an expert and has been given authority by society, he can pass judgment on the social-personal conduct of the client.

As discussed above, the superior position of the therapist, his almost complete authority over the client's behavior, is clear in inpatient settings. A similar but hidden authority and control over the clients also extends to outpatient settings. This superiority has frequently led therapists to act in a smug and pompous manner toward clients.

As can be seen, the issue of control—of the social power, authority, and status of the therapist—is an important one in psychotherapy. If the therapist's superior position is not accepted by the client, the therapist is likely to spend many hours trying to convince the client to accept it. If the client refuses to do so, continuation of therapy is not likely. Indeed, under such conditions most therapists have a built-in rationalization to foreclose therapy. They maintain that the client is not ready to explore himself or that he lacks the motivation to change.

Clients' Social and Psychological Status

Clients' psychological orientation to psychotherapy plays an important role in facilitating or detracting from the process of therapy and the resolutions of the clients' conflicts. Like other people, clients both want to know and are afraid to know themselves. They are afraid that the therapist will reveal their "madness" and the seamy side of their lives, or rather that they may encounter these aspects of their personalities during the course of therapy. Frequently, therefore, clients are fearful of opening up and reluctant to investigate their own lives.

Generally, when a client comes to therapy, he brings feelings about himself and his expectations of therapy. By the time a client comes to therapy, he has struggled with his difficulties, has talked to others about them, and has been unable to resolve them. He enters therapy with a feeling of low self-esteem. In addition, the therapist and the client are strangers to each other. Yet the client is expected to shed

his inhibitions and discuss the intimate details of his life. The require-
ment of psychotherapy to talk about one's personal life may present an
additional struggle for the client unless he is helped by the therapist.

Clients have certain expectations of therapy and the therapist.
These expectations may take various forms. Some expect to discover
the "right" way of acting, feeling, and living. Some wish to obtain guidance, advice, and collaboration from the therapist (Heine and Trosman
1960). Some expect to find allies in their life struggles, and some expect comfort and nurturing. Others expect to find a role model or a
neutral critic (Apfelbaum 1958). The client may expect the therapist to
function as an active, directive, and supportive teacher (Chance 1957);
or he may expect the therapist to be passive, detached, and objective
(Begley and Lieberman 1970).

The psychotherapy literature attaches great significance to the
client's expectations of therapy and also to the expectation of the therapist with regard to the client's satisfaction with therapy and the client's
continuation in therapy. If the expectations of the client and the therapist about psychotherapy are too divergent, the client is unlikely to
continue (Heine and Trosman 1960; Overall and Aronson 1963). The
mutuality of expectation was held to be a key factor in successful continuation of psychotherapy.

The effect of clients' expectations of psychotherapy appears to
be complex. In fact, it is difficult to determine from the studies what
constitutes an expectation or "expectancy effect" (Wilkins 1975). Thus,
the findings have been unclear and frequently contradictory.

Duckro, Beal, and George (1979) exhaustively reviewed the
literature on the disconfirmed client role expectation in psychotherapy. They maintain that the studies done prior to 1962 show that unfulfilled expectations had a negative effect on therapy. However, "a review of the available empirical literature since 1962 revealed that the
validity of the disconfirmed expectations—negative effects hypothesis—has not been established with certainty. The research was almost
evenly divided in terms of support for and lack of support for the
hypothesis."

Other reviewers concur in this conclusion. Lambert (1979)
states that while

initial work in this area did show a relationship between expectation for
change and actual improvement, recent reviews are more cautious. . . . Controversy in the conclusions has been obvious and as yet it must be concluded

that the place of the variety of concepts and behaviors, loosely referred to as "expectation" in psychotherapy outcome, is yet to be determined.

Several reasons explain why the disconfirmed expectations of the client do not generate a consistently negative effect in therapy. The first reason could be described as methodological. In many of the studies where no difference was found between the expectancy versus the nonexpectancy group, the experimental subjects were instructed at the beginning of therapy that they were participating in a study dealing with a therapy technique that has been demonstrated to be effective. The control group was given no instructions (Wilkins 1971). It was assumed that the instructions would be internalized by the subjects and would constitute some form of expectation. It is possible that the experimental instruction did not affect the client's motivation or emotional response; therefore, it had no effect, positive or negative, upon the process or the outcome of therapy.

"The question of whether the clients' expectations were confirmed or disconfirmed (asked in most studies) is too simplistic when asked alone. One must also ask whether the person (client) wanted or did not want what he or she expected" (Duckro et al. 1979). For instance, a client may expect a detached and quiet therapist. This expectation may be disconfirmed where the therapist is involved and active. The client may like it. Thus, a client may have either a negative or positive expectation which may be confirmed or disconfirmed. Unless the expectancy variable is further defined, it will remain difficult to generalize from the existing studies about the unconfirmed expectations in psychotherapy.

Furthermore, it appears that the client's expectations of the therapist and the therapeutic process are multidimensional. For instance, a client may hold more than one expectation when he goes to therapy. He may expect to find moral guidance, help, criticism, clarification, change, advice, support, self-expression; he may expect a quiet listener, an active participant, an ally in his struggle to discover secrets of his life, and so on. Disconfirmation may occur in any of these expectations but not all (or most). Hence disconfirmation of expectation may result in diminished client satisfaction only when several expectations are not fulfilled. Disconfirmation of any one expectation may not be in itself an important factor in psychotherapy (Duckro et al. 1979).

The client's attitude and his expectations of therapy will vary if he goes under direct or indirect coercion. If under coercion, the client often displays a guarded suspicion of the therapist's social power and neutrality. He feels that he is expected to make some form of gesture to stay in therapy while he may have little interest and motivation to do so. The client may begin therapy, but he generally looks for situations and opportunities to drop out. Such clients may state publically their commitment to change while privately they attempt to sabotage it.

Some clients in this group expect the therapist to confirm their normality or sanity. If the client is coming to therapy under threat or coercion of the law court, he may wish to obtain a statement from the therapist that he does not need psychotherapy. Hence, he will present no problems, portray his life as relatively conflict free, and minimize his role in any conflict in which he was an active participant.

How should a therapist handle the client's expectations? Should he ignore them? Should he discuss them with the client? Should he wait for the client to bring them up, or should he initiate the discussion? Being aware of the client's expectations and discussing them helps the therapist, especially in the early stage of therapy, to avoid any serious misunderstanding with the client. Generally, confirmation of the client's positive expectations helps the successful completion of therapy. If, however, the negative expectations were confirmed, the client probably dropped out, the therapy was not successful, or the client was not satisfied. In sum, it behooves the therapist to discuss with the client, at least in general terms, the client's expectations in the beginning phase of therapy.

There is general but consistent evidence that the therapist's positive expectations have a direct and salubrious effect upon the client's progress and therapy (Heller and Goldstein 1961; Goldstein 1962; Wilkins 1973; Sloane et al. 1975).

The Setting of Therapy and Its Implications

The therapist and the client interact within a therapeutic setting. The setting and its structure communicate certain assumptions about the relationship between the therapist and the client. Therapists use various settings to meet with their clients. Each has its own significance, advantages, and disadvantages.

The current setting of psychotherapy, in which the client goes to see a therapist regularly at a specified time, evolved over many years

(Fenichel 1946). Previously other structural settings were used; for example, the client's home or a neutral setting in a restaurant or a park, where meetings occurred irregularly.

In such settings, a number of variables affected the client—external stimuli, home conditions, the presence of people involved in the client's life, and so on. It was difficult for the therapist to determine which set of conditions, external or internal, stimulated the conflicts of the client. For the client it was difficult to focus upon himself. Over the years, therefore, an attempt was made to find a constant setting that would minimize the variables affecting the thoughts and feelings of the client. The hope was that if the impact of extraneous variables affecting the client could be reduced, then the client's inner motivational conflicts would emerge.

Extraneous variables were minimized by seeing the therapist at the same time of the day or week for a definite period of time (constancy of time), in the therapist's office (constancy of environment), and with the same person (constancy of personal interaction). The assumption was that once the client's inner conflicts emerged and the client understood his motives and the source of his conflicts, changes in his daily life or behavior would follow.

The setting for psychotherapy that emerged was (and is), at least in outpatient situations, the therapist's office. Many reasons have been given for this practice. First, if the therapist goes to the patient's home, the patient may manipulate the therapist; he may not be ready for the therapy session, or get interrupted by telephone calls, friends dropping in, and so on. Second, the patient's home may represent a social situation rather than a therapeutic one and thus is not conducive to serious exploration of the client's life struggles. Third, it may encourage the client's dependency and regression, because the client is being attended to. Finally, as Szasz (1963) has stated, the therapeutic situation is a very intimate one with a thin line between words and actions. Hence, to avoid the temptation of physical involvement, home visits should be avoided and the protection of an office situation used.

There are two other reasons for creating a neutral environment within which to conduct psychotherapy. These reasons are seldom mentioned in the literature, but they play an important part in the therapeutic process. The first reason is that in all therapies with adult clients, an assumption is made that the client is an active, although unwitting, participant in bringing his troubles and difficulties upon himself. (This assumption is not made in the case of children, because others hold physical and social power over them.) Hence, he must be active in acknowledging his role in his troubles and be active in reducing it. The client demonstrates his willingness to be active when he goes to the therapist's office of his own volition. When the therapist goes to the client's home, it implies that the client is a passive victim of the conflicts and should be looked after, and that he has had little or no active part in bringing his troubles upon himself. His difficulties "happened" to him (Szasz 1961).

The second reason for the evolution of the present setting, also infrequently mentioned in the literature, is that if the therapist goes to the client's house, he has little control over the client's behavior. The therapist will have little authority over what the client does or does not do in his own home, whereas he may be able to exercise some control over the client's behavior in his own office (Older 1977).

During the past two decades, the therapist's office has not always been the sole site of therapy, except for classical analysts. Therapists working with seriously disturbed adult clients, with disturbed children, and in outreach programs (community psychiatry) have recommended home visits. These visits, they maintain, give the therapist a true picture of the client's living space, and his interaction with family members. With children, the therapist can witness the interaction between the child and his parents. Without making a home visit, the therapist cannot thoroughly comprehend how the physical, social, and interpersonal forces in the client's life contribute to his conflicts.

Others have advocated that it may not be necessary to see the clients in the office; clients can be seen in neutral public places such as restaurants, parks, student unions. Such an arrangement, they say, will reduce the stigma (of being crazy) that becomes attached to the client when he goes to see a therapist. Furthermore, such an arrangement generates a sense of equality between the therapist and the client because in public places the therapist has little control or power over the client. Feelings of equality are difficult to generate in an office setting.

The inpatient setting of therapy, in which the client is hospitalized, has certain implications for the client. In such a setting, he has little or no power; he cannot leave the setting, whereas the therapist can and does. Others have control over the client's life. In this structure, therefore, the relationship between the therapist and the client is that of powerful versus powerless or controller versus controlled.

For any setting the therapist chooses, he should remember that each arrangement has limitations and advantages. For example, if the therapist goes to a client's home to do psychotherapy, there is a possibility of psychological and emotional complications. Further, the therapist will have little power over the client in his own home. The advantage could be that the therapist can observe the client in his own physical and social settings. If the therapist regularly sees a client in a neutral place, the client will have difficulty focusing upon himself and will be able to evade the disturbing issues of his life. The therapist will have little idea of what is influencing the client, although the client may feel free, less controlled by the therapist, and more his equal.

If the therapist wishes to maintain some control in the therapeutic situation and wishes to avoid personal entanglement with the client, it may be advisable to meet in an office setting where the client comes to see him. The disadvantages could be that such a setting is likely to give the client a feeling of inequality and of being under the therapist's control.

The Therapist's Office   When the therapist and the client meet, the client should be (relatively) physically comfortable and free from distracting stimuli so that he may be able to focus upon his mental and emotional state. There should be as few interruptions as possible during the session, for it distracts both parties from focusing upon the task at hand. Since therapeutic sessions are organized around time, an easily visible clock should be a part of the setting. A psychotherapist should avoid (especially if he is a nonmedical therapist) any display of anatomical charts, bottles of pills and drugs, or any other medical paraphernalia, since his task has little to do with curing a disease or an illness.

Books, periodicals, and journals are commonly found in a therapist's office. Many therapists also display their degrees and diplomas on the wall, which tend to convey to the client the therapist's knowledge and expertise and his legitimacy as a therapist. Generally, clients are curious about what is in the therapist's office and may wish to initiate some kind of discussion of any of the objects displayed. The setting should convey a sense of privacy (not secrecy) so that the client feels encouraged to delve into his private world.

Some therapists like to tape-record their sessions with clients. Under such conditions, the client's permission must be obtained beforehand. It is generally preferable that the tape recorder be out of the client's sight.

Contradictions of Therapy and Their Resolution

As this chapter attempts to show, the matrix of psychotherapy consists of a series of social forces, role relations, role expectations of the participants, and the conceptual model held by the therapist. Many of them contradict each other. A therapist has to resolve these contradictions, which are either embedded in the matrix of psychotherapy or embodied in the role of a therapist.

The role of the therapist requires that when he is in a power position vis-à-vis the client, he learn to relinquish his power; that he see the client's conflicts through the client's eyes, cooperate with the client, and develop a working alliance, while at the same time point out the client's attempts to manipulate and outwit the therapist. He may view the various actions of the client as games, yet he must take them seriously. A therapist has to fulfill his part of the therapeutic contract, yet he has to be nonbusinesslike and display warmth and concern for the client. The therapist may view the client's conflicts as transactions between different parts of his personality, yet he must perceive the client as a unitary whole.

Similarly, a therapist has to resolve various contradictions inherent in his approach and the conceptual model he uses in therapy. Although he may choose to follow a particular model, he may have to incorporate other models contradictory to the one he uses. And the setting in which he chooses to work may have its own contradictions.

In view of contradictory models, Prochaska (1979) has advocated the development of a

trans-theoretical therapist who strives to go beyond the relativism of eclecticism through a commitment to creating a higher order theory of therapy. Trans-theoretical therapists make an epistemological commitment more than an ethical commitment. Such a commitment is based on the belief that the current relativism can be transcended by discovery or creation of concepts and processes that cut across or transcend present theories (and models) of therapy.

Only when a therapist is able to unify the opposing forces in his conceptual model and his techniques, and embody such unity in himself, will he be able to help his clients resolve their conflicts successfully. If the therapist is not successful in doing so, he is likely to become a partisan, leaning toward or favoring one aspect of the contradictory forces which beset his work.

Summary

The social context of psychotherapy and how the therapist approaches therapy are two important variables which have a significant influence on the course of therapy. Various schools of therapy assign different significance to the social context within which psychotherapy takes place. Some try to divest therapy of its social context; others advocate that therapy is entirely dependent upon its social context; still others acknowledge the social context of therapy and view it only as a backdrop.

Four separate but interacting variables make up the social context and the conceptual structure of psychotherapy. They are the conceptual model of therapy used by the therapist to conduct therapy, the therapist's social position, the client's socioeconomic and psychological status as well as cultural background, and the setting of therapy. Each of these variables affects the course of therapy in a significant way.

The conceptual model of therapy held by the therapist predetermines the approach a therapist is likely to take. The therapist understands and interprets the material presented by the client within the confines of his conceptual model, and he emphasizes or deemphasizes various aspects of the client's behavior in accordance with it. Because no existing conceptual model is broad enough to encompass the diversity and the complexity of human behavior, therapists begin to incorporate aspects of other conceptual models.

The therapist's social position is also an important variable which affects the moves of the therapist in therapy. Generally, therapists have a higher social status and more social-legal power than the client. Therapists expect to direct the client's conduct during the course of therapy. If the client does not readily submit to the therapist's power, then some form of conflict is likely to take place.

The socioeconomic and psychological status as well as cultural background of the client are also important variables in the course of therapy. Clients are anxious when they come to therapy about relating the intimate details and secrets of their lives to a stranger. They also bring certain expectations with regard to the process of therapy and the therapist. If these two aspects are not properly handled, the client is likely to drop out.

The setting in which therapy is conducted—the therapist's office, the confines of a mental institution, the client's home—also exerts an influence over the course of therapy. For example, if therapy is conducted in a therapist's office, then the therapist has a certain control over the client's conduct, whereas if therapy is conducted in a client's home, then he has little control.

Various forces impinge upon the role of a therapist. Many of them are contradictory in nature; for example, a therapist may believe that the client and the therapist should be equals, yet the therapist has social-legal power over the client. He would have to divest himself of his power to be a client's equal. A therapist's role is replete with contradictions, and he must be able to reconcile them before he can successfully help a client.

References

Agel, J., ed. 1971. *The radical therapist*. New York: Ballantine Books.

Apfelbaum, B. 1958. *Dimensions of transference in psychotherapy*. Berkeley: University of California Press.

Begley, C., and L. Liberman. 1970. Patient expectation of therapist techniques. *Journal of Clinical Psychology* 26:112–16.

Berne, E. 1964. *Games people play*. New York: Grove Press.

———. 1961. *Transactional analysis in psychotherapy*. New York: Grove Press.

Brenner, C. 1973. *An elementary textbook of psychoanalysis*. New York: Doubleday-Anchor Books.

Brown, P., ed. 1971. *Radical psychology*. New York: Harper and Row.

Brunink, S. A., and H. E. Schroeder. 1979. Verbal therapeutic behavior of expert psychoanalytically oriented, gestalt and behavior therapists. *Journal of Consulting and Clinical Psychology* 3:567–74.

Bursten, B. 1973. *The manipulator*. New Haven: Yale University Press.

Cartwright, R. D. 1966. A comparison of the response to psychoanalytic and client centered psychotherapy. In L. A. Gotschalk and A. H. Auerbach, eds., *Methods of research in psychotherapy*, 517–29. New York: Appleton Century Crofts.

Chance, E. 1957. Mutual expectations of patients and therapists in individual treatment. *Human Relations* 10:167–78.

Chessick, R. D. 1974. *Technique and practice of intensive psychotherapy*. New York: Jason Aronson, 112.

Colby, M. K. 1951. *A primer for psychotherapists*. New York: Ronald Press.

Duckro, P., D. Beal, and C. George. 1979. Research on the effects of disconfirmed client role expectations in psychotherapy: A critical review. *Psychological Bulletin* 2:260–75.

Ellis, A. 1962. *Reason and emotion in psychotherapy*. New York: Lyle Stuart, 89.

Fenichel, O. 1946. *The psychoanalytic theory of neurosis*. New York: W. W. Norton.

Fey, W. F. 1958. Doctrine and experience: Their influence upon psychotherapists. *Journal of Consulting Psychology* 22:403–9.

Fiedler, F. 1950. A comparison of therapeutic relationships in psychoanalytic, non-directive and Adlerian therapy. *Journal of Consulting Psychology* 14:436–45.

———. 1951. Factor analysis of psychoanalytic, non-directive and Adlerian therapeutic relationships. *Journal of Consulting Psychology* 15:22–28.

Freud, S. 1950. Analysis terminable and interminable (1937). In J. Strachey, ed., *Collected papers*, Vol. 5, 316–58. London: Hogarth Press.

Frey, D., and H. F. Raming. 1977. Primary factors in American counseling. *Psychotherapy: Theory, Research and Practice* 14(3):273–85.

Garfield, S. 1982. Eclecticism and integration in psychotherapy. *Behavior Therapy* 13:610–23.

———. 1980. *Psychotherapy: An eclectic approach*. New York: Wiley, 133, 135, 136.

Garfield, S., and R. Kurtz. 1976. Clinical psychologists in the 1970s. *American Psychologist* 31:1–9.

———. 1977. A study of eclectic views. *Journal of Consulting and Clinical Psychology* 45:78–83.

Glasser, W. *Reality therapy*. 1967. New York: Julian Press.

Goldstein, A. 1962. *Therapist-patient expectancies in psychotherapy*. New York: Pergamon Press.

Haley, J. 1963. *Strategies of psychotherapy*. New York: Grune and Stratton, 72, 74.

Halleck, S. 1971. *The politics of psychotherapy*. New York: Science House.

Halmos, P. 1966. *The faith of the counselors*. New York: Schocken Books.

Harris, T. A. 1969. *I'm OK, you're OK*. New York: Harper and Row.

Heine, R. W., and H. Trosman. 1960. Initial expectations of the doctor-patient interaction as a factor in continuance in psychotherapy. *Psychiatry* 23:275–78.

Heller, K., and A. Goldstein. 1961. Client dependency and therapist expectancy as relationship maintaining variables in psychotherapy. *Journal of Consulting Psychology* 5:371–75.

Henry, W. E., S. H. Sims, and S. L. Spray. 1971. *The fifth profession*. San Francisco: Jossey-Bass.

Ho, D. F. Y. 1978. The conception of man in Mao Tse-Tung thought. *Psychiatry* 41(4):377–91.

Hurvitz, N. 1977. The status and task of radical therapy. *Psychotherapy: Theory, Research and Practice*, 14(1):65–73.

Lambert, M. J. 1979. *The effects of psychotherapy*, Vol. 1. Montreal: Eden Press, 13.

Lick, J., and R. Bootzin. 1975. Expectancy factors in the treatment of fear: Methodological and theoretical issues. *Psychological Bulletin* 6:917–31.

Lowe, C. M. 1969. *Value orientation in psychotherapy*. Cranston: Carol Press.

MacKenzie, T. B., S. D. Rosenberg, B. J. Bergen, and G. J. Tucker. 1978. The manipulative patient. *Psychiatry* 41:264–71.

Menninger, K. A., and P. S. Holzman. 1973. *Theory of psychoanalytic technique*. New York: Basic Books.

Munro, D. J. 1977. *The concept of man in contemporary China*. Ann Arbor: University of Michigan Press.

Norcross, J., and J. Prochaska. 1982. A national survey of clinical psychologists: Affiliations and orientations. *The Clinical Psychologist* 39:1–7.

———. 1983. Clinicians' theoretical orientation: Selection, utilization and efficacy. *Professional Psychology: Research and Practice* 14:197–208.

Older, J. 1977. Four taboos that limit the success of psychotherapy. *Psychiatry* 40:197–204.

Overall, B., and H. Aronson. 1963. Expectations of psychotherapy in patients in lower socioeconomic class. *American Journal of Orthopsychiatry* 33:421–30.

Parloff, M. 1976. Shopping for the right therapy. *Saturday Review*, Feb. 21, 14–16.

Patterson, C. H. 1967. Divergence and convergence in psychotherapy. *Journal of Psychotherapy* 2:4–17.

Perls, F. S., R. F. Hefferline, and P. Goodman. 1951. *Gestalt therapy*. New York: Julian Press.

Prochaska, J. O. 1979. *Systems of psychotherapy: A transtheoretical analysis*. Homewood, Ill.: Dorsey Press, 366.

Raimy, V. 1975. *Misunderstandings of the self*. San Francisco: Jossey-Bass.

Richert, A. J. 1976. Expectations, experiencing and change in psychotherapy. *Journal of Clinical Psychology* 32:438–44.

Rogers, C. 1942. *Client-centered therapy*. Boston: Houghton-Mifflin.

Science for the People. 1974. *China: Science walks on two legs*. New York: Avon Books.

Singer, E. 1965. *Key concepts in psychotherapy*. New York: Random House.

Sloane, R. B., R. G. Staples, A. H. Cristol, N. J. Yorkston, and K. Whipple. 1975. *Psychotherapy versus behavior therapy*. Cambridge, Mass.: Harvard University Press.

Smith, D. 1982. Trends in counseling and psychotherapy. *American Psychologist* 37:802–9.

Strupp, H. 1960. *Psychotherapists in action*. New York: Grune and Stratton.

Sundburg, D. M., and E. N. Barker. 1962. The orientation of psychotherapists. *Journal of Consulting Psychology* 26:201–2.

Szasz, T. S. 1961. *Myth of mental illness*. New York: Hoeber and Harper.

Wilkins, W. 1973. Expectancy of therapeutic gain: An empirical and conceptual critique. *Journal of Consulting and Clinical Psychology* 40:69–77.

Wogan, M., and C. Norcross. 1985. Dimensions of therapeutic skills and techniques. *Psychotherapy* 22:61–74.

Part Two

Technical Aspects of Psychotherapy

5

Beginning Therapy: The First Encounter

It is difficult to give an accurate analysis of the interpersonal dynamics and forces experienced by the participants in therapy. What follows is a schematic and somewhat sterile representation of what takes place in a therapy session. As mentioned in Chapter 4, each of the participants brings his fears, hopes, and questions to the therapy session. The client has to talk to a person he has never met before (although they may have talked over the telephone) about his troubles and conflicts of life. The client may not understand the process of therapy nor does he know what will be expected of him. Generally, therefore, the client is anxious and nervous before and during the first few sessions. Usually he has a great deal on his mind. One session is simply not enough for him to tell his troubled story.

The therapist has to listen to the client's troubles. Some of the conflicts will be clear and understandable. Other aspects of the client's story may be vague, confused, or cryptic. The therapist will have to clarify them for himself and the client. The therapist may have to ask numerous questions to develop a picture of the client's conflicts. The therapist will have to present some form of contract to the client so that the process of therapy may take a form, have some ground rules, and delineate the roles of each of the participants. He may have to answer the client's inquiries. For the therapist too, one session may not be enough to do all this.

Stieper and Wiener (1965) maintain that psychotherapy has a rhythm or phases (stages).

The first three sessions may represent a "get acquainted" period during which the patient and therapist quickly assess each other to find out if they can work together, or if they like each other. A high proportion of pairs apparently find they cannot. Termination at this point is generally at the initiative of the patient, perhaps because the therapist feels pressures against throwing in the towel so easily.

Other studies seem to concur that a large percentage of attrition occurs during the first three sessions (Meyers 1977). (See also Chapter 6 on dropouts.)

Given this psychological background, the therapist's task becomes twofold. First, he will have to create an atmosphere in which the client feels accepted, respected, and free to express himself. In other words, a therapist will have to establish rapport with the client. Second, the therapist will have to clarify his role in the process of therapy. For these reasons, the first meeting and the early phase of therapy are important.

Usually, during the first and/or second session (the early phase) the client summarizes for the therapist his life. The importance of the summary lies in the fact that a considerable part of therapy will deal with the issues raised, albeit in a condensed form, in their myriad ramifications. When the therapist asks the client what has brought him to therapy, the client briefly tells him his troubles and their history and background. The client gives an overview of his life, the details of which will have to be filled in with the unfolding of therapy.

Generally, the presenting difficulties of the client are the denouement in a long series of interpersonal conflicts in which the client has been an active participant. The client may have lived with his troubles for many years. Hence, it requires a concerted struggle on the part of the client to change his situation. Therefore, although he may come to therapy to alleviate his troubles, the client may not be eager to explore and change his life since it will involve confronting his own role in it. In this sense, the client's presenting difficulties are also his resistances.

Thus, the early meetings give the therapist a vague idea of the client's struggles and mode of operation. The first few meetings tend to confirm or disconfirm the client's expectations, fears, and trepidations about psychotherapy and the therapist. And they begin to give both the client and the therapist an idea of whether they can work together.

How to Begin and What to Do in the First Session

For a beginning therapist, the first few sessions are difficult to handle properly. The therapist is uncomfortable and sometimes nervous. During the session, he frequently feels confounded and lost. The therapist is not clear about which aspects of a client's life to explore, what questions to ask, and how to broach certain issues. Furthermore, the beginning therapist has read a considerable amount of literature on therapy. He may subscribe, or be asked by his supervisors to subscribe, to a certain school of therapy. He may be eager to fit the client into a theoretical framework but isn't sure of how to accomplish it.

In spite of the fact that much is written in the literature (Fromm-Reichman 1950; Colby 1951; Saul 1958; Wolberg 1967; Chessick 1974) about the first session(s), a few general principles are worthy of mention and may be helpful to a beginning therapist.

First, the therapist should know the name of the client and should greet him in the waiting room by name, addressing him as Mr., Miss, or Mrs., as one does in any initial meeting. The same courtesy and dignity should be accorded to the client as to any individual one meets for the first time. After a preliminary conversation (I usually ask about the parking problem, difficulty in finding the office, and so on), the therapist could ask, "For what kind of troubles and difficulties have you decided to come?" or simply "What brings you to me?"*

Second, if the therapist knows anything about the client's trou-

---

*Many therapists ask, "What kinds of problems are you having?" or "What is your problem?" The author avoids the use of the term *problem* because it implies an external mathematical-like solution, unless one interprets the client's life or the client himself as the problem. It should be noted that there are hardly any solutions to one's life problems; only resolutions.

bles through a third party—perhaps the person who referred the client to the therapist—he should briefly tell the client what he knows. If the client himself called the therapist and briefly told him about his troubles over the telephone, then the therapist could now recapitulate what was said and ask the client to elaborate upon it.

Some clients bring with them their written autobiographies or journals describing their troubles or conflicts. Other clients, who have been in therapy before, may bring their case histories and diagnostic evaluations. When such clients are asked about their conflicts, they present the therapist with the written material and say, "It's all in here." Under such conditions, my general remark is, "Your efforts to understand your troubles through studies are commendable. However, in this situation it is better to hear them directly from you." The reason for saying this is that it makes the client talk to the therapist. It gives the client a clue that he is expected to express himself verbally. Otherwise, the client hides behind the printed matter.

Third, a therapist should respect the client. Some authors maintain that three attitudes of the therapist—accurate empathy, nonpossessive warmth, and genuineness,*—are basic ingredients to any form of therapy (Rogers 1967; Berenson and Carkhuff 1967). These three attitudes affect the patient in four indirect ways: (1) they reinforce positive aspects of the patient's self-concept; (2) they reinforce self-exploratory behavior; (3) they eliminate anxiety and fear response; and (4) they reinforce human relations (Truax and Mitchell 1971). Since many clients have a vague feeling of defeat and suffer from low self-esteem (see Chapter 1), an accepting and respectful attitude helps alleviate such feelings to a certain extent.

A therapist must always be sympathetic with the client's struggles, whether they be homosexuality, marital troubles, or inability to speak up or to control aggression. Only sympathy to the client's struggles will enable the therapist to see the client's life as the client sees it; only then will the therapist be able to present negative confrontational material to the client for his examination. In fact, a sympathetic attitude

---

*Some studies question the validity of the distinctive roles of the three attitudes. Factor analysis revealed one factor which the authors labeled a "good-guy trait" (Muehberg et al. 1969). Other studies show a negative correlation between warmth and the other two. Garfield and Bergin (1971) found a negative correlation between genuineness and the other two. For a more detailed discussion on this issue, see Traux and Mitchell (1971) and Bordin (1974).

toward the client's struggles should be maintained throughout the course of therapy.

Attitudes of smugness, pomposity, or impatience and lack of humility on the part of the therapist are antithetical to an accepting and self-respecting atmosphere. Such attitudes do not create an atmosphere where the client can begin self-exploration.

Fourth, it is inadvisable to sit in silence or to believe that one should not break silence (Colby 1951). Silence makes the client more anxious and hesitant to talk and makes his task more difficult. Szasz (1965) observes about the patient who finds it difficult to begin:

I think it unpardonable for the therapist to sit silently during the first or second interview and wait for the patient to say something. This early in the relationship the patient does not know the sort of game he is expected to play. Courtesy and tact, as well as analytic principles, require that the therapist discover why the patient cannot proceed beyond stating the initial complaint.

Fifth, an attempt should be made to encourage the client to talk freely and to ruminate about his life difficulties (unless the client is too voluble). Beginning therapists find this difficult to do. Sooner or later they fall into a question/answer type of dialogue with the client. This form of relationship and exchange begins to acquire a courtroomlike atmosphere where the therapist asks questions and the client answers them. Otherwise, the client sits in silence. Such an atmosphere hinders the development of rapport between the therapist and the client.

A few simple methods to encourage the client to express himself could be mentioned. First, therapists' questions or inquiries should be presented in an open-ended way, so that the client's reply involves expressing his opinions, thoughts, and feelings, rather than simply providing yes or no answers. Second, a therapist could preface his inquiry by saying something like, "You have thought about and struggled with these dilemmas rather extensively and for some time; can you tell me a little more about such and such." As discussed in Chapter 1, the client indeed has struggled with his troubles, has done some thinking about them, and usually has little difficulty talking and explaining.

The therapist should avoid making any assumptions about a client's life, at least in the beginning phase of therapy. Therapists often draw conclusions about a client's life from a paucity of data, but the temptation should be avoided. Whatever the therapist wishes to know about a client's life, he should ask directly. A client may not wish to answer it, however. That remains his choice and privilege, and his response should be accepted without question.

A therapist should avoid joining the client in blaming and attacking a third party (the client's spouse, supervisor, or parents) for his troubles and conflicts. If a therapist acquiesces with the client in blaming the third party for his troubles, then obviously the client is not an active agent in creating his difficulties. Therefore, there is little in the client's life that needs change.

The principle that the therapist should not join the client in attacking others but should clarify the client's role in the conflict has been customarily, albeit unwittingly, used by therapists to defend the established authorities and institutions, the status quo, and even the injustices meted out to the client. Frequently when the clients criticize or hold the external agencies and agents responsible for their conflicts, the therapists ignore the client's statements as unreliable or distorted (Wolberg 1967). Instead, therapists are eager to bring out the client's part in the conflict. The existing inequities of the external (social) agencies and agents which may provoke indignation and generate conflict remain protected by the therapists' focusing upon the client's actions and feelings.

Such a nondialectical approach—that is, ignoring the interaction between the subjective and objective—almost invariably tends to put the onus of both the internal (subjective) and external (objective) upon the client, and he has to bear the burden of the existing inequities (Tennov 1975). A therapist's role, however, demands that he avoid any support of the existing inequities. Therefore, they have to be acknowledged and brought out before the client's role in the conflict is discussed. Otherwise, a therapist, regardless of his denials, becomes a defender of the status quo.

A thirty-two-year-old female computer programmer, who was having severe interpersonal difficulties with her parents, children, supervisors, ex-husband and coworkers, was being seen at the clinic. One day she took her sick child to a local hospital of which she was a prepaid member. In the community this hospital is known for delays in service, long hours of wait, and poor medical attention. In the therapy session following her visit to the hospital, the client described and complained to the therapist of the poor service and of an argument with the attending physician. The therapist proceeded to analyze the client's role in it by saying that she always has had difficulty in her interpersonal relations and this was one more example of the same. The client bitterly complained about the therapist's perception and approach to the problem, missed the next session and called the therapist at home to declare that she would not return for future sessions.

Finally, during the first or the second session, a therapist should ask the client whether he has had any previous therapy. If the client did, then one should ask: How long did it last? What, if anything, did the client gain from it? What brought about the termination of the previous therapy? The client's answers to these questions give the therapist an idea of the therapeutic sophistication of the client. The pattern of behavior and relationship which may emerge in the present therapy may be similar to the one in previous therapy. From this similarity, the therapist may be able to develop some idea of what to expect during the course of therapy and may be able to ward off a similar fate or a repetition of the previous therapy.

A thirty-nine-year-old single professional woman who lived with her parents called for therapy because of intense anxiety after the breakup of her engagement. She wanted to find out why she could not sustain a relationship with a man, why she was still living with her parents, and why she had developed colitis. Five years prior to coming to therapy she was an obese woman, weighing three hundred pounds. By sheer determination and strength of will to stay on a diet for about four years she was able to bring her weight down to 125 pounds. Then she discovered she had colitis and sometimes could not control her bowel movements, which was very embarrassing for her. She had been in therapy before with a local psychiatrist for approximately eight and a half months. At the end of this period, she had felt better and quit. After about nine months of therapy with this author, she said that she was feeling better and did not have much more to say. It was brought to her attention that she had quit the previous therapy too when she began to feel better. She was told that thus far in the present therapy she had scarcely touched upon the conflicts and dilemmas for which she came. After that it took another year of work with her to resolve some of the conflicts that had originally brought her to therapy.

Three groups of clients deserve to be singled out for discussion to caution a beginning therapist. In passing it should be mentioned that, generally, if a therapist likes a client he thinks that the client will be easy to work with (Merbaum and Butcher 1982). However, such an assumption, as all experienced therapists have learned, is an erroneous one.

The first group consists of those clients who are voluble, enjoy talking about themselves and their troubles, and fill up the hour easily. They dislike any interruptions or questions by the therapist and are eager to present their side of the story to whomever is willing to listen. A beginning therapist welcomes such clients for there are no silences, difficult moments, or need for questions on his part. He has only to sit and listen.

Such clients may appear to be easy to work with since the therapist drifts along with them, feeling that therapy is progressing since the client is expressing himself. Soon the sessions turn into the client's repetitious monologue. The therapist finds himself at a loss and without any leverage to change the flow of the sessions. He finds himself frustrated and begins to become angry and resentful. With such clients he should not hesitate to raise questions similar to those he raises with other clients. The therapist's inquiries may make the client irritated or angry, but he should be willing and able to absorb the client's negative feelings.

A second group of clients are those whose story is full of lurid and sordid details, usually of sex and violence. The life stories and activities of such clients have a great fascination for a middle-class therapist. The therapist becomes titillated, and consequently abdicates his role as a therapist, losing his direction in the mire of sexuality and violence.

A forty-year-old ex-prison inmate called for therapy because of extreme anxiety and fear of losing control. He had been in prison for the past fifteen years for the murder of his pregnant wife. He had been released on probation six months prior to the call. During these six months he had married a call girl. He was having difficulties at home and found he was more attracted to homosexuals and visited local homosexual bars but had to hide all this from his wife. He was assigned to a third-year graduate student who soon became enmeshed in the lurid details of murder, sex, and homosexuality (both inside and outside of prison). The result was that the client became more upset and anxious, since his main troubles were scarcely being alleviated. Only after intense supervision and guidance for one and a half years was the young therapist able to change his therapeutic strategy and help the client to be partially rehabilitated.

The third group of clients are those who come to therapy with physical (psychosomatic or hypochondriacal) complaints. Before coming to therapy such clients have gone through numerous physical checkups and examinations. Since no physical basis could be found for their troubles, they are referred for therapy. In the literature such clients have been noted for a poor prognosis. However, during the beginning phase, such clients specifically focus upon the history of their physical troubles, complaining that the physicians have been unable to find anything physically wrong with them, or have given them the wrong kind of treatment. Frequently they ask the therapist if he can recommend a good specialist. With such clients a beginning therapist is likely to get involved either in recommending a more qualified physician or in attempting to prove to the client that there is nothing physically wrong with him. Usually he lets the client spend the session talking about his physical troubles.

The therapist should avoid taking any of these three positions—finding a more qualified physician, becoming an antagonist by trying to disprove the client, or being a passive listener to his physical complaints. Rather the therapist's main focus should be the life history (not a history of the physical troubles) of the client; he should not allow the client to dwell on his physical troubles and complaints.

> *A twenty-five-year-old Chinese student now studying in a U.S. university was referred by an opthamologist for psychotherapy because the client was having trouble with his eyes, but the physician had been unable to find any physical cause. The client was deeply preoccupied with the shape of his eyes and felt that he could not see through them clearly. Because of this he was unable to study. His history revealed that since the age of fifteen he had been to numerous opthamologists both in Hong Kong and in the U.S.*
>
> *The therapist, a second-year graduate student, advised the client that no physical problem with his eyes had shown up in the numerous examinations. He returned to this point of demonstration again and again and soon was locked into a position of disproving the client's fears and trepidations. After ten sessions, the client dropped out of therapy, stating that it was not helping him.*

Anxiety and the Therapist's Task

Every client is apprehensive about the first meeting. But he will have difficulty telling his story if he is too anxious or nervous. Under such circumstances the client's anxiety should be reduced. This can be done by being sympathetic toward his dilemmas and offering reassurance; by helping the client state clearly whatever he is trying to say; by not getting upset or frightened by the client's conflicts and dilemmas; and by offering explanations to the client of his anxiety whenever it appears to be of help.

> *A thirty-two-year-old female client, mother of two children, was referred by a school psychologist because her children were having difficulty in school. After interviewing the parents, the school psychologist referred the mother for psychotherapy. During the preliminary conversation, when the*

therapist asked what had been upsetting her, she said it was very difficult for her to talk. She felt nervous and tense and did not know what to say. The therapist explained that it would be natural to feel this way since they were strangers to each other; yet she was supposed to tell about her private conflicts and turmoils. He understood that this must make her feel more nervous and anxious than usual. This approach seemed to calm her a bit, and she was able to talk for the rest of the session.

If the client is rambling and scattered in his narrations, jumping from one theme to another, the therapist should help him focus on one theme so that he can tell his story more coherently. This helps the client express his thoughts in a relatively more systematic manner and gives him a feeling of mastery over his thoughts.

Frequently, the client who comes to therapy under duress or coercion to please others is tense, reticent, and reluctant to talk. Under these conditions, the therapist may talk a little more than usual, may discuss more diverse topics, and may choose not to push the client to discuss the circumstances of his life that brought him to therapy. This approach helps the client feel more free and relaxed so that he can talk.

With every client attending under coercion, it is important that the therapist make his social role clear to him during the first or second session, that is, whether he is the client's agent or that of some other party. After explaining his social role, the therapist must leave the choice up to the client whether he wants to continue therapy.

A married couple of Chinese descent in their early forties came for marital therapy. The wife was born in the United States and the husband, an aeronautical engineer, was born on mainland China. The wife had been seen for the past three years by a local psychiatrist, who had put her on tranquilizers. She had tried to initiate joint therapy with her husband. The psychiatrist saw the two of them for two sessions, but the husband dropped out saying that the psychiatrist sided with the wife and was negative toward him. When he mentioned this to his wife, the wife asked him to find a "neutral" therapist. The husband called me for an appointment.

In our second meeting, I mentioned to the wife that she must feel implicitly coerced to come since she was not eager to see another therapist; still, she had to show her husband that she wished to preserve the marriage. I said that under such conditions she must feel that I wouldn't quite be on her side because the husband had sought me out. She replied affirmatively to both of my remarks. I mentioned that she might wish to reconsider coming to me under these conditions of implied duress. She agreed to think about it, and cancelled our subsequent appointments.

Client's Questions to the Therapist

After the client has talked during the session, he should be offered an opportunity to ask whatever questions he wants and to satisfy whatever doubts and curiosities he may have about the therapist and the process of therapy. Therapists handle a client's questions in various ways. Some therapists invite the client's questions but inform the client that they will answer questions pertaining to psychotherapy, but not pertaining to their personal lives. Other therapists do not invite the client's questions. If the client has any, the therapist may or may not choose to answer the questions. Still other therapists do not invite any questions and if the client asks, they do not answer (Colby 1951). Personally, I encourage the client to ask questions by saying something like, "You may have certain questions and curiosities about me or therapy which you are free to bring up."

Generally, clients are curious and do have questions about the therapist and the process of therapy. Often when the client is invited to ask questions during the first or the second session, he may not have any immediate ones, but some do arise in subsequent sessions. Clients' questions can be divided roughly into six categories:

(1) Questions pertaining to the process by which therapy will help resolve the client's conflicts; for example, "How can talking help me get along better with my wife?" "Is it all we are going to do, talk, or are you going to give me some sort of advice or hypnotize me?"

(2) Questions pertaining to the therapist's education, training, experience, background (including ethnic origin); for example, "Where did you go to school?" "How long have you been working with clients?" "Have you worked with someone who had problems like I do?" "Where did you originally come from?"

(3) Questions pertaining to the different kinds of therapeutic approaches or school of therapy; the difference between psychologists, psychiatrists, and social workers; whether different methods and techniques of therapy are used by each of the professional groups.

(4) Questions pertaining to the client's mental-emotional state or diagnosis; for example, "Do you think I need therapy?" "Can I be helped?" "Am I crazy?" "Am I neurotic or psychotic?" "What is my diagnosis?"

(5) Questions pertaining to the duration of therapy; for example, "How long will therapy last?" "Can it be shortened?"

(6) Questions pertaining to injunctions in therapy; for example, "Is it all right to talk to my spouse about what we discuss here?" "Do I have to start (or stop) doing certain things?"

The client's questions will be predetermined by the limits a therapist has imposed upon the kinds of questions he will entertain. As a rough guide to answering clients' questions, questions of fact (whether personal or otherwise) should be answered factually. Questions of opinion should be largely avoided. For example, when a client asks whether the therapist is a registered Democrat or a Republican, it is a question of fact; but when the client asks whether the Democrats or Republicans are better for the country, it is a question of opinion. The first one should be answered; the second one should be avoided. A factual or informational statement will help the client clarify his relationship with external (social) realities. The reason for avoiding the second one is that the therapist's opinions influence the client's opinions and outlook. It does not help the client to think through the problem on his own and formulate his own opinions.

I try to answer every question of fact as best I can, including personal facts. I avoid answering questions of opinion. I convey to the client that his questions cannot be answered factually, that whatever I say will be my opinion; my opinion is as bad or as good as that of the client.

Although there are no prescribed answers to clients' questions, a few general guidelines may be of help.

The question about therapy requires a brief explanation of the process of psychotherapy. It could be: "When you talk about your life struggles and upsetting experiences while the therapist listens and clarifies, it facilitates exploring your thoughts, feelings, and life-style. Many things which may be unclear now begin to become clear and understandable. This understanding of yourself and your difficulties may help you to change your own behavior and the conditions and circumstances that produce conflict.

The questions about the therapist should be answered factually if the therapist has agreed to answer this category of question.

The questions about different kinds of therapeutic approaches demand a certain knowledge about the field. If the therapist is familiar with the various forms of therapies the client is asking about, a brief explanation should be given; if the therapist is not familiar, then he should say so. The therapist should answer factually questions about his academic background and training. Studies do not suggest any significant differences among the three professional groups—psychologists, psychiatrists, and social workers,—either in the procedures and methods of therapies used or the success rates (Strupp 1973; Bergin and Suinn 1975; Jones and Zoppel 1980). The legal fact that a psychiatrist can write prescriptions, give shock treatments, and hospitalize the client while the other two cannot should be clearly explained to the client.

Questions about the client's mental-emotional state can be answered by saying, "From what you have told me about your troubles and torments, it may be helpful to talk to someone." When the client asks whether he is neurotic, psychotic, or crazy, a similar answer is warranted. "From your description it appears that your life has been a turbulent and tormented one." "The label people may try to put on your life is irrelevant."

In answering questions about the duration of therapy, the therapist should remember that it is difficult to estimate the length of therapy. This should be clearly conveyed to the client. As a general answer, a therapist could say, "It has taken you many years to develop these conflicts; you should allow some time for their resolution, although it is quite understandable that anyone who is going through mental anguish would like to resolve them as soon as possible."

Questions about injunctions in therapy can be answered by stating that a client should be free to do whatever he wishes to do, without first checking with the therapist.

Those therapists who do not invite questions from the client are under no obligation to answer the client's questions. This fact should be conveyed to the client during the first few sessions. Most therapists, however, do not wish to appear closed or reticent about answering questions since they profess to believe in an atmosphere of freedom for the client to say whatever he wants to (Chessick 1974). Therefore, they at least acknowledge the client's freedom to ask questions. Frequently when the client asks questions, particularly ones having any bearing upon the background, training, or experience of the therapist, the therapist avoids answering them in a straightforward manner. Instead, he circumvents the questions by saying, "I don't think it will help our work here." (Weiner 1975). Or he turns the question back on the client: "Do you think it will alleviate your problems if I answer that?" Or he asks about the client's motives for raising the questions: "I wonder why you ask that question?" (Colby 1951; Wolberg, 1967).

Such answers are less than honest. They are intended to create an illusion that the therapist is an open and candid person. In fact he is acting reticent and closed but alleging that his reticence helps the client. Such maneuvers give the client a feeling of one-up-manship by the therapist, inequality of status between the two of them, and arbitrariness on the part of the therapist.

Fees *

Much has been written about, and a considerable significance has been attached to, the issue of fees in psychotherapy. It has been said that if a client does not pay or pays less than he can reasonably afford, therapy will not go well (Haak 1957; Davids 1964). Menninger and Holzman (1973) state, "The analysis will not go well if the patient is paying considerably less than he can reasonably afford to pay. It should be a definite sacrifice for him, and not for someone else." It is further believed that those clients who do not pay feel obligated to the therapist. Additionally, if a client does not pay, or pays less than he can afford, he may feel that the quality of therapy may not be high. Studies suggest that neither psychologists, social workers, nor psychiatrists agree about treating any client, be he on welfare or middle class, on a no-fee basis. . . . Most of the professional groups support a fee schedule based on ability to pay. The fee is charged to maximize the client's benefit from the therapy (Dightman 1970).

Some poorly controlled studies also show that those who pay for therapy feel that they are making a sacrifice (monetary); they work hard in therapy and hence show more improvement than those who do not pay (Koren and Joyce 1953; Goodman 1960). Such beliefs and myths about the role of fees in psychotherapy need clarification.

In a capitalist society, the bourgeoisie, or the middle class, has a dual but contradictory attitude toward money and fees. This seems to hold true for both the therapist and the client. One set of values dictates that one pay as little as possible for whatever one is shopping for. The other set of values dictates that the more you pay, the better the goods or services must be. Both of these attitudes show up in the pro-

---

*See also Chapter 9, Money as a Source of Counter-transference.

cess of therapy, just as in every interaction and transaction around money and fees.

A private practitioner in psychotherapy is a private entrepreneur. His livelihood depends upon the fee he collects. Therefore, he attaches a great deal of importance to the fee. Freud (1950), a private practitioner, attached a great significance to two things in therapy—time and money. Obviously a private practitioner has to collect his fee. The more he can collect the better off he is and the more social status he derives from it in a capitalist society. Since a therapist is an entrepreneur in an open market, his fee has to be determined by the market value of psychotherapeutic services at a given time and in a given area (Fromm-Reichman 1950). Hence, the recommended rule for setting one's fee is to charge the going rate in the community (Chessick 1974).

The simple fact that the therapist is a private entrepreneur has been convoluted by presenting the issue of the fee as a psychological conflict of the client (Kubie 1950). Hence, some say that the therapist should charge a fee for the benefit of the client, or that the fee should be used as a therapeutic tool (Allen 1971).

The growing empirical evidence, however, does not seem to support the existing beliefs about fees (Mintz 1971). A study of the nonpaying clients of the Psychoanalytic Clinic of the State University Medical Center shows that

the difficulties encountered in this new milieu of treating the patients without charge were very little different from the general difficulties which are found in the office practice. The reports of the supervisory analysts about the treatment which they conducted showed that the difficulties were only somewhat different quantitatively and not qualitatively (Lorand and Console 1958).

Empirical studies on the effect of fees

indicate that fees assessed for individual therapy fail to exert any independent effect on outcome, number of appointments, or reliability of attendance. Taken out of context, certain aspects of the data offer false support for the wide-spread belief that patients should pay, and for theoretical constructs relating fees to the psychotherapeutic process. The fifth major group of tests, in which socio-economic status and diagnosis were confounded with fee, seemingly generates statistical support for the idea that fees influence psychotherapy. (Pope, Geller, and Wilkinson, 1975).

Other experimental studies (Lievano 1967; Balch et al. 1977; DeMuth and Kamis 1980) and clinical observations (Schjelderup 1955; Meltzoff and Kornreich 1970) substantiate the findings of Pope et al.

that neither the source of payment—payment made by the client; or by a third party, that is, insurance company or medical aid—nor the amount of fee significantly influences the number of sessions or the utilization of clinical services. In view of these findings it appears that the prevailing belief that it is in the client's interest to pay a fee is incorrect; rather, the fee, as is expected, serves the therapist's interest and is a remuneration for his work.

With this background, a few principles about setting the fee can help a beginning therapist. First, a therapist should not hesitate to engage in a full and frank discussion of the client's income, expenses, and indebtedness. Whatever fee is settled upon should be mutually agreeable. Clients should not be left completely on their own to say what they can afford to pay; the client would like to pay as little as possible for what he gets, and he may not know the minimum fee acceptable to the therapist and how flexible the therapist can be.

Frequently, therapists do not have a fixed fee but a fee range within which they are willing to work with a client. In that case, the range must be mentioned, either over the phone or during the first session. From then on, the therapist can negotiate his fee and agree upon a sum.

Clients prefer to pay according to their budgetary convenience—monthly, weekly, by cash or check. A client should have some say and flexibility in the manner and frequency of payment. What is important is that whatever the method and the frequency of payment agreed upon, it must be adhered to. If the client fails to pay, the issue of the fee must be discussed again with the client and the reasons for nonpayment should be brought out in the open.

Many times a therapist will have to work with a client who is able to pay only the minimum fee. In that case, the stipulation is made that if the client's income increases, the therapist will raise his fee. If the client's income does increase, it is incumbent upon the therapist to raise the fee.

Diagnosis

A nonmedical-model therapist does not need to make a psychiatric diagnosis of the client (except for the purpose of insurance claims). As discussed in Chapter 2, not only does a diagnosis have a pejorative connotation about a person's life; it also has little relationship to the course and success of therapy (Fromm-Reichman 1950; Draguns and Phillips 1971).

It is, however, natural that both the client and the therapist try to assess each other when they meet in the first and succeeding sessions. In other words, the therapist does make some sort of assessment of the client's life, his failures and successes, his methods and style of operating in daily life, and his assets and liabilities, (intelligence, social and interpersonal skills, goal direction, confusion of thoughts and feelings).

A clear distinction should be made between assessment and psychiatric diagnosis. Even in everyday life, one assesses one's friends and relatives; one does not make a psychiatric diagnosis of them. Only when one tries to fit one's assessment into a preestablished sickness-health category is a diagnosis made.

Any assessment of the client's personality should be made as tentative hypotheses, which are to be confirmed or disconfirmed by the behavior of the client. A therapist should always remain open to changes in his assessment of the client. Studies suggest that it is not an easy task. Soon after making the initial assessment of the client a therapist begins to foreclose the possibility of changing his evaluation of the client's problems (Meehl 1960). Furthermore, with the passage of time, a therapist becomes more confident of his assessment of the client's personality even though he may have judged incorrectly in the first place. Thus, his assessment is difficult to change.

A therapist should always keep in mind that any conflict or turmoil in a client's life is not the result of a single causative or sustaining factor; rather, it is the culmination of interpersonal conflicts, conflicting values, and ethical and moral dilemmas which affect his beliefs, perceptions, and habits. If the client's troubles had a single cause or source, then he probably could have handled them without the therapist. For this reason, the therapist should avoid looking for a single cause of the client's troubles, for example, oral or anal conflict, schizophrenic mother, fixation at a particular psychosexual stage, and so on. He should try to assess the client's interpersonal interactions and the behavioral–cognitive–affective systems which sustain and perpetuate the client's troubles and turmoils. The implication for therapy is that since there is not a single cause or sustaining factor supporting the conflicts, the therapist will have to help the client seek resolution at various levels and in different aspects of the client's day-to-day functioning.

Setting the Goals of Therapy

During the initial phase of therapy,—the first three sessions—a therapist should set the goals. It is important to do so for several reasons. The goals help the therapist know whether he will be able to treat the client successfully and whether he should take on the process of therapy. If no goals are set, the therapist (especially the beginner) has no sense of direction in therapy; frequently therapy begins to flounder. The goals indicate the distance a therapist has to travel in therapy. Toward the later phase, when one begins to think of termination, the goals set in the beginning give both the therapist and the client an idea of what has been achieved and when it is time to stop. Without goals, the therapist has no way to know when to consider termination.

Some therapists have preconceived ideas of the goals of therapy, which they directly or indirectly try to impose upon the client. These preconceived goals take various forms. They may be theoretical. For example, psychoanalysts maintain that making the unconscious conscious, and achieving genital primacy are the goals of therapy or analysis (Saul 1967; Whitehorn 1967). They could be cryptic moral goals. For example, if a spouse comes for therapy because he is troubled about his marital situation, the therapist may feel that the best goal for the client may be to get along with the spouse, and he may induce the client to accept this goal. Other therapists have certain beliefs about what "cures the symptoms" of the clients. They impose their "tested beliefs" upon the client as the goal of therapy. For instance, some may believe that catharsis, the recovery of traumatic childhood memories, or primal scream, are the curative factors. Such therapists would then try to convince the client to accept these goals.

Still other therapists have abstract ideals as goals of therapy. For instance, a therapist may want the client to be mentally healthy or "to uncover the unique fundamental structure of his personality and to commit himself to the actualization of this structure" (Van Kaam 1967).

These goals do not take the client's actual life struggles into account. Directly or indirectly, they are formulated by the therapist. Therefore, when the therapist discusses or presents the goals to the client, they appear alien and tangential to the client's struggle. In view of the therapist's goal setting, it is not surprising to hear the complaints of Carl Rogers. He states,

For the past two years I have encouraged my seminar of psychiatric residents to discuss goals of therapy, either in general, or in regards to a particular client we are considering. Such discussion reveals the most profound differences. We are not agreed whether the goal is removal of symptoms, reorganization of personality, curing a disease, or adjustment to culture. . . . In my experience the only therapists who agree on goals of therapy are those who have been strongly indoctrinated in the same dogma (Rogers 1963).

The goals of therapy should be set in a straightforward manner, without any preconceived notion on the part of the therapist. After the client has discussed his conflicts, a therapist could ask, "In what way would you want to change your life?" or "How would you want to live differently from the way you have been living?" These questions allow the client to set his own goals, rather than have them thrust upon him by the therapist. Even with seriously disturbed clients, the issue of goals should be approached in a similar manner. Obviously, the goals of therapy will be different for each client.

It is possible that what the client wishes to change in himself or in his life may not be possible through therapy. For example, a client who is not very bright may say he would like to be intelligent. Under such conditions, the therapist should clarify how therapy can help the client and whether he would want to work with this client.

It is helpful to both the therapist and the client to avoid abstract goals and to set goals as concretely as possible. Concrete goals of therapy provide behavioral referents which can be observed and discussed both by the therapist and the client. Abstract goals leave much to the subjective interpretation of the therapist about which a client may have little to say.

In passing, it should be emphasized that the time of the therapy session should also be mutually agreed upon. The client's convenience must be given serious consideration. Many therapists give the client little choice in this regard. Studies suggest that external inconveniences—the inability to get away from work for the session, transportation difficulties, and so on—play an important role in attrition (Garfield 1963). (See Chapter 6.)

Filling in the Picture—Dimensions of the Client's Behavior

Like any individual, the client interprets his role in his life uniquely. Hence, during therapy sessions he reports his life experiences in unique ways. Some clients simply describe what they do or what happens to them between sessions, while others spend the session discussing their feelings about something or someone. Still others try to find genetic causes and motivational roots of their troubles and conflicts.

A beginning therapist may find it difficult to develop a coherent picture of a client's life from his description since he usually receives incomplete or biased information. Hence the therapist has to fill in the sketchy picture and at the same time delineate some of the forces affecting the client's life, including the client himself. In order to do this, he has to understand many dimensions of the client's behavior or experience, which he does by following a simple procedure. First, he has to obtain the physical and temporal dimensions of the client's behavior and interactions—the "what, where and when" (Eckartsberg 1966).

Another dimension of the client's behavior pertains to the active role he plays in generating the experiences about which he generally complains. The therapist has to ask what part the client played in the situation, how the situation came about. The therapist might also discuss motives for the client's behavior—why he did what he did.

During the therapy sessions, clients generally discuss some of these dimensions of their behavior. Indeed, they emphasize some aspects and underplay or ignore others. When a client has omitted mentioning an aspect of his behavior, the therapist should guide him in filling in omitted parts.

One may ask what happens if the therapist ignores a particular aspect of the client's behavior. For instance, if the therapist ignores the physical and temporal dimensions of the client's experience, therapy is less likely to be linked to the real life situation. Many authors have stated that clients frequently use isolation of therapy from real life as a form of resistance (Fenichel 1945; Wolberg 1967). By not raising the issues pertaining to the place and time of the client's behavior, a therapist may abet the development of such a resistance.

A thirty-seven-year-old married woman, mother of two children aged sixteen and nineteen, came to therapy because the older son and the husband were constantly fighting, and she had to play the role of mediator. Beside the fact that there was no peace at home, she was tired of her role. When asked the cause of the fights, she was unable to recall although she had just finished describing a fight on the previous day. She was also unable to tell how she makes peace. However, she was able to remember what the son said to the father and what the father said to the son. When this was brought to her attention she became quite anxious and nervous.

The client's actual moves, his style of doing things, and his active participation in his life experiences need to be brought out. If the therapist does not point out the client's role in his own conflicts, then it is very difficult to know what aspects of the client's behavior need to be focused on in therapy.

A forty-two-year-old, twice-married woman of Mexican-American descent, who was employed as a social worker, came for therapy because she was confused as to what was happening in her life. Both marriages were to Caucasian men. She had been married the first time for eighteen years and had three children from this marriage. Her second marriage had taken place seven months before she came for therapy. She had known and worked with her husband for about eight years prior to her marriage and had gone out with him seriously for about a year prior to that. During this period, she became pregnant three times by this man and had three abortions. They also had violent fights during which he beat her severely, requiring her to seek medical attention.

Her husband was quite emotionally disturbed. During the early phase of therapy, she described his temper and called him crazy and paranoid. It was difficult for her to remember or describe how the fights began. During this early phase, much of the focus was upon her role in the fights, which were caused by her flirting with other men in front of her husband. When the husband would object to her behavior, she would say that he was insecure and needed therapy. This made him furious and sometimes physically abusive toward her.

If the "why" of client's behavior is not discussed, then his motivation cannot be explored. Behavioral therapists maintain that understanding the motivational roots or the psychic origin of one's behavior is not important to bring about changes in a client's life. Yet it is understandable that a therapist and client may wish to delve into these roots of behavior. This could be done after the first two dimensions of the client's behavior (what, where, when; and how) are clarified. After these aspects are discussed, generally clients themselves offer explanations for their motivation and even try to find genetic origins. Attempts on the part of the therapist to explore the motivation or genetic origins of a client's conflicts before clarifying the other aspects leave a certain ambiguity in the client's understanding because he has to search for the roots of a poorly delineated kind of behavior.

The time and place, the method, and the motivation of the client's actions pertain to the cognitive aspects of behavior. They do not deal with the client's feelings and emotions. In therapy literature, it has been repeatedly stressed that feelings and emotions are the most important aspects of the client's conflicts and should be the primary focus in therapy. While it is true that emotions are quite important, they do not occur in a vacuum or in isolation in the client's life. A client experiences his emotions (or avoids experiencing them) in relation to someone or something. Usually they are experienced in the structural context of the client's behavior, or are generally intertwined with behavior. Frequently, clients describe and reexperience some of their feelings while narrating an incident or describing their life condition. Only when the client has not expressed some of his feelings and emotions during his narrations should a therapist bring them out and help the client to reexperience some of them. Focusing solely upon the client's feelings, while minimizing his behavior and his participation in the situations of which he complains tends to reduce the link between psychotherapy and the client's outside life.

A thirty-year-old married woman, mother of two children who worked as a secretary-receptionist at a local mental health clinic, came to therapy because of anxiety and confusion. She had been in therapy before for approximately one and a half years. During the early phase of therapy she essentially spoke of emotions and feelings about whatever had happened in her life. While talking about other people in her life (husband, children, friends, and so on) she would describe their feelings. It was difficult for her to describe the events of the previous week; she was unclear about when many of the things had happened and how she had done certain things, although she was quite willing to describe and experience her feelings. Thus, her life had developed a vague and nebulous quality. Much of the therapy from then on consisted of focusing on specific and concrete details.

The Contract

The concept of a contract in psychotherapy has gained a great deal of popularity in recent years. In fact, so popular has the concept become that some therapists have begun to identify themselves as contractual therapists, and consumer groups have begun to urge clients to demand a contract from their therapist (Adams and Orgel 1975). Szasz (1965) was the first to examine the usefulness of the contract in a psychotherapeutic situation. He called it the "analytic contract."*

---

*Although Menninger and Holzman (1973) and others also discuss the concept of contract, they discuss it from a medical-model viewpoint, where the client's part in the contract is to submit to the physician-therapist rather than to bring some form of equality into the situation.

Some practitioners of therapy and consumer advocate groups recommend that early in therapy a contract be drawn up between the client and the therapist. What is a contract and what is its purpose?

In legal theory contract is defined as a promise or set of promises protected from breach by law. . . . Thus, the legal definition of contract recognizes that contracts may be broken. . . . The analytic contract, like the legal contract, seeks clarity rather than vagueness and specifies the remedies available should one of the contracting parties fail to keep his promises. They also differ, however, for ordinary contracts are written, whereas analytic contracts are verbal; also, the participants understand that neither legal nor even social sanctions are available for punishing the party who breaks the contract (Szasz 1965).

More recently, however, many have begun to suggest that for a variety of reasons a written contract should also be drawn up in psychotherapy (Adams and Orgel 1975; Hare-Mustin et al. 1979).

A contract is, by and large, an arrangement between equals. There cannot be a contract if one of the parties is under coercion or threat or in a subordinate position. Therefore, it is difficult to draw up a therapeutic contract with hospitalized patients, with adolescents who are legally forced to live with their parents until a specified age, with prisoners, detainees, or children (Szasz 1965). Therapists who attempt to draw up therapeutic contracts with such clients soon discover that the contract has no meaning for the client; nor does he attach any significance to it other than placating the therapist.

Most clients entering psychotherapy are seeking help, not self-protection. The client is in a poor position to negotiate. Further, therapy is a novel situation for most clients. They do not know what role to assume, and they do not know their rights. Finally, some clients entering therapy may not be capable of protecting their rights. They may be members of groups that historically have been denied power, such as women or racial minorities. For these reasons, the clients generally rely on the therapist to provide the structure, and it is the therapist's role to present the contract to the client (Goldberg 1977).

The therapist should present the contract in such a way that the client retains the right to reject it or to disagree with certain items in it. The client should feel that he may present his own contract to the therapist if he so desires.* Thus, it has to be arrived at through negotia-

---

*It should be mentioned that it is not an easy task for the therapist to present such a contract since, implicitly, it threatens the therapist's superior social position.

tion. The contract, then, is a statement (usually by the therapist) about the procedures, goals, and expectations (promises) which each party undertakes.

Generally, the contract should bring relative freedom to both parties by letting each fulfill his own part of it. A contract holds the individual as an equal and autonomous being when the responsibilities of each are specified. It also reduces the status and power of the therapist by establishing a mutual and routine accountability between the client and the therapist. A contract thus makes clear to both parties that the process is a mutual effort which entails mutual responsibilities.

What are the consequences of no contract in therapy? First, therapy may begin to drift without ground rules for the participants to follow. Then the client will have little understanding of the process of therapy, his own role, and the role and function of the therapist. Second, a therapist can take advantage of his power position. For example, if therapy is not progressing well, a medical therapist may put the client on shock treatments or pills, or hospitalize him. A therapist might demand sexual or other favors of the client in a noncontractual situation. A client would have little recourse against such demands except to drop out of therapy.

A contract between the therapist and the client should explain, minimally, the following items:*

(1) The role of the client and what is expected of him.

(2) The role and functions of the therapist—procedures, policies, and practices.

(3) The number of meetings per week.

(4) The place of meeting.

(5) The fee and frequency and method of payment.

(6) The issue of confidentiality—who the therapist would or would not communicate with and under what conditions.

(7) The penalties if the contract is broken, if appointments are broken without adequate (agreed upon) notice, and the policy about vacation, sickness, and so forth.

(8) The freedom to renegotiate the contract at certain or specified times.

---

*For a detailed analysis of contractual items, see Goldberg (1977).

Only after such a contract has been discussed between the parties and agreed upon should a therapist or a client proceed with therapy. The importance of the contractual items cannot be overemphasized, for without the protection of the contract for both of the parties, therapy soon runs into various entanglements which are difficult to resolve.

Summary

The first session and the beginning phase of psychotherapy are important because during this period the therapist must be alert to many factors to launch therapy successfully. The early phase is therefore a difficult one for the beginning therapist. It is not unusual for a beginning therapist to be uncomfortable during this phase. A few general principles may help alleviate the discomfort. The therapist should know the client's name and should greet him in a cordial manner. He should accord the client dignity and respect and be sympathetic to his life struggles. He should not let too many silences develop during the first session; rather, he should encourage the client to express his thoughts and feelings about the issues troubling him. Most clients are anxious and nervous during the first sessions. A therapist should attempt to alleviate the client's anxiety so that the client can talk freely.

Clients are always curious about the therapist and the therapeutic process and may have many questions pertaining to both of them. Before a therapist invites the client's questions, he should make it clear what kinds of questions he is willing to answer.

The therapist should also set the fee for therapy during the beginning phase. Many therapists believe that if the client does not pay then he will not work hard in therapy, that he will feel he is not getting good service, or that he will feel obligated to the therapist. Such beliefs have not been substantiated by the existing empirical studies.

During the beginning phase of therapy, the therapist must establish goals for therapy. He should ask the client what he would like to change in his life. If the therapist does not establish some goals for therapy, he is not likely to have a clear direction as therapy begins to unfold.

Establishing a therapeutic contract with the client is strongly recommended. A contract is a statement about the procedures, goals, and expectations which each party undertakes. A contract should bring relative freedom to both the parties by letting each fulfill his part of the contract. If a therapeutic contract is not stipulated, then therapy lacks the ground rules, and the therapist may take advantage of the client. Only when some of the basic items of the contract are agreed upon by the parties—time and frequency of meetings, confidentiality, fee, and role and obligation of the participants—should a therapist begin psychotherapy.

References

Adams, S., and M. Orgel. 1975. *Through the mental health maze*. Washington, D.C.: Health Research Group.

Allen, A. 1971. The fee as a therapeutic tool. *Psychoanalytic Quarterly* 40: 132–40.

Balch, P., J. Ireland, and S. Lewis. 1977. Fees and therapy: Relation of source of payment to course of therapy at a community mental health center. *Journal of Consulting and Clinical Psychology* 45:504.

Berenson, B. G., and R. R. Carkhuff, eds. 1967. *Sources of gain in counseling and psychotherapy*. New York: Holt, Rinehart and Winston, 358–92.

Bergin, A. E., and R. M. Suinn. 1975. Individual psychotherapy and behavior therapy. In M. R. Rosenwerg and W. O. Porter, eds., *Annual review of psychology*, vol. 26, 509–56. Palo Alto, Calif.: Annual Reviews.

Bordin, E. S. 1974. *Research strategies in psychotherapy*. New York: John Wiley and Sons.

Chessick, R. D. 1974. *Technique and practice of intensive psychotherapy*. New York: Jason Aronson, 113.

Colby, K. M. 1951. *A primer for psychotherapists*. New York: Ronald Press.

Davids, P. S. 1964. The relation of cognitive-dissonance theory to an aspect of psychotherapeutic practice. *American Psychologist* 19:329–32.

DeMuth, N., and E. Kamis. 1980. Fees and therapy: Clarification of relationship of payment source to service utilization. *Journal of Consulting and Clinical Psychology* 48:793–95.

Dightman, C. R. 1970. Fee and mental health services: Attitudes of the professionals. *Mental Hygiene* 54:401–6.

Draguns, J., and L. Phillips. 1971. *Psychiatric classification and diagnosis: An overview and critique*. Morristown, N.J.: General Learning Press.

Eckartsberg, R. 1966. On situation analysis. *Psychotherapy: Theory, research and practice* 4:167–70.

Fenichel, O. 1945. *Psychoanalytic theory of neurosis*. New York: W. W. Norton and Company.

Freud, S. 1950. Further recommendations in the technique of psychoanalysis. In *Collected papers*, vol. 2, 342–65. London: Hogarth Press.

Fromm-Reichman, F. 1950. *Principles of intensive psychotherapy*. Chicago: University of Chicago Press.

Garfield, S. 1963. A note on the patients' reasons for terminating therapy. *Psychological Reports* 13:38.

Garfield, S. L., and A. E. Bergin. 1971. Therapeutic conditions and outcome. *Journal of Abnormal Psychology* 77:108–14.

Goldberg, C. 1977. *Therapeutic partnership*. New York: Springer Publishing Co.

Goodman, N. 1960. Are there differences between fee and non-fee cases? *Social Work* 5:46–52.

Haak, N. 1957. Comments on the analytic situation. *International Journal of Psychoanalysis* 38:183–95.

Hare-Mustin, R. J., J. Marecek, A. G. Kaplan, and N. Liss-Levinson. 1979. Rights of clients, responsibilities of therapists. *American Psychologist* 1:3–17.

Jones, E., and C. Zoppel. 1980. Impact of client and therapist gender on psychotherapy process and outcome. *Journal of Consulting and Clinical Psychology* 50:259–73.

Koren, K., and J. Joyce. 1953. The treatment implication of payment of fees in a clinical setting. *American Journal of Orthopsychiatry* 23:350–57.

Kubie, L. S. 1950. *Practical and theoretical aspects of psychoanalysis*. New York: International Universities Press, 136.

Lorand, S., and W. Console. 1958. Therapeutic results in psychoanalytic treatment without fee. *International Journal of Psychoanalysis* 39:59–64.

Lievano, J. 1967. Observations about payment of psychotherapy fees. *Psychiatric Quarterly* 41:324–38.

Meehl, P. 1960. Cognitive activity of the clinician. *American Psychologist* 15:19–27.

Meltzoff, J., and M. Kornreich. 1970. *Research in psychotherapy*. New York: Atherton Press.

Menninger, K. A., and P. S. Holzman. 1973. *Theory of psychoanalytic technique*. New York: Basic Books, 31.

Merbaum, M., and J. Butcher. 1982. Therapists' liking of their psychotherapy patients: Some issues related to severity of disorder and treatability. *Psychotherapy: Theory, Research and Practice* 19:69–76.

Meyers, C. T. 1977. *A follow-up study of clients' reasons for dropping counseling*. Master's thesis, California State University, Sacramento.

Mintz, N. L. 1971. Patient fee and psychotherapeutic transactions. *Journal of Consulting and Clinical Psychology* 36:1–8.

Muehberg, N., R. Pierce and J. Drasgow. 1969. A factor analysis of therapeutically facilitative conditions. *Journal of Clinical Psychology* 25:93–95.

Pope, K. S., J. D. Geller, and L. Wilkinson. 1975. Fee assessment and outpatient psychotherapy. *Journal of Consulting and Clinical Psychology* 6:835–41.

Rogers, C. R. 1967. The conditions of change from a client-centered viewpoint. In B. Berenson and R. Carkhuff eds., *Sources of gain in counseling and psychotherapy*, 71–85. New York: Holt, Rinehart and Winston.

———. 1963. Psychotherapy today or where do we go from here. *American Journal of Psychotherapy* 17:5–16.

Saul, L. J. 1967. Goals of psychoanalytic therapy. In A. R. Mahrer, ed., *The goals of psychotherapy*, 41–51. New York: Appleton-Century-Crofts.

———. 1958. *Techniques and practice of psychoanalysis*. Philadelphia: J. B. Lippincott Company.

Schjelderup, H. 1955. Lasting effect of psychoanalytic treatment. *Psychiatry* 18:109–33.

Stieper, D. R., and D. Winer. 1965. *Dimensions of psychotherapy*. Chicago: Aldine Publishing Co., 42–43.

Strupp, H. 1973. Technique, professional affiliation and experience level. In H. Strupp, ed., *Psychotherapy: Clinical research and theoretical issues*, 173–86. New York: Jason Aronson.

Szasz, T. 1965. *The ethics of psychoanalysis*. New York: Basic Books, 105–6, 161.

Tennov, D. 1976. *Psychotherapy: The hazardous cure*. Garden City, N.Y.: Anchor Press, 93–100.

Truax, C. B., and K. M. Mitchell. 1971. Research on certain interpersonal skills in relation to process and outcome. In A. E. Gergin and S. L. Garfield, eds., *Handbook of psychotherapy and behavior change*, 299–344. New York: John Wiley and Sons.

Van Kaam, A. 1967. The goals of psychotherapy from the existential point of view. In A. R. Mahrer, ed., *The goals of psychotherapy*, 145–62. New York: Appleton-Century-Crofts.

Whitehorn, J. C. 1967. The goals of psychotherapy. In A. R. Mahrer, ed., *The goals of psychotherapy*, 59–73. New York: Appleton-Century-Crofts.

Weiner, I. B. 1975. *Principles of Psychotherapy*. New York: Wiley.

Wolberg, L. R. 1967. *The technique of psychotherapy*. New York: Grune and Stratton, 557–69.

6

Dropping Out of Therapy

It is generally assumed in therapy that a minimum of contact with the client is necessary to institute any change in his life. If the client drops out of therapy before the number of sessions which the therapist believes are necessary to resolve the client's conflicts, then it is believed little change will occur in the client's life (Rosenthal and Frank 1958). Therapists look askance upon a client's premature termination without their approval or recommendation. They believe that the longer a client stays in therapy, the greater his chances of improvement. Generally, studies support such tenets (Rosenthal and Frank 1958; Garfield and Affleck 1959; Brown and Kosterlitz 1964; Luborsky et al. 1971). Those who stay longer in therapy are likely to be rated as improved and their therapy a "success" (Cartwright 1955), whereas those who drop out are likely to be rated as unimproved, their therapy a "failure" (Rosenthal and Frank 1958).

Every practicing therapist is aware that many clients do not show up for their first appointment, even though they may have applied to the clinic for the specific purpose of obtaining psychotherapy. Frequently, clients who start therapy do not keep their appointments, often without explanation, and simply withdraw from therapy. Thus, the incidence of dropouts in psychotherapy is sufficiently high to warrant the serious attention of any practitioner (Garfield and Kurz 1952; Kurland 1956; Rosenthal and Frank 1958; Weiss and Schaie 1958; Raynes and Warren 1971; Vail 1978).

Generally, a dropout is defined as one who stops coming to therapy against the implicit or explicit recommendation of the therapist to continue. A client could be a dropout at any stage of therapy, after any number of sessions. Traditionally, however, therapists do not consider a client a dropout after he has been in therapy for a certain number of sessions, usually about twenty or so. This is in spite of the fact that he stops coming to therapy sessions against the therapist's recommendation to continue. The reasons for not counting such clients as dropouts center around three assumptions. Therapists believe that since the client has been regular in coming to therapy thus far, to a certain extent he has fulfilled his therapeutic contract—to be present in the therapist's office every week. Second, it is believed that some changes must have occurred in his life during this period or the client would have stopped coming earlier. Third, since most of the clients drop out early in therapy (see below), attending a certain number of sessions, is considered a success. Some clients apply to the clinic, are accepted for therapy, but do not come for the first interview. They are called the "no shows" or pre-therapy dropouts, to differentiate them from "in-therapy" dropouts.

For many reasons the definition of a dropout remains vague and ambiguous. Authors and researchers use arbitrary criteria to define them (Pekarik 1985). For instance, some authors consider those who miss the first or the second session as dropouts (Fiester and Rudestam 1975). Others use the third session as the indicator (Shapiro 1974; Vail 1978). Some use the fourth session (Frank et al. 1957; Hiler 1958; Afflect and Garfield 1961; Cole and Magnussen 1967), while others use the fifth session (Rogers et al. 1958), the sixth session (Heilbrun 1961); the eighth session (Affleck and Mednick 1958); the ninth session (Auld and Eron 1953; Kotkov and Meadow 1953; Salzman et al. 1976); the tenth session (Freedman et al. 1958; Cartwright et al. 1980); one year (Grotjahn 1972); or three years (Aronson and Weintraub 1969).

The researchers' choice of a specific session to differentiate the dropouts from remainers assumes a qualitative difference between them. For example, if the fourth session is used as a criterion, and a client drops out in the fifth or sixth session he will be considered a remainer and his behavioral dynamics will be considered different from those of the client who terminated on or before the fourth session. Yet the behavioral dynamics are not likely to be much different between clients who drop out in the fourth session or in the fifth or sixth session. Thus it is not surprising that few studies have been able to find any difference between the dynamics of dropouts and remainers (Gliedman et al. 1957; Garfield et al. 1963; Mendelsohn and Geller 1967; Fiester et al. 1974).

In order to quantify the difference between the dropouts and remainers, some authors have established that the fourth and fifth sessions be used as the criteria for dropouts and the twelfth or twentieth sessions for the remainers (Rubinstein and Lorr 1956; Hiler 1958; Cole and Magnussen 1967). This method has yielded some fruitful results.

However, many studies count both the pretherapy dropouts and the in-therapy dropouts, while other studies clearly differentiate between these two groups. To add to the confusion, most studies do not distinguish between clients who initiate termination themselves and those whose termination is instigated by the therapist (Garfield and Affleck 1959; Brandt 1965). In each of these situations, the motivation and the dynamics of the dropouts are different, yet the studies treat them as a homogeneous group. Obviously it is difficult to do comparative studies and differentiate the behavioral dynamics of the different categories of dropouts.

Some authors refuse to accept the concept of a dropout at all. They maintain that all dropouts, regardless of when the termination occurred, are failures. Hence, in their studies there are no dropouts, only failures and successes of psychotherapy (Rachman and Wilson 1980).

The type and location of the clinic or the therapist has many implications for dropouts. Authors typically neglect to mention the demography of the clinic reporting dropouts. It is extremely important to recognize whether the clinic is rural, semirural, or urban; whether it caters to a particular religious or ethnic group; whether it is a university clinic, affiliated with a training institute, and so on. Each kind of clinic caters to a different type of clientele whose socioeconomic level, educational background and sophistication about the issues of mental health vary. Such demographic variations seriously influence the drop-out rates. But authors have compared the dropout rates from clinics of divergent demographies.

For all these reasons, studies on dropouts are ambiguous. Most of the studies proliferate the findings without developing a system-atic behavioral/dynamic pattern of the dropouts. In spite of all these problems, some general conclusions can be drawn from the exist-ing studies.

Statistical Aspects

Two sets of facts concerning dropouts are important for the stu-dent as well as the practitioner of psychotherapy. In outpatient clinics, a high percentage of clients who apply for therapy and are accepted do not even come for their first appointment. Figures for pretherapy dropouts vary between 4 and 37 percent, depending upon the nature of the clinic, namely whether it is a university clinic catering to a stu-dent population, a community mental health clinic, a hospital-affiliated clinic; and so on. The low figure of 4 percent no-shows applies to uni-versity clinics as reported by Brown and Kosterlitz (1964). The drop-out rates at mental health clinics and V.A. clinics are reported to be much higher. Koren et al. (1951) report a 20 percent no-show rate. A rate of 30 to 33 percent no-shows is reported by Garfield and Kurz (1952), Kurland (1956), Rosenthal and Frank (1958), Weiss and Schaie (1958), and Raynes and Warren (1971a, 1971b). Thus the pretherapy dropouts appear to be a regular part of the outpatient clinic and should be anticipated in any setting.

Second, of those clients who do enter therapy, approximately half of them drop out or terminate prematurely during the early phase. Most studies seem to concur that dropout rates are highest in the early phase of therapy. The precise number of sessions by which the clients drop out is not clear. Straker et al. (1967), and Dodd (1970) reported a dropout rate of 48 percent by the fourth session; Kurland (1956) found that by the fifth session 36 percent had dropped out of therapy. Garfield and Kurz (1952) and Rosenthal and Frank (1958) found that by the sixth session, half the clients who started in therapy had dropped out; by the tenth session, about 66 percent had dropped out; by the twentieth session more than 80 percent had dropped out.

Brown and Kosterlitz (1964) reported that 59 percent of the clients had dropped out before the fifth session. Some studies report that by the twelfth session 50 percent dropped out (Garfield and Affleck 1959).

Haddock and Mensh (1957) found that "about two-thirds of the patients were seen for less than five interviews; about one-fifth (20 percent) for 5–9 hours; half of that number (11 percent) for 10–19 hours." Gabby and Leavitt (1970) found that 45 percent of the four hundred clinic patients were seen for fewer than five interviews, with a majority simply discontinuing therapy. Fiester and Rudestam (1975), studying the population of three clinics, found that between 37 and 45 percent of adult outpatients terminate psychotherapy after the first or the second session.

Annual statistical reports for psychiatric clinics in the states of New York and Maryland show that the majority of patients are seen for fewer than five interviews (Gordon 1965). Rogers (1960) also found that in the government-supported clinics, a majority of patients have left treatment before the eighth interview.

Recent studies of clients going to private therapists suggest that the dropout rate of clients seen in private practice is only slightly lower than those seen in outpatient clinics (Koss 1979, 1980). "Clients attended a median of eight sessions over 2.5 months. Half of the clients had terminated by the tenth session and two-thirds by the fifteenth. Only 20% of the clients remained in treatment longer than 25 sessions" (Koss 1979). Only a handful of studies do not support these findings (Leif et al. 1961; Cartwright 1955; Gundlach and Geller 1958). Studies thus seem to concur that attrition is highest in the early phases of psychotherapy.

Salzman et al. (1976) attempted to discover when or at what session a client decides to drop out of therapy. He found that by the third session it is relatively clear which clients may drop out. They report,

The strongest relationship between third session dimension scores and persistence in treatment confirms the expectation that this discrimination can be made early. It had not been anticipated that the peak effect would occur at the third session nor that the effect would subsequently taper off. . . . At the end of the first session, the relationship remains quite tentative. . . . After three sessions, however, the viability of the relationship is becoming evident. The strengths and the weaknesses of the therapeutic alliance are now strongly reflected in the quality of the experience in the therapeutic situation.

. . . The vast majority of them (13 out of 20) persisted through the third session, during which they experienced widespread dissatisfaction with the therapeutic relationship, signalling the large exodus (11) that followed Sessions 4 and 5. The pattern of the data suggests the further possibility that the drop out phenomenon is a complex one composed of a set of waves peaking in rapid succession. . . .

Some authors maintain that a certain group of clients—those whose self-respect is fragile and easily threatened—go through a failure zone in therapy, during which the client is likely to drop out. Such a period usually falls between the sixth and tenth sessions (Weitz et al. 1975). Others delineate this period between the thirteenth and twenty-first sessions (Cartwright 1955; Taylor 1956; Standal and Van Der Veen 1957; Kirtner and Cartwright 1958; Fulkerson and Barry 1961). These authors postulate that a critical period exists because some clients fear the emergence of conflicting material during the forthcoming sessions of therapy which may threaten their self-respect. The client may not be willing or strong enough to face such material. These authors hypothesize that the critical period occurs at different sessions because therapists of different persuasions tend to confront the client with self-threatening material at different rates.

In view of the existing empirical evidence, it appears that in most settings approximately one-fourth to one-third of the clients who are accepted for therapy do not show up for their first interview. Conservatively speaking, approximately half the clients drop out by the seventh session of therapy. Furthermore, by the twenty-fifth session, approximately 80 percent of the clients who started out in therapy (not counting pretherapy dropouts) have dropped out. Thus, beyond the twenty-fifth session, a therapist works with 20 percent of those who started in therapy.* It is thus instructive for any therapist, especially a beginning one, to understand and analyze the factors that encourage a client to continue in therapy or to drop out.

---

*These statistics contradict the subjective experience or the belief of successful therapists. Yet any conscientious therapist should know that a considerable number of clients drop out in the referral process. Moreover, a very select group of clients are referred to "successful" therapists. Hence their dropout rates are usually much lower than the statistics indicate.

Who Drops Out

Before we discuss the factors that contribute to dropping out, it is helpful to mention those factors that do not significantly contribute to the attrition of the client. Existing empirical studies suggest that the following are not significant factors.

Neither the age* nor the sex of the therapist, nor of the client are related to termination of therapy (Cartwright 1955; Rubinstein and Lorr 1956; Rosenthal and Frank 1958; Affleck and Garfield 1961; McNair et al. 1963; Yalom 1966; Garfield 1977). The psychiatric diagnosis of the client is not a significant factor (Rosenthal and Frank 1958; Garfield and Affleck 1959; Affleck and Garfield 1961; Brown and Kosterlitz 1964; Shapiro 1974), nor is the professional background of the therapist (nurse, psychiatrist, social worker, psychologist) (Hiler 1958; Lorr and Rubinstein 1958; Sullivan et al. 1958; McNair et al. 1963; Riess and Safer 1973). Finally, the marital status of the client is not a factor (Rubinstein and Lorr 1956; Lorr et al. 1958; Brandt 1965).

Many studies have attempted to isolate the specific factors which do contribute to premature termination, but most have not been successful in this endeavor. The reason seems to be that a single factor rarely results in the client's dropping out; it is a combination of factors or a pattern of interaction between the client and therapist that determines the course of the client's participation in psychotherapy.

Mentioned below are factors which alone may not cause premature termination, but which in combination with other factors affect the client's decision to terminate or continue in therapy.

SOCIAL CLASS. Clients belonging to the lower socioeconomic strata, tend to drop out early in therapy (Garfield 1980; Pekarik 1985). Garfield (1980) states, "Those variables that appear to show the most reliable relationships to continuation in therapy are again social class variables, even though the findings are by no means uniform or consistent." (See Chapter 1.)

ETHNICITY. As discussed in Chapter 1, clients belonging to cultural or ethnic groups other than that of the therapist tend to drop out early in therapy as compared to white American clients.

---

*Contrary to these studies, Carpenter et al.'s study (1981) found "that 18–24-year-old patients were more likely to drop out . . . of outpatient psychotherapy prematurely."

COERCION. Clients who go to therapy under duress and/or coercion tend to drop out early (Rickles et al. 1950; Koren et al. 1951; Raynes and Warren 1971). Reasons for their termination have been discussed in Chapter 1. Clients who seek therapy on their own volition, the self-referred clients, tend to stay longer (Frank et al. 1957; Raynes and Warren 1971).

WAITING LIST. A waiting list at a clinic or in a practitioner's office has many psychological implications for the public at large. Surprisingly, a long waiting list does not appear to have negative implications, such as a shortage of qualified staff, mismanagement at the institution, tardiness or the lack of efficiency at the clinic, and so on. Rather it implies that the clinic or the practitioner must be in demand, that the quality of service is superior or satisfactory, that the institution or the practitioner must have some sort of status or prestige with the result that it [he] has a waiting list (Heyder 1965), that one may be better off waiting to get better service than to go somewhere else where there is no waiting list but the quality of service may be inferior.

There is a myth that has developed in the field of psychotherapy regarding the waiting list as a test of the client's motivation. It is assumed that those clients who can wait long enough to get into psychotherapy will show a stronger motivation to continue, whereas those who do not wait will be more likely to drop out of therapy sooner than otherwise. Hence a long waiting list is deemed desirable.

Studies of psychotherapy clients who were placed on waiting lists suggest that such is not the case; rather the findings contradict the prevailing beliefs. Rogers and Dymond (1954) found that clients who were asked to wait sixty days (the control group of the study) before beginning therapy "were less likely to become involved in therapy, became more extreme in their social attitudes, liked the counselor less when they began their interviews, and showed less benefit from therapy. From this evidence in a small number of cases, it appeared that having to wait for therapy . . . makes therapeutic gain less likely."

Similarly, Uhlenhuth and Duncan (1968) found that "patients who enter treatment soon after the psychiatric consultation improve more than patients who must wait longer. . . . Patients who still want treatment after a prolonged waiting period are, by and large, less likely to respond readily to therapeutic influences. . . ."

Although these authors do not explicitly state that the waiting list clients are likely to drop out, on the basis of the behavior of the waiting list clients when they are in therapy, one can surmise that their potential for dropping out is much higher as compared to those who were not on the waiting list.

Rayes and Warren (1971) found that in a hospital-based clinic "the drop out rate increases precipitously after the fifteenth day, and there is no difference in the drop out rate from 0–15 days although the rate then increases steadily with increased length of waiting list."

In a follow-up telephone interview study of the no-shows, Carpenter et al. (1981) found that a long wait to get the initial appointment was given as a reason by about 12 percent of the no-shows. Roth et al. (1964) and Uhlenhuth and Duncan (1968) found that a long and mandatory wait between applying for psychotherapy and beginning it is inversely related to outcome.* Robin (1976) studied patients who were offered delayed versus immediate appointments. Patients who took immediate appointments kept their initial appointments at a significantly greater rate than those who chose delayed appointments.

In view of these findings, some authors have observed that the waiting list serves the purposes of the clinic, whatever they may be, rather than those of the client (Graziano and Fink 1973). It is probably safe to state that the longer the waiting list, the higher the probability of pretherapy and in-therapy dropouts, for numerous reasons. First, the client is not a passive individual; generally, he struggles to resolve his conflicts and dilemmas in one way or another. If help is not forthcoming within a reasonable time from one clinic (usually two to three weeks) he may look for it elsewhere. Or he may find other means of coping with his dilemmas and troubles: he may try to make new friends who would listen to him and give him support and encouragement so that he can handle his problems. Other events may occur: he may change jobs, get divorced, leave the geographical area, take a trip, and so on.

Second, it is usually a considerable struggle for a client to admit that he cannot cope further with his life problems. (See Chapter 1.) When he calls and finds out that assistance is not immediately avail-

---

*Rosenthal and Frank's (1958) study is an exception to these findings. They had a ten-week waiting period between the time the client was seen for "diagnostic interview" and the time he started in therapy. They claim that the waiting period did not increase the drop-out rate, which was about the same as for other clinics—about 33 percent no-shows, and a drop-out rate of 50 percent by the sixth session for those who started therapy.

able, he may feel discouraged, disappointed, or even offended that his request has not been heeded quickly. Thus he may not show up even for the first interview. For these reasons, therefore, many authors recommend that one way to reduce the drop-out rate is to abolish the waiting list (Korner 1964; Heyder 1965). Korner states that by abolishing the waiting list, their clinic was able to reduce the dropout rate between intake and postdiagnostic interview by 30 to 50 percent.

EXTERNAL FACTORS. Little attention has been paid in the psychotherapy literature to physical and social factors contributing to the dropout of clients. Generally, it has been assumed that dropouts occur fundamentally because of internal, motivational factors. However, many studies show that many external factors contribute to the client's dropping out of therapy.

The distance from the client's workplace or home to the therapist's office or the clinic has been cited by many studies as a reason for termination (Rickles et al. 1950; Koren et al. 1951; Kline et al. 1974; Acosta 1980). Having to take time off from work regularly to see a therapist has also been mentioned by many studies as a cause of attrition. These two factors become even more important when the clients belong to the working class. Unlike a professional, a blue-collar worker does not easily take time off regularly from his job. Most of the clinics are open during his working hours. Hence these clients find it difficult to keep their regular appointments. Therefore, some therapists have recommended that for therapy with such clients, clinics should stay open during the evening hours (Rickles et al. 1950).

Garfield (1963) found that the most frequently mentioned reasons for termination were transportation or babysitting problems. Frequently overlooked also is the fact that many clients cannot comfortably afford to pay for therapy. Thus, the cost of therapy has also been mentioned as a factor in premature termination (Rickles et al. 1950; Riess and Safer 1973; Klein et al. 1974).

History of Clients Dropping Out

A good predictor of clients dropping out of therapy is their therapeutic history (Rogawski and Edmundson 1971). Some clients experiment with therapy. They go to a therapist or a clinic and soon drop out. They apply again for therapy and repeat the process. Others shop around for a suitable therapist. Some are searching for a high-quality or prestigious therapist, some for a therapist of the same sex, some for a bargain therapist, and so on. Such clients rarely settle down in therapy. Clinical and supervisory experience suggests that these clients are highly prone to dropping out.

These clients use the same or similar reasons for termination as they did in their previous encounters with therapists. For example, a client may say that he cannot come anymore as he has too many commitments, or that the spouse is against therapy, or that he feels better and hence does not need to continue. It is therefore advisable for a therapist to spend some time with a client discussing his previous therapy experiences, the length of time involved, and his reasons for terminating. A similar pattern will more than likely repeat itself with the present therapist.

The Therapist's Reaction as a Factor

Therapists contribute to the client's termination in a variety of ways. Generally they have difficulty in accepting or recognizing their contribution to the client's attrition. Sometimes they overtly instigate a client's termination, while at other times their contribution is subtle, unrecognized, and insidious. For instance, a therapist may be verbally accepting of the client, but may show little interest or warmth toward him. After the client senses this, he may soon drop out. Or a therapist may have difficulty understanding the client's troubles and struggles and not be helpful in abating his confusions or in reducing his conflicts. The client may feel that he is not accomplishing much and terminate.

Perhaps the most frequently mentioned attitude which encourages the client to drop out is the therapist's lack of interest in and/or dislike of the client. In an interview study of the clients who terminated prematurely (that is, dropped out of therapy after a maximum of two sessions), the most frequently mentioned reason for termination was that the therapist was not interested in them. The second most frequent cause for leaving was the feeling that the therapist was insensitive or inappropriate to the client's particular needs (Kline et al. 1974).

Other studies substantiate these findings. Hiler (1958) found that "cold" therapists are able to keep only highly motivated clients in therapy, while "warm" therapists are able to retain both the motivated and those who are likely to drop out. Shapiro and Budman (1973) found that "patients who dropped out of therapy tended to explain their doing so as a negative reaction to the therapist's behavior." Shapiro (1974) found that, although the dropouts were not perceived as clinically more disturbed than the continuers, "the way therapists feel about their patients may result in patients deciding to continue in treatment or quit prematurely."

Koren et al. (1951) found that the therapist significantly contributes to the clients' dropping out through the problems of transference and countertransference. Feifel and Eells (1963) state that, in their study, "unsuccessful therapy was associated essentially with noninterest on the part of the therapist and assignment to multiple therapists (i.e., changing therapists in a clinic). . . ."

McNair et al. (1963) also found that "remaining in therapy is related to the degree of interest the therapist expressed in the type of problem presented by the patient. This relationship was consistently significant both among predicted Quitters . . . and among predicted Stayers. . . ."

The therapist's liking of the client affects his commitment to therapy in other ways, too. Shapiro et al. (1976) found that

if patient and therapist liked each other, their respective rating of improvement varied between 77% and 96%. However, if the therapist did not like the patient, the improvement reported by the therapist varied between 52% and 62%. Of even more importance, if the patients did not like their therapists, only 21% to 35% reported themselves improved at 1–6 months, and none reported improvement at 7–12 months.

Thus, if the client shows no improvement because the therapist does not like him, then the likelihood of the client's dropping increases. He may feel that there is nothing to be gained in continuing therapy.

To summarize, strong evidence supports the belief that one of the critical factors contributing to the client's attrition is the therapist's feelings and attitudes toward him. For whatever reasons, if the therapist does not like the client or display warmth toward or interest in him, the client is likely to drop out. If the client does not like the therapist, he is also likely to drop out. Thus, mutual like, warmth, and interest between the therapist and the client are crucial factors to continuation of therapy.

Personality Variables of the Client

Many studies have attempted to sort out the client's personality factors which contribute to his dropping out of therapy. Psychological tests, interviews, diagnostic categories (purporting to show certain personality characteristics of the client) have all been used to sort out the variables that may predict attrition. Few studies have been successful in pinpointing specific variables. What seems to emerge from these studies is a vague composite picture of the personality of the client who drops out early in therapy. In other words, one finds clusters of variables which are likely to predict premature termination.

The following personality traits have been found to be significant in the client's dropping out of therapy: (1) lack of anxiety or unwillingness to admit to being anxious (Lorr et al. 1958; Taulbee 1958; Salzman et al. 1976); (2) a history of antisocial or aggressive behavior (Shapiro et al. 1976), or a history of trouble with the law (Lorr et al. 1958); (3) impulsive, nomadic, or restless behavior (Rubinstein and Lorr 1956; Lorr et al. 1958); (4) low or weak motivation for therapy, little interest in change, or lack of involvement in therapy (Cartwright and Lerner 1963; Yalom 1966; Grotjahn 1972; Salzman et al. 1976; Greenspan and Kulish 1985); (5) the use of repression as a defense mechanism so that the client responds to a very limited range of emotional stimuli (Gibby et al. 1953; Taulbee 1958; Yalom 1966); (6) rigidity, defensiveness, or unwillingness to reveal anything about oneself (Rubinstein and Lorr 1956; Yalom 1966); (7) the expression of difficulties in the form of somatic complaints (Frank et al. 1957; Hiler 1958; Brown and Kosterlitz 1964); and (8) paranoia (Sullivan et al. 1958). Baekeland and Lundwall (1975) note that "a cluster of variables connected with dependence needs and their expression (or suppression) seems to bear an important relationship to whether the patient in psychotherapy drops out of or continues in treatment. Furthermore, a client who conforms most to cultural stereotypes of masculinity tends to terminate early (Heilbrun 1961b). Finally, both a high need for approval and conformity to expected cultural stereotypes of femininity have been correlated with dropping out (Heilbrun 1961 a and b; Strickland and Crowne 1963).

The following personality traits and variables have been found significant in the client's staying in therapy: (1) a history of less impulsive and less antisocial behavior (McNair et al. 1963); (2) ability to show anxiety and to admit to being anxious (Gibby et al. 1953; Frank et al. 1956; Taulbee 1958; McNair et al. 1963); (3) dissatisfaction with one-self and/or poor interpersonal relationships (Rubinstein and Lorr 1956; McNair et al. 1963); (4) evidence of more disturbance or higher elevation on the MMPI Symptoms Scales (Taulbee 1958); (5) more education and better jobs (Sullivan et al. 1958; McNair et al. 1963; Rosenweig and Folman 1974); (6) higher motivation for therapy (Koren et al. 1951; Gibby et al. 1953; Rosenthal and Frank 1958; Cartwright, Lloyd, and Wicklund 1980); and (7) sensitivity, little rigidity, responsiveness to the environment, and openness and trust with the therapist (Taulbee 1958; Yalom 1966; Salzman et al. 1976).

Can Dropouts Be Predicted

Researchers have tried to predict dropouts with the Rorschach (Auld and Eron 1953; Gibby et al. 1953; Kotkov and Meadow 1953; White et al. 1964) and the M.M.P.I. (Borghi 1968; Walters et al. 1982), and/or on the basis of the first interview with the client or the transcript of the first session (Affleck and Garfield 1961; Garfield et al. 1963). Although most of the tests report initial success, on a cross-validation most have yielded indeterminate results (Fulkerson and Barry 1961).

Prediction of dropouts is a tricky issue. Since approximately half the clients terminate by the sixth or the seventh session, and about two-thirds by the twelfth session, the level of accuracy of prediction increases with the number of sessions. To be more accurate, a judge has only to raise the percentage of termination with the increase in the number of sessions.

Likewise, the level of accuracy in predicting dropouts in the early phase of therapy (fewer than five sessions) decreases. Thus, Garfield et al. (1963) and Affleck and Garfield (1964) found that neither the judges nor the therapists were able to predict who would drop out before the fifth session. The accuracy rate of the judges was 14 percent. However, they were able to predict the dropouts with 86 percent accuracy beyond the tenth session. Similar successes of prediction of dropouts beyond the tenth session have been reported by other researchers who used the ad hoc test batteries (Gibby et al. 1953; Rubinstein and Lorr 1956; Lorr et al. 1958). On the basis of empirical studies, it is difficult to predict successfully the early dropouts, although later dropouts can be reasonably predicted.

Characteristics of the No-Shows

Are there any differences between the no-shows (pretherapy dropouts) and those who come for the first appointment. Researchers have found various reasons for the no-shows. Gottsfeld and Martinez (1972) interviewed 100 who did not keep their first appointment and 100 who did. They found that those who said that their problems had become less acute prior to their appointment were less likely to keep their appointment, while those who said that their problems had become more acute prior to their appointment were more likely to keep the appointment. This finding is supported by the studies of Noonan (1973) and Carpenter et al. (1981), who found that one of the largest groups of no-shows comprised those who stated that between the initial call and the appointment their problems had improved sufficiently so that they did not need any help. Noonan, however, also found that "the largest group [of no shows] was composed of those subjects who essentially were unable to explain why they did not attend, usually stating that they had forgotten or had no specific reason for missing their appointment." Lowe (1982) found that no-shows were less impaired at the time of intake as compared to those who came for treatment.

Noonan's and Carpenter et al.'s follow-up interviews with the dropouts show that more no-shows gave vague or evasive reasons for seeking help (for example, a personality problem, a family problem, or just a problem). In contrast, a significantly greater number of those who came to the first session gave their reasons for seeking help in terms of specific personal problems (such as obsessive thoughts, frigidity, and so forth). "A . . . smaller number of subjects stated that they had not arrived because of anxiety regarding what they might encounter or become involved in" (Noonan 1973). Kline et al. (1974) also found that a certain number of patients did not come for the first interview because they lost their resolve. On the basis of these studies a no-show is usually an individual who seeks immediate help for his troubles; if such help is not available he is not willing to wait. He is evasive and somewhat bewildered by his troubles and problems.

In contrast to these studies, other studies suggest that no-shows comprise two rather distinct groups: those who seriously seek therapy elsewhere, and those who do not. Brandt (1964) maintains that no-shows are not a homogeneous group. In his follow-up study of the pretherapy dropouts, 63 percent reported that they had either entered or were trying to enter therapy elsewhere. Thirty-seven percent had made no effort to obtain other therapy. Brandt, therefore, suggests that the pretherapy dropouts form two distinct groups: (1) those who change their mind concerning treatment and (2) those who obtain treatment elsewhere. Both of these groups probably could not be identified by a single test.

In a follow-up study of dropouts at their clinic, Riess and Brandt (1965) found that approximately 37 percent of the no-shows had either started or applied for therapy elsewhere. Chaneidas and Yamamoto (1973) also report similar findings. Kline et al. (1974) found that

approximately 50% of the patients who discontinued treatment prematurely also sought additional help. This strongly suggests that at least 50% of the patients we were able to contact did not feel their problems were resolved nor were they unmotivated. It is suggested that out-patient clinic in some way failed to meet their needs or expectations.*

Carpenter et al. (1981) state,

Our follow up of the patients who did not keep their appointments indicated that about half of them either sought help at another treatment division at the same facility, scheduled a subsequent out patient appointment, or made contact with another treatment facility.

It would thus appear that anywhere between 35 and 63 percent of the no-shows attempt to seek therapy elsewhere. The rest do not seem to make much of an effort. The negative image of a no-show presented by the therapists and/or the researchers applies mostly to those who do not seek therapy elsewhere.

Unlike this group of no-shows, the in-therapy dropouts do not seem to seek therapy elsewhere. Riess and Brandt (1965) found that 92 percent of those who dropped out before the seventh session did not apply for therapy again. These studies suggest that the no-shows are more likely than in-therapy dropouts to seek therapy elsewhere.

Although therapists tend to equate dropouts with failure, some studies show that this may not be the case. Feister and Rudestam (1975) found that

one of the many complex factors causing the patient to unilaterally terminate is the judgment that he/she is ready to try to handle problems on his/her own

---

*It is not clear from this study whether premature termination includes those who were in therapy and then dropped out (that is, in-therapy dropouts) or both the in-therapy dropouts and the no-shows.

without further help. Apparently such a decision may be reached without therapist concurrence after the cathartic relief of even a single session. . . . A sizeable number of dropout patients receive benefit from their short clinic contact as revealed by their self-reported initial session experiences. The proposition that patients leave therapy solely as a function of dissatisfaction with the services they receive seems at best tenuous in light of the findings of this study. The results suggest that early psychotherapy termination cannot be equated with failure in all cases.*

Preventing Dropouts

In the prevention of dropouts, two sets of factors have to be taken into consideration. The first set pertains to the structural and procedural aspects of an institution, including methods of intake and screening, methods of communication with the clients (form letters, individualized letters, telephone calls, and other means), explanation of the policies of the institution, and so on. The second set pertains to the process of therapy and the therapist. The two sets of factors are interrelated, but for schematic purposes we shall discuss them separately.

The issue has been frequently raised whether an institution should make any efforts to reduce its dropout rates. Some argue that the potential dropouts, to begin with, show poor motivation for therapy. Sooner or later (generally sooner) they will drop out prematurely. Hence, it is not worthwhile to pour professional time and effort into preventing their attrition.

Other have argued that dropouts are serious therapy seekers (Brandt 1964; Garfield 1977) who should be helped to continue in therapy. If they can be helped to overcome one of their major resistances, namely dropping out, they constitute potentially good therapy clients. In passing, one should note that in private practice the question of dropouts is an important one. A therapist cannot afford to be casual about the dropouts since his livelihood depends on keeping clients in therapy.

With regard to the structural and procedural aspects of an institution, a multipronged effect has to be made to reduce the dropouts. Because a single factor rarely contributes to the client's dropping out,

---

*Pekarik's (1983) study supports this finding.

alleviating or improving a single factor will not reduce the number of dropouts significantly. Some of the factors that may help prevent the dropouts are discussed below. By no means do they constitute a complete list; rather, they are some of the obvious factors that have been frequently mentioned in the literature.

Generally an explanation or even an exposition of institutions' procedures and policies helps prevent dropouts. Noonan (1973) states,

It is valuable to provide the caller with some orientation regarding the clinic procedure and philosophy at the time of original contact. In addition to informing the client of what might realistically occur, it would allow those individuals with fears of treatment an opportunity to express their concerns and hopefully to be placed at ease.

As discussed earlier in the chapter, a short waiting list helps reduce the potentiality of dropouts. If it is not possible to start a client in therapy soon after his call, then it helps the client to know exactly when he can start. If the period between the client's intake and the start of therapy is long, it is advisable to contact the client by phone during the interim period. This keeps the client's hopes up, makes him feel that help is forthcoming, and lessens his feelings of being neglected; his resentment does not build up excessively.

Several authors have suggested that a better screening procedure helps reduce the dropout rate. Weinberger and Gay (1949) mentioned that a dual screening procedure by the social worker and the psychiatrist helped reduce the dropout rate. Other authors found that the more screening a client went through before being accepted for therapy, the lower the dropout rate (Rogers 1960). Still others have found that the clients who fill out some sort of pretherapy forms or are willing to take psychological tests are less likely to drop out (Dodd 1970; Koran and Costell 1973) than those who are not willing to do so. Wirt (1967) found that in private practice, those who completed the MMPI at the beginning of therapy stayed in therapy significantly longer than those who did not complete it.

These reports do not make clear what criteria they used in screening which helped to reduce the dropout rate. One guess is that they are assessing the client's motivation for therapy or the initial commitment that a client is willing to make for therapy. Noonan (1973) recommends that the client should be recontacted "on the day prior to his scheduled appointment to confirm it. Those who had not made a true commitment to treatment might choose to cancel at that time."

Similarly, Turner and Vernon's study (1976) suggests that "no-show rates could be reduced 20% by having an administrative staff member deliver a personalized telephone reminder to the client several days before his appointment."*

Still others recommend that dropouts can be reduced by selecting clients for therapy who show

a high social engagement factor—job, responsibility for living with children, and living with spouse [because these are] important correlates of intensive utilization of psychotherapy services. The reason is that the greater a person's social engagement, the greater his willingness and ability to undertake yet another socially engaging experience, namely, psychotherapy. (Udell and Hornstra 1975)

Noonan (1973) suggests that "finally the caller might well be required to provide a relatively specific, personal statement of his reasons for contact. Since such statements were associated with lower rates of pre-therapy dropping out it might be that such behavior reflects or insures greater commitment on the part of the caller."

How much each of these factors contributes to the prevention of dropouts is not known; nor is it clear which factors are more important than the others. Yet, taken together, these factors should help reduce significantly the dropout rates. The implementation of these factors is obviously time-consuming and laborious, but there are no short-cuts to reducing the dropout rate.

The Therapist's Role

What is the therapist's role in a client's dropping out of therapy. Should he try to prevent it in the belief that if the client stays in therapy long enough he may be able to resolve some of his problems, including his tendency to drop out? Or should the therapist let the client drop out, accepting his right to choose whether or not to stay in therapy? A therapist may believe that even though clients drop out they derive some benefit from the brief contact with the therapist, or that

---

*Burgoyne et al.'s study (1983) does not support this finding. They believe that dropping out of therapy is a class phenomenon.

one of the reasons for the client's dropping out is that one of the participants has negative feelings toward the other. Hence it is better to separate than to get embroiled in a conflict. These are some of the dilemmas a therapist has to face with a potential dropout.

A few general observations are in order on this issue. This author believes that it is preferable to keep a client in therapy, not through intimidation, cajoling, or bribery but on a voluntary basis, rather than to let him drop out. If the client continues in therapy, it may be possible to explore with him the factors leading to his wish to drop out; otherwise no such exploration is possible.

A case in point is a thirty-seven-year-old counselor, mother of four children, who came to therapy because of marital quarrels and dissatisfactions, impending divorce, and general turmoil in the household. She had been in therapy twice before. Both times she had dropped out; once in the early stages and the other time after about eighteen sessions. Early in therapy with this author she began to hint at dropping out. The main task of the therapist then became to discuss her desire and method of dropping out. She was quite candid in her discussion of her desire to terminate. After this discussion, she came for a few more sessions and hinted again at dropping out. Again, her motives for dropping out were discussed. This process recurred four or five times during the course of therapy, which lasted a little over a year and a half. Toward the end of therapy, many of the things that were troubling her had abated and were resolved. She was, more or less, satisfied with the results of therapy and thanked the therapist for not letting her quit.

Every therapist should remember that a large number of dropouts occur in the early stages of therapy. Knowing this, he should try to be sensitive to a client's indications that he may terminate. Some of these indicators have been discussed earlier in the chapter. It is difficult to judge which factors are most significant. However, on the basis of subjective clinical and supervisory observations and experience, I would list the following factors roughly in order of their importance: (1) Those who come under duress or coercion; (2) mutual negative feelings, or the therapist's negative feelings toward the client; (3) ethnic and class difference between the therapist and the client; (4) a previous history of the client's attrition; (5) poor or weak motivation for therapy; and (6) personality variables of the client.

As discussed above, these factors are not isolated or independent; they interact with each other, constituting a force which leads the client to drop out. For instance, there may be cultural differences between the client and the therapist, and the client may have a history of dropping out as well as psychosomatic complaints. In this case, the probability of dropping out is high.

The multitude of factors that facilitate a client's premature termination are numerous and difficult to control. Yet if a therapist wishes to work with a client, he should make some effort to remember with each client which forces are operating in his life that are likely to contribute to his dropping out. Awareness of specific factors with particular clients will help the therapist to bring up such factors for discussion with the client and prevent him from dropping out.

The therapist plays a key role in the client's dropping out. This fact has not been frankly acknowledged in the literature. Myers and Auld (1955) found that about 11 percent of the dropouts are almost a direct result of the therapist's attitude and/or behavior. Garfield and Affleck (1959) report that the therapist-initiated (or therapist-instigated) dropouts are much higher than is believed. This fact was markedly noticeable in their study made between the ninth and twenty-first sessions, when the therapist begins to take stock of progress (or lack thereof) and suborns the client to drop out.

Of the many ways in which a therapist contributes to the attrition of the client, perhaps by far the most significant is his negative feelings toward the client and/or his discomfort and/or diffidence of handling the client's troubles and problems. The client will sense the therapist's negative feelings and withdraw from therapy. Hence, a therapist's honesty, with regard to his feelings toward the client or toward his problems, can help prevent the termination of many clients.

Many therapists are reluctant to open up a discussion of the client's dropping out, even when they are aware of the presence of certain factors in the client's life and/or in themselves. They may vaguely deny the presence of such factors and hope that the client will keep coming; they may feel that they will offend the client by raising such issues or that they will initiate such a discussion at the wrong time and trigger the client's dropping out. They may be afraid that their own feelings and attitudes will come under scrutiny. Or they may have a narcissistic self-image and think that the client cannot leave them.

By and large, whenever there is a hint from a client that he is thinking of dropping out, the therapist should encourage him to express his thoughts and feelings on it. He should then explore with the client his reasons and motives for dropping out. The client's reasons may or may not appear valid to the therapist; or the therapist may have a different assessment of the client's motivation to drop out. Yet he should maintain a neutral stance while exploring the client's motives for leaving.

It is difficult for a therapist to discuss in an unbiased manner the reasons and motives for the client's dropping out, for in many ways it reflects upon his own competence. Thus, many therapists may become angry or vindictive, or belittle the client who is thinking of dropping out. If the therapist wishes the client to be honest and open with him in discussing his feelings and motives, he will have to create an atmosphere of openness and impunity. If he cannot create such an atmosphere, he forfeits the right to expect or demand honesty from the client.

After discussion, a client may still drop out of therapy. But the therapist has performed his therapeutic duty and should feel satisfied that he has done his best. If he does not raise the issue of the client dropping out, however, then he has fallen short of his obligation.

Summary

Dropping out of psychotherapy is a pervasive phenomenon. Of all the clients who are accepted at a clinic for therapy, approximately one-third do not even show up for their first appointment. Of those who start therapy, a very large number of clients drop out in the early stages of therapy. Calculating conservatively, by the seventh or eighth session approximately 50 percent terminate. By the twenty-fifth session, 85 percent of those who started in therapy have stopped coming.

Clients have various reasons and motives for dropping out. Some drop out because of ethnic or socioeconomic differences with the therapist; some drop out because they came to therapy under duress and want to leave as soon as possible. Others drop out because of the therapist's negative feelings toward them; some because they had to wait too long to get into therapy; some because of the distance, time, and expense; and some because of personality factors.

Various suggestions have been made and procedures recommended to reduce the percentage of dropouts: explaining to the client the procedures and policies of the clinic when he calls; abolishing the waiting list; developing better screening procedures; calling the client a day before his initial appointment; and reducing the negative feelings of the therapist toward the client.

Generally, the role of a therapist demands that whenever he feels that a client is thinking of dropping out, he should explore the client's feelings and reactions. The client may still drop out, but the therapist has performed his therapeutic duty.

References

Acosta, F. 1980. Self-described reasons for premature termination of Psychotherapy by Mexican American, Black American, and Anglo-American patients. *Psychological Reports* 47:435–43.

Affleck, D. C., and S. Garfield. 1961. Predictive judgments of therapist and duration of stay in psychotherapy. *Journal of Clinical Psychology* 17:134–37.

Affleck, D. C., and S. Mednick. 1959. The use of the Rorschach test in the prediction of the abrupt terminator in individual psychotherapy. *Journal of Consulting Psychology* 23:125–28.

Aronson, H., and W. Weintraub. 1969. Certain initial variables as predictors of change with classical psychoanalysis. *Journal of Social and Abnormal Psychology* 74:490–97.

Auld, F., and L. Eron. 1953. Use of Rorschach scores to predict whether patients will continue psychotherapy. *Journal of Consulting Psychology* 17:104–9.

Baekeland, F., and L. Lundwall. 1975. Dropping out of treatment: A critical review. *Psychological Bulletin* 82:738–83.

Borghi, J. 1968. Premature termination of Psychotherapy and patient-therapist expectation. *American Journal of Psychotherapy* 22:460–73.

Brandt, L. W. 1964. Rejection of psychotherapy: The discovery of unexpected number of pseudorejectors. *Archives of General Psychiatry* 10:310–13.

———. 1965. Studies of "dropout" patients in psychotherapy: A review of findings. *Psychotherapy: Theory, Research and Practice* 2:6–13.

Brown, J. A., and N. Kosterlitz. 1964. Selection and treatment of psychiatric outpatients. *Archives of General Psychiatry* 11:425–38.

Burgoyne, R., F. Acosta and J. Yamamoto. 1983. Telephone prompting to increase attendance at a psychiatric outpatient clinic. *American Journal of Psychiatry* 140:345–47.

Carpenter, P., G. Morrow, A. Del Gandio, and B. Ritzer. 1981. Who keeps the first appointment. *American Journal of Psychiatry* 138:102–5.

Cartwright, D. S. 1955. Success in psychotherapy as a function of certain actuarial variables. *Journal of Consulting Psychology* 19:357–63.

Cartwright, R. D., and B. Lerner. 1963. Empathy, need to change, and improvement with psychotherapy. *Journal of Consulting Psychology* 27:138–44.

Cartwright, R., S. Lloyd, and J. Wicklund. 1980. Identifying early dropouts from psychotherapy. *Psychotherapy: Theory, Research and Practice* 17:263–67.

Chameides, W., and J. Yamamoto. 1973. Referral failures: A one year follow up. *American Journal of Psychiatry* 130:1157–58.

Cole, J., and M. Magnussen. 1967. Family situation factors related to remainers and terminators of treatment. *Psychotherapy: Theory, Research and Practice* 4:107–9.

Dodd, J. 1970. A retrospective analysis of variables related to duration of treatment in a university psychiatric clinic. *Journal of Nervous and Mental Disease* 151:75–84.

Feiffel, H., and J. Eells. 1963. Patients and therapists assess the same psychotherapy. *Journal of Consulting Psychology* 27:310–18.

Fiester, A., and K. Rudestam. 1975. A multivariate analysis of early dropout process. *Journal of Consulting and Clinical Psychology* 43:528–36.

Fiester, A. R., A. Mahrer, L. Giambra, and D. W. Ormiston. 1974. Shaping a clinic population: The dropout problem reconsidered. *Community Mental Health Journal* 10:173–79.

Frank, J., L. Gliedman, S. Imber, E. Nash, and A. Stone. 1957. Why patients leave psychotherapy. *Archives of Neurology and Psychiatry* 77:283–99.

Freedman, N. D., D. Engelhardt, L. Hankoff, B. Glick, H. Kaye, J. Buchwald, and P. Stark. 1958. Dropout from outpatient psychiatric treatment. *Archives of Neurology and Psychiatry* 80:657–66.

Fulkerson, S. L., and J. Barry. 1961. Methodology and research on the prognostic use of psychological tests. *Psychological Bulletin* 58:177–204.

Gabby, J., and A. Leavitt. 1970. Providing low cost psychotherapy to middle income patients. *Community Mental Health Journal* 6:210–14.

Garfield, S. 1963. A note on patients' reasons for terminating therapy. *Psychological Reports* 13:38(a).

———. 1977. Further comments on "Dropping out of treatment": Reply to Baekeland and Lundwall. *Psychological Bulletin* 84:306–8.

———. 1980. *Psychotherapy: An eclectic approach.* New York: Wiley.

Garfield, S. L., and D. C. Affleck. 1959. An appraisal of the duration of stay in outpatient psychotherapy. *Journal of Nervous and Mental Disease* 129:492–98.

Garfield, S., D. C. Affleck, and R. Muffly. 1963. A study of psychotherapy interaction and continuation in psychotherapy. *Journal of Clinical Psychology* 19:473–78.

Garfield, S., and M. Kurz. 1952. Evaluation of treatment and related proce- *Quarterly* 26:414–24.

Gibby, R. G., B. A. Stotsky, D. Miller, and E. W. Hiler. 1953. Predictions of duration of therapy from the Rorschach test. *Journal of Consulting Psychology* 17:348–54.

Gliedman, L., A. Stone, J. D. Frank, E. Nash, and S. Imber. 1957. Incentives for treatment related to remaining or improving in psychotherapy. *American Journal of Psychotherapy* 11:589–98.

Gordon, S. 1965. Are we seeing the right patients? Child guidance intake: The sacred cow. *American Journal of Orthopsychiatry* 35:131–37.

Gottsfeld, H., and H. Martinez. 1972. The first psychiatric interview: Patients who do and do not come. *Psychological Reports* 31:776–78.

Graziano, A. M., and R. S. Fink. 1973. Second-order effects in mental health treatment. *Journal of Consulting and Clinical Psychology* 40:356–64.

Greenspan, M., and N. Kulish. 1985. Factors in premature termination. *Psychotherapy* 22:75–82.

Grotjahn, M. 1972. Learning from dropout patients: A clinical view of patients who discontinued group psychotherapy. *International Journal of Group Psychotherapy* 22:306–19.

Gundlach, R., and M. Geller. 1958. The problem of early termination: Is it really the termin? *Journal of Consulting Psychology* 22:410.

Haddock, H., and I. Mensh. 1957. Psychotherapeutic expectations in various clinic settings. *Psychological Reports* 3:109–12.

Heilbrun, A. B. 1961. Clients' personality patterns, counselor dominance and duration of counseling. *Psychological Reports* 9:15–25(a).

———. 1961. Male and female personality correlates of early termination in counseling. *Journal of Counseling Psychology* 8:31–36(b).

Heyder, D. W. 1965. A contribution to overcoming the problem of waiting lists. *American Journal of Orthopsychiatry* 35:772–78.

Hiler, E. W. 1958. An analysis of patient therapist compatibility. *Journal of Consulting Psychology* 22:341–47.

Kirtner, W., and D. Cartwright. 1958. Success and failure in client-centered therapy as a function of client personality variables. *Journal of Consulting Psychology* 22:259–64.

Kline, F., A. Adrian, and M. Spevak. 1974. Patients evaluate their therapist. *Archives of General Psychiatry* 31:113–16.

Koran, L. M., and R. M. Costell. 1973. Early termination from group therapy. *International Journal of Group Psychotherapy* 23:346–59.

Koren, L., P. Goertzel, and M. Evans. 1951. The psychodynamics of failure in psychotherapy. *American Journal of Psychiatry* 108:37–41.

Korner, H. 1964. Abolishing the waiting list in a mental health center, pt. 2. *American Journal of Psychiatry* 120:1097–1100.

Koss, M. P. 1979. Length of psychotherapy for clients seen in private practice. *Journal of Consulting and Clinical Psychology* 47:210–12.

———. 1980. Descriptive characteristics and length of psychotherapy of child and adult clients seen in private psychological practice. *Psychotherapy: Theory, Research and Practice* 17:268–71.

Korner, H. 1964. Abolishing the waiting list in a mental health center, pt. 2. *American Journal of Psychiatry* 120:1097–1100.

Kotkov, B., and A. Meadow. 1953. Rorschach criteria for continuation in individual psychotherapy. *Journal of Clinical Psychology* 17:16–20.

Kurland, S. H. 1956. Length of treatment in a mental hygiene clinic. *Psychiatric Quarterly Supplement* 30:1–8.

Leif, H., V. Leif, C. Warren, and R. Heath. 1961. Low dropout rate in a psychiatric clinic. *Archives of General Psychiatry* 5:200–211.

Lorr, M., M. Katz, and E. Rubinstein. 1958. The prediction of length of stay in psychotherapy. *Journal of Consulting Psychology* 22:321–27.

Lowe, R. 1982. Responding to "no-shows": Some effects of follow up methods on community mental health center attendance pattern. *Journal of Consulting and Clinical Psychology* 52:602–3.

Luborsky, L., A. H. Auerbach, M. Chandler, J. Cohen, and H. M. Bachrach. 1971. Factors influencing the outcome of psychotherapy: A review of quantitative research. *Psychological Bulletin* 75:145–85.

McNair, D., M. Lorr, and D. Callahan. 1963. Patient and therapist influences on quitting psychotherapy. *Journal of Consulting Psychology* 27:10–17.

Mendelsohn, G. A., and M. H. Geller. 1967. Similarity, missed sessions and early termination. *Journal of Consulting Psychology* 14:210–14.

Myers, J. K., and F. Auld. 1955. Some variables related to outcome of psychotherapy. *Journal of Clinical Psychology* 11:51–54.

Noonan, J. R. 1973. A follow up of pretherapy dropouts. *Journal of Community Psychology* 1:43–45.

Pekarik, G. 1983. Follow-up adjustment of outpatient dropouts. *American Journal of Orthopsychiatry* 53:501–11.

———. 1985. The effects of employing different termination classification criteria in dropout research. *Psychotherapy* 22:86–92.

Rachman, S. J., and G. T. Wilson. 1980. *The effects of psychological therapy*. New York: Pergamon Press, 55–57.

Raynes, A. E., and G. Warren. 1971. Some characteristics of drop-outs at first contact with a psychiatric clinic. *Community Mental Health Journal* 7:144–50.

———. 1971. Some distinguishing features of patients failing to attend a psychiatric clinic after referral. *American Journal of Orthopsychiatry* 41:581–88.

Rickles, N., J. Klein, and M. Basson. 1950. Who goes to a psychiatrist. *American Journal of Psychiatry* 106:845–50.

Riess, B., and L. Brandt. 1965. What happens to applicants for psychotherapy. *Community Mental Health Journal* 1:175–80.

Riess, B., and J. Safer. 1973. Some causes and correlates of psychotherapy termination: A study of 500 cases. *International Mental Health Research Newsletter* 15:4–7.

Robin, A. 1976. Rationing outpatients: A defense of the waiting list. *British Journal of Psychiatry* 128:138–41.

Rogawski, A., and B. Edmundson. 1971. Factors affecting the outcome of psychiatric interagency referral. *American Journal of Psychiatry* 127:925–34.

Rogers, C., and R. Dymond. 1954. *Psychotherapy and personality change*. Chicago: University of Chicago Press, 423–24.

Rogers, D., J. Knauss, and K. Hammond. 1958. Predicting continuation in psychotherapy by means of the Rorschach test. *Journal of Consulting Psychology* 15:368–71.

Rogers, L. S. 1960. Drop out rates and results in psychotherapy in government-aided mental hygiene clinics. *Journal of Clinical Psychology* 16:89–92.

Rosenthal, D., and J. P. Frank. 1958. The fate of psychiatric clinic outpatients assigned to psychotherapy. *Journal of Nervous and Mental Disease* 27:83–93.

Rosenweig, S., and R. Folman. 1974. Patient and therapist variables affecting premature termination in group psychotherapy. *Psychotherapy: Theory, Research and Practice* 11:76–79.

Roth, I., P. J. Rhudick, D. Shaskan, M. Slobin, A. Wilkinson, and H. Young. 1964. Long term effects on psychotherapy of initial treatment conditions. *Journal of Psychiatric Research* 2:283–97.

Rubinstein, E., and M. Lorr. 1956. A comparison of terminators and remainers in outpatient psychotherapy. *Journal of Clinical Psychology* 12:345–49.

Salzman, C., M. Luetgert, C. Roth, J. Creasser, and L. Howard. 1976. Formation of a therapeutic relationship: Experiences during the initial phase of psychotherapy as predictors of treatment duration and outcome. *Journal of Consulting and Clinical Psychology* 44:546–55.

Shapiro, A. K., E. Struening, E. Shapiro, and H. Barten. 1976. Prognostic correlates of psychotherapy in psychiatric outpatients. *American Journal of Psychiatry* 133:802–8.

Shapiro, R. J. 1974. Therapist attitudes and premature termination in family and individual therapy. *Journal of Nervous and Mental Disease* 159:101–7.

Shapiro, R. J., and S. H. Budman. 1973. Defection, termination and continuation in family and individual therapy. *Family Process* 12:55–67.

Straker, M., H. Davanloo, and A. Moll. 1967. Psychiatric clinic dropouts. *Laval Medicine* 38:71–77.

Standal, S. W., and F. Van Der Veen. 1957. Length of therapy in relation to counselor estimates of personal integration and other case variables. *Journal of Consulting Psychology* 21:1–9.

Strickland, B. R., and D. P. Crowne. 1963. Need for approval and premature termination of psychotherapy. *Journal of Consulting Psychology* 27:95–101.

Sullivan, P., C. Miller, and W. Smelser. 1958. Factors in length of stay and progress in psychotherapy. *Journal of Consulting Psychology* 22:1–9.

Taulbee, E. S. 1958. Relationship between certain personality variables and continuation in psychotherapy. *Journal of Consulting Psychology* 22:83–89.

Taylor, J. W. 1956. Relationship of success and length in psychotherapy. *Journal of Consulting Psychology* 20:332.

Turner, A. J., and J. C. Vernon. 1976. Prompts to increase attendance in a community mental health center. *Journal of Applied Behavioral Analysis* 9:141–45.

Udell, B., and R. Hornstra. 1975. Good patients and bad: Therapeutic assets and liabilities. *Archives of General Psychiatry* 32:1533–37.

Uhlenhuth, E., and D. Duncan. 1968. Subjective change in psychoneurotic outpatients with medical student therapists. II. Some determinant of changes. *Archives of General Psychiatry* 18:532–40.

Vail, A. 1978. Factors influencing lower-class black patients remaining in treatment. *Journal of Consulting and Clinical Psychology* 46:341.

Walters, G., G. Solomon, and V. Waldon. 1982. Use of M.M.P.I. in predicting psychotherapeutic persistence in groups of male and female outpatients. *Journal of Clinical Psychology* 38:80–83.

Weinburger, J., and E. Gay. 1949. Utilization of psychiatrist and social worker as an intake team. *American Journal of Psychiatry* 106:384–88.

Weiss, J., and K. W. Schaie. 1958. Factors in patient failure to return to clinic. *Diseases of the Nervous System* 19:429–30.

Weitz, L., S. Abramowitz, J. Steger, and F. Calabria. 1975. Number of sessions and client judged outcome: The more the better. *Psychotherapy: Theory, Research and Practice* 12:337–40.

White, A. M., L. Fichtenbaum, and J. Dollard. 1964. Measure for predicting dropping out of psychotherapy. *Journal of Consulting Psychology* 28:326–32.

Wirt, W. M. 1967. Psychotherapeutic persistance. *Journal of Consulting Psychology* 31:429.

Yalom, I. D. 1966. A study of group therapy dropouts. *Archives of General Psychiatry* 14:393–414.

Young, H. 1964. Long term effects on psychotherapy of initial treatment conditions. *Journal of Psychiatric Research* 2:283–97.

7

Movement and Stagnation:
The Lack of Desire to Change

For any individual, it is not easy to change behavior patterns, ways of interaction, and general life-style. Many reasons may account for the difficulty on the part of the client to change. First, the process of learning about oneself and to change accordingly requires a great deal of struggle with oneself. Some are willing to do so no matter how difficult it may be. Others may wage the struggle half-heartedly; still others may pretend to struggle but privately have no desire to change.

Second, the client has developed a certain behavioral pattern or habits. Old habits, however faulty and cumbersome, are difficult to modify. Third, over a period of time the client learns to use such habits and behavior patterns to his advantage or begins to derive certain "secondary gains" from them. To extract these gains from his troubles and conflicts the client may have to pay a heavy price. Yet such gains may be the few gratifications the client derives from his conflicted life. Fourth, the client's new understanding of himself and the new pattern of behavior he is trying to achieve are still risky in terms of bringing satisfactions and rewards, whereas the old pattern of behavior is a familiar and tested one.

For all these reasons the client tends to resist change. But he also desires to change, as manifested by his seeking therapy. Hence, from the beginning of therapy a dual set of forces—desire to change and to resist change—is present in every client.

Definition and Attributes of Resistance

One could define resistance broadly as a force within the client that opposes his becoming aware of himself or of changing (Menninger and Holzman 1973). It has also been defined as opposition to uncovering "anxiety and terror-producing material" (Singer 1965).

Existential writers maintain that resistance reduces the client's authenticity in life (Bugental 1965). Because of his dread, the client does not let himself fully experience certain thoughts and feelings. By holding back the client tries to preserve as much as possible of what he considers authentic in himself. Thus, resistance is a compromise between the reality of his experience and the client's attempt to preserve a certain remnant of self. Resistance is a way of life for the client; it is a difficult pattern for him to change.

Just as resistance reflects the client's unwillingness to alter his way of life, or a sort of despair, similarly the therapist's efforts to challenge and remove resistance reflect the therapist's hope and faith that the client can find alternative ways of life (Singer 1965).

The preferred methods of resistance generally represent survival in the face of experiences perceived as a threat to the client's integrity (Singer 1965). Since the client prefers resistance, one may expect that whatever he does in his daily life he would prefer to do the same in therapy. Hence the mode of resistance and the methods of defense a client employs in his daily life should enlighten the therapist as to what kind of resistances to expect in therapy.

The question has been frequently asked whether resistances are unconscious or conscious, whether the client resists wittingly or unwittingly. In psychoanalytic literature, resistances have been viewed as unconscious, as a counterpart of repression (Freud 1950). Thus, the client is not aware that he is resisting. Most therapists, however, generally do not completely accept this assumption in their work with clients. They proceed on the belief that the client is vaguely aware of resistances in his feelings, attitudes, or mental activity. They argue that if the client were not at least partially aware of his resistances, the therapist would be unsuccessful in convincing the client that he is resisting.

If the therapist is not successful in removing the client's resistances, the therapeutic process begins to stall and gradually becomes stalemated or frozen, and communication between the therapist and the client is diminished. For all these reasons, one of the prime tasks of the therapist is to remove the client's resistances as they emerge (Menninger and Holzman 1973).

Types of Resistances

From the above discussion, one sees that anything which blocks communication or hinders change can be interpreted as resistance. Authors have attempted to categorize resistances in various ways. One group has categorized them as dichotomies: ego alien versus ego syntonic (Greenson 1967; Chessick 1974), blatant versus subtle (Fine 1971; Menninger and Holzman, 1973), and long-term (baseline) versus short-term (intercurrent) (Colby 1951). This approach, however, gives the therapist no indication of how to handle the resistances.

Others have provided a list of resistances the client is likely to use in therapy. Here is a partial list compiled from writers in the field.

1. Lateness or forgetting of appointments
2. Suppression or repression of thoughts and emotions
3. Intensification of symptoms
4. Self-devaluation
5. Flight into health
6. Dissociation of treatment hour from real life
7. Contempt of normality
8. Intellectualization
9. Transference or fear of losing the therapist if the client improves
10. Anxiety
11. Acting out
12. Erotization of therapy
13. Aggression
14. Lack of reference to future
15. Silence (prolonged) during the session

This list is only partial because any behavior can be used by the client as resistance. Furthermore, the cataloging of a client's behavior as resistance tells the therapist little about why certain behavior should be treated as such. The list also does not tell the therapist whether under certain circumstances these behaviors may not constitute resistances, or whether they are to be treated as resistances in a categorical manner.

Nine Sources of Resistances and How to Manage Them

Rather than providing a long list of resistances, it is more productive for the therapist to recognize the sources from which resistances develop. Doing so helps the therapist handle them in a relatively more direct fashion. Clinical observations and a search of the literature suggests the following nine sources of resistances.

1. Resistance to the Client's Role   Certain clients have difficulty in assuming the role of a client, that is, examining their actions, feelings and relationships; opening themselves to their thoughts and feelings; being cooperative with the therapist and sincerely participating in the therapy. Such clients seem to have only a partial interest in effecting any change in themselves and in their lives. They may be challenging and argumentative about the benefits of therapy or the competence of the therapist, or they may be suspicious and doubtful of the therapeutic process. Frequently, such clients mention that perhaps their problems are not serious enough to warrant psychotherapy, especially when they compare them with those of other people.

This resistance arises early in therapy, often in the beginning. It is in the beginning of therapy that a client has difficulty in assuming his role, perhaps because he may have conflicts about what it means to be a client (Weiner 1975). He may interpret it as a sign of weakness, submission, craziness, dependency, inner confusion, low self-esteem, and so on. Hence, if he does not assume the client's role wholeheartedly, he may feel that he has none of the aforementioned traits or characteristics.

This form of resistance should be the first thing that the therapist handles in therapy. Unless it is confronted, the possibility is slim that therapy can be launched with success or that any changes can be brought about in a client's life. This form of resistance—difficulty in assuming the client's role—should be brought to the client's attention in a straightforward manner. After noticing the resistance the therapist could say, "From what you have mentioned here, it seems that you have doubts about the usefulness of therapy or of my competence; or you believe your problems are not serious enough to proceed with therapy."

2. *Ego Resistances*   For lack of a more precise expression I have borrowed the title of this section from the psychoanalytic literature (Freud 1926; Fenichel 1941). This form of resistance means that for reasons of embarrassment, shame, guilt, or emotional upsets the client unconsciously withholds, distorts or blocks his actions, reactions, and experiences as they might have occurred. He manifests such behavior in therapy because, first, he is attempting to protect his self-image, whatever it may be, both in his real life and in therapy. He wishes to present himself in a favorable light, both to himself and to the therapist. Any behavior that contradicts his self-image will have to be forgotten or distorted. Second, the emotional conflicts that lie behind the client's behavior may be too painful to remember or re-experience, and be hurtful or upsetting to him.

This behavior constitutes resistance in therapy for two reasons. First, because of the client's conflicts and feelings, his active role and participation in his life events are not faced squarely. This minimizes the possibility of change. Second, this kind of behavior creates a discontinuity in the client's emotional life, and, as it were, leaves certain "blank spots" in his emotional experiences.

This form of resistance is subtle and difficult to detect. A client may leave out or forget some parts of a story; he may report his feelings and reactions in a distorted way; or he may deny the occurrence of certain feelings or actions. Because the therapist has no independent data on the client's life, he cannot verify the completeness or the veracity of the client's narrations; he must accept the client's word at face value. The therapist devotes a certain amount of time and work to piecing together or juxtaposing the contradictory aspects of the client's behavior in an effort to detect the distortions and blocking. A therapist therefore should allow such resistances to develop and unfold by encouraging the client to explore his feelings and emotions. As a client begins to do so, the therapist should note when and how this form of resistance emerges—whether in the client's affective life, in the recollection of his past, in the description of his behavioral interactions, and so on. Only when the therapist has collected such data (or noted the contradictions) should he bring them to the client's attention. For instance, he could say, "I have observed that when you discuss certain topics (for example, your relationship with your wife), you have difficulty recalling such and such, or you leave out what you said or felt." After the client becomes convinced that he does indeed behave in this manner, the therapist may then begin to search for the motivation for such behavior.

3. *Lack of Desire to Change Owing to Secondary Gain*   A client learns to extract some benefit or pleasure—however convoluted and perverted it may be—from his troubles and conflicts. Such gratification usually becomes intertwined with certain aspects of a client's behavior, which may result in his resistance to any change in his behavior. This form of resistance is difficult to detect because it is hidden or submerged in the client's conflicts and troubles. A therapist is likely to pay more attention to the client's troubles and conflicts than to the gratification that the client derives from them. Once the therapist has recognized the form of resistance, it may take even longer for a client to be convinced that he is extracting certain gratifications from the troubles and conflicts in his life. To help the client overcome his resistance, a therapist may have to assure him that using a different method of gratifying the same needs may be more worthwhile and rewarding. Simultaneously, he may have to encourage the client to seek gratification in different ways.

4. *Old Behaviors and Habit Patterns as Resistances*   It is difficult for any individual to change his behavior and habit patterns because they have been reinforced for a long time and have acquired a quasi-reflexive quality. A person becomes accustomed to them or set in his ways, and they develop an inertia of their own; to change them may require energy and effort which an individual may be reluctant to invest. In psychoanalytic thought and therapy, this mode of operation has been given the label of *repetition-compulsion resistance* (Freud 1926).

Many recent authors and therapists have recommended behavior modification techniques for changing old habit patterns. Psychotherapy literature contains many successful reports of changing the habit hierarchy either through desensitization or through some form of conditioning. Through encouragement or rewards, a therapist may convince the client to make such changes in his behavior.

5. *Rigid Morality*   Sometimes a client adheres to a semi-

absolutistic standard of morality, which can become a tool for him to resist change. In this case, the individual grows so inflexible that he forecloses any possibility of change, preferring to live (or suffer) with his morality and take the consequences.

Adhering to such rigid moral standards is frequently explained in the literature by citing the client's "need for punishment." Or it is viewed as his "atonement for guilt feelings through sufferings" (Menninger and Holzman 1973). While such interpretations of a client's motivation and behavior may sometimes be accurate, a therapist should not accept such generalized interpretations as resistances unless strong evidence from the client's life supports such conclusions. A client who lives by rigid moral standards may, for a number of reasons, be willing to pay a price for his moral inflexibility.

> *A forty-four-year-old policeman came to therapy because he was troubled about his home life. He had been married for twenty-four years, and had three children, two of whom had left home. His wife had several "psychotic" breakdowns, and for the past several years had refused to have sex with him. He was on the "night beat" and would pick up girls after the bars closed at two* A.M. *After spending the night with them, he would become quite fond of them and they of him, for he was a decent person. Some of the women had wanted to marry him. When asked if he had thought of getting a divorce and marrying one of them, he replied, "When I walked up to that altar twenty-four years ago, I said for better or for worse; it turned out for worse. There is nothing I can do about it."*

First, the therapist needs to ascertain that such morality constitutes a "resistance" in relation to those goals which a client has set for himself in therapy. If it does, then the therapist must work to break through the client's rigid morality. This could be done by analyzing the source of the morality; by determining the reasons why the client accepts such morality; by uncovering the client's fears or anxiety about changing such morality; and by encouraging the client to construct a new morality.

6. *Wallowing in Affects and Feelings*   A certain group of clients resist change in their relationships and behavior by continuously expressing their emotions. Such a stance begins to constitute resistance in therapy because expressions of feelings and emotions brings little change in the client's life. The client's behavior excludes the social and intellectual comprehension of his troubles; it reduces his potential to take action in changing his life and focuses exclusively on his

inner state rather than considering the relationship between his inner and outer life.

To help the client overcome this form of resistance, the therapist must demonstrate to him that he does not relate his behavior to external events; that he does not comprehend or analyze his behavior in cognitive terms; that he does not see the impact of his behavior upon others; and that he does not actively strive to change his relationship and behavior.

7. *Attachment and Attraction to the Therapist*   If the client's attachment to the therapist develops beyond a certain point, it can also function as a resistance. When this happens, the client becomes more interested in preserving the status quo rather than in working toward changing himself. The client may fear the termination of a relationship which has begun to provide him with certain assurances and gratifications. Shapiro (1972) states that the more meaningful the relationship with the therapist, the more difficult change becomes because it will threaten the loss of the relationship.

Generally, such resistance develops after the therapist and the client have met for a certain length of time and have developed some kind of bond between them. In the psychoanalytic literature a lack of desire to change due to this reason has been called *transference resistance.*

Recognizing such resistance should not be difficult for a therapist (see Chapter 8). Clients express such feelings and attachments through words, behavior, and gestures. The client's feelings become resistance only when they develop beyond a certain level of intensity; that is, when the client becomes rather preoccupied or consumed by the therapist's thoughts. When this occurs, the therapist should bring it to the client's attention. Then, the therapist may have to discuss the reasons for the client's reluctance to change and his desire to preserve the therapeutic relationship. In short, the therapist may have to persuade the client to seek gratification in his real life rather than in therapy.

8. *Therapist's Errors as Client's Resistances*   Frequently, a therapist (especially one just beginning to practice) is not successful in focusing on the issues and the dilemmas with which the client is struggling at a particular time. The therapist may focus upon feelings and affects when he should focus upon cognition, or vice versa. Or he may choose to pursue a direction in the therapy sessions that the client feels is unwarranted by his own concerns and conflicts. Thus, a therapist makes errors of judgment and interpretations. If these errors be-

come frequent, a client may feel at odds with the therapist; he may not open up to the therapist, or he may hold back material during subsequent sessions. Therapy may become temporarily stalemated.

Under this condition, the therapist constitutes the source of the client's resistance. It is difficult for a therapist to become aware of the problem since presumably he does not knowingly make erroneous interpretations. Therefore, a therapist should consider himself as the possible source of the client's resistance, and he should be modest enough to acknowledge it. Perhaps the best way to overcome the source of such resistances is for the therapist to supervise his own work or to consult with colleagues.

9. Acting Out As a form of resistance, acting out has been accorded a prominent place in the psychoanalytic literature (Fenichel, 1947; Greenacre 1950; Bellak 1965; Menninger and Holzman 1973) and in all psychoanalytically oriented therapies (Wolberg 1967; Weiner 1975). It has remained a vague concept, difficult to define, poorly understood, and frequently difficult to delineate. According to Fine (1971), "The borderline between ordinary action and neurotic acting out may frequently be a most difficult one to define with any precision." However, the concept of acting out is extensively used in the literature, and therefore it is necessary to discuss it. (See also Chapter 8, especially the section on the acting out of transference.)

Classical psychoanalysis defines the concept as

an acting which unconsciously relieves inner tension and brings a partial discharge to ward off impulses . . . the present situation, somehow associatively connected with the repressed content, is used as the occasion for the discharge of the repressed energies; the cathexis is displaced from the repressed memories to the present 'derivatives' and this displacement makes the discharge possible (Fenichel 1945).

Menninger and Holzman (1973) state,

It is the tendency to substitute an act or a series of acts for episodes that the analysand cannot remember or at least fails to report. In other words, the patient remembers not in words, but in behavior and thus repeats a piece of language behavior. He repeats it, without, of course, knowing that he is repeating it. This is an extremely effective kind of resistance since, like a dream, it offers some discharge of tension. It is like a charade played between two parts of the ego.

In quoting Greenace (1950), Menninger and Holzman further declare, "Since in its very nature acting out is ego syntonic, and the patient is not aware of its destructive nature, it comes to the attention of the analyst in most instances after its occurrence (if at all) and sometimes is not reported or only indirectly."

Robertiello (1965) states that

the important issues then in acting out are (1) the gratification of childhood unconscious impulses in a present situation which has some parallels or similarities to the original situations and (2) the maintenance of the repression through the patient's not seeing the present day behavior is inappropriate, or at least, his viewing it as ego-syntonic and not connecting it with reliving a past situation. Both of these conditions are essential to calling a piece of behavior acting out.

According to Weiner (1975), "Acting out refers to the resolution of psychological conflicts by translating anxiety provoking impulses directly into behavior. Because acting out behavior replaces intrapsychic grappling with conflictual impulses, it is temporarily anxiety reducing. However, because acting out behavior is also typically impulsive and poorly planned, it tends to generate new sources of anxiety."

These theoretical definitions of acting out suggest that it has four aspects. First, it is an unconscious (impulsive) act to discharge energy or anxiety. Second, it substitutes actions for words (or thoughts). Third, acting out is intrinsically ego-syntonic, or pleasurable, although its consequences may be harmful. Finally, the acts in question generally have an unconventional, quasi-antisocial, or harmful quality.

In actual practice, however, a therapist generally attaches the label of "acting out," after the fact, to four kinds of client behavior. First, client behavior which may have an anti-social or "immoral" quality is likely to be labeled as "acting out" (for example, stealing or having an extramarital affair). Second, it is attached to behavior whose motivation or purpose the client cannot clearly and easily explain. For example, if a client says that when he got home he started shouting at his wife on a slight provocation, but didn't quite know why, his behavior may be labeled as "acting out." Third, behavior whose explanation may seem beyond the theoretical framework of the therapist is likely to be called "acting out." For instance, if a client engages in certain mystical rituals to attain certain goals (mystical ritualistic behavior exists beyond the framework of most therapeutic systems) this may be labeled as "acting out." Finally, client behavior that is not discussed with the therapist prior to its appearance (or which appears to have been performed impulsively) is likely to earn the label of "acting out." Thus the term *acting out* has a negative connotation.

It is noteworthy that the positive action of the client, which may fulfill most of the criteria of the resistance, is not labeled as "acting out." In fact, there is little in the literature to suggest that acting out may include positive behavior. For instance, without discussing it with the therapist a client may buy certain unstable stocks. During the subsequent therapy he may not be able to explain satisfactorily why he bought such stocks; he may say he doesn't know, or that he bought them impulsively. If during the course of the next few weeks or months the price of the stock falls and the client loses money, his behavior will be labeled as "acting out." However, if the price of the stock rises and the client makes money, it will rarely be regarded in the same way.

There are some suggestions in the literature that the therapist may unwittingly motivate such behavior and then label it as "acting out." Strupp (1960) found that "therapists giving a negative prognosis were more likely to expect the patient to act out than therapists whose prognosis was favorable." In other words, acting out may become a kind of self-fulfilling prophecy created by the therapist for a client toward whom he is unfavorably disposed.

Acting out is considered a resistance for two reasons. First, the client avoids discussing in therapy the thoughts and feelings which bother him. He is expected to do so. Hence, acting out conflicts with the assumptions and demands of psychotherapy. Second, rather than discuss these issues in therapy, the client acts them out elsewhere. For these reasons, such conflicts cannot be resolved in psychotherapy and the client cannot modify his behavior.

Various methods of handling acting out have been mentioned in the literature. Strupp (1960) found that for many therapists "the preferred methods of handling the problem were . . . interpretation and control, by firmness, strictness, or setting limits. . . . Rogerians recommended understanding, clarification and reflection."

Bellak (1965) differentiates between the management of long-term and short-term acting out. Following Greenacre (1950), he recommends three techniques for handling long-term acting out: prohibition, interpretation, and strengthening the ego. He also recommends systematic and intentional use of prediction. If a therapist can tell the patient in advance that he is likely to act out because of an approaching set of circumstances or situations, he will go a long way toward aborting the behavior.

Furthermore, according to him, patients acting out tend to forget the moods and events of the previous sessions. Hence, therapy sessions should routinely begin with recalling and reviewing the previous sessions. The need for current action should be related to the events and feelings of the past. Such a method helps strengthen the synthetic functions of the patient's ego. Therefore, such a method is likely to reduce the possibility of acting out.

For the management of short-term acting out, Bellak (1965) makes the following recommendations:

1. Remove the patient from the situation which triggers acting out. Or, in some cases, change the social milieu.
2. Encourage cathartic interpretation to deal directly with the drive expressed in acting out.
3. Point out the repetitive and harmful nature of acting out, and point out that the patient is a victim of his unconscious distortions.
4. Urge the patient to wait—a day, a week, or a month—before taking any action. Since immediate action is a large factor in all acting out, any delay, of itself, will tend to interfere with this behavior. Benefits of waiting are that the urgency of the moment may be bypassed, and one gains time to interpret usefully.
5. In extreme cases, enlist the help of others to curb harmful acting out.
6. Attempt to strengthen the super ego.
7. Appeal to the patient's conscience and point out to him the social implications of his behavior and the detrimental effect it may have on others. Attempt to ally with the part of the patient's personality that wishes to control the impulse. At those times, when the danger of acting out is acute, be available to the patient by telephone or personal contact in order to delay or deter the episode.

Although not usually mentioned in the literature, the following technique may be recommended. If the therapist feels that a client may "act out," in certain situations or under certain circumstances he may give his telephone number to the client, suggesting that the client call him. Thus the client's tensions, anxieties, and feelings could be discussed before he delves into certain kinds of behavior.

A thirty-year-old female insurance underwriter, the mother of two children, came to therapy because she was married but enjoyed having extramarital affairs, which got her into trouble. She had grown up on a small farm in Oklahoma, where her father attempted to have incest with her when she was sixteen. After her marriage, her parents would visit her every two years, and the visit was neither pleasant nor easy for her. When the parents left, she would engage in various extramarital affairs. She began therapy following one of these visits. Her pattern of behavior after her parents' visits was brought to her attention. During the subsequent visits of her parents she was encouraged to call the therapist if she felt that she might engage in extramarital affairs. She did not call between the sessions, nor did she engage in extramarital affairs.

Some General Principles of Handling Resistances

As discussed in the earlier part of this chapter, resistances may appear at the beginning of therapy. The client comes to therapy with certain built-in resistances, a fact that a beginning therapist is likely to overlook if he believes that resistances develop only later in therapy. For this reason, the therapist should be alert to the manifestations of resistances from the time therapy begins. A client's past behavior will provide the therapist with some clues as to when and what sort of resistances to expect.

Generally, resistances do not appear in their pure form, as described above. Frequently, they have a complex character and combine more than one source. In other words, they are multiply determined. While some resistances may be easy to observe, others are not, especially when they are subtle or innocuous on the surface and/or are supported by the prevailing culture.

For instance, a young woman belonging to the middle class may be quite concerned about her looks, clothes, dates, sexual presentation of self, and so forth. She may spend a great deal of time talking about these issues in therapy. At one level, this may be a narcissistic form of resistance, and yet the expectations of her social class and the demands of the culture may support her concerns and behavior. Thus the client's resistances are embedded in and/or supported by the culture and may be difficult to isolate. Beginning therapists frequently overlook these causes of resistance as long as the client comes to therapy and talks.

When the therapist realizes that the resistance is interfering with the progress of therapy, he should bring it to the client's attention. Declaring it a resistance on the basis of one instance, however, generally will not convince the client to try to change his behavior. To demonstrate to the client that his behavior may be a resistance, the therapist needs numerous instances. For example, if a client comes late for a session, and the therapist tells him that he may be resisting, the client can always come up with an answer, such as "I got caught in a traffic jam." Only when such behavior occurs repeatedly can a therapist point out that (1) he has noticed that the client has been late for so many sessions, (2) the client has not allowed enough time to get to the session on time, and (3) he may therefore be unwilling to examine certain things or may be resisting.

What happens if such resistances are not brought to the client's attention? Basically, this means that those conflicts which may be creating difficulties for the client are not made apparent and therefore cannot be examined. Hence, such resistances continue to impede the client's progress in therapy. When the therapist misses an opportunity to bring to the client's attention a part of his behavior which may be creating his difficulties, the client's behavior has little chance of being modified.

The Role of Reassurance in Handling Resistances

Conflicts with cultural taboos attached to them—for example, lesbianism, masturbation, sexual impotence in men, and so forth—are difficult for the client to discuss. The client may feel too embarrassed, ashamed, or guilty to raise these issues. Hence, because of their cultural context, these topics are likely to become resistances in therapy. Under such conditions, a certain degree of reassurance from the therapist assists the client in overcoming his initial resistance (Weiner 1975).

A twenty-six-year-old male bachelor client was struggling with his homosexual fears. At periodic intervals he would hint about this conflict and then would change the topic or lapse into silence for a few minutes. First, it was brought to the client's attention that his silences were preceded by a certain kind of discussion. Then, it was pointed out that there are certain life interests which are difficult to talk about and still more difficult to face because one may feel ashamed, guilty, or less worthwhile. Yet the therapist would want the client to be courageous enough to discuss them as best he could.

However, when a client begins to show more than the usual amount of anxiety or nervousness about any topic, then too the therapist must reassure the client so that he may calm down and develop some control over himself. Only after the client has attained some mastery over his emotions will he be able to attempt to change. A client's general state of anxiety and nervousness, frequently seen in certain seriously disturbed (schizophreniclike) conditions, begins to constitute a form of resistance.

Generally, a therapist should mix his observations of a client's resistances with encouragement, reassurance, or support. Remarks by the therapist which reflect only the client's resistance—for example, "you don't want to change" or "you have something on your mind which you are afraid to say," or "you are resisting becoming aware of such and such,"—are experienced by the client as "nagging" (Bugental 1965). They make the client defensive and self-conscious, and they blunt his spontaneity. The same kind of remark could be formulated as an observation, and couched in the following language: "Although you came to therapy to change and you have struggled to do so, you still seem to have difficulty in accepting certain things which may need to change."

Yet, a single observation or remark about the client's resistance is not sufficient to change the client's behavior. The total pattern of every resistance has to be brought to the client's attention, and it must be dealt with many times before any stable change can be expected. A resistance is a part of the client's life-style, his way of being in the world, and it is reinforced by many aspects of the client's daily existence.

After the therapist has taken the aforementioned steps, he may try to understand, in cooperation with the client, the meaning and purpose of the client's resistance. In what ways is the client resisting change? Why is he resisting? In short, what is the meaning and purpose of resistance? If the therapist is able to arouse the client's curiosity about his own behavior, he becomes far more helpful to the client in dissolving the resistance (Weiner 1975).

Resistances and the Therapist's Role   The client's resistance to change poses many problems for the therapist, in much the same way that negative transference does. Indeed, many authors have equated resistance with the client's negative transference (see Chapter 8). The client's resistance to change usually generates a counter-resistance—an annoyance or irritation—in the therapist. When a resistance emerges, psychotherapy seems to lose its momentum and begin to develop a stalemate. The therapist not only has to handle his own feelings and emotions, but he must make the therapy "move." The client's attempt to overcome his own resistance may require special efforts from the therapist. Thus, a resistance becomes a test of the therapist's skill and his understanding of a client's struggles.

A resistance does not dissolve simply because the therapist

points it out to the client. Before the client can overcome the various manifestations of his resistance, the therapist must help him recognize how the resistance affects his relationships, actions, thoughts, and feelings. This, too, requires more than the usual amount of work on the part of the therapist.

Frequently, clients' resistances have served as a convenient alibi for the therapist's own shortcomings in his work, his inability to develop suitable techniques and the proper understanding of a client's problems. For instance, if after a certain period of time a client does not make satisfactory progress, or if a stalemate develops in therapy, a therapist may put the onus for the lack of progress on the client. He may state that the client is too resistant, that his resistances are too deeply rooted to be changed, or that he is too manipulative to benefit from therapy (Colby 1951; Wolberg 1965; Singer 1965; Menninger and Holzman 1973; Chessick 1974; Saltmarsh 1976). Because this exculpates the therapist, he may not examine the shortcomings of his own motivations, methods, and techniques.

Resistances in a client call for the therapist to take on a dual role. On the one hand, the therapist is required to bring the resistances to the client's attention, analyze them, and help the client overcome them. On the other hand, since a client's resistances are likely to generate counter-resistance in a therapist, they call for self-examination on the therapist's part. The therapist must avoid blaming the client and examine objectively and dispassionately his own role and participation in therapy.

Summary

The client generally comes to therapy to understand himself, to resolve his conflicts, and in general, to change his life. Yet the client is also resistant to change. Both sets of forces operate in therapy from the beginning. It is a therapist's task to keep the balance of forces tilted in the direction of change.

Resistances can arise from a number of sources. Each of these requires careful handling by the therapist. If the client is not motivated to overcome his resistances, therapy is likely to become stalemated. The client's resistances generate a series of feelings and reactions in the therapist which are generally negative. This makes the therapist's task more difficult. He has to struggle with his own reactions and almost simultaneously help the client overcome his resistance. Thus, the client's resistances become a test of a therapist's skill and understanding.

References

Bellak, L. 1965. The concept of acting out: Theoretical considerations. In L. E. Abt and S. L. Weissman, eds., *Acting out*. New York: Grune and Stratton, 3–20.

Bugental, J. 1965. *The search for authenticity*. New York: Holt, Rinehart and Winston, 93–113.

Chessick, R. 1974. *Technique and practice of intensive psychotherapy*. New York: Jason Aronson.

Colby, K. M. 1951. *A primer for psychotherapists*. New York: Ronald Press Co.

Fenichel, O. 1945. Neurotic acting out. *Psychoanalytic Review* 32:197–206.

———. 1941. Problems of psychoanalytic technique. *Psychoanalytic Quarterly*. Albany, N.Y.: Psychoanalytic Quarterly.

Fine, R. 1971. *The healing of the mind*. New York: David McKay Co., 128.

Freud, S. 1950. *Beyond the pleasure principle*. New York: Liveright Publishing Corporation, 20.

———. 1959. *Inhibitions, Symptoms and Anxiety* (1926), standard ed., vol. 20. London: Hogarth Press, 87–174.

Greenacre, P. 1950. General problems of acting out. *Psychoanalytic Quarterly* 19:455–67.

Greenson, R. 1967. *The technique and practice of psychoanalysis*, vol. 1. New York: International University Press.

Menninger, K., and P. Holzman. 1973. *Theory of psychoanalytic technique*. New York: Basic Books, 103–12.

Robertiello, R. C. 1965. Acting out or working through. In L. E. Abt and S. L. Weissman, eds., *Acting out*, 40–48. New York: Grune and Stratton.

Saltmarsh, R. E. 1976. Client resistance in talk therapies. *Psychotherapy: Theory, Research and Practice* 1:34–39.

Shapiro, R. J. 1972. Resistance revisited: The therapist as surrogate family. *American Journal of Psychotherapy* 1:112–22.

Singer, E. 1965. *Key concepts in psychotherapy*. New York: Random House, 223, 231, 243–65.

Strupp, H. 1960. *Psychotherapists in action*. New York: Grune and Stratton, 88.

Weiner, I. 1975. *Principles of psychotherapy*. New York: John Wiley, 167–93.

Wolberg, L. 1967. *The technique of psychotherapy*, vols. 1 and 2. New York: Grune and Stratton.

8

Client's Feelings toward the Therapist:
The Transference

In any form of therapeutic relationship, clients develop feelings toward the therapist (and the therapist toward the client; see Chapter 9). The client's feelings could be negative or positive, mild or intense, specific or diffuse; they could be directed toward the person of the therapist, or they could become enmeshed in the process of therapy (Freud 1954). However, these feelings are found in other relationships—between boyfriend and girlfriend, between teacher and student, between parent and child, or between physician and patient. Are the feelings of the client toward the therapist different from the feelings in other relationships? If so, in what ways are they different? If not, why are they accorded a special status in psychoanalysis and psychotherapy?

In psychoanalysis (and in certain other forms of therapies), the client's feelings have been given a particular label—"transferences." The feelings of the client in therapy or psychoanalysis are said to reflect those feelings which were once directed toward the client's parents or other significant figures in his past. In technical language, the patient displaces emotions belonging to an unconscious representation of a repressed object to a mental representation of an object of an external world. This object represented within the ego is the analyst, on whom emotions and ideas belonging to the repressed unconscious objects are projected. The repressed objects belong to the past, mostly to the patient's early childhood, and are thus unreal. (Nunberg 1951)

Transference has become one of the shibboleths of psychoanalysis,* the other is resistance. In fact, it is on the basis of these two concepts, transference and resistance, that psychoanalysis itself is defined (Freud 1938).

The popularity, utility, and acceptance of the concept of transference has led to its liberal use in schools of therapy other than psychoanalysis, with the result that no other topic in psychoanalysis and psychotherapy has been so extensively written about, accepted so uncritically, and so generally assumed to be understood (McAlpine 1950).

How is the term *transference* defined? What is the history of the concept of transference (or of transference neurosis)? How does it manifest itself and what purpose does it serve in therapy? What happens if a therapist conceptualizes a client's feelings in therapy as transference? How should it be handled in therapy? These are some of the issues discussed in this chapter.

Freud's Concept of Transference

Freud himself never clearly defined the concept of transference. He used the term in different ways from time to time, and the concept became amorphous and confused. Possibly such variation in the use of the concept occurred because Freud worked with many different kinds of patients over his long years of practice. Some of his patients were seriously disturbed, while others were only mildly so. He saw some of his patients quite frequently, five or six times a week,

---

*Some authors maintain that it is not the transference, but the "transference neurosis" which is the "central technical and conceptual vehicle of psychoanalysis" (Wallerstein 1967). Present-day psychoanalysts, agreeing with Freud, maintain that the fundamental distinction between psychoanalysis and other psychotherapies should be made on the basis of the management and resolution of the transference neurosis (Gill 1954; Rangell 1954). For a distinction between transference and transference neurosis, see below.

while others were seen less frequently. Some were female; others were male. In each case, the intensity and variety of the client's emerging feelings toward the therapist may have been different.

Freud defined the concept of transference according to the kinds of clients he may have been working with at a given time, always taking into consideration the feelings of the clients he encountered. In addition to his clinical observations, he speculated in a philosophical vein about the nature of transference, as, for example, in *Beyond the Pleasure Principle* (1950). Such philosophical speculation did not require any empirical evidence, with the result that clinical observations, clinical interpretation, and philosophical speculation became welded together in the concept of transference. For many of these reasons, he could not, or did not, arrive at a standard definition of transference.

Although Freud used the term *transference* in his earlier writings (Breuer and Freud 1937), his first clinical definition came in 1905 with his discussion of the case of Dora:

What are transferences? They are new editions or facsimiles of the tendencies and phantasies which are aroused and made conscious during the progress of the analysis; but they have this peculiarity, which is characteristic of their species, that they replace some earlier person by the person of the physician. To put it another way: A whole series of psychological experiences are revived not as belonging to the past, but as applying to the person of the physician at the present moment. (Freud 1950e)

Freud returns to the definition of transference he formulated in the early *Papers on Techniques*. In "Observations on Wild Psychoanalysis" (1910), he describes transference as an affective relationship to the physician which might imply no more than "rapport." Orr (1954) summarizes the next phase in Freud's development of the concept:

In the three papers entitled "*Further Recommendations in the Technique of Psychoanalysis*" (1913, 1914 and 1915), Freud employs the term *transference* in a somewhat confusing variety of ways. In some instances Freud appears to mean no more than rapport; in others he clearly means the transference neurosis; and in still others he implies some intermediate variety of displacement and intensities of affective relationships. In the third of these papers, subtitled "Observations on Transference—Love," Freud is exclusively preoccupied with the erotic transference of female patient to male therapist.

In 1920, Freud returned to the topic of transference in *Beyond the Pleasure Principle*. In this book, Freud discusses the theme of repetition compulsion. Transference is one example of repetition compulsion, which is viewed as such with particular force in the "transference neurosis." In *An Outline of Psychoanalysis* (1949), Freud stresses four aspects of transference:

[a] the ambivalence of transference; [b] the reincarnation of figures from childhood in the person of the analyst; [c] the analyst as a new super ego being thus in a position to correct errors of early upbringing—a position that must not be abused, however, lest one type of dependent relationship replace another; [d] the transference neurosis as marked by a confusion of the present with the past so that the analyst must tear the patient away each time from the menacing illusion to show him again and again that what he takes to be new real life is a reflection of the past.

Freud's definition and the characteristics attributed to the concept of transference have been accepted almost on faith by subsequent writers and clinicians. Modifications of the concept have not altered its nature or its structure in any substantive manner. Those therapists who do not use the concept in their work with clients have dropped the use of the concept altogether.

Transference and Transference Neurosis

A survey of the literature suggests that in its classical form the term *transference* is used to describe various feelings and reactions of the client which emerge in different intensities during the course of therapy and which may be directed toward the therapist. To describe, encompass, and comprehend the variety of clients' feelings and reactions during therapy, various terms have been used liberally in the literature—*transference relationship, transference cure, indirect transference, transference resistance, transference neurosis, infantile neurosis*, and so on. Some of these terms are used interchangeably. Sometimes one term may subsume the other, while at other times the terms may be used with distinctly different connotations. Consequently, the definition and the implied meaning of these terms frequently become confusing for the beginning student and require a great deal of research in order to make much sense of the concept. Here, from the literature, is a typical example of an attempt at a definition of the concept.

In its widest sense, as we here use the word, transference is the exact repetition of any former reaction without adjusting it to fit the present situation. In a more specific sense, transference is the neurotic repetition with relation to the analyst of a stereotyped, unsuitable behavior pattern based on the patient's past—the transference "relationship," then, is the relationship which obtains within the therapeutic situation wherein the therapist is indeed the representative of a figure of importance from the patient's past.

When defined this way, the transference relationship becomes identical with the transference "neurosis" except the transient neurotic transference reactions are not usually signified with the name of "transference neurosis." Thus transference "neurosis" may be defined as that mass of stereotyped neurotic behavior patterns (evidenced in the analytic situation) which are based on the past and do not take into account the differences between the present and the past. . . . (Alexander and French 1946)

Nor have attempts by more recent writers to clearly distinguish between transference and transference neurosis (and infantile neurosis) been successful (Hoffer 1956; Ruesch 1961; Tarachow 1963; Kepecs 1966; Calef 1971; Weinshel 1971). Thus, the distinction between the two concepts of transference and transference neurosis remains diffuse and amorphous. Szasz (1963) maintains that

the difference between transference and transference neurosis is one of degree. Analysts generally speak of transferences when referring to isolated ideas, affects, or patterns of conduct which the patient manifests toward the analyst and which are repetitions of similar experiences from the patient's childhood; and they speak of transference neurosis when referring to a more extensive and coherent set of transferences.

The imprecision in this usage stems from a lack of standards as regards the quantity of transferences required before one can legitimately speak of transference neurosis. In other words, we deal here with a quantitative distinction but possess neither measuring instruments nor standards of measurements for making quantitative estimates. Thus, the distinction between transference and transference neurosis remains arbitrary and impressionistic. (Szasz 1963)

A review of the literature on this topic suggests a general consensus on the following characteristics of the concept of transference. (However, it is not necessary to discover all five characteristics in order to interpret a client's feelings as transference; most authors generally settle for three or four.)

First, the patient feels and behaves toward the therapist as he did toward his parents or important figures in his past; or the patient unconsciously experiences the therapist as his father or as another important figure (Bugental 1965). The feelings originally associated with parental figures are displaced, albeit unconsciously, onto the analyst, and the analytic situation is perceived as an infantile one (Freud 1949; Colby 1951; Glover 1955; Greenson 1967).

Second, the feelings and attitudes attributed to the therapist or analyst are unreal, illusory, or misplaced; they do not belong in the therapeutic situation (Freud 1949; Nunberg 1951; Ruesch 1961; Dewald 1964; Menninger and Holzman 1973).

Third, the patient behaves in this manner under the influence of "repetition compulsion" (Freud 1946; Silverberg 1948; Freud 1950). Hence, the patient's behavior reveals a stereotyped reaction pattern, without adjusting to fit the present situation (Alexander and French 1946; Zetzel 1956; Saul 1958).

Fourth, transference develops due to regression (to a childhood stage) induced in the analytic situation. For these reasons, the phenomenon of transference shows the nature of the patient's past conflicts with his parents; it shows how his past affects his present life (Freud 1949; McAlpine 1950; Greenacre 1954; Waelder 1956; Wolstein 1960; Singer 1965; Menninger and Holzman 1973; Weiner 1975).

Fifth, transference is a form of resistance in which the patient defends himself against remembering his infantile conflicts by trying to relive and gratify them (Fenichel 1941; Wolstein 1954; Zetzel 1956; Gill 1982).

With this survey as background, we may now raise two questions with regard to the concept of transference. First, what were the sociohistorical and psychological antecedents which led to the development and formulation of the concept of transference? In other words, why did it become necessary to formulate such a concept? To understand this, we need to trace the concept's historical development. Second, is there existing empirical evidence which may suggest that the phenomenon of transference, as defined by various authors, occurs during the course of therapy?

History of the Concept of Transference

Bertha Pappenheim (called "Anna O." in the literature) was born in Vienna on February 27, 1859. The Pappenheims were a wealthy, orthodox Jewish family, and by tradition a very moral one (Freeman 1972). The husband, Mr. Pappenheim, was a wealthy merchant and dealer in grain futures. Mrs. Pappenheim (whose maiden name was Recha Goldschmidt) was the daughter of one of the wealthiest international bankers of Frankfurt (Freeman 1979). The Pappenheims had a country home on the outskirts of Vienna, a little over an hour away by carriage, where the family traditionally spent the summer (Freeman 1972). During the rest of the year they stayed in a large third-floor apartment in Vienna, only a few blocks from Breuer's home.

Of the four children* born to the Pappenheims, the older two daughters had died before they reached adolescence. Only Bertha and her younger brother, Wilhelm, had survived to adulthood (Freeman 1979). "That she thought her birth was a disappointment to her parents can still be detected in the essay Bertha Pappenheim wrote in December 1934" (Edinger 1968).

Bertha attended a Catholic school in Vienna. Apparently, she felt that she learned little at the school (Jensen 1970). She was fluent in several languages, including English, French, and Italian (Edinger 1968; Ellenberger 1972). Like daughters of most well-to-do families, she had a governess (Jensen 1970). She led the usual life of a young lady of high Viennese society, engaging in outdoor activities, such as horseback riding, and doing a great deal of needlework. Bertha visited theaters and was interested in Shakespeare's plays (Ellenberger 1972). Breuer and Freud (1937) describe her in the following passage:

> She had a keen intuitive intellect, a craving for psychic fodder, which she did not, however, receive after she left school. She was endowed with a sensitiveness for poetry and fantasy, which was, however, controlled by a very strong and critical mind—only arguments, no assertion had any influence upon her.

Her parents were reported to be "nervous but healthy" (Breuer and Freud 1937). Ellenberger (1972) suggests that Bertha had difficulties with her "very serious" mother, whom Jones (1953) describes as "somewhat of a dragon." Bertha sometimes quarreled with her younger brother. Some accounts suggest that she resented the fact that her brother had been given the opportunity to pursue a higher education while she had been deprived of it. By all accounts her relationship with her father was a very close and intimate one. She adored her father (Breuer and Freud 1937); she had a "passionate love for her father who pampered her" (Ellenberger 1972).

Physically, she was a very attractive and vivacious woman: "She

---

*According to Ellenberger (1972), "They had three children all of them born in Vienna. Henriette, born on September 2, 1849, Bertha, born on February 27, 1859, Wilhelm, born on August 15, 1860. Henriette, who was ten years older than Bertha, died in early youth."

was absolutely bewitching in a group of men. . . . She had many admirers. . . . Even as an old woman she could be very seductive with men" (Freeman 1979). A stubborn opposition to religion added a negative streak to her personality: "She is thoroughly unreligious. . . . Religion played a role in her life as an object of silent struggles and silent oppositions, although, for her father's sake, she outwardly followed all the religious rites of her strictly orthodox Jewish family" (Ellenberger 1972).

In July 1880, when she was a little over twenty-one years of age, her father developed a peripleuritic abscess (presumably tuberculosis) which did not yield to treatment (Breuer and Freud 1937). From that time on she saw her father "sinking": "She knew [he] would soon be dead, buried and fleshless" (Freeman 1979). On April 5, 1881, her father died. Her first hallucination developed during her father's illness. During the night of July 17–18, 1880, while the father was sick and the family waited for the arrival of a surgeon from Vienna, Bertha was by her father's bedside, where she experienced the hallucination.

She saw a black snake crawling out of the wall to kill her father. She wanted to drive it away, but could not move her right arm; she saw her fingers as transformed into as many little snakes with skulls, instead of the nails. She was filled with anguish, tried to pray, but could not speak until she found an English sentence. At this point the spell was interrupted by the whistling of an engine; it was the train which brought the surgeon from Vienna. (Ellenberger 1972)

Other symptoms began to appear.

"Many of them occurred during a peculiar state of absent-mindedness which she termed (in English) "time missing." Her visual perceptions were strangely distorted. Looking upon her father, she saw him as a skeleton and his head as a skull. After having once been shaken by her brother she became momentarily deaf but from that time on a transient deafness always appeared whenever she was shaken.

At the beginning of September 1880, the family went back to Vienna (it is not stated where they were before). Bertha devoted herself to nursing her sick father. Her symptoms were aggravated, a "nervous cough" appeared. Breuer saw her for the first time at the end of November due to the "hysterical cough"; he recognized at once that she was mentally sick . . . something that had escaped her family's notice. (Ellenberger 1972)

On December 11, 1880, she became bedridden and remained so until April 1, 1881, four days before her father's death. "Bertha's both legs were paralyzed, as was her right arm. Because of a paralyzed muscle in her neck she could hardly turn her head. And her visual disturbances were so severe that she could no longer read or write. The nerve and the eye specialist her mother had consulted could find no physical cause for any of these physical symptoms" (Freeman 1979). Her attention would wander off as if she was hallucinating. She appeared not to hear what was being said to her and when she spoke, she frequently broke off in mid-sentence. She would say, "I see death's head—skulls—fleshless bones, grinning at me" (Freeman 1972).

She became weak and anemic and evidenced a disgust for nourishment; she would eat only a few oranges fed to her by a nurse (Freeman 1972). "During the afternoons she remained in a state of somnolence, which continued until about an hour after sunset. She then awoke and complained that something was tormenting her, or rather she always repeated the infinitive, 'to torment, to torment'" (Breuer and Freud 1937).

Since Bertha was ill and had developed a severe cough a few months prior to her father's death,

she was not allowed to see him and had continuously been told lies about his condition. . . . [She told Breuer] she used to get up in the night, put her stockings on and go to listen at his door until one night she was caught by her brother. . . . In spite of her lasting anxiety, there had been some improvement in Bertha's illness and she had got up for the first time on April 1. On April 5, at the moment when her father was dying, she called her mother and asked for the truth, but was appeased and the lie went on for some time. When Bertha learned that her father had died, she was indignant; she had been "robbed" of his last look and last word. From that time on, a marked transformation appeared in her condition; anxiety replaced by a kind of dull insensitivity with distortions in her visual perceptions. Human beings appeared to her as wax figures. In order to recognize someone she had to perform what she called (in English) a "recognizing work." The only person she immediately recognized was Breuer. She manifested an extremely negative attitude toward her mother and to a lesser degree, toward her brother. (Ellenberger 1972)

Treatment by Breuer   Breuer treated Bertha Pappenheim on a regular basis for approximately eighteen months—from the second week in December 1880 until June 7, 1882 (Freeman 1972). During the course of his treatment he used various techniques and approaches. In the beginning, he hypnotized her. Instead of asking her to give up her symptoms, he asked, "Is something troubling you?" This question allowed her to express her feelings and emotions (Freeman

1972). Hypnotic sessions were conducted daily at Bertha's home, usually in the evenings. After approximately four months of treatment—by the beginning of April 1881—her condition began to improve. On April 1, 1881, she got out of her bed and was able to walk across the room by herself (Freeman 1979).

On April 5, 1881, Bertha's father died. The father's death wiped out most of the gains she had made during the preceding four months. For several days after her father's death she

showed violent excitement, which was followed by a deep stupor, lasting for about two days, from which she awoke in a very alienated state. At first she was quiet, and her feeling of anxiety was essentially diminished. The contractures of both arms continued. She also showed a high degree of narrowing of the visual field. She also complained that she could not recognize people—all the human beings appeared to her like wax figures without any relationship to herself (Breuer and Freud 1937).

Because of Breuer's treatment she began to calm down slightly after her father's death. About ten days after his death, around April 15, 1881, Breuer had to leave Vienna. A new consultant was called in to look after her during Breuer's absence* (Breuer and Freud 1937). While Breuer tried to demonstrate the peculiarities of the patient to the new consultant, Bertha completely ignored him. The consultant tried to make himself noticeable, but in vain. "He finally succeeded in attracting her attention by blowing smoke in her face. . . . She then suddenly saw a stranger, rushed to the door, grabbed the key, but fell to the floor unconscious. This was followed by a short outburst of anger, and then by a severe attack of anxiety, which I could calm with a great deal of effort" (Breuer and Freud 1937).

When Breuer returned after many days of absence, he found that "her condition had markedly aggravated. Throughout the whole time she was entirely absent-minded and full of anxiety. Her hallucinatory absences were filled with terrifying images of skulls and skeletons" (Breuer and Freud 1937). Ellenberger (1972) describes what happened next:

In view of the difficulties of keeping Bertha at home and because of several suicidal attempts,** it was decided to transfer her to Inzersdorf.***

---

*According to Ellenberger (1972), Krafft-Ebing was the consultant.
**Breuer and Freud (1937) state that she showed intense suicidal impulses; they do not mention any suicide attempts on her part.
***Located on the outskirts of Vienna.

However, it was not in the fashionable sanitarium of Drs. Fries and Brelauer, but in a kind of a cottage near the sanitarium (Breuer called it in a Villa, in 1895 a Landhaus), where she could be attended daily by the sanitarium psychiatrists and visited by Breuer every few days. The transfer was performed "without deceit, but by force" on June 7, 1881 (Ellenberger 1972).

Breuer and Freud (1937) report that "a disturbance of three days and three nights followed immediately after her removal to the country. During this period she remained sleepless, took no nourishment and was full of suicidal ideation . . . and evidenced hallucinations."

Breuer continued to visit her every three or four days and she would wait in anticipation for his visit. She remained quiet after Breuer's visit; but during the intervals, she had to be given fairly high amounts of chloral (Ellenberger 1972).

When Bertha returned to Vienna at the beginning of November 1881, her mother had bought a new, one-story house. Breuer saw her regularly and decided to change his techniques. He increased his visits, coming now twice a day, in the morning and evening. "He now asked her, under hypnosis when it was necessary, to concentrate her thoughts on one symptom at a time and tell him about all the occasions she could remember on which that symptom appeared (Freeman 1979). Gradually her symptoms began to disappear, with the last one being the paralysis of her right arm.

On June 7, 1882, as Bertha was preparing to leave for her country home, she expected that Breuer would continue to visit her regularly as he had done during the previous year (Freeman 1979). Instead, Breuer told her that she was well and no longer needed him.* Amicably, they said goodbye to each other.

That evening, as he was eating dinner with his family, Breuer received an urgent message from Bertha's mother to come immediately; there was an emergency. He found Bertha thrashing around on her bed, writhing as in acute pain. After observing her for a few minutes, Breuer realized that she was going through the throes of an imaginary childbirth.

And out of her lips came the words, "Now Dr. Breuer's baby is coming! It is coming!" writhing all the while as though giving birth.

Breuer felt a strange panic, nothing like this had ever happened to

---

*Ellenberger (1972) states that 'the patient had decided and announced in advance that she would be cured in June 1882, on the anniversary of her transfer to the country house, and in time for her summer vacation."

him, and he did not understand it. Not once during the entire eighteen months had she spoken of sex. She had never mentioned falling in love with any man, much less him. He had thought it surprising that she did not speak of love. She seemed astonishingly underdeveloped sexually in spite of her attractiveness, charm, and capacity for passion. How could she imagine she had become pregnant by him and hallucinate the birth of his baby? It was an alarming idea. (Freeman 1972).

He managed to calm her down by hypnotizing her, then gave her a posthypnotic suggestion: "When you wake in the morning, you will feel better, [and] will realize that what you have just gone through was an imaginary experience" (Freeman 1972). He left Bertha Pappenheim's home about two hours later.*

Breuer entrusted her future care to another physician. Bertha's condition deteriorated. Her mother took her away from Vienna, and on July 12, 1882, she was hospitalized in Sanatorium Bellevue in the town of Kreuzlinger, Switzerland. She stayed there until October 29, 1882, just about three and a half months. After her return from Switzerland she was "reinstitutionalized three times at Sanatorium in Inzersdorf near Vienna (from July 30 to January 17, 1884, from March 4 to July 2, 1884, and from June 30 to July 18, 1887)" (Sulloway 1979).

During this period she was placed on heavy medication of chloral and morphine for her facial neuralgia. She became a morphine addict (Ellenberger 1972). It took her about six years to recover her mental and emotional balance (Freeman 1979). Bertha and her mother moved from Vienna to Frankfurt in November 1888 (Edinger 1968), and in 1895 she "officially began her social work career" (Jensen 1970).

Breuer, Freud, and Anna O. Five months after Breuer stopped seeing Bertha—on November 18, 1882—he told his friend Freud about his treatment of her, of "how her physical and mental symptoms had vanished as she was able to recall experiences that had been painful, fearful, humiliating, angering, or frustrating" (Breuer and Freud 1937). Breuer's description of Bertha's case seemed to have led Freud to ask how talking could cure physical ailments. He urged Breuer to write an article so that other doctors would know about it. "Breuer refused, saying that he had had enough of hysterical women;

---

*Ellenberger (1972) casts doubt on the authenticity of this incident. He states, "Jones's version of the false pregnancy and hysterical birth throes cannot be confirmed and does not fit into the chronology of the case." This author concurs with Ellenberger's skepticism about this incident.

they were an ordeal, and he was giving them up as patients" (Freeman 1979). Breuer then began to practice only internal medicine (Freeman 1979).

It should be added here that Sulloway (1979) clearly contradicts Freeman's, Jones's, (1953; see below), and other similar accounts. He states

Albrecht Hirschmuller (1978), who has published the German text of the various documents discovered by Ellenberger, has found other equally relevant materials at the Sanatorium Bellevue. These new documents show that Breuer treated at least seven other patients for psychical disorders; six of them after Anna O. Moreover, several of these cases involved clear-cut sexual etiologies according to Breuer's hand-written diagnosis. So much for the myth about "timid" Breuer, retreating from the distasteful implications of his own momentous discoveries! . . .

Freud's account shows that Breuer never mentioned to him the incident of the hallucinated childbirth which led to his termination of the treatment of Bertha Pappenheim. In a letter written from Hohe Warte (a suburb of Vienna) on June 2, 1932, to Stefan Zweig, to correct an error that Zweig had made in describing the case of Anna O. in his book, *Mental Healers*, Freud said:

What really happened with Breuer's patient I was able to guess later on, long after the break in our relations, when I suddenly remembered something Breuer had once told me in another context before we had begun to collaborate and which he never repeated. On the evening of the day when all her symptoms had been disposed of, he was summoned to the patient again, found her confused and writhing in abdominal cramps. Asked what was wrong with her, she replied: "Now Dr. Breuer's child is coming."

At this moment he held in his hand the key that would have opened the "doors to the Mothers,"* but he let it drop. With all his great intellectual gifts there was nothing Faustian in his nature. Seized by conventional horror, he took flight and abandoned the patient to a colleague. For months afterwards she struggled to regain her health in a sanitarium.

I was so convinced of this reconstruction of mine that I published it somewhere. Breuer's youngest daughter . . . read my account and asked her father about it [shortly before his death]. He confirmed my version, and she informed me about it later (Freud 1960).**

---

*Allusion to an image in Goethe's *Faust*, II.
**Contrary to Freud's account, Sulloway (1979) states "Breuer apparently told Freud about the details of his unusual case as early as 18 November 1882, according to an unpublished letter written by Freud to Martha Bernays the following day (Jones

Jones (1953) continues the narrative of Freud's attempt to re-kindle Breuer's interest in the case:

> In the late eighties and still more in the early nineties, Freud kept try-ing to revive Breuer's interest in this problem of hysteria. . . . In this endeavor he met with strong resistance, the reason for which he could not at first understand. . . . It gradually dawned on Freud that Breuer's resistance was connected with his disturbing experiences with Frl. Anna O. . . . so Freud told him of his own experience of a female patient suddenly flinging her arms around his neck in a transport of affection, and he explained to him his rea-son for regarding such untoward occurrences as part of the transference phe-nomenon characteristic of certain types of hysteria.* This seems to have had a calming effect on Breuer. . . . At all events Freud ultimately secured Breuer's cooperation, it being understood that the theme of sexuality was to be kept in the background. Freud's remarks evidently made a deep impression, since when they were preparing the *Studies* together; Breuer said apropos of the transference phenomenon, "I believe that is the most important thing we both had made known to the world."

Thus, out of these two episodes—Breuer and Anna O, and Freud and his female patient—the concept of transference was born. Using these episodes as models of transference development, future therapists were cautioned against the intense transferences that a hys-teric (female) patient is likely to develop toward her therapist. Over the years, the concept of transference became the cornerstone of all dynamic psychotherapies.

The Breuer Episode and Its Relation to Transference   Certain facts of this episode should be emphasized, since they bear almost di-rectly upon our discussion of the topic of transference. First, in pre-Breuerian therapy, a physician's task was to respond directly to the manifest "symptoms" that the patient presented. If a woman was neur-asthenic, it was the physician's job to make her more energetic; if a man was impotent, the task was to make him potent again. Any further "exploration of the symptoms" was precluded. Thus, a "therapeutic

---

1953; 226)." He goes on to say, "As Freud reveals in this letter to Zweig, he had forgot-ton about this [phantom pregnancy] aspect of the case, which Breuer never repeated, and [Freud] only recalled it several decades later when writing his 'History of the Psycho-Analytic Movement'."

*Clark (1980) doubts the veracity of this incident. He states, "Freud himself recalled the occasion when a patient impetuously threw her arms around his neck; his salvation from further embarrassment was the apparently fortuitous entry of a maid—a somewhat incongruous story since one must assume that psychoanalytic sessions were not usually interrupted by servants."

homeostasis," or status-quo situation, prevailed between the physician and the patient. The patient's symptoms provided a kind of buffer zone between the feelings and emotions of physician and the patient. Breuer trespassed this buffer zone; he disturbed the status quo or therapeutic homeostasis by trying to translate the patient's hysterical body language into ordinary speech (Szasz 1961). In attempting to do this, he had to develop a personal relationship with the patient. He had to give up the protection of the buffer zone provided by the patient's symptoms. Bertha's mother told him: "You are giving her so much time. Other doctors would have spent one or two hours with her and then never returned" (Freeman 1972). Once the translation from body language to speech was effected, the feelings and emotions underlying the patient's symptoms surged. Bertha was no longer a pitiful, symptom-ridden patient, but a sexually aroused, attractive female. "Breuer, as we know, could not cope with this new situation, and fled from it. Freud, however, could, and thereby established his just claim to scientific greatness" (Szasz 1963).

Second, although Breuer classified Bertha as hysteric, by modern criteria she would be diagnosed as psychotic, and possibly as paranoid or catatonic schizophrenic (Goshen, 1952).* Although Breuer and Freud tried to protect Bertha's identity in their writings by giving her fictitious name, Anna O., some of her relatives knew she was Anna O., that in her early twenties she had suffered a "serious breakdown" (Jensen 1970; Freeman 1972).** In other words, the relatives viewed her "breakdown" as a "psychotic" break, rather than a hysterical condition. Frequently Breuer himself used the word *psychotic* to describe her condition (Breuer and Freud 1937). Breuer classified her as hysteric because during that era nearly every form of psychological disturbance, especially among female patients, was labeled hysteria (Szasz 1962, 1966).

Third, in spite of the multiple symptomatology which she presented, Bertha was, by all accounts, intelligent, cultured, and "extremely attractive in physique and personality" (Jones 1953). Fourth,

---

*Pollock (1972) states, "Her reactions had features of melancholia and hysterical psychosis."

**Sulloway (1979), quoting Hirschmuller, states, "Even as late as 1895, when Breuer and Freud finally published *Studies On Hysteria*, Bertha Pappenheim's identity as "Anna O." became immediately evident to many Viennese readers of that book."

Breuer used a minimal amount of medication: "Breuer felt that drugs did not reach the root of illness, they were temporary expedients. Only in emergencies he used chloral so that the young patient might get some sleep" (Freeman 1972). Rather he preferred to talk with her, either directly or under hypnosis. Bertha used the expression *talking cure** to describe Breuer's method of treatment (Freeman 1972).

Fifth, the psychotherapeutic treatment was quite intense, sometimes involving two sessions a day. Also, during the course of treatment, the time limit of one hour was not quite strictly followed; instead the sessions seemed to have a somewhat open-ended quality.

Sixth, Breuer used hypnosis quite frequently; sometimes he hypnotized her every day, and on some occasions twice a day. Such an extensive use of hypnosis combined with the intensity of the relationship, made Bertha quite dependent upon Breuer;

this created wild swings in her moods. When he came to see her she was ecstatically happy. But when he failed to show up, no matter what the reasons, she sank into a depressed mood or flailed about in fury. . . . On every occasion Breuer reported her as depressed or angry, or refusing to eat or talk; he had not seen her for a few days, with one exception—when she sank into depression after her father died. That she was able to give up some of her excessive grief so quickly, that she did not kill herself as she threatened was, no doubt, due to Breuer's presence. (Freeman 1972)

Seventh, the personal characteristics of the therapist should not be overlooked in the episode. Breuer has been described as

almost Christlike in character . . . wise, restrained, lofty in spirit, with that rare balance between the inquiring, intuitive mind and thorough, objective appraisal and research. He was a modest man—he would talk to the chambermaid the way he would to an emperor—he was an extremely compassionate man. When he retired from regular practice he continued to treat those patients who could not afford to pay—he spoke many languages—he liked literature and music . . . (Freeman, 1972)

When, on October 31, 1883, Freud wrote to his fiancee, Martha Bernays, to reassure her that his patients would not fall in love with him, saying "For that to happen one has to be a Breuer" (Jones 1953), he seemed to be referring to Breuer's "celebrated charm" (Freeman

---

*It should be noted that even today many of the unsophisticated patients in mental hospitals use the expression *talk treatment* to describe psychotherapy sessions with their therapists in the hospital setting.

1979). Later writers were to recognize the role of the therapist's personality in influencing the nature of regressive transferences (Kepecs 1966).

Eighth, various accounts suggest that "Breuer had developed what we now term a strong counter-transference to his interesting patient. At all events he was so engrossed with the case that his wife became bored at listening to no other topic, and before long, jealous" (Jones 1953). "The jealousy grew into depression and there were rumors that Mrs. Breuer threatened suicide unless her husband gave up his young patient" (Freeman 1979).*

Finally, many of the issues which simmered in the background of therapy—termination, the client's attachment to the therapist, and counter-transference—were not openly discussed by the participants.

Many of the features of the relationship between Breuer and Anna O. became woven into the concept of transference. Some aspects of their relationship have been explicitly recognized by subsequent writers as influences upon the development of transference; while others—such as the role of the therapist's counter-transference in stimulating the client's transference—have been barely acknowledged in the literature (Hollender 1980).

The Therapy Situation and the Significance of Transference

What is the significance of transference in therapy? To understand this we must take a close look at the therapy process. In therapy two people meet alone, frequently, in an atmosphere of mutual respect and acceptance. The patient reveals his most guarded secrets; the therapist pledges to keep the patient's confidence. The patient is encouraged to experience and express his feelings and emotions. Such a situation tends to make the relationship a close one for both the therapist and the patient, although more so for the patient. When feelings and emotions are aroused they do not demand explanation, but gratification. The question is, what prevents the therapist from gratifying his emotions in therapy? Szasz answers succinctly, "Not much"

---

*Pollock (1972) speculates that Breuer developed counter-transference owing to the many similarities between him and Anna O. Breuer's mother had died when she was young and attractive and when Breuer was between three and four years of age, at the height of Oedipus stage. His mother had the same first name, Bertha, as Anna O; one of Breuer's daughters was named Bertha, and Anna O. was young and attractive.

(1963). In fact, sexual affairs and erotic relationships between client and therapist are not uncommon (see Chapter 9). Yet, therapists, for the most part, seem to withstand the impact of the client's powerful feelings for and against him.

Four sets of factors appear to help the therapist to withstand temptations. First are the therapist's gratifications in his personal life. If a therapist's material, emotional, erotic, and ego gratifications are lacking in his life outside psychotherapy, then there is a higher probability that he may seek gratification within the therapy sessions and through the client.

Second is the personality of the therapist. A therapist must be ascetic to a certain extent. He should be able to distance himself from his emotions and temptations, and he should have a greater-than-average ability to refrain from acting.

The third factor is the formal setting where therapy is conducted including use of a professional office, the regularity of appointments, the payment of fees for services rendered, and so forth.

The fourth and final factor is

the concept of transference, the belief of a therapist that the patient's feelings and emotions are directed not toward the therapist but toward internal objects. In other words, if the patient loves or hates the therapist, and if the analyst can view these attitudes as transferences, then, in effect, the analyst has convinced himself that the patient does not have these feelings and dispositions toward him. The patient does not really love or hate the analyst but someone else . . . (Szasz 1963).

By defining the situation in this manner, a therapist can avoid reacting to the client's feelings and emotions. He has only to acknowledge it and try to analyze it.

"Thus," says Szasz, "although in psychoanalytic theory the main function of the transference is to serve as a logical construct, in the psychoanalytic situation, i.e., in therapy, it is to serve as a psychological defense of the analyst" (1963).

The Judgment of Transference, the Projection of Feelings, and the Role of Sexuality

In the literature the term *transference* is generally used as a self-explanatory concept, whose behavioral correlates are presumed to be self-evident and can be reliably observed by independent observers. The presumed correlates are the inappropriateness of feelings, affects, and reactions; the projection of feelings directed toward the parents upon the therapist; and the development of erotic-sexual feelings toward the therapist.

Before we examine how valid this claim is, three questions should be asked. First, how is it decided in therapy which of the feelings constitute transference and which do not? Second, does the client believe that his feelings in therapy are unconsciously directed toward his parental figures and that he may be projecting such feelings upon the therapist, or are such feelings projected upon the therapist without the client's awareness? Finally, do the clients (especially female) develop sexual feelings toward therapists (male) and long to have sexual affairs with them?

The Judgment of Transference   How is it decided in therapy which of the client's feelings and reactions are based on reality and which ones are projections or distortions? A general belief, frequently stated in the literature and prevalent among practitioners, holds that if the feelings and reactions of the client are inappropriate they constitute "transference reactions" (Ruesch 1961; Weiner 1975). As one analyst puts it: "We must determine the diagnostic signs which enable us to distinguish transference from ordinary behavior . . . that transference manifestations are characterized by their inappropriateness. This inappropriateness is on the one hand a quantitative and on the other a qualitative one" (Spitz 1956).

Who decides what is an appropriate or inappropriate affect or behavior? Rarely, if ever, is such a decision reached through a mutual discussion between the therapist and the client. Generally, it is the therapist who interprets the client's feelings and reactions and decides which are appropriate feelings and which are not. Further, because the client's feelings and reactions are perceived by the therapist as transference—and therefore, as inappropriate projections—it then seems that the therapist's judgment is more accurate, more oriented to reality, than that of the client (Fenichel 1941; Nunberg 1951; Menninger and Holzman 1973; Gill 1982). In other words, through such a role definition of himself and the client, and through such a definition of the client's feelings, the therapist preempts the right to label the client's feelings as "transferences."*

---

*An examination of Yalom and Elkin's study (1974), where both the therapist and the client took independent notes on many therapy sessions, suggests that it is the therapist who judges and labels clients' feelings (many of them hardly even mentioned by the client in her notes) as transferences.

Understandably, with more seriously disturbed clients or in certain blatant situations, the therapist may with little difficulty make a distinction between appropriate and inappropriate feelings and reactions
or between "transference" (projection) and reality. However, most of
the time a therapist does not deal with blatant situations, but with a
client's subtle and complex sets of feelings and reactions. Therefore,
he must make a delicate distinction between reality and fantasy (or
projections) in the client's feelings and reactions.

An example from Szasz illustrates this point: "Suppose the
therapist believes that he is a kindly and sympathetic person, whereas
the patient thinks that he is arrogant and self-seeking. Who shall now
say which is reality and which is transference?" (Szasz 1963). The therapist does not find the client's feelings and reactions prelabeled; he
must infer which to consider transferences (Luborsky et al. 1973).
Thus, the term *transference* is not a neutral description of the client's
emotions but rather the therapist's inferred judgments of them (Szasz
1963).

Is It Conscious or Unconscious?   Therapists commonly believe that most of the clients' feelings which are labeled transference
are unconscious. Freud (1950a) stated that "transference is made conscious to the patient by the analyst." Gill (1982) maintains "that without
the analyst's initiative in interpretation, these ideas [labeled trans-
ference] will not become explicit."

Before we examine the conscious versus the unconscious status
of transference, a few general remarks about the client's feelings in
therapy are in order. First, one of the reasons that a client initiates therapy is that he is confused and conflicted (and sometimes helpless)
about his feelings and reactions toward many people in his life. Obviously, therefore, his feelings in therapy and toward the therapist will
also be confused and conflicted.

Second, a patient usually experiences a fairly wide range of
emotion during a therapy session (Howard, Orlinsky, and Hill 1970).
These feelings, for instance, may include the desire to be cared for, to
be listened to, to receive approbation, affection, praise, and so forth;
erotic feelings and feelings of apprehensiveness, comradeship, anger,
hate, jealousy, vengeance, and loneliness. The client's feelings during a
session also fluctuate and may vary from one session to the next (Howard, Orlinsky, and Hill 1970).

Given such a context, it is not unusual for the therapist to present the image of himself as a benign "father figure" (Snyder 1961) rather than as a neutral figure. A certain degree of encouragement on the therapist's part may encourage the client to look upon the therapist as a parental figure, and some of the client's feelings, originally directed toward his parental figure, may be deflected onto the therapist.

Reports of clients about feelings they have experienced during therapy sessions (reported immediately after each session) suggest that on certain occasions clients view their therapists as symbolic parental figures; for example, the client may state that the therapist reminds him of, or acts like, a rejecting father or a domineering mother (Snyder 1961). Other studies suggest that while going through stress or anxiety during the course of therapy, the client's behavior toward the therapist becomes similar to his behavior toward parental figures in the past, as the client now remembers his past behavior (Mueller 1969).

Clients who are not seriously disturbed can discern that the feelings they attribute to the therapist are either based on reality, are symbolic reactions to the therapist, or are based on a resemblance (or continuity) between their past and present feelings.

A twenty-six-year-old single unemployed male came to therapy because nothing in life interested him. He had stopped looking for work and had moved in with his mother eight months prior to initiating therapy. His father was once a wealthy man but had lost his photography business because of mismanagement and his own negligence. The family then moved to a modest house, and the mother took a job as a social worker. The parents subsequently separated, and the client and his younger sister lived with the mother. His father then became a shadowy figure who would come and go, sometimes being absent for months.

As therapy progressed, the client began to discuss and express his hatred and anger toward his parents. He also expressed compassion toward his parents and sister. Gradually, he began to express some homosexual fears, although he was functioning as a successful heterosexual. During the course of these sessions, he would frequently remark that he wished he had a father like the therapist with whom he could have discussed all his fears and feelings. Then he would not have to come to therapy, and his life would have been less confused and conflicted. He would have been able to find a direction in his life and by now, possibly, would have settled into a professional career.

He also began to express compassion and sympathy for his father, since according to the client, the father had struggled hard in his life. He began to propose various business ventures to his father, in which they both could work together. However, the ventures never got off the ground. He then took a job as a medical equipment salesman and married a local schoolteacher.

Sexuality In Transference   The emergence and development of erotic feelings toward the therapist is considered basic to the structure of transference. Literature is replete with examples in which the client develops erotic feelings and fantasies and longs to have an affair with the therapist. Apparently, and for a variety of reasons discussed below, considerable confusion has arisen about the role of sexuality in transference.

The first of these confused interpretations could be called "reductionistic-theoretical." Freud emphasized that the roots of all feelings can be traced to sexual feelings:

We have to conclude that all feelings of sympathy, friendship, trust and so forth which we expend in life are genetically connected with sexuality and have developed out of purely sexual desires by an enfeebling of their sexual aim, however pure and non-sexual they may appear in the forms they take on to our conscious self-perception. To begin with we knew none but sexual objects; psycho-analysis shows us that those persons whom in real life we merely respect or are fond of may be sexual objects to us in our unconscious mind still. (Freud 1943)

This form of reductionism to sexual motivation encourages the therapist to interpret the client's feelings and behavior as sexual in nature. Hence, when the client develops any feelings toward the therapist, he will interpret them as sexual feelings.

The second source of confusion is the paradigm of transference. As Szasz maintains, "Freud's [1914] classic paradigm of transference, it will be recalled, was the phenomenon of transference-love, that is, the female patient's falling in love with the male therapist. Just what is this phenomenon? According to the patient, it is being in love with the analyst; according to Freud [1916–1917], it is an illusion" (Szasz 1963). Freud himself believed in such a paradigm. Uncritical acceptance of the paradigm led subsequent writers and practitioners to attribute, a priori, a factual status to the emergence of sexual feelings of the (female) client toward the male therapist during the course of therapy.

Freud tried to apply the same paradigm to men. He said that men show the "same attachment to the physician, the same overestimation of his qualities, the same adoption of his interest, the same jealousy against all those connected with him" (Freud 1943). The paradigm, however, did not make fit comfortably the interaction between a male client and a male therapist or between a female client and female therapist. Clients rarely fall in love with or long for affairs with therapists of the same sex (barring perhaps those clients who may be struggling with their homoerotic conflicts). The question arose: Should there be two paradigms? one for male therapists and female clients (a relationship which, according to the theory, unfolds uniquely), and the other for dyads of the same sex.* This issue was never clearly confronted, with the result that the concept of transference was never tied to empirical data, thus leaving a large gray area for various therapists to fill in according to their personal interpretations and experiences.

The converging evidence suggests that in male (therapist)–female (patient) dyads the reported frequency of the occurrence of erotic feelings or the longing to have affairs on the part of the client is not as high as it is believed to be or as it is generally presented in the literature (Orlinsky and Howard 1975; Applebaum 1977).

Female patients (who had male therapists) in long-term therapy were asked to recall their feelings and reactions toward the therapist. They reported warm and trustful feelings, feelings of being accepted and of showing confidence in their therapists. Reports of the frequency of sexual and erotic feelings toward the therapist seem to vary. Some studies report the occurrence of erotic feelings in about one-third of the clients (Snyder 1961); in other studies, clients report developing sexual feelings about 18 percent of the time (Strupp et al. 1969; Howard, Orlinsky, and Hill 1970).

The third source of confusion arises because what have been described in the literature as the client's erotic or libidinal feelings toward the therapist seem to comprise at least two sets of feelings experienced by the participants. The two kinds of libidinal feelings seem to evoke two different kinds of responses in the therapist. One set of feelings could be called a parental type of feeling. Which of the client's attitudes, dispositions, and behaviors in therapy evoke parental feelings in the therapist is not clear. Nevertheless, these feelings are expe-

---

*It is interesting to note that there are hardly any empirical studies or clinical case reports in the literature which discuss the "sexual aspect of transference" where the therapist is female and the client is male.

rienced by the therapist comfortably during the course of therapy (Singer 1965; Orlinsky and Howard 1975).

The other set of libidinal feelings could be called erotic or sexual. These feelings generate considerable anxiety in both the participants (Orlinsky and Howard, 1975). "Male therapists were most distressed and disturbed by feelings evoked when their female patients were high on Erotic Transference Resistance, whereas female therapists responded more positively to such stimulation" (Howard, Orlinsky, and Hill, 1969). In a male–female dyad,

There was a private awareness of sexual arousal in each of the participants, and a considerable amount of defensiveness attendant upon it. Although each participant was uncomfortably aware of his own sexual arousal, this state of affairs was not explicitly communicated between them. . . . The patient tended to block and found it difficult to express herself to the therapist. Her behavior, as she saw it, was hostile and provocative.

The therapist was viewed by the patient as being accepting but also non-commital, unwilling to take initiative with respect to her. From the therapist's point of view, this was with good reason; he was disturbed by his sexual responsiveness to the patient and did not trust himself to take initiative. He experienced himself as passively and somewhat hostilely detached from the patient. (Orlinsky and Howard 1975)

Thus, the issue of sexuality in transference appears to be far more complex than what has hitherto been believed. First, it appears that the client's sexual feelings toward the therapist, as discussed in the literature, do not develop in all the (female) clients; nor do they appear to develop as often as has been believed. They develop only in a certain percentage of clients. Rather, what appears to be a more pervasive development is the positive affect (attachment, trust, warmth) of the client toward the therapist, which may then be interpreted by the therapist as "sexual" in nature.

Second, the development of sexual feelings toward the therapist seems to be related to the members of the therapeutic dyad, namely, whether they are of the same sex or of the opposite sex, their ages, their ethnicity, and so forth. Third, the issue of sexuality seems to be interwoven with the interpretation of the term *sexuality*. If the word is used by one who believes that most motives can be reduced to sexual ones, then the client would seem to experience many more sexual feelings toward the therapist than otherwise. Finally, the emergence of sexual feelings toward the therapist seems to depend upon the quality of interaction between the two participants. If the therapist instigates, tantalizes, and reciprocates the feelings of the client, then the emergence of sexual feelings in the client will be more likely than otherwise.

Mutuality of Interaction: Transference and Counter-transference

Empirical studies of the process of therapy suggest that "the therapist does not 'do' therapy as if it were a skilled but detached application of impersonal techniques. On the contrary, the therapist tends to feel genuinely and warmly involved precisely when [both therapist and client] experience themselves as functioning most effectively. Some forms of involvement, of course, are undoubtedly quite uncomfortable and perhaps counterproductive as well (e.g., erotic transference–countertransference) . . ." (Orlinsky and Howard 1977).

Clearly, the therapist becomes emotionally involved during the session. Orlinsky and Howard's study (1977) indicates the extent to which therapists are conscious of their participation in the emotional dynamics of therapy. Therapists felt warmly toward, interested in, and involved with their clients. Other feelings, frequently reported, included confidence, optimism, cheerfulness, playfulness, relaxation, and pleasure. In about half to three-fourths of the sessions, therapists reported feeling intimate (sympathetic, close, and affectionate), while also feeling inadequate (uncertain) on about 25 percent of the occasions observed. Therapists felt demanding, ill, and disturbing sexual arousal (sexually stimulated, annoyed and attracted) quite rarely by their own report, generally in about 10 percent of the sessions observed. Similarly, other studies, based upon surveys of clients, suggest some form of emotional involvement on the part of the therapist. In a questionnaire study of ex-therapy clients, Strupp, Fox and Lessler (1969) found that a "good" therapist "did not stimulate angry feelings and he did not assume an impersonal role; instead, he actively participated in the verbal exchange, kept the patient 'moving,' and pointed out constructive modes of behavior".

Clients viewed "poor" therapists as those who were

causing (or allowing) the patient to experience intense anger toward him; making him feel like "just another patient"; using abstract language (which, presumably, the patient did not understand); failing to understand his "real" feelings; passive (admittedly a very vague phrase but apparently interpreted by the respondents to mean being unresponsive and doing nothing); and being neutral (evidently interpreted as an indication of lack of interest and concern)" (Strupp, Fox, and Lessler 1969).

Thus, there appears to be a definite interaction between the feelings, attitudes, and behavior of the therapist and the client. Some of the feelings expressed in therapy seem to be influenced by the client, while other feelings are influenced by the therapist (Howard, Krause, and Orlinsky 1969). Other studies seem to confirm the general findings that both the therapists' and the clients' behavior during the course of therapy are determined by the interaction between them (Moos and Clemes 1967; Mueller 1969; Moos and MacIntosh 1970). Snyder's conclusion to his 1961 study maintains that "the similarity between the affect toward the therapist coming from each client and the affect directed toward the client by the therapist is one of the most striking findings of this research."

In view of the reciprocity of interaction between the therapist and the client during the course of therapy, transference and counter-transference seem highly correlated (Snyder 1961). As one observer puts it: "Transference and counter-transference are so closely connected, and although no analogy is perfect, they might be regarded as two sides of the same magnetic tape. Both are inextricably involved with each other and share a common fabric; nevertheless they make different sounds and in some senses move in opposite directions" (Cox 1978).

The textbook conception of a therapist, which is accepted by most therapists, views him as only a technical agent who reacts minimally to clients' feelings and excludes his personal feelings and reactions, serving as an object upon whom the client projects those feelings directed toward parental figures. This view of the therapist is not quite substantiated by existing studies; nor is it true of Breuer or Freud, both of whom were actively involved with their clients' lives (Freeman 1972; Freud 1950b).

Current Status

The concept of transference remains vague because it lacks a clear operational definition for therapeutic practice and because so few empirical studies have been conducted on this topic. Many modern therapists who use transference in their work have tried to modify some of the dimensions of the concept formulated by the classical analysts.

Therapists who use transference as an operational concept believe that it has three dimensions. The first is the feelings and attitudes expressed by the client during the course of therapy could be directed toward any significant figure in his past, and not necessarily toward his parents. In this respect, therapists prefer to use the term *parataxic distortion* rather than *transference* and *counter-transference*. "Parataxic interpersonal experiences are distortions in patients' present interpersonal relationships. They are conditioned by carry-overs of a person's previous interpersonal experiences prevalently from infancy and childhood but not always or necessarily from entanglements with his parents" (Fromm-Reichman 1950).

Second, the client's feelings are not strictly a projection, but a mixture of fantasy and reality (Fromm-Reichman 1950). Third, the client expresses his feelings and attitudes toward the therapist in two ways: in a generalized form, which the client shows in any of his relationships, and more specifically, in a mode directed toward a particular therapist in a particular setting. This dual set of feelings, subsumed under the concept of transference by the modern therapists, has been described by various writers as "earned" versus "unearned" transference (Snyder 1961) and as "generalized" versus "specific" transference (Weiner 1975).

For modern therapists the concept of transference seems to encompass all of the client's feelings expressed during the course of therapy, regardless of whether they are based on reality, distorted, or directed toward parental figures. Studies suggest that modern therapists, (the judges involved in the following study, who were asked to make judgments of transference from the taped sessions)* "respond primarily to the affect, rather than to the distorted attitude toward the therapist as manifestation of transference. . . . The explicit reference to the influence of past attitudes on present relationships was not a striking aspect of the judges' response. . . . In practice most analysts refer to transference as the expression of any or all aspects of the patient's involvement with the analyst" (Lower et al. 1973).

---

*These judges were themselves practitioners of psychotherapy of many years' standing.

Many therapists explicitly do not believe in transference as a working concept. Instead, they hold that

the patient becomes attached and forms a meaningful interpersonal relationship not on the basis of his irrational and unreasonable expectations but on the basis of the reality of the situation. It is an experience with a human being who is different, who can be trusted, irrespective of the contents of the patient's disturbing feelings or impulses (Strupp 1960).

Therefore, in view of the findings that exist, a more faithful formulation of transference would maintain that generally the client develops feelings of attachment with the therapist. The client reacts toward the therapist in ways not much different from what the client does in his other relationships where he is accepted and becomes affectively involved. Some of the feelings and reactions expressed by the client in his affective relationships (including those with the therapist) may be feelings he has learned with his parents and siblings, in the context of peer group relationships, or through the course of his personal life. Some of his feelings could be derived from fantasies, while other feelings and reactions may result from the social role he is expected to adopt within the prevailing sociocultural context—for example, a female client's effort to present herself as a sexually desirable object. Thus, the client's feelings toward the therapist during the course of therapy are the result of a mixture of feelings and attitudes derived from the past and the present, from reality and fantasy. (Applebaum 1977).

Conditions and Emergence of Transference Neurosis

In the phenomenon of transference, as it is generally described in the literature, the client regresses to a childhood stage, confuses the past with the present, transfers his feelings from his parents to the therapist, and desires an affair with the therapist, while the therapist remains unaffected, rational, and beyond temptations. However, this scenario does not take place very frequently in therapy sessions. Yet, one must ask if there are conditions under which the phenomenon of transference (or transference neurosis) does happen as it is described in the literature? Our observation suggests that such a phenomenon of transference seems to occur under three sets of conditions.

The first set of conditions exists when the client is seriously disturbed. The client's ego strength, his relations with external reality, and his interpersonal relationships are already precarious. Added to his emotional state is his dependence on, attachment to, and/or suspicion of the therapist. The combination of these conditions creates for the client a certain amount of difficulty in distinguishing the feelings he directs toward the therapist from those he directs toward others, including his parents. His past and present feelings are liable to overlap and become confused. This seems to have been true of the relationship between Anna O. and Breuer, in which, by all accounts, the client was seriously disturbed and was extremely dependent upon her therapist. Frequently, she would confuse many of her past feelings with those that she experienced at the present moment.

The second set of conditions in which the phenomenon occurs involves the client who is seen in therapy five or six times a week, and who is encouraged to regress to a childhood stage. In this intense relationship, the therapist encourages the client to assume a childlike role vis-à-vis the therapist. The client may become dependent upon the therapist, and then may experience himself as a child, reviving some of his childhood feelings. Simultaneously the client may perceive the therapist as a parental figure. He may then transfer the feelings directed toward his parents onto the therapist. Therefore, the client may not be very successful in making a sharp distinction between his present and his past feelings. In the Breuer and Anna O. episode, something of this nature transpired. Breuer saw her at least five or six times a week, and sometimes from ten to twelve times a week, hypnotizing her frequently. In becoming dependent upon him, she revived many of her childhood feelings and directed them toward him.

The third set of conditions arises when the therapist induces the client to experience the feelings which the client had toward his parents. The therapist encourages the client to view him in a parental framework, rather than allowing the client to develop his own image of the therapist. Under these conditions, it is not unusual for a therapist to become attached to the client, and he may not wish to open up many of the issues pertaining to his own feelings. In this connection, one must note that the personality and personal qualities of the therapist— such as his interest, concern, physical and mental alertness, looks, flexibility, playfulness, seductiveness—all become important factors that begin to affect the development of transference. Although Breuer did not directly urge Anna O. to feel toward him as toward her parents, he did encourage her to become dependent upon him, and he developed a counter-transference toward her, almost never raising the issue of his own feelings. Breuer's personal charms and attractiveness further exacerbated the situation for Anna O.

The client's feelings that emerge under the three above-mentioned conditions are described as "transference neurosis." They have been defined as "psychoticlike" states where the distinction between the inner and the outer (projection) is blurred. The literature, however, ignores two factors which significantly contribute to its development. First is the role of the therapist: A therapist frequently encourages the emergence of such "psychoticlike" feelings (transference neurosis). Second is the disturbed state of the client; the more seriously disturbed a client is, the more he is likely to develop such transference neurosis or the psychoticlike state.

Under conditions in which therapy is not directed by the therapist in a predetermined way, it remains a moot question whether the feelings of transference as described in the literature would develop in most clients. One may surmise that a phenomenon would emerge similar to what the client feels and projects in his other relationships. However, since most therapists believe that therapy will unfold in a preordained fashion in which the client will or should regress to the childhood stage, fall in love with the therapist, and project the feelings directed toward his parents upon the therapist, they are liable to become involved in creating a self-fulfilling prophecy.

Handling the Clients' Feelings Toward the Therapist

Handling the clients' feelings toward the therapist during the course of therapy is crucial for the continuation and successful conclusion of therapy. When clients express their feelings toward therapists, therapists react in a variety of ways. Some become afraid or confused and baffled, withdrawing behind a veil of "techniques." Others encourage the client to express more of the same feelings, or to express sexual feelings. Some therapists may ask the client to express only positive feelings, while others will be more comfortable with the client's negative feelings. Still others maintain a "proper" distance, involvement, and balance in helping the client to explore and resolve feelings toward the therapist. The resolution of the client's feelings toward the therapist is important because otherwise his feelings become a stumbling block and impede the therapeutic progress.

Clients begin to develop feelings toward the therapist in the early stages of therapy. These feelings are as diverse as the clients themselves; they vary in intensity from mild to strong, and they may be diffuse or specific, direct or indirect. In the beginning of therapy, neither the client nor the therapist may be very clear about the client's feelings toward the therapist because the client is usually burdened and preoccupied by his conflicts. However, as some of the client's confusion begins to abate, he grows more aware of his feelings toward the therapist. What kinds of feelings would a client develop toward the therapist and in what manner would he reveal them or conceal them? One may answer these questions somewhat naively: He would develop similar feelings toward the therapist as he does in any affective relationship in which he is involved. However, in the client's daily life, people tend to react to his feelings directly or indirectly, whereas in therapy these feelings are, ideally, accepted, explored, understood, and rechanneled.

As therapy progresses, the client's feelings may begin to manifest themselves through innocuous, indirect references which appear in his reactions or associations pertaining to the therapist. These oblique references may allude to the therapist's office, dress, furniture, decorations, books, and other possessions. Sometimes such references may occur in the client's dreams, where the therapist may appear in a role other than that of a therapist. Weiner (1975) calls these references "indirect transference."

When indirect references appear in their inchoate form in the early stages of therapy, it is advisable to let them evolve into more direct references. Frequently, indirect references do not develop into direct ones. In an attempt to capitalize on indirect references and accelerate the development of transference, many therapists link them either to the client's past—to the client's relationship with his parents (or to the oedipal situation)—or to themselves personally. The client may feel that the links the therapist is making have little significance in his own mental and emotional reality. An examination of case studies by therapists, in which the therapist attempts early in therapy to link the client's feelings and conflicts to his oedipal situation, reveals that such efforts have few beneficial results for the client (Malan 1976).

The therapist should explain to the client that for various reasons it is not uncommon in psychotherapy for the client to develop certain feelings toward the therapist. First, the intimacy of psychotherapeutic situation encourages the client to reveal many "secrets" he has not revealed before. Second, the client is encouraged to express just about anything, a process which also facilitates the development of certain feelings in therapy that the client has not previously experienced or expressed. Third, the therapist listens to the client's troubles and remains nonjudgmental about the client's life. All of these factors help to generate in the client certain feelings toward the therapist. The therapist's explanation of this process usually helps the client to feel more at ease in expressing his emotions toward the therapist, and allow indirect references to become more direct.

During the course of therapy, clients may develop unrealistic expectations, and their perceptions may become distorted. They may also attempt to gratify some of their wishes and desires through the process of therapy and/or through the person of the therapist. Attempts to gratify some wishes are understandable since clients come to therapy with conflicting interpersonal relationships, troubled lives, and many unfulfilled desires. In contrast to their lives outside, the therapeutic relationship is (or should be) an accepting one; therefore the client may feel that he should be able to gratify his unfulfilled desires because they will also be accepted.

To say that the client's feelings and reactions are distortions is to imply that there is a discrepancy between the client's viewpoint (his intent, expectations, perceptions) and that of the therapist. It is the therapist's task to bring the distortions into open discussion where they can be examined. First, the therapist may have to convince the client that he is distorting or misjudging the situation. If the therapist can link the client's distortions to analogous examples from other aspects of the client's life, he may try to demonstrate to the client that such feelings, perceptions, and reactions may not be in accord with the perceptions of other people. He may point out that the client's feelings and reactions are common in his other interpersonal relationships, where he may have learned to feel and react in this fashion. For whatever reasons, such methods must serve some useful purpose in the client's life. To derive some satisfaction, the client may have to stretch the existing facts to suit his learned behaviors. The therapist should then assist the client in perceiving his situation and the people in his life (including the therapist) more accurately, encouraging the client to gratify his feelings in real life.

After the client's distortions have been resolved and the methods of his distortions clarified, the therapist may wish to explore the interpersonal context in which the client learned to project his feelings and conflicts upon others. These interpersonal contexts could include familial and peer-group situations and social and cultural expectations. That these interpersonal contexts usually overlap should then be revealed.

To assist the beginning therapist in helping the client sort out the distortions, a few guidelines may be useful. First, if the therapist feels that there is distortion or projection on the part of the client, he should remember that such distortions are the result of a mixture of reality and fantasy, and a confusion of the past with the present. Second, the client's patterns of distortion tend to be similar to those that occur in his other affective interpersonal relationships. Third, if a therapist can maintain his neutral position (which is not one of disinterest or unconcern) during the course of therapy, he will be able to offer the client greater assistance in unraveling his distortions. Obviously, the less counter-transference a therapist develops, the easier it will be for him to show the client his distortions, since the therapist's own projections will not intrude on his assessment of the client's perceptions.

Acting Out of Transference   Much has been written in the literature about the "acting out of transference." (See also the section on acting out in Chapter 7.) In fact, the acting out of transference is considered inevitable in intensive psychotherapy, or psychoanalysis (Strupp 1960). What does it mean, and how does it manifest itself? Generally, it is believed that during the course of therapy a client develops feelings toward the therapist which he is too embarrassed or ashamed to express in the sessions. Instead, he may act out these feelings in his life outside therapy. His behavior is considered a direct result of the unexpressed feelings or unresolved conflicts which have begun to emerge in therapy and which he is unwilling to face and explore. It is considered a resistance in therapy because, instead of attempting to understand his feelings and conflicts, the client tries to gratify them. Or instead of striving to remember his past, he tries to relive it. It is maintained that a client makes his decision "unconsciously," unaware of the motives of his actions and behavior. It then follows that actions whose motivations are not understood are likely to make the individual's life more difficult.

Here is an example from a well-known authority in the field.

States of excitement and overactivity developing during psychotherapy are signs of "acting out" or manifestations of ego shattering. During acting out the patient may engage in destructive, antisocial or perverse sexual behavior. In attempting to understand acting out, our first suspicion is that the patient is protecting himself from awareness of transference by projecting it away from the therapist. Hostile or aggressive outbursts, delinquency, criminality, homosexuality and marked promiscuity are often products of hostile and sexual impulses toward the therapist which the patient is unable to acknowledge.

The only way to resolve such acting out is to explore the patient's feelings and attitudes toward the therapist, to determine which of these are rooted in realities and which are irrational carry-overs of the past. So long as he is unaware of, and cannot verbalize his proclivities towards the therapist, the patient will continue to "blow off steam" outside therapy. Skillful use of the interviewing process that brings out verbalization related to the transference may put a halt to the patient's destructive patterns." (Wolberg 1967)

Thus, by definition, "acting out" has negative connotations. Because acting out happens outside therapy, without prior discussion with the therapist, and contains antisocial elements, it frequently comes as a surprise to the therapist when the client mentions it in subsequent sessions.

Before the therapist accepts the concept of acting out, he should ask if it is a necessary result of "transference," that is, of the development of the client's feelings toward the therapist? Should it be considered undesirable even under those conditions in which the client does not get himself into difficulties? Is it always "destructive"? Are there any sets of circumstances in which it is not undesirable? Again, the reader is reminded that the client's "positive" behavior is not considered as acting out (see chapter 7).

Certain clients may have a tendency to express their personal feelings and conflicts before or during the discussion of their feelings in therapy. (As discussed in earlier chapters, lower-class clients usually fall into this category.) There may also develop certain situations in which the client becomes more comfortable in expressing his feelings outside therapy. Generally, the life history of a client who has a propensity to live out his feelings will indicate to the therapist the method and manner that he follows; this, in turn, should provide a clue as to the timing involved in a situation in which the client may "act out."

However, if the atmosphere of therapy is egalitarian, nonthreatening, and nonjudgmental, it is not unusual for a client to offer hints about his expression of feelings outside therapy. If a client in therapy alludes to what he might do outside therapy, the therapist should ask him what is stopping him from discussing and expressing his feelings and conflicts in therapy; in other words, why is it necessary for him to act before exploring his feelings? The client, even after expressing his feelings in therapy, may still wish to act them out in his real life; that, however, remains his choice.

A thirty-six-year-old Certified Public Accountant working for a medium-sized company was urged to go to therapy by his wife because he was dissatisfied with his life. He was a bridge player of national reputation, playing for the national bridge team. Before he took the job, he had struck an agreement with his employer that he would need time off to play in bridge tournaments but would complete his work on time, even if he had to work weekends or nights. His employer had agreed to this arrangement.

After two years, the employer became dissatisfied with the client's behavior and fired him, although according to the client his work was satisfactory. He was very angry and upset about it. He felt that the employer had backed out of their agreement and had not treated him justly and fairly. He wanted to get even with his employer.

Soon thereafter, both the client and the therapist (for different reasons) moved to another town 120 miles away and resumed therapy. A year later, the client said that he was still very angry with his previous employer and wanted revenge. He discussed his plan of retaliation in considerable detail with the therapist. He said that he still had the key to the safe, although the books had shown that he had returned it. He had contacted the janitor of the building who still worked there and had convinced him to let the client into the building. In return, he would give the janitor half the money they found in the safe. The janitor agreed, and they stole the money and divided it. They were never caught.

During the therapy sessions, the therapist pointed out that the client was free to do whatever he wanted to do in his life; however, if he was caught, he knew the consequences of his actions very well. Furthermore, if the client was apprehended the therapist would under no circumstances testify in court or write a letter stating that the client was "mentally ill" and had acted under the influence of an "irresistible impulse." The client agreed to such a stipulation before he embarked upon his venture.

Sexuality and Acting Out

In intensive psychotherapy, a male-female dyad is likely to engender a sexual "acting out" because, it is believed, the client readily develops erotic feelings toward the therapist. Because of the repression of such feelings, cultural values and mores, and the role relationship between the therapist and the client (with the therapist generally considered a symbol of stability and authority), the client is generally embarrassed or ashamed to express her erotic-sexual feelings and conflicts. The client may then express such feelings outside therapy, or act them out.

A few remarks about handling such behavior, should it occur, are in order. First, the frequency of such occurrences is not as high as it is believed to be. Some clients have facetiously complained about not falling in love with their therapist, although they were looking forward to it when they started therapy.

The therapist should encourage the client to express such feelings in therapy when he notices them emerging. Frequently, reassuring comments are helpful in reducing the client's embarrassment and in helping her express her emotions. For instance, when a client develops erotic feelings toward a therapist, the therapist may say, "It is not unusual to develop such feelings toward the therapist in therapy situations." After providing the client with the list of reasons mentioned above, he might add, "Being aware of your feelings will help you work out some of the important and conflicting emotions in your interpersonal relationships. Recognizing the feelings that you have toward me is a step in your ability to feel and to relate to other people."

If the client, however, is unable or unwilling to express her feelings, the resistance should be brought to her attention, and the shame, guilt, or embarrassment associated with such feelings should be explored. When the client expresses her feelings, the therapist should accept them in the same manner as any other set of feelings expressed by the client during therapy.

The therapist should help the client understand what these feelings mean in her life. For a female client who is indiscreet in her sexual life, sexuality may mean that she is able to break away from the restrictions of her family. Or it could provide her with a confirmation of her female identity. Similarly, for a male client, sexual indiscretion could mean a number of things, such as being overpowering, winning in competition with others, or gratifying his narcissism.

Finally, if none of the techniques mentioned thus far help the client stop "acting out," some form of injunction may be recommended. For instance, a therapist may say to the client, "When you feel like doing such and such, try to do certain other things" (which the therapist may then discuss with the client). Some therapists take such injunctions a step further, telling the client, "If you do such and such again, I shall stop seeing you in therapy."

Studies suggest that "the preferred method [of therapists] for handling the problem [of acting out] . . . [was] interpretation and control, by firmness, strictness or setting limits. Miscellaneous recommendations were made for supportive measures, including reassurance, focus on the patient's personality assets, and re-education" (Strupp 1960). Rogerian therapists, however, recommend "understanding, clarification, and reflection to handle 'acting out'" (Strupp 1960).

In the literature, the term *acting out* is used for a wide variety of clients who have a propensity for living out their feelings in their lives outside therapy. They are generally called "acting out characters." Clients of various diagnostic categories are included under this rubric; among them, psychopaths, delinquents, alcoholics, drug addicts, hysterics, and clients afflicted with obesity, psychosomatic illness, and other maladies (Abt and Weissman 1965). This group of clients, it is maintained, does not develop transference in a classic sense because they dissipate feelings outside therapy which should be expressed in therapy sessions. While such patients may not develop transference in a classic sense, they do develop positive or negative feelings toward the therapist. If, therefore, one were to use the definition presented above, they do develop "transference." The feelings of such clients toward the therapist should be handled in the same way as those of any other client.

Negative Transference

The concept of negative transference is diffuse and amorphous. Sometimes, it is used for the client's negative feelings derived from his early childhood relations with his parents. At other times, it refers to any negative feelings shown by the client during the course of therapy. Frequently, the client's negative feelings are interpreted as "resistances." Hence, the concepts of negative transference and resistance are frequently used synonymously (Snyder 1961). Other authors maintain that all transference is negative, be it negative or positive in nature, because it is used by the client in the service of resistance (Fromm-Reichman 1950; Singer 1965; Gill 1982).

Studies suggest that positive transference and resistance are separate and distinct variables (Rawn 1958). Positive transference does not appear to lead to resistance. Studies of long-term trends among patients in psychoanalysis generally confirm the evidence that resistance and positive transference are not related (Graff and Luborsky 1977). Thus, the therapist should bear in mind that when he interprets a client's feelings and attitudes as "negative transference" he is also interpreting them as resistance and vice versa.

During the course of therapy, a client shows negative feelings and attitudes, that is, resistance or negative transference, toward the therapist. Reports vary with regard to the frequency with which clients express negative feelings during the course of therapy. One study states,

our data indicates that negative transference feelings did not occur with any frequency. A number of factors, singly or in combination, seem to have kept them to a minimum. The first concern in most forms of therapy is to build a positive working relationship, which is essential to therapeutic change. Furthermore, such a relationship serves as a counterbalance to negative feelings, which always must be dealt with in psychotherapy, even if they are driven underground. A patient who harbors strong hostility toward authority figures, for example, is likely to transfer such hostility to a therapist who remains a fairly shadowy figure, and most therapists in our sample, perhaps unwittingly, counteracted such feelings by quickly establishing a well-defined relationship with their patients. (Strupp et al. 1969)

Other studies equate resistance and negative transference.

We found that the poorer clients most characteristically showed their resistance by a general inability to relate to the therapist. . . . They were more critical of the therapist and his methods than were the clients in better groups. . . . Three major factors were involved in producing this negative transference. First, these clients were the most maladjusted of the group, several of them having been classified as schizoid. . . . Second, . . . some of them were reluctant to admit to themselves that their personal deficiencies might have contributed to their problems. These clients tended to focus on situational problems. . . . Third, the defensiveness, the hostility, the differences in values of some of these clients tended to cause the therapist to respond less warmly to them than would be considered ideal. (Snyder 1961)

In this and other studies, the negative transference seems to develop because the therapist (for whatever reasons) shows distance, coolness, irritation, and other feelings toward the client. In turn, the client develops negative feelings (negative transference or resistance) toward the therapist. Both sets of studies suggest that the therapist is an important factor in the development and attenuation of negative transference. His reactions and attitudes can either exacerbate or reduce the negative feelings of the client in therapy.

Generally, both negative and positive feelings are present in the beginning of therapy. Negative feelings commonly reported by clients include an open hostility toward or criticism of therapy (Snyder 1961) and the fear of being rejected by the therapist (Snyder 1961). However, in successful therapy negative feelings begin to abate; in unsuccessful therapy negative feelings seem to remain much the same (Snyder 1961).

For a variety of reasons, the negative feelings of the client in therapy are difficult to handle. First, they generate a negative attitude in the therapist, which may result in his retaliation, defensiveness, or self-justification. Thus, the possibility of the client's negative feelings being accepted is reduced (Heller et al. 1963). Second, such feelings or attitudes on the part of the client carry an implicit criticism of the therapist's professional competence which may not be easy for the therapist to accept. Third, when a client projects hostility and negative feelings, a therapist is more likely to act in a less friendly manner or to avoid the discussion or exploration of the client's negative feelings (Bandura et al. 1960); he is more likely to seek control over the client's behavior by trying to direct it (Ashby et al. 1957). It is not surprising, therefore, to find that therapists perceive clients' expressions of aggression and hostility as the second most stressful behavior in therapy, suicidal statements being the first (Farber 1983).

The therapist should bear in mind the possibility that he may react negatively toward the client when the client expresses negative feelings. When the client shows hostility toward the therapist, there is also a great temptation to interpret such feelings as being directed toward one of the client's parental figures.

The therapist should struggle to overcome such overt or covert reactions and try to accept the client's negative feelings. He may then explore with the client the source of such feelings, attempting to discover whether such reactions are distortions of earlier feelings or the result of the therapist's actions and behavior.

Summary

This chapter suggests that what has been called "transference" (a client's feelings toward the therapist, which are not necessarily derived from his childhood) is not formed independently by the client in therapy, as has been believed. One of the major factors in the development of the client's feelings is his interaction with the therapist. The client's feelings could be either exacerbated or alleviated by the therapist's reactions. Thus, contrary to the prevailing belief, a therapist can play a direct role in the emergence and evolution of transference.

Szasz (1962) argues that the concept of transference used in classical literature (in which the client's feelings are directed toward his parental figures and only symbolically toward the therapist) is a necessary concept for any long-term therapy. This concept protects the therapist from the client's negative and positive feelings. Without it, it would be impossible to conduct successful therapy because the therapist is likely to react directly to the client's emotions instead of remaining detached.

Others have maintained that transference is not necessary for effective therapy (Butler 1952). Yet the fact that the client has (or develops) certain feelings in therapy and toward the therapist is incontestable. The client's feelings should be allowed to take their own evolutionary course (unless, of course, the client is psychotic, in which case the techniques should be different). In this process, the therapist's role should be neutral as opposed to disinterested or unconcerned. He should welcome the development and expression of the client's feelings.

References

Abt, L. E., and S. L. Weissman, eds. 1965. *Acting out*. New York: Grune and Stratton.

Alexander, F., and T. French. 1946. *Psychoanalytic therapy*. New York: Ronald Press Co., 73.

Applebaum, S. 1977. *The anatomy of change*. New York: Plenum Press, 130–32.

Ashby, J. D., D. H. Ford, and R. L. Guerney. 1957. Effects on clients of a reflective and a leading type psychotherapy. *Psychological Monograph* 71:453.

Bandura, A., D. H. Lipsher, and P. E. Miller. 1960. Psychotherapists' approach-avoidance reaction to patients' expression of hostility. *Journal of Consulting Psychology* 24:1–8.

Breuer, J., and S. Freud. 1937. *Studies in hysteria*. Boston: Beacon Press, 14–19, 230.

Bugental, J. 1965. *A search for authenticity*. New York: Holt, Rinehart and Winston, 103.

Butler, J. M. 1952. The interaction of client and therapist. *Journal of Abnormal and Social Psychology* 47:366–78.

Calef, V. 1971. Concluding remarks. *Journal of American Psychoanalytic Association* 19:89–97.

Clark, R. W. 1980. *Freud*. New York: Random House, 129–30.

Colby, K. 1951. *A primer for psychotherapists*. New York: Ronald Press, 107.

Cox, M. 1978. *Structuring the therapeutic process*. New York: Pergamon Press, 127.

Dewald, P. A. 1964. *Psychotherapy: A dynamic approach*. New York: Basic Books.

Edinger, D. 1968. *Bertha Pappenheim: Freud's Anna O*. Highland Park, Ill.: Congregation Solel.

Ellenberger, H. 1972. The story of Anna O.: A critical review with new data. *Journal of the History of Behavioral Sciences* 8:267–79.

Farber, B. A. 1983. Psychotherapists' perceptions of stressful patient behavior. *Professional Psychology: Research and Practice* 14:697–705.

Fenichel, O. 1941. *Problems of psychoanalytic technique*. Albany, N.Y.: Psychoanalytic Quarterly, 129.

Freeman, L. 1979. Immortal Anna O. from Freud to feminism. *The New York Times Magazine*, (30) Nov. 11, 79–91.

———. 1972. *The story of Anna O*. New York: Walker and Co., 5, 7, 14–18, 20, 26, 57, 205, 218–19, 221–23.

Freud, A. 1946. *Ego and the mechanism of defense*. New York: International University Press.

———. 1954. The widening scope of indication for psychoanalysis. *Journal of the American Psychoanalytic Association* 2:607–20.

Freud, E. L., ed. 1960. *Letters of Sigmund Freud*. New York: Basic Books, 266.

Freud, S. 1950(a). *An autobiographical study*. London: Hogarth Press, 43.

———. 1950(b). Analysis of a case of hysteria. In *Collected papers*, vol. 3. London: Hogarth Press.

———. 1950(c). *Beyond the pleasure principle*. New York: Liveright Publishing Corp.

———. 1950(d). *Collected papers*, vol. 2. London: Hogarth Press, 319.

———. 1950(e). *Collected papers*, vol. 3. London: Hogarth Press, 139.

———. 1950(f). Further recommendations in the technique of psychoanalysis. In *Collected papers*, vol. 2. London: Hogarth Press.

———. 1943. *General introduction to psychoanalysis*. Garden City, N.Y.: Garden City Publishing Co., 384, 387.

———. 1938. History of the psychoanalysis movement. In A. A. Brill, ed., *The basic writings of Sigmund Freud*, 931–81. New York: Random House.

———. 1933. *New introductory lectures on psychoanalysis*. New York: W. W. Norton and Co.

———. 1950(g). Observations on wild psychoanalysis. In *Collected papers*, vol. 2. London: Hogarth Press.

———. 1949. *Outline of psychoanalysis*. New York: W. W. Norton, 68–69.

Fromm-Reichman, F. 1950. *Principles of intensive psychotherapy*. Chicago: University of Chicago Press, 6, 100, 112.

Gill, M. 1982. *Analysis of transference*, vol. 1. New York: International University Press, 61.

———. 1954. Psychoanalysis and exploratory psychotherapy. *Journal of American Psychoanalytic Association* 2:771–97.

Glover, E. 1955. *The technique of psychoanalysis*. New York: International University Press.

Goshen, C. E. 1952. The original case material of psychoanalysis. *American Journal of Psychiatry* 108:830–34.

Graff, H., and L. Luborsky. 1977. Long term trends in transference and resistance: A report on a quantitative-analytic method applied to·four psychoanalyses. *Journal of American Psychoanalytic Association* 25:471–90.

Greenacre, P. 1954. The role of transference: Practical considerations in relation to psychoanalytic theory. *Journal of American Psychoanalytic Association* 2:671–84.

Greenson, R. 1967. *The technique and practice of psychoanalysis*, vol. 1. New York: University Press, 105.

Heller, K., R. A. Myers, and L. Kline. 1963. Interviewers' behavior as a function of standardized client role. *Journal of Consulting Psychology* 27:117–22.

Hoffer, W. 1956. Transference and transference neurosis. *International Journal of Psychoanalysis* 37:377–79.

Hollender, M. 1980. The case of Anna O.: A reformulation. *American Journal of Psychiatry* 137:797–800.

Howard, K., M. Krause, and D. Orlinsky. 1969. Direction of affective influence in psychotherapy. *Journal of Consulting and Clinical Psychology* 5:614–20.

Howard, K., D. Orlinsky, and J. Hill. 1970. Affective experience in psychotherapy. *Journal of Abnormal Psychology* 3:267–75.

———. 1969. The therapist's feelings in the therapeutic process. *Journal of Clinical Psychology* 25:83–93.

Jensen, E. M. 1970. Anna O. A study of her later life. *Psychoanalytic Quarterly* 39:269–93.

Jones, E. 1953. *The life and work of Sigmund Freud*, vol. 1. New York: Basic Books, 224–26, 245–55.

Kepecs, J. 1966. Theories of transference neurosis. *Psychoanalytic Quarterly* 35:497–521.

Lower, R. B., P. J. Escoll, R. B. Little, and P. B. Ottenberg. 1973. An experimental examination of transference. *Archives of General Psychiatry* 29:738–41.

Luborsky, L., H. Graff, S. Pulver, and H. Curtis. 1973. A clinical-quantitative examination of consensus on the concept of transference. *Archives of General Psychiatry* 29:69–75.

Malan, D. H. 1976. *Toward the validation of dynamic psychotherapy*. New York: Plenum Publication Corp., 32–132.

McAlpine, I. 1950. The development of transference. *Psychoanalytic Quarterly* 19:501–39.

Menninger, K., and P. Holzman. 1973. *Theory of psychoanalytic technique*. New York: Basic Books, 83.

Moos, R., and S. Clemes. 1967. Multivariate study of the patient-therapist system. *Journal of Consulting Psychology* 31:119–30.

Moos, R., and S. MacIntosh. 1970. Multivariate study of the patient-therapist system: A replication and extension. *Journal of Consulting and Clinical Psychology* 3:298–307.

Mueller, W. J. 1969. Patterns of behavior and their reciprocal impact in family and in psychotherapy. *Journal of Counseling Psychology*, no. 2, pt. 2, 1–25.

Nunberg, H. 1951. Transference and reality. *International Journal of Psychoanalysis* 32:1–9.

Orlinsky, D., and K. Howard. 1977. The therapist's experience of psychotherapy. In A. S. Gurman and A. M. Razin, eds., *Effective psychotherapy*, 566–90. New York: Pergamon Press.

———. 1975. *Varieties of psychotherapeutic experience.* New York: Teachers College Press, Columbia University, 165–67.

Orr, D. 1954. Transference and counter transference: A historical survey. *Journal of American Psychoanalytic Association* 2:771–97.

Pollock, G. H. 1972. Bertha Pappenheim's pathological mourning: Possible effects of childhood sibling loss. *Journal of American Psychoanalytic Association* 20:476–93.

Rangell, L. 1954. Similarities and differences between psychoanalysis and dynamic psychotherapy. *Journal of American Psychoanalytic Association* 2:734–44.

Rawn, M. L. 1958. An experimental study of transference and resistance phenomenon in psychoanalytically oriented psychotherapy. *Journal of Clinical Psychology* 14:418–25.

Ruesch, J. 1961. *Therapeutic communication.* New York: W. W. Norton, 170–71.

Saul, L. 1958. *Technique and practice of psychoanalysis.* Philadelphia: J. B. Lippincott Co., 189.

Silverberg, W. 1948. The concept of transference. *Psychoanalytic Quarterly* 17:303–21.

Singer, E. 1965. *Key concepts in psychotherapy.* New York: Random House, 249, 276.

Snyder, W. V. 1961. *The psychotherapy relationship.* New York: Macmillan, 166, 181, 204–33.

Spitz, R. 1956. Transference: The analytic setting and its prototype. *International Journal of Psychoanalysis* 37:380–85.

Strupp, H. H. 1960. *Psychotherapists in action.* New York: Grune and Stratton, 50, 55, 114, 297.

Strupp, H. H., R. Fox, and K. Lessler. 1969. *Patients view their psychotherapy.* Baltimore: Johns Hopkins Press, 19–43, 80–81, 117.

Sulloway, F. J. 1979. *Freud, Biologist of the Mind.* New York: Basic Books, 58, 79, 80, 84.

Szasz, T. 1963. The concept of transference. *International Journal of Psychoanalysis* 44:432–43.

———. 1966. Mental illness is a myth. *The New York Times Magazine*, June 12, 90–92.

Tarachow, S. 1963. *An introduction to psychotherapy*. New York: International University Press.

Waelder, R. 1956. Introduction to the discussion of problems of transference. *International Journal of Psychoanalysis* 37:367–68.

Wallerstein, R. 1967. Reconstruction and mastery in the transference psychosis. *Journal of American Psychoanalytic Association* 15:551–83.

Weiner, I. 1975. Principles of Psychotherapy. New York: John Wiley.

Weinshel, E. M. 1971. The transference neurosis: A survey of the literature. *Journal of the American Psychoanalytic Association* 19:67–88.

Wolberg, L. 1967. *The Technique of Psychotherapy*. Part 1 and 2. New York: Grune and Stratton.

Wolstein, B. 1954. *Transference*. New York: Grune and Stratton.

———. 1960. Transference: Historical roots and current concepts in Psychoanalytic theory and practice. *Psychiatry* 23:159–72.

Yalom, I. and G. Elkin. 1974. *Everyday gets a little Closer*. New York: Basic Books.

Zetzel, E. 1956. Current concepts of transference. *International Journal of Psychoanalysis* 37:369–75.

9

Therapist's Feelings Toward the Client: The Counter-transference

Just as a client develops certain feelings toward a therapist (transference), a therapist develops feelings towards a client (counter-transference). As a therapist's feelings will vary from one client to another, they may also vary in relation to the same client from time to time; in the beginning of therapy a therapist may have one set of feelings toward the client which will have changed by the time therapy has substantially progressed.

Certain feelings that the therapist experiences toward the client are necessary and important for therapy—for example, empathy, warmth, and compassion. A therapist is able to help the client through empathic understanding of his struggles. Frequently, however, the therapist's feelings and reactions may develop beyond the point of being useful to become a stumbling block that hinders the therapist's understanding of the client's conflicts.

A therapist's feelings toward the client are not independent of the feelings a client shows toward the therapist. The two seem to be closely related. For instance, if a client develops negative feelings toward the therapist, a therapist is also likely to develop some sort of negative feeling toward the client. If a client shows positive feelings toward the therapist, it is likely that the therapist may develop positive feelings toward the client (Heller, Myers, and Kline 1963; Beery 1970). "During those sessions when neurotic patients are depressed, the therapist tends to be more depressed than otherwise. With schizophrenic patients, a therapist is more anxious when the patient shows thought disorder, anxiety or silence" (Tourney et al. 1966); while passive dependent clients elicit a significant degree of directiveness on the part of the therapist (Bohn 1965). Thus, the feelings and reactions of the therapist (counter-transference) and the feelings and reactions of the client (transference) are intricately interwoven and difficult to separate.

Little attention has been paid in the literature to counter-transference and its effect upon the course of therapy (Little 1951). In fact, many of the standard works on psychoanalytic therapy do not contain a chapter on this topic, and at best mention it only in passing (Colby 1951; Saul 1958; Tarachow 1963; Bugental 1965; Greenson 1967; Chessick 1974; Basch 1980; Storr 1980). Several reasons may account for this absence.

The first reason is a historical one. Wolstein (1959) states that

it was easy enough to deduce from the concept of the analyst's role as a tabula rasa that the emergence of his distortions would be ruled out in practice. This prolonged neglect of countertransference may also have been rooted in the hypnotherapeutic situation: Though the hypnotist's personal qualities were important for the induction of the trance, he presumably withdrew once the subject became entranced and kept his personality out of his subject's way as best as he could.

The second is a theoretical reason. It is generally expected that a therapist (or analyst) will go through personal analysis. During the course of personal therapy, he will become aware of his unconscious needs and conflicts. Since lack of awareness and control of one's unconscious conflicts triggers counter-transference, presumably a well-analyzed (or successfully analyzed) therapist would not project his unconscious feelings and reactions onto the client. Thus, the likelihood of the development of counter-transference is minimal.

The third is a personal reason. Many therapists have displayed a lack of candor in discussing their feelings and reactions toward the client. Since most of the writing on the topic of psychotherapy is done by the therapists, they have failed to open this issue to scrutiny. Possibly, if clients would write about the enterprise of psychotherapy, we might learn different things about counter-transference.

History and Definition

The concept of counter-transference, sometimes called the "untoward feelings" of the therapist (Wolberg 1977), remains as ill defined and amorphous as the concept of transference. Partly because the usage of the term *counter-transference* has changed over time and because authors have used the concept with different meanings, little consensus has been reached on what sorts of feelings should be included under this rubric (Little 1951, 1957; Epstein and Feiner 1979).

Freud first used the term in 1910:

Other innovations in technique relate to the physician himself. We have begun to consider the "counter-transference" which arises in the physician as a result of the patient's influence on his unconscious feelings, and have nearly come to the point of requiring the physician to recognize and overcome this counter-transference in himself. . . . Anyone who cannot succeed in this self analysis may without more ado regard himself as unable to treat neurotics by analysis. (Freud 1950)

Freud's statement has four implications, and in one form or another, all four have been accepted by subsequent writers and practitioners. These implications have also been woven into the definition and the conceptual structure of counter-transference. First, Freud's use of the prefix "counter"* implies that the therapist's reactions are to the transferences of the client. Otherwise, a more appropriate term would have been *transference of the therapist*. Various authors and clinicians have accepted Freud's position (Fenichel 1945; Glover 1955; Gitelson 1952; Ruesch 1961; Baum 1969; Menninger and Holzman 1973).

The second implication is that the client's transference influ-

---

*According to Greenson (1967), "Countertransference is a transference reaction of an analyst to a patient, a parallel to transference, a counterpart of transference. The counter in countertransference means analogue, duplicate of, like the counter in counterpart. It is not like the counter in counteract or counterattack, where it means opposed to or contrary, etc." However, it is rather clear in Freud's writings that "counter" meant "as a reaction to," albeit an unconscious one, as shown by the above quotation.

ences the therapist's unconscious (his needs and conflicts). The therapist, therefore, reacts unconsciously to the material presented by the client (Reich 1951, Kernberg 1965; Racker 1968; Baum 1973; Menninger and Holzman 1973; Wolberg 1977). And because the therapist reacts unconsciously, his reaction is derived from his repressed and infantile feelings and conflicts and follows the same genetic history as transference; the analyst reacts to the patient as though the patient were an important figure from the analyst's past (Berman 1949; Reich 1951; Spitz 1956; Tower 1956; Greenson 1967).

Third, it is implied that the therapist is not likely to develop counter-transference on his own (Fenichel 1945; Ruesch 1961; Menninger and Holzman 1973). Finally, the remedy for correcting the therapist's counter-transference is either self-analysis or further analysis of the therapist (Cohen 1952; Weigert 1954; Spitz 1956; Wolberg 1977).

Isn't it likely that the therapist's conscious and semiconscious attitudes and reactions can become a hindrance to his understanding of the patient's conflicts? If they can, then why not include these conscious and semiconscious attitudes under the heading of counter-transference? To resolve this contradiction, many authors began to differentiate among the various feelings and reactions of the therapist toward the client, dividing counter-transference into various categories: libido versus ego (Stern 1924); acute (arising out of the therapeutic situation) versus permanent (arising out of the therapist's personality conflicts) (Reich 1951); healthy versus unhealthy (Sharpe 1947); reactions to patient's transferences versus the analyst's own transference to the patient (Gitelson 1952; Orr 1954; Hoffer 1956); rational (or appropriate) versus irrational (or inappropriate) (Weiner 1975); total, or generalized, versus specific (Kernberg 1965), and so on.

Other authors began to widen the definition of counter-transference. They began to include a wide variety of therapists' reactions, regardless of their conscious or unconscious character, under the term *counter-transference*. Cohen (1952) states, "When in the patient-analyst relationship anxiety is aroused in the analyst with the effect that communication between the two is interfered with by some alteration in the analyst's behavior (verbal or otherwise), then countertransference is present." Singer (1965) elaborates upon Cohen's definition:

What emerges from an examination of the theoretical literature is a widely held position which suggests that countertransference appears when the therapist is made anxious by the patient, when he fears feelings and ideas which therapeutic investigation may arouse in him, and when his desire to avoid anxiety and its dynamic roots force him to assume defensive attitudes. . . . Thus, in broadest terms, countertransference is thought of as a manifestation of the therapist's reluctance to know and/or learn something about himself, as a reflection of his wish to remain oblivious to certain facets of himself, and to leave unresolved conflicts buried.

The meaning and usage of the term *counter-transference* began to change, becoming broad enough to incorporate the conscious and the unconscious, the total and specific reaction of the therapist, and sometimes any and/or all feelings of the therapist toward the client (Peabody and Gelso 1982).

For our purposes, we shall define counter-transference as any conscious or unconscious feelings, attitudes or reactions of the therapist toward the client which hinders the therapist's understanding of the client's conflicts and troubles and/or generates anxiety in him. Since nearly any attitude, feeling, or reaction of the therapist—fear, jealousy, sexual attraction, competitiveness, overinvolvement, ethnic and class difference, excessive need for money, egotism, narcissism, possessiveness, diffidence—can become a hindrance in his understanding of the client's struggles all of those factors may show up as counter-transference.

Indications of Counter-transference

What are the signs and clues to the therapist's counter-transferences? In the literature a series of therapists' attitudes and reactions are mentioned as indicators of his counter-transference. Here is a partial list (Cohn 1952; Gitelson 1952; Holzman 1973; Weiner 1975).

1. Inability to understand certain kinds of material.
2. Depressed or uneasy feelings before or after the therapy session.
3. Being habitually late; forgetting appointments; frequently over-running the sessions.
4. Persistent drowsiness; going to sleep during the session.
5. Too permissive in financial arrangement.
6. Repeated erotic feelings toward the client.
7. Trying to impress or argue with the client.
8. Too much anticipation.
9. Unreasonable dislike for the patient.
10. Liking the patient excessively; feeling that he is his best patient.
11. Overconcern about the confidentiality of his work with the patient.

12. Feeling compelled to do something active.
13. Sadistic and/or sharp formulations when confronting or interpreting material presented by the client.
14. Cultivating client's dependency upon him.
15. Tendency to ask favors of the client in some form.
16. Trying to elicit affects from the patient—for instance, by provocative or dramatic statements.
17. Feeling that the patient consistently misunderstands the analyst's interpretations or never agrees with him.
18. Strong positive or negative emotional reactions to a patient's comments.

If a client were to reveal any (or some) of the above attitudes or reactions during the course of therapy, the therapist would interpret them as positive or negative transference. Hence, if a therapist shows the same (or similar) attitudes and feelings during the course of therapy, they should be interpreted in the same way. Ruesch (1961) states that

countertransference is transference in reverse. The therapist's unresolved conflicts force him to invest the patient with certain properties which bear upon his own past experiences rather than to constitute reactions to the patient's actual behavior. All that was said about transference, therefore, also applies to countertransferences, with the addition that it is the transference of the patient which triggers into existence the countertransference of the therapist.

In other words, although many authors see a structural similarity between the client's feelings (transference) and the therapist's feelings (counter-transference) they believe that the roots of the client's feelings and the therapist's feelings are different. The client's feelings emerge independently in therapy (Racker 1957; Ruesch 1961), while those of the therapist emerge as a reaction to the feelings of the client. This position, as we shall learn in this chapter, is not an accurate reflection of the studies on this topic. Rather, the studies suggest that the therapist develops many "untoward feelings and reactions" the source of which lies within the therapist as well as, of course, in the therapist's interaction with the client.

Sources of the Therapist's Counter-transference

What are the sources of the therapist's counter-transference? In the literature a series of possibilities are presented. Here is a partial list (Wolberg 1977): character distortions in the therapist; tendencies toward passivity and submissiveness; impulse toward detachment, which may become a defense against entering into a close contact with some patients; living through the patient vicariously because of a deprived life situation; the therapist's neurotic ambitiousness; the therapist's anxiety and guilt; fear of hostility; overemphasis on fees and payment. Each of these factors, in one form or another, could become the source of counter-transference and thereby affect the work of the therapist and the course of therapy.

All of the aforementioned sources of counter-transference have to do with the personality of the therapist. I wish to suggest that a more productive method of categorizing counter-transference would make its source relatively easy for the therapist and the supervisor to discern. For schematic and didactic purposes, the following categories are proposed:

1. Initial like or dislike of the client.
2. Therapist's counter-transference to the client's negativity.
3. Personality conflicts of the therapist.
4. Therapist's diffidence as a source of counter-transference.
5. Erotic counter-transference of the therapist.
6. Differences in values and ideology.
7. Money as a source of counter-transference.

We shall discuss each of these categories below.

1. Initial Like or Dislike of the Client   It is not unusual for a therapist to like or dislike the client from the initial phase of therapy. Many reasons may account for such a reaction. However, such feelings have a definite effect on the assessment and understanding of the client and on the course of therapy. Strupp (1958) found that

the therapists who indicated a dislike for the patient tended to choose more pejorative diagnostic labels, such as psychopath, paranoid or character disorder. They predicted a poor prognosis for the patient. They anticipated encountering certain kinds of problems in treatment, such as countertransference feelings of anger and resentment. These therapists were more inclined to be strict, active, and to suggest a briefer and more supportive type of therapy which might be terminated by unworkable countertransference reactions. On the other hand, therapists who expressed a positive attitude toward the patient tended to diagnose him "hysteric" and to describe him as experiencing much anxiety. They felt he had a good pronosis with treatment and suggested a long term, intensive, insight-oriented therapy. While these therapists could predict some countertransference responses, they felt they could deal with them therapeutically. Thus, there was a significant dichotomy in the sample of therapists, with one group tending to be more therapeutic, permissive, tolerant, and warm and the other group appearing more directive, disciplinarian, unrealistic and harsh.

Therapists may also show preferences for certain kinds of clients with whom they want to work. Generally, they prefer clients who are cooperative, hard-working, suggestible, and nonhostile. These kinds of clients do not threaten the therapist, and he can easily develop positive feelings toward them. The therapist's feelings tend to influence his perception of the client; friendly clients are said to improve more than less friendly ones, and they tend to stay longer in therapy (Shapiro 1974).

However, if the client is hostile, resistant, and unmotivated, the therapist is uncomfortable with him and finds it hard to establish a relationship. Such clients are described as "not making progress." Further, "poor clients" are also frequently classified as hostile and resistant (Rosenweig and Folman 1974).

More specifically, the emotional responses of the therapist to the client (liking the client, feeling comfortable with him) are intertwined with the therapist's clinical judgment about the client.

When the client is doing well in therapy, is making progress, the therapist likes him. If however, the client shows "sicker behavior" (belligerent, complaining, regressed, psychotic) the therapist shows negative attitudes towards the client. Even if the patient shows "less obtrusive sick behavior" (depression, self-deprecation, withdrawal, etc.) the therapist has negative attitudes toward the client.

When, however, the patients' attitudes and behavior are consistent with the therapist's professional and personal interests, providing confirmation of his effectiveness (and his science), the therapist finds the clients more likeable and savor more their work together. (Rabiner et al. 1971)

A similar phenomenon of counter-transference is seen on the wards of mental hospitals. Patients who are attractive and liked by the staff are rated as mentally healthy; patients who are not liked by the staff are rated as mentally ill. Further, patients who are liked are rated as making more improvement, while patients who are disliked are rated as making less improvement (Katz and Zimbardo 1977).

These studies suggest that the initial like or dislike of the client is an important parameter of counter-transference. If it is not properly assessed or handled from its inception, this factor may develop into countertransference, which, in turn, will affect the course of therapy.

2. Therapist's Counter-transference to Client's Negativity   No other set of feelings that the client reveals is likely to evoke more counter-transference in the therapist than his negative, hostile, and friendly attitude in therapy (see Chapter 6). The client's hostility and aggressive behavior generally create a strong anxiety in the therapist (Russell and Snyder 1963). The therapist reacts to the client's negativity with reduced friendliness or by avoiding the hostility (Bandura et al. 1960). As the client becomes more aggressive or hostile, the therapist seeks more control over him by being directional. Generally, the client's hostile behavior generates similar behavior in the therapist (Winnicott 1949; Heller et al. 1963).

These reactions of the therapist seem to be particularly common when the client expresses his hostility and anger directly toward the therapist. When the client's hostility is directed toward others, however, the therapist does not seem to react with the same feelings (Gamsky and Farwell 1966).

The reactions are common also when the hostility is expressed by a client of the same sex as the therapist. In an interesting study, Langberg (1979) found that

therapists would approach the hostile comments of their opposite sex clients more frequently, but avoid similar comments made by persons of the same sex. Results indicated that males approach 44% of the direct hostility coming from females and none of that coming from males. Female therapists approach 100% of direct male hostility, but only 33% of direct female hostility.

Not all therapists, however, react to the client's hostility with counter-hostility, avoidance, or dislike. Some studies suggest that therapists who tended to express their own anger directly and who had little need for approval were more likely to respond to the expression of anger by attempting to further explore the client's feelings (Bandura 1956).

3. Personality Conflicts of the Therapist Feelings related to the therapist's personality conflicts in contrast to feelings which may be generated by external stimuli, seem to be the ones that are most difficult to detect as counter-transferences. The therapist's personality conflicts seem to assume an "unconscious" form in their expression during the course of therapy, thus surreptitiously interfering in the management and movement of therapy.

Clinical experience and empirical studies (Cutler 1958) show that a therapist is much less accurate in reporting his own and the patient's behavior in psychotherapy when the topics are related to the therapist's personality conflicts. Furthermore, when the therapist works with the patient on issues that are also a problem for the therapist, his interventions are judged to be significantly less effective than when he works with neutral material.

Other studies corroborate such findings.

When the therapist's unmastered personality problems [during the course of therapy] come in contact with a similar problem in his patients, he was as ineffective in recognizing or dealing with it analytically as he was in resolving it within himself.

The therapist reacted inappropriately. He would, for example, perceive his patients' typical and expectable therapeutic resistances as a desire to move away from him and therapy and would react to his own misinterpretations in a sufficiently irrational manner to put enough pressure on his patients to drive them away from therapy. The therapist, because of his lack of awareness of his own problems, was not able to accept the behavior of his patient, nor go to the underlying causes. (Fielding 1972)

These studies as well as clinical observations suggest rather convincingly that the therapist's personal conflicts and problems directly affect his behavior in therapy, his reporting (and presumably remembering) of the interaction with the client, and ultimately the course of therapy. It is possible that such counter-transference on the part of the therapist may not be pervasive; it may be circumscribed to certain aspects of his life—for example, his relationship with his father—but nevertheless it has a clearly unfavorable bearing upon therapy.

4. Therapist's Diffidence as a Source of Counter-transference
A therapist may sometimes encounter certain behavior during the course of therapy which the client may not have manifested before. Such behavior may include a suicidal threat or attempt (which generates more diffidence in a nonmedical therapist), running away from home, starting an extramarital affair, or development of some form of "psychotic episode." The therapist may view the client's behavior as disturbed or "sick," or as a manifestation of "underlying psychosis" or "deep regression." For a beginning or an anxious therapist, such behavior creates a great deal of diffidence.

Generally, the therapist (especially the beginner) reacts to such situations with a certain form of counter-transference. Sensing his own diffidence, the therapist may (a) abandon his therapeutic role and drift along with the client and his life activities; (b) moralize, pontificate, or lecture to the client to mend his ways; (c) subtly try to drive the client away; or (d) encourage the client to drop out of therapy. Usually, the client intuitively "reads" the therapist's communication, sensing what the therapist expects of him. Frequently, the client is somewhat baffled by the therapist's message. He may feel that his behavior is bizarre enough to make the therapist feel uncomfortable and try to get rid of him. Sensing the therapist's discomfort, some clients may behave in the opposite way, engaging in a battle of wills with the therapist, and knowing that the therapist wants them to quit they may deliberately refuse to do so.

A forty-year-old, female second-year graduate student, who was working in the university clinic as a therapist trainee, was seeing a seriously disturbed client in therapy. It is the policy of the center not to make a psychiatric diagnosis of the applicant. The therapist developed a good rapport with the client and during the first eleven sessions was able to help the client reduce some of his anxieties and mental confusions. She encouraged him to look for work, which the client was rather actively pursuing. In general, the client seemed to be progressing well. During one of the supervisory sessions, in a general discussion, the supervisor mentioned that if the client were to be seen in a setting where diagnostic labels are attached to the client, he would be diagnosed by all criteria as borderline schizophrenic. This took the therapist by surprise, for she had never thought of him as "crazy" or as a "schizophrenic" and felt that she was not qualified to work with schizophrenics. From that day on, she lost her confidence and was unable to give direction to therapy. Subtly, she began to encourage the client to drop out of therapy and to seek therapy in a medical setting where he might receive medication. Five sessions after this incident, the client dropped out of therapy.

    5. Erotic Counter-transference of the Therapist   As late as 1966 there was very little in the literature dealing with the nature of the therapist-client erotic or sexual contact.* It is possible that the freedom of sexuality in Western culture—the so-called sexual revolution beginning in the mid-1960s—encouraged the frequency of writings about erotic and sexual relationships between client and therapist since then. Whether the increased attention reflects an increase in the actual frequency of erotic-sexual contact or more freedom to write on this topic will never be known.

It is well known by now that both client and therapist develop erotic and positive feelings toward each other. When the therapist's erotic feelings develop beyond a certain level—a mildly positive lik-

---

*Perhaps exceptions to this could be the Freud-Ferenchi correspondence on this issue (Jones 1957), and Jung-Freud correspondence pertaining to Jung's affair with his patient Sabina Spielrein (Carotenuto 1984).

ing for clients and emotional support for their life struggles—they begin to hinder the therapist's understanding of the client's troubles and conflicts. Frequently, a therapist develops erotic feelings toward a client which take the form of persisting erotic fantasies and dreams. In other cases, there may be erotic embracing, kissing, and hugging between the two. At times, the therapist may engage in sexual intimacy with the client.

Earlier writers maintained that therapists indulge in sexual intimacy with their clients for the benefit of the client, that is, for altruistic purposes (McCartney 1966; Van Emde Boas 1966; Shepard 1971). McCartney (1966) suggests, for example, that

some patients need to do more than just talk about their feelings toward their therapist. They need to caress, fondle, observe and examine the body of the therapist, and, in some instances, share in sexual intercourse. In those cases where the patient cannot find an appropriate person outside of the analytic situation to be a surrogate in acting out, the analyst of the opposite sex may have to remain objective and yet react sexually appropriately in order to lead the immature person into full maturity.

Shepard (1971) reported ten case histories in which there was a sexual relationship (both heterosexual and homosexual) between the therapist and the client. He states, "In summation, I would say that these cases indicate that as many people are aided by intimate involvement with their therapist as are hurt, and no blanket prejudgements concerning the ethicalness or validity of intimacy per se ought to be made." Some authors, directly or indirectly, place the onus of a sexual affair upon the female client, by saying that the client had an "ego defect" (Ulanov 1979).

The active role of the therapist in instigating sexual affairs with clients began to emerge somewhat guardedly. An examination of the case histories of those clients who have had sexual relations with their therapists (many of them recorded verbatim) suggest that in a majority of cases the therapist was the active instigator of some form of sexual relationship (Shepard 1971; Nancy 1973; Freeman and Roy 1976).

Using data from nine cases, Dahlberg (1970) concludes, "It is more than likely that these nine therapists were simply ordinary aging men in a depressive period who somehow let themselves be convinced by their patient's fantasies that they might recapture a real or fantasied youth." Marmor (1970, 1972) states that in cases where there is sexual intimacy between the therapist and the client, the "psychoanalyst or psychotherapist is himself beset by deeply rooted, often unconscious needs that tend to foster or stimulate impulses toward physical closeness toward his patient."

Surveys (Kardener et al. 1976; Holroyd and Brodsky 1977), studies (Butler and Zelen 1977), and reports of other research (Masters and Johnson 1970) about the beliefs and practices of therapists show the incidence of erotic contacts (such as kissing, petting, and caressing) to be from 12 to 13 percent, while the incidents of sexual intercourse (relations) average between 5 and 6 percent. Erotic contacts occur overwhelmingly between male therapist and female client, who is often much younger than the therapist (Dahlberg 1970; Taylor and Wagner 1976; D'Addario 1977; Holroyd and Brodsky 1977; Bouhoutsos et al. 1983).

Many authors speculate that sexual relations between therapist and client may be far more prevalent than the literature reveals. First, indulging in and admitting to sexual relations with clients is contrary to the ethical code of any professional organization to which therapists presumably belong; in fact, sexual behavior toward clients is considered taboo by the professional organizations. Further, such behavior on the part of the therapist generally does not agree with the professed self-image of the therapists who state that their role is helping their clients. Finally, admission of such behavior may result in an impending threat of legal action against the therapist. For all these reasons, the figures mentioned above should be considered as a minimum estimate (Taylor and Wagner 1976; Stricker 1977; Davidson 1977).

Contrary to existing beliefs that the therapist only reacts to the client's erotic transferences with an erotic counter-transference, empirical studies suggest that the therapist is an active agent in instigating and initiating sexual affairs with his client. Furthermore, his personal needs and motivations overwhelmingly contribute to the sexual contact. Therapists acknowledge their needs as a factor in initiating sexual contact (although not necessarily at the time it occurs, according to some studies). Such needs have been described as crises involving the therapist's vulnerability, loneliness, dissatisfaction with his marriage, a recent separation and/or divorce, a demotion or loss of job, fear of aging, alienation from his children, or a combination of these factors (Butler and Zelen 1977; D'Addario 1977).

How does the sexual contact develop?

In most cases the therapist in his leadership role, would bring up the issue of his sexual attraction to the patient. In many cases, the patient responded favourably to these innuendoes. Subsequently, there was an acceptance of the mutuality of this attraction and the therapist lost control of the therapeutic hour. . . . In some situations the therapist's innuendoes led to further discussion of the mutual attraction, and then resulted in intercourse. (Butler and Zelen 1977)

Thus, sexual contact may serve the therapist's needs more than those of the client. This seems to be true regardless of the motivation for the sexual affair—whether the therapist's neurotic needs come into play (Marmor 1970, 1972), whether the therapist rationalizes that he is engaging in sexual affairs for the good of the patient (McCartney 1966; Shepard 1971), or whether the therapists were vulnerable and lonely at the time the affair began (Butler and Zelen 1977; D'Addario 1977).

Surveys show that a small proportion of therapists (3 percent) believe that if the therapist is not personally in need of sex the erotic contact can be useful for the patient under four conditions:

for specific purposes, if a person were crippled by inferiority feelings based on the conviction of being unacceptable to anyone for anything; if one is having severe doubts of sexual identity and truly does not know the mechanics of sexual intercourse; if the erotic contact and/or intercourse are not outside the boundaries of the therapy relationship, i.e., psychotherapy per se should not exclude the obvious such as the need and desire to touch, stimulate and explore the boundaries of contact and intimacy; if the use of sexual energy, up to and including actual intercourse between therapist and client, can have a considerable healing effect for the client. (Holroyd and Brodsky 1977)

Some authors attempt to differentiate between erotic contact and nonerotic contact. They believe that nonerotic physical contact can be useful, at least occasionally, to both male and female clients, and they suggest four situations or conditions in which it can be beneficial: (1) for socially or emotionally immature clients (children, schizophrenics, patients with a history of maternal deprivation); (2) for periods of acute distress such as grief, trauma, or severe depression; (3) for more general emotional support, including warmth, reinforcement, contact, and reassurance; (4) for greeting or at termination of a therapy session (Kardener et al. 1976; Holroyd and Brodsky 1977).

What is the effect of a sexual relationship upon the therapist and the client? The answer to this question is difficult to determine for many reasons. First, there exists a lack of candor on the part of both participants. There is also sampling bias, since most of the respondents are either volunteers or are included in the studies because of complaints against the therapist or client. Second, many therapists and/or clients report from memory, which may or may not be quite accurate. Finally, the criteria for the affair's helpfulness or harmfulness are difficult to determine and agree upon. Given these limitations, some studies "based upon material presented in the case histories or by the patient's ratings of involvement show that . . . 21% of the relationships had positive effects. Mixed effects occurred in 32% of the relationships, and 47% of the cases involved a negative outcome to either the client, the therapist or both" (Taylor and Wagner 1976).

Reports of the effects of sexual affairs also vary depending upon whether the male therapist or the female client is interviewed. One study, based mostly upon interviews with male therapists, states that

25 percent of the clients terminated therapy immediately after the onset of sexual behavior* . . . 30 percent maintained therapy and the sexual behavior simultaneously throughout the course of their relationship. The remaining 45% who continued therapy without sex reported constant questioning of their own motives. ("I was never certain what I was doing, and whether or not I was harming the patient.") Those therapists who terminated therapy immediately reported better, and less conflicted experiences. They referred to those relationships which involved both therapy and sexual behavior as exploitive of the therapist.

. . . A wide range of conflicts [were] experienced by the therapists. Nineteen of the 20 participants reported conflicts, fears and guilt, yet despite their continued ambivalence, sexual acting-out behavior continued. Only 40 percent sought help for their conflicts. When they did, a friend who was a professional colleague was consulted. (Butler and Zelen 1977)

Therapists report both positive and negative aspects to the relationships:

The relationships were growthful, there seemed to be a commitment from both participants to deal with any and all problems that arose from their relationship. The negative aspects were: The inequality between the participants, particularly in relation to the powerful role of the therapist, the tremendous conflicts experienced by both, and especially the eventual feeling of anger, hurt and damage to the patient after the relationship dissolved. (Butler and Zelen 1977)

Studies which focused on female clients who had sexual intercourse with their therapists suggest, in most cases, that effects were detrimental, destructive, and sometimes even devastating. Most of the female clients needed further therapy to overcome the effects related to previous therapy and the sexual affair with the therapist (Belote 1974; D'Addario 1979; Bouhoutsos et al. 1982).

The weight of existing studies and reports would suggest that an overwhelming number of affairs occur between the male therapist and the female client. Sexual affairs with the therapist prove deleterious for the clients. From the viewpoint of common sense, this is quite understandable. A client does not go to a therapist to seek a sexual affair; she could easily have an affair outside therapy. Rather, the client seeks support and clarification of her struggles, some of which may be sexual in nature. Even if the client is seductive, as many authors report, a sexual affair with the client during the course of therapy is a testimony to the therapist's lack of control and discipline to overcome his temptations; he has succumbed to the client's seductiveness, and has been unable to offer the client what she came for—understanding, support, and clarification of her confusion.

6. *Differences in Values and Ideology*   As discussed in Chapters 1 and 3, the two major sources of differences between the values and ideology of therapist and client are class and ethnicity. Of course, there are other differences in values, such as those dividing married from single persons, traditionally from radically oriented individuals, and males from females (or feminists). However, the latter could be subsumed under class and ethnicity values and ideological differences.

As mentioned in Chapters 1 and 5, an overwhelming number of therapists belong to the middle class. In more than one way a therapist espouses and propagates the values and ideology of the middle class. The ideology of psychotherapy itself is akin to middle-class ideology. Hence, if a client does not espouse many of these values, discord is quite likely to develop with the therapist.

When there is a divergence of values and ideology, a therapist may develop counter-transference feelings toward the client. By definition, values and ideology are not easily amenable to scrutiny unless they are confronted by other, usually opposing values and ideology. Thus, when a clash develops between the therapist and client on these issues, the therapist's forbearance is put to the test. He must either examine his own values and ideology or attempt to justify them in trying to change the client's values and ideology.

It is not unusual for a therapist to try to change the client's values through various ways, particularly arguing with the client, trying to prove him wrong, giving interpretations which may be embedded in his own value structure, and so forth. Obviously, when such divergence exists between them, the therapist and the client are using different moral standards to assess and evaluate behavior. Hence, the likelihood of agreement about a change of behavior is rather slim.

A thirty-two-year-old black male came to therapy because he was confused. He had been in prison on a felony charge and had turned to the Bible for guidance. When the client got out of prison, he worked as a pimp. His prostitute (who, according to him, sometimes also claimed to be his wife) had tried to leave him because she could solicit her own business from a higher class of clientele. This left him at loose ends, upset and confused. When the therapist, a second-year graduate student, asked what kind of work the client did, he replied that his wife worked, that he had never had a regular job, and then he hinted cryptically at what he did. The therapist asked if it did not seem somewhat strange to the client that he had never held a steady job. Would it not be helpful to him and his wife if he took a regular job so that many of the debts, of which the client complained, could be gradually paid off? The client protested somewhat ineffectually, but said that he would look for one in the near future. The next few sessions were devoted to the discussion of a job and the client's debts. A few sessions later, the client dropped out of therapy, thanking the therapist but also mentioning that the therapist didn't quite understand his struggle.

7. *Money as a Source of Counter-transference**   A therapist enters the profession of psychotherapy, at least in part, to make a living. He spends many years and considerable sums of money to obtain the training necessary for him to attain professional status. Yet the question of his fees has not been openly discussed, or at best it has been stated only cryptically and tangentially (Group for Advancement of Psychiatry 1975). Furstein (1971) observes that "my own experience, and that of many therapists I have spoken with, suggests that therapists, as well as patients, tend to avoid the topic of personal income and personal financial resources."

Therapists hold various beliefs and rationales about fees and money.** Freud (1950) says, "It is well known that the value of treatment is not enhanced in a patient's eyes if a very low fee is asked." Others maintain that since the therapist has spent many years in training he has a right to collect a high fee (Bar-Levav 1979). Still others believe that free treatment increases a client's neurotic resistances

---

*It is not clear from the study at whose initiative—the therapist's or the client's—therapy was terminated. Bouhoutsos et al's. study (1983) shows that 67 percent of the clients and 15 percent of therapists terminated therapy after the initiation of sexual relations.

**As discussed in Chapter 5 (in the section on fees) the paying versus the nonpaying client, the amount of fee paid, and the source of payment (client, insurance, third party, and so on) does not exert an independent influence upon therapy. The beliefs about money mentioned here are held by therapists despite contrary evidence.

(Eissler 1974) or that "lowering the fee would reinforce any patient's unhealthy demand that someone else be his 'keeper' or play God to him" (DiBella 1980). Menninger and Holzman (1973) believe that "analysis would not go well if the patient is paying considerably less than he can reasonably afford to pay. It should be a definite sacrifice for him, for him and not for someone else." Mowrer (1963) believes that "in neurosis we are dealing . . . with real guilt . . . [and] persons undergoing 'treatment' will interpret the financial cost and other associated sacrifices as repayment for past misconduct . . ."

A therapist evolves his attitudes toward money and fees on the basis of his personal monetary and financial ideology. These attitudes provide the framework for the emergence of "fee-money counter-transference." Empirical studies show that fee setting is one of the ten most common mistakes made by a beginning therapist (Buckley et al. 1979); the therapist is either hesitant to set a fee, sets it too high or too low, or is too inflexible about it.

Many authors acknowledge that fees can and sometimes do become a source of counter-transference in private practice (Goodenough et al. 1957; Schonbar 1967). Even when a therapist works in a clinic where patients pay fees, and in which the therapist may be a paid employee or trainee, the development of counter-transference remains a serious possibility.

Three major sources seem to generate fee-money counter-transference. The first source could be described as socioeconomic in nature. A private practitioner of psychotherapy is a private entrepreneur. In the role of entrepreneur, he is likely to be more motivated by profit than by service to the needy. As an individual entrepreneur selling a service, he is in competition with others in his profession selling the same or a similar service (Chodoff 1964). Therefore, he needs a regular supply of paying clients, particularly those who can pay his highest fee. The higher the rate of his fee collection from the client, the more successful he is as an entrepreneur.* For this reason, the amount of money collected (or not collected) in the form of fees is likely to provide a framework in which counter-transference develops. This can assume various forms:

---

*It should be noted that turning unpaid clients' bills over to collection agencies is a common practice among therapists. Tarachow (1963) says that he has even sued clients to collect his money.

1. CLIENTS WHO PAY LOWER FEES. A low-paying client makes the same demands upon the therapist as a high-paying client. The therapist has to give him the same attention, provide him with the same empathy, and show him the same concern as he would a high-paying client. Under such circumstances, the therapist may begin to compare the monetary returns from different clients for the same amount of effort. If he feels that he is not getting an equitable return, the therapist may begin to develop a sense of being deprived and exploited by the low-paying client. The result is frustration, anger, and detachment on the part of the therapist (Berman 1979).

2. CLIENTS WHOSE FINANCIAL STATUS CHANGES DURING THE COURSE OF THERAPY. Frequently, a therapist begins to work with a client on a contingency basis. If the client is unable to pay the therapist his full fee at the beginning of therapy, the therapist may stipulate that as the client's income increases he may raise his fee. On the other hand, the therapist may lower his fee if the client's income goes down. As long as the therapist increases his fee there is no problem for him. However, lowering the fee increases the likelihood of counter-transference.

Circumstances which may lead a therapist to lower his fee can result from a variety of situations. For instance, a client may be able to pay a therapist's full fee because both the husband and the wife are working. If the couple separates during the course of therapy, the income of one person may not be enough, and the fee contract will have to be renegotiated. The therapist may have to lower his fee if he wishes to work with the client. He may also transfer the client to group therapy; send him to community mental health agencies, where the fee may be lower; shorten the length of therapy sessions; terminate therapy; or transfer the client to another therapist who charges a lower fee (Bergman 1979). If a therapist lowers his fee, he may begin to feel that he negotiated a poor financial contract at the beginning of therapy. Or he may develop a feeling of martyrdom because he feels that he is sacrificing his income. If he transfers the client to a person or institution charging a lower fee, he may feel that money is more important to him than helping troubled individuals.

A therapist may find himself in a similar situation when a major part of the payment is made by a third party (an insurance company or Medicare, for example). Generally, insurance companies pay for a fixed number of therapy visits per year. If the number of therapy sessions exceeds the number paid for by the insurance company, the therapist may have to renegotiate his fees. Similarly, if a client loses his job while he is in therapy, he may not be able to pay for the therapist's services. Under all these conditions, the therapist may feel his relationship with the client and influence in the therapeutic process are affected in a debilitating way.

3. CLIENTS WHO PAY HIGHER FEES. A very different kind of counter-transference is likely to develop with high-paying clients. Generally, a therapist may allow them to bend the therapeutic ground rules, which he may not allow other clients to do (Bergman 1979). For example, a therapist may attempt to see such clients more frequently during the week than he would ordinarily see low-paying clients. And he may not think of terminating such clients, even when conditions warrant it. Consequently, therapy comes to be controlled by the client. A therapist may wish to break loose of such control, ineffectually try to retaliate, feel helpless to do anything, or feel resentful because he may need the high-paying client. Under such circumstances, therapy deviates from its optimal effectiveness.

4. CLIENTS IN CLINICS AND INSTITUTIONS. Empirical studies and observations suggest that the following types of counter-transference problems are not unusual in clinics and institutions where a fee for therapy is charged.

Frequently, therapists prefer not to collect the fee themselves; instead, the receptionist (or some other agent) transacts the financial arrangement (Meyer 1976), or "if the patient must pay, that the arrangement be made according to a mechanically operating set of rules, preferably administered by the clinic" (Schonbar 1967). Therapists usually avoid a direct discussion of the fee with the client. They feel that a therapist's job is to help the client and not to collect money from him.

If a clinic uses a sliding scale or charges according to the client's ability to pay, eager or overzealous therapists may overcharge the client and frequently expect him to pay for every missed session regardless of the circumstances of the absence. The client begins to feel punished, unjustly treated, and/or resentful toward the clinic or the therapist. In turn, he may sabotage therapy by retaliating in various ways.

Other therapists rarely raise the issue of the fee with the client. If the client falls behind in payments, he begins to feel indebted to and dependent upon the therapist and may feel hesitant in openly expressing his thoughts and feelings, especially those which he feels may be contrary to the beliefs of the therapist. Under these circumstances, therapy begins to have a stifling rather than a liberating effect upon the client.

A second source of fee-money counter-transference has cultural roots. The various attitudes of the therapist toward money become enmeshed with the symbolic significance that the culture attaches to money (Weiner and Raths 1960). Schonbar (1967) maintains that "in our culture money is also a symbol of worth, prestige, competence, masculinity, freedom, control, and security, focal points in many people" [sic].

Bar-Levav (1979) maintains that in a "materialistic society a person's worth is often superficially determined by how much he earns."* Laythrop (1979) feels that "money, which is a form of energy, tends to be in the arena of power (as opposed to relatedness)." In a materialistic society, money signifies worth to the members of the society, including the therapist.

The therapist's attitudes and feelings toward money may surface in therapy. Many therapists announce how high their fee is, declaring that they do not accept a client who cannot afford to pay their high fees. Hence, they equate money with their self-worth and/or competence. At the same time, they feel that those who do not charge as high a fee as they do, or who work with low-paying clients, must not have a very high regard for themselves.

Symbolically money (and sex) represent many things to a person both consciously and unconsciously (Schwartz and Wolf 1969). In discussing money and/or sex, many of the issues, problems, and conflicts in the client's life can be brought to the foreground in therapy. Therefore, therapists often make money (or sex) the central theme of discussion thereby imposing their own value systems, albeit symbolically, upon the psychotherapeutic process. They steer therapy in a direction determined more by their values than those of the client.

In psychoanalysis, a dual symbolic significance is attached to money (and hence to the fee). Freud (1950) declares:

The analyst does not dispute that money is to be regarded first and foremost as the means by which life is supported and power is obtained, but he maintains that, besides this, powerful sexual factors are involved in the value set upon it; he may expect, therefore, that money questions will be treated by

---

* In this quotation, the word *superficially* reflects Bar Levav's beliefs or wishes, and not the reality of the materialistic (and capitalistic) society.

cultured people in the same manner as sexual matters, with the same inconsistency, prudishness and hypocrisy. He is therefore determined beforehand not to concur in this attitude, and in his dealings with patients to treat of money matters with the same matter-of-course frankness that he wishes to induce in them towards matters relating to sexual life.

Other psychoanalysts maintain that a preoccupation with money (or with fees) is either a reaction formation against or a sublimation of interest in feces. Hence, money is symbolically equated with feces (Fenichel 1945; Ferenczi, 1950). Psychoanalytic theory holds that symbolic significance is attached to money in the unconscious of both patient and therapist, where such matters as secrecy, prudishness, withholding, and aggressiveness may be the sources of fee-money counter-transference.

A third major source of fee-money countertransference arises from a conflict built into the therapist's role. By his own admission, the therapist assumes the role of helping others, devoting himself to a humanitarian endeavor (Edelwich 1980). Yet, at the same time, he must charge money for helping others, and refuse to help if the client can't afford to pay. As DiBella notes, "in our culture all must cope with two greatly contradictory ethics regarding money: altruistic, humanistic, selfless Judeo-Christianity versus capitalistic individualism" (1980).

The therapist's conflict, which in turn affects his relations with the client and the course of therapy, becomes noticeable when a client with marginal ability to pay the therapist's fees seeks therapy (Furstein 1971). The therapist then must struggle with his value system, which may potentially lead to the development of counter-transference.

A thirty-three-year-old housewife, the mother of three daughters, came to therapy because of marital discord and dissatisfaction with her life. She was married to an engineer who had just begun his professional career. When the issue of fee was discussed, she indicated that she could not comfortably pay the therapist's minimum fee. She was willing to pay as much as her budget allowed, and would try to find more money, but she was not sure that it would meet the therapist's minimum fee. The therapist mentioned that although he was financially more comfortable than she, his "professional principles" forced him not to accept less than what he had set as his minimum fees. She said that she understood the therapist's position but still requested that he see her. After all, she insisted, her life was in turmoil. The therapist agreed to work with her, urging her to pay the minimum. For about four months she did not pay the minimum fees. Therapy sessions were marred by discussion of fees. The therapist began to develop conflicting (and negative) feelings and was relieved when the client cancelled the ses-

sions. Fortunately, her husband got a promotion shortly afterward, and she was able to pay the minimum fees. Therapy became easier for both the therapist and the client.

Communication of the Therapist's Counter-transference

How does the therapist communicate his counter-transferences to the client? Since there are few studies on this topic, one can only infer from existing studies the manner and method of the therapist's communications. They may vary from a direct expression of feelings and reactions to indirect and subtle nonverbal and body-language communication.

Many writers in recent years have recommended that the therapist express his feelings directly to the client in order to facilitate open communication (Mullan 1964; Jourard 1971a, b; Weiner 1978). Obviously, self-disclosure is usually a conscious and direct communication from the therapist to the client in relation to what the client has said during the therapy session. Self-disclosure, according to Patterson (1974), occurs when "the therapist reveals information about himself, his ideas, values, feelings and attitudes. He may reveal that he has had experiences or feelings similar to those of the client. . . ."

A therapist may engage in self-disclosure in various ways. He may reveal intimate thoughts and feelings, or he may offer only the superficial ones; he may spend considerable or little time in revealing his thoughts and feelings, and he may disclose much or little information. Thus, according to Cozby (1973), self-disclosure has three dimensions: intimacy, duration, and breadth.

Proponents of self-disclosure maintain that for numerous reasons it has a beneficial and liberating effect upon the client and the therapeutic process. First, "to a shocking extent, behavior begets its own kind. Manipulation begets counter-manipulation. Self-disclosure begets self-disclosure" (Jourard 1971a). Thus, because the therapist reveals himself the client is likely to disclose more of himself. Second, the self-disclosure of the therapist presents the client with a role model of uncontrived honesty with which the client may be able to identify and thus be able to develop a greater sense of self-honesty (Jourard 1971a, b). Third, it enhances the client's definition of the therapist as a real person and his perception of the actual patient–therapist relationship (Weiner 1978). Fourth, it provides feedback about the impact of the patient on others (Weiner 1978). Finally, because in self-disclosure the therapist actively participates in an immediate relationship with the client, each responding to the other and exploring together (Mullan 1964; Patterson 1974), it has a facilitative effect upon the client and the therapeutic process.

Other observers hold a somewhat contrary view:

The common-sense idea that disclosure begets disclosure is supported by questionnaire studies and by direct observation of persons in laboratory, work and social settings.

A different picture emerges in the psychotherapist–patient relationship. Unfortunately, much of the research in this area is naive and based on studies of quasi-patients in pseudotherapy. The data suggest that self-disclosingness per se does not consistantly augment patient disclosure. Neither high therapist disclosure nor high patient disclosure consistently correlates with improvement in psychotherapy. (Weiner 1978)

Self-disclosure by the therapist can also lead to a worsening of the patient's condition, a fact that has been noted by Weiner (1978), among others. It is reasonable to assume that self-disclosure which creates an impasse or a deterioration in therapy has more likely developed into some kind of counter-transference. Some authors noted the conditions under which self-disclosure brings impasse or deterioration:

when it is a manipulation of a patient's feelings; when it is designed to meet the therapist's needs, be they social or sexual or pathological; when it is the therapist's attempt to defend against his own feelings; when it helps the therapist avoid facing his incompetence or indifference to the patient; when it reinforces the patient's pathological pattern of defense through an untimely attack or inappropriate gratification; when it increases the patient's need for active intervention or gratification by the therapist; when it obstructs the possibility for the patient to eventually leave the therapist; when it pushes the patient into action with which he cannot cope or which is detrimental to him; when it leads to identification with an unhealthy aspect of the therapist. (Weiner 1978)

Mullan (1964) implies that there are two kinds of self-disclosure: beneficial and harmful. He calls the beneficial kind "the therapist's expression of subjective response, and the harmful one the expression of neurotic needs. Subjective response is an attempt to lessen self-deception and attain meaning in the therapeutic situation while neurotic needs are those which are expressed for other purposes."

How does the therapist know when he is manipulating a patient's feelings, or expressing himself without regard for the client's needs? How does the therapist know whether he is expressing his neurotic or nonneurotic needs during self-disclosure? These are some of the questions that have not been asked openly by advocates of self-disclosure; rather, they have assumed that the therapist's judgment is sound, that the therapist's behavior is judicious, and that during the process of self-disclosure the therapist maintains a certain altruistic attitude.

Under what conditions is the therapist's self-disclosure helpful to the client? At the risk of presenting an oversimplified solution, one may state the following. With a client who is diffident in talking and in expressing himself, a certain amount of self-disclosure provides identification and impetus for him to be open. Self-disclosure also appears to help more seriously disturbed clients who withdraw, develop muteness, and suffer other difficulties. Self-disclosure, as long as it is in direct relationship to the mental and emotional state of the client, can be used to convey the therapist's empathy, to illustrate a point, and to share the emotions of the client—his sorrows, joys, achievements, anger.* Self-disclosure is likely to become detrimental when it is meant to serve the therapist's own needs or desires (McCarthy and Betz 1979; Reynolds and Fisher 1983).

How intimate should the self-disclosure of the therapist be so that it is useful to the client and the therapeutic process? Some theorists recommend a mildly personal self-disclosure; for example, the expression and/or sharing of feelings. Lewis (1978) maintains that the more urgently the therapist feels a need for self-disclosure, and the more personal its content, the greater will be his need to consider carefully his reasons for the proposed act. Jourard (1971b) recommends a greater degree of personal self-disclosure. On balance, however, it appears that self-disclosure which is too intimate is likely to confuse the client, for it is he and not the therapist who is expected to reveal himself; it may appear to the client that the therapist is unburdening himself; and finally, psychotherapy may veer away from the client's troubles and conflicts.

Studies suggest that there is a curvilinear relationship between

---

*Curtis's study (1982) contradicts this point. However, an examination of his data suggests that in his study empathy and self-disclosure, two rather distinct variables, became confounded.

the therapist's and the client's self-disclosures. A warm and intermediate level of self-disclosure by the therapist helps the client to follow his lead (Chaikin et al. 1975; Mann and Murphy 1975; Halpern 1977), while too much and/or too little self-disclosure seems to have a negative influence on therapy (Giannandrea and Murphy 1973; Mann and Murphy 1975).

Indirect expression of the feelings that hinder the therapist's understanding is far more common than their direct expression. The reactions of the therapist that evolve into counter-transferences are more subtle, insidious, and cryptic. The therapist conveys his feelings and reactions to the client through indirect suggestions and innuendos (Butler and Zelen 1977), or through changes in the "tone of his voice (cold, cheerful, tense, eager), his facial expressions and such minutiae as the way he walks, his breathing habits, his bodily stance, and so on" (Sherman 1965). Such cues convey to the client the therapist's values and morality and his approval or disapproval of the client's behavior.

Concealing the Counter-transference

As this discussion suggests and as the studies show, counter-transference is much greater than is commonly supposed (Singer and Luborsky 1977). In fact, some therapists state that "it seems probable, although there is no statistical evidence to support the conclusion, that countertransference accounts for a large percentage of mistakes and failures in psychiatric treatment" (Levine 1952). In view of the widespread prevalence of counter-transference, one may ask why it is written about and discussed so rarely (Little, 1951). One reason could be that the therapist may conceal his counter-transference even from himself (and therefore from others). If so, how does he do this? It appears that a series of psychological and ideological maneuvers occur.

First, a therapist may rationalize his counter-transference through a theory of therapy. For instance, a therapist who cannot help his client at a certain stage of therapy because of his counter-transference may state that the client is seductive or manipulative and is interested in using others. The client, therefore, is not interested in examining himself. Or he may decide that the client is unwilling to explore himself. Here, there is no motivation for the therapist to examine his own counter-transference.

Second, a certain group of therapists and analysts believe that since they have gone through therapy themselves, they are aware of their "unconscious conflicts." They hold that counter-transference arises from unconscious conflicts, and so there is little likelihood that they will develop it. Hence, they hardly entertain the notion that their own confused feelings may get in the way of understanding the client's conflicts.

Third, the issue of counter-transference hardly arises for therapists who use the medical model. These therapists believe that the "patient" is "mentally ill or sick"; hence, his feelings are also "sick." The therapist, on the other hand, is "mentally healthy," and his feelings, whatever they may be, are also healthy. In this conceptual framework, the issue of counter-transference can arise only as a contretemps.

Fourth, many analysts believe that although the therapist may develop a counter-transference, of which he may be aware, it should be used to investigate the feelings of the client (Heimann 1950; Weiner 1978; Baum 1973; Kernberg 1965; Little 1951). In other words, a therapist should focus not upon himself but upon the client and why he is trying to evoke certain feelings in the therapist. Such an approach, according to these writers, will explore the unconscious dynamics of the client's conflicts. Again, in this framework, the focus is upon the client; a therapist does not have to examine the conflicts and feelings that hinder his understanding.

Fifth, a therapist may not be aware of his counter-transference, and how it prevents him from understanding the client's conflicts, until it is brought to his attention by someone else—by his colleagues or supervisor.

Uses of Counter-transference in Therapy

Sandler, Holder, and Dare (1970) state that "Freud did not take the step [which he took in relation to transference] of regarding counter-transference as a useful tool in analytic work." Instead, he implicitly considered it to be harmful to the therapeutic process. Consequently, many therapists developed a negative attitude toward their own feelings and reactions in therapy. However, many subsequent writers believe that the therapist's counter-transference can be a useful tool for diagnostic purposes, for the therapeutic process, and for the patient himself (Tauber 1954).

Hill (1956), for instance, states that irritation in the doctor can suggest a diagnosis of hysteria in the patient. Kernberg (1965) says that "when dealing with borderline or severely regressed patients . . . the countertransference becomes an important diagnostic tool, giving information on the degree of regression in the patient and the predominant emotional position of the patient toward the therapist and the changes occurring in this position."

Little (1950, 1951) maintains that the communication of the analyst's counter-transference to the patient often can be a valuable therapeutic tool. For example, when the therapist, motivated by his countertransference, says or does something that may be mistaken or poorly timed, not only should he correct it but

its origin in the unconscious countertransference may be explained, unless there is some definite contraindication for doing so, in which case it should be postponed until a suitable time comes, as it surely will. Such explanations may be essential for the further progress of the analysis and it will have only beneficial results, increasing the patient's confidence in the honesty and goodwill of the analyst, showing him to be human enough to make mistakes, and making clear the universality of the phenomenon of transference and the way it can arise in any relationship.

Heimann (1950) maintains that the analyst's countertransference is an instrument of research into the patient's unconscious. From the point of view I am stressing, the analyst's counter-transference is not only part and parcel of the analytic relationship, but it is the patient's creation; it is a part of the patient's personality.

The emotions aroused in the analyst will be of value to his patient, if used as one more source of insight into the patient's unconscious conflicts and defences.

Racker (1957) believes that

countertransference reactions have specific characteristics (specific contents, anxieties and mechanisms) from which we may draw conclusions about the specific character of the psychological happenings in the patient. . . .

[He recommends] countertransference as a tool for understanding the mental processes of the patient (including especially his transference reactions), their contents, their mechanisms and their intensities.

Racker (1968) holds that "counter-transference is dominated by the law of talion which follows simple rules and allows retranslation of the complicated-subtle experiences." In other words, if a therapist harbors hostile feelings toward the client, then the client must also feel some form of hostility toward the therapist; otherwise the therapist would not have such feelings. The therapist's hostility can thus be used as a springboard to analyze the client's unconscious feelings of hostility.

While discussing their own adverse feelings, attitudes, and reactions toward the client, this group of therapists makes the client rather than themselves the subject of study. They ignore the possibility of focusing upon themselves and their own dynamics—what it is in the therapy sessions that may be generating their conflicts, how it may hinder their understanding of the client's troubles, how it may deflect or freeze therapy into those conflicts of the client with which they may be uncomfortable, and so forth. Thus, one could say that in helping the client resolve his conflicts the therapist avoids understanding his own.

It appears that counter-transference can be useful and beneficial if the therapist is honest enough to use it as an opportunity to explore his own conflicts and prejudices—how they affect his reactions toward the client, how they affect the course of therapy, and how they may hinder his understanding of the client's conflicts as well as their source.

Managing the Counter-transference

For a series of reasons, it is difficult to suggest a set of simple rules for handling one's counter-transferences. First, what has been called counter-transference—the untoward feelings of the therapist—is difficult to detect since frequently it is an "unconscious reaction." Second, the therapist is directly involved in the actions and reactions of the process. It is therefore more difficult for the therapist to attain the distance necessary to judge it. Third, to detect those feelings and reactions that make him uncomfortable and anxious, a therapist must be honest with himself and open to self-examination. This may not be possible for many therapists. In addition, it requires a certain amount of struggle on the part of the therapist to face his adverse feelings, to accept them, and to change them. Finally, given the therapist's role of authority, power, and prestige in a therapeutic relationship, it is easy for him—and especially for the beginning therapist—to attribute many of his own conflicts and anxieties to the client, and thus remain unaware of his counter-transferences.

In spite of what is said above, perhaps the first step in the therapist's awareness of his counter-transference is to recognize in himself one of the eighteen feelings and reactions mentioned above. This will be a signal for the therapist to examine his own feelings, anxieties, values, and conflicts in light of his counter-transferences.

Wolberg (1977) mentions that

in order to sensitize himself to neurotic manifestations when they appear, the therapist may advantageously subject himself to self-examination throughout the course of therapy. Such questions as the following are appropriate:

1. How do I feel about the patient?
2. Do I anticipate seeing the patient?
3. Do I overidentify with or feel sorry for the patient?
4. Do I feel any resentment or jealousy toward the patient?
5. Do I get extreme pleasure out of seeing the patient?
6. Do I feel bored with the patient?
7. Am I fearful of the patient?
8. Do I want to protect, reject or punish the patient?
9. Am I impressed by the patient?

Should answers to any of the above point to problems, the therapist may ask himself why such attitudes and feelings exist. Is the patient doing anything to stir up such feelings? Does the patient resemble anybody the therapist knows or has known, and if so, are any attitudes being transferred to the client that are related to another person? Mere verbalizations to himself of answers to these queries permits a better control of unreasonable feelings. Cognizance of the fact that he feels angry, displeased, disgusted, irritated, peeved, uninterested, unduly attentive, upset, or overly attracted, may surface to bring these emotions under control. In the event untoward attitudes continue, more self searching is indicated. . . .

One of the generally accepted methods of resolving counter-transference is self-analysis. Here, some writers state that inadequately analyzed therapists develop counter-transference (Wolberg 1952; Weigert 1954). Others have suggested that anxious therapists are more likely to develop counter-transference (Yulis and Kiesler 1968). Hence many authors recommend further analysis of the therapist to help him overcome his counter-transference.

In extending the concept of self-analysis, Ross and Knapp (1962) have suggested that "a useful technique of self-analysis of the counter-transference which seems to provide a further tool of value for the analyst is using the analyst's associations to his visual images of his patients' dreams. . . . [This] technique can be applied either when a countertransference problem has already been suspected or, routinely, to test for countertransference, even without other clues."

Perhaps the most widely accepted method of detecting and resolving counter-transference is the supervision of the therapist, either by a superior or by a peer group.* It is generally recommended that if during the course of supervision counter-transference becomes noticeable, the supervisor should bring to the therapist's attention how the counter-transference may be hindering his understanding of the client's problems, how the movement of therapy is being blocked, and so forth. If a supervisor can assist the therapist by suggesting various means, methods, and devices to handle his counter-transference in therapy, he should do so.

In the literature, it remains a moot question whether the supervisor's role should be limited to pointing out the therapist's counter-transference, its effects upon the client and the process of therapy, and certain means of overcoming it; or whether the supervisor should analyze the dynamics of the therapist's counter-transferences. From this author's point of view, the first alternative appears to be the most judicious. The roles of supervisor and of therapist seem contradictory or incompatible since they begin to confuse the teaching of therapy with therapy itself.

Sometimes it is helpful for the therapist to discuss his counter-transference feelings and attitudes with the client. Little (1951) is perhaps alone in suggesting that the therapist should discuss his counter-transference with the client as well as explain its origin. It is difficult to point out what kind of counter-transference—among those dealing with sexuality, hostility, or differences in values—should be discussed with the client. However, for a number of reasons, it is not easy for the therapist to discuss his counter-transference with the client.

First, to engage in an honest discussion of his own conflicts, a therapist must speak to the client without the protection of his "superior role position." If the therapist cannot divest himself of his "role superiority," there cannot be an honest encounter with the client.

Second, once a therapist admits his own conflicts, anxie-

---

*Goin and Kline's study (1976) shows that during supervisory sessions, half of the supervisors (twelve out of twenty-four) avoided discussing the therapist's countertransference. Four approached the subject indirectly, and eight made direct and open reference to it.

ties, temptations, and prejudices, which may lie at the source of his counter-transference, then the client is free (or should be free) to judge and criticize the therapist in his role. This would reverse the role relations in therapy where, usually, it is the therapist who does the judging. A therapist may find it difficult to accept such a role reversal.

Third, a client may question (either openly to the therapist or secretly to himself) whether the therapist's life is managed any better than his own; hence, perhaps the therapist has no right to fill the role he is in.

It is not unusual for the therapist, while discussing his counter-transference with the client, to maintain a foothold in the realm of therapeutic authority. In this case, the therapist will be unable to create an atmosphere of equality in which the client can honestly express his reactions to the therapist. If a therapist is unable to shed his authority, he is best advised not to discuss his counter-transference with the client.

Finally, the following device may help the therapist to check his counter-transference. A conscientious therapist should keep notes on each session with every client. A beginning therapist is also advised to jot down from time to time his own reactions to the client and to the sessions. A periodic study of these notes, some self-reflection on his own feelings about the client, and an analysis of the movement of therapy or the lack of it should help the therapist discover whether he may be developing or has developed any counter-transference.

Summary

A therapist develops various feelings toward the client, particularly toward one of the opposite sex. The therapist is aware of some of these feelings, while he is only vaguely conscious of others. Some of his feelings and reactions may be innocuous; other sets of feelings, when developed beyond a certain point, become detrimental to therapy.

It is not rare for a therapist to seek gratification of his feelings through the client. Generally, if the therapist's own life is not satisfactorily managed, he will be more likely to develop a counter-transference as well as attempt, however indirectly, to seek gratification through the client.

A therapist reacts, almost directly, to the feelings and emotions which the client expresses in therapy. These reactions can become a stumbling block to the therapist in attempting to understand the client's conflicts. Frequently, a therapist may conceal his feelings from himself and others by convincing himself that he is above such adverse reactions. Various methods and techniques for the correction of counter-transference have been recommended; it appears to this author that perhaps the most useful one is self-honesty, the ability to examine oneself openly.

References

Balint, M., and A. Balint. 1939. On transference and counter-transference. *International Journal of Psychoanalysis* 20:223–30.

Bandura, A. 1956. Psychotherapists' anxiety level, self insight, and psychotherapeutic competence. *Journal of Abnormal and Social Psychology* 52:333–37.

Bandura, A., D. H. Lipsher, and P. E. Miller. 1960. Psychotherapists' approach-avoidance reactions to patients' expression of hostility. *Journal of Consulting Psychology* 24:1–8.

Bar-Levav, R. 1979. Money: One yardstick of the self. *Voices* (Journal of American Academy of Psychotherapists) 14:24–30.

Basch, M. F. 1980. *Doing psychotherapy*. New York: Behavioral Science Book Service.

Baum, E. 1969. Countertransference. *Psychoanalytic Review* 56:621–37.

———. 1973. Further thoughts on countertransference. *The PsychoAnalytic Review* 1:127–40.

Beery, J. W. 1970. Therapist response as a function of level of therapist experience and attitude of the patient. *Journal of Consulting and Clinical Psychology* 34:239–43.

Belote, B. J. 1974. Sexual intimacy between female clients and male psychotherapists: Masochistic sabotage. Ph.D. diss., California School of Professional Psychology, San Francisco.

Bergman, R. 1979. Fees and clinical judgement. *Voices* (Journal of American Academy of Psychotherapists) 14:11–15.

Berman, L. 1949. Countertransference and attitudes of the analyst in the therapeutic process. *Psychiatry* 12:159–66.

Bohn, M. J. 1965. Counselors' behavior as a function of counselors' dominance, counselors' experience and client type. *Journal of Counseling Psychology* 12:346–51.

Bouhoutsos, J., J. Holroyd, H. Lerman, B. Forer, and M. Greenberg. 1983. Sexual intimacies between psychotherapists and patients. *Professional Psychology: Research and Practice* 14:185–96.

Buckley, P., T. Karasan, and E. Charles. 1979. Common mistakes in psychotherapy. *American Journal of Psychiatry* 136:1578–80.

Bugental, J. 1965. *The search for authenticity*. New York: Holt, Rinehard and Winston.

Butler, S., and S. Zelen. 1977. Sexual intimacies between therapists and patients. *Psychotherapy: Theory, Research and Practice* 2:139–45.

Carotenuto, A. 1984. *A Secret Symmetry*. New York: Pantheon Books.

Chaikin, A. L., V. J. Derlega, B. Bayma, and J. Shaw. 1975. Neuroticism and disclosure reciprocity. *Journal of Consulting and Clinical Psychology* 43:13–19.

Chessick, R. D. 1974. *Techniques and practice of intensive psychotherapy*. New York: Jason Aronson.

Chodoff, P. 1964. Psychoanalysis and fees. *Comprehensive Psychiatry* 5: 137–45.

Cohen, M. B. 1952. Countertransference and anxiety. *Psychiatry* 15:231–43.

Cohn, R. 1966. Sexual fantasies of the psychotherapist and their use in psychotherapy. *Journal of Sex Research* 2:219–26.

Colby, M. K. 1951. *A primer for psychotherapists*. New York: Ronald Press.

Cozby, P. C. 1973. Self disclosure: A literature review. *Psychological Bulletin* 79:73–91.

Curtis, J. 1982. The effect of therapist self-disclosure on patients' perception of empathy, competence and trust in an analogue psychotherapeutic interaction. *Psychotherapy: Theory, Research and Practice* 19:54–62.

Cutler, R. 1958. Countertransference effects in psychotherapy. *Journal of Consulting Psychology* 22:349–56.

D'Addario, L. J. 1977. Sexual relations between female clients and male therapists. Ph.D. diss., California School of Professional Psychology, San Diego.

Dahlberg, C. 1970. Sexual contact between patient and therapist. *Contemporary Psychoanalysis* 6:107–27.

Davidson, V. 1977. Psychiatry's problem with no name: Therapist-patient sex. *American Journal of Psychoanalysis* 37:43–50.

DiBella, G. A. 1980. Mastering money issues that complicate treatment: The last taboo. *American Journal of Psychotherapy* 34:510–22.

Edelwich, J. 1980. *Burn-Out*. New York: Human Science Press, 46–47.

Eissler, K. 1974. Some theoretical and technical problems regarding the payment of fees for psychoanalytic treatment. *International Review of Psychoanalysis* 1:73–101.

Epstein, L., and A. H. Feiner, eds. 1979. *Countertransference*. New York: Jason Aronson.

Fenichel, O. 1945. *Psychoanalytic theory of neurosis*. New York: W. W. Norton and Co., 580.

Ferenczi, S. 1950. *Sex in psychoanalysis*. New York: Basic books.

Fielding, B. 1972. Aspects affecting premature termination of psychotherapy at a training clinic. *American Journal of PsychoTherapy* 26:268–76.

Freeman, L., and J. Roy. 1976. *Betrayal*. New York: Stein and Day.

Freud, S. 1950. Further recommendations in the techniques of psychoanalysis (1913). In *Collected papers*, vol. 2. London: Hogarth Press, 351–52.

————. 1950. Future prospects of psychoanalytic therapy (1910). In *Collected papers*, vol. 2. London: Hogarth Press, 285–96.

Furstein, C. 1971. Money as a value in psychotherapy. *Journal of Contemporary Psychotherapy* 3:99–104.

Gamsky, N., and G. F. Farwell. 1966. Counselors' verbal behavior as a function of client hostility. *Journal of Counseling Psychology* 13:184–90.

Giannandrea, V., and K. C. Murphy. 1973. Similarity self disclosure and return for a second interview. *Journal of Counseling Psychology* 20:545–48.

Gitelson, M. 1952. The emotional position of the analyst in the psychoanalytic situation. *International Journal of Psychoanalysis* 33:1–10.

Glover, E. 1955. *The technique of psychoanalysis*. New York: International University Press.

Goin, M., and F. Kline. 1976. Countertransference: A neglected subject in clinical supervision. *American Journal of Psychiatry* 133:41–44.

Goodenough, D., H. Klein, and H. Potter. 1957. Problems related to personal costs of psychiatric and psychoanalytic training. *American Journal of Psychiatry* 113:1013.

Greenson, R. 1967. *The technique and practice of psychoanalysis*. New York: International University Press, 348–50.

Group for the Advancement of Psychiatry. 1975. *The effect of the method of payment on mental health care practice*, vol. 9, report no. 95. (New York), 499–636.

Halpern, T. P. 1977. Degree of client disclosure as a function of past disclosure, counselor disclosure and counselor facilitativeness. *Journal of Counseling Psychology* 24:41–47.

Heimann, P. 1950. On countertransference. *International Journal of Psychoanalysis* 31:81–84.

Heller, K., R. A. Myers, and L. V. Kline. 1963. Interview behavior as a function of standardized client roles. *Journal of Consulting Psychology* 27:117–22.

Hill, D. 1956. Psychiatry. In J. S. Richardson, ed., *The practice of medicine*, 231–65. London: Churchill Publishers.

Hoffer, W. 1956. Transference and transference neurosis. *International Journal of Psychoanalysis* 37:377–79.

Holroyd, J., and A. Brodsky. 1977. Psychologists' attitudes and practices regarding erotic and non-erotic physical contact with patients. *American Psychologist* 10:843–50.

Jones, E. 1957. *Life and work of Sigmund Freud*, vol. 3. New York: Basic Books, 163–64.

Jourard, S. 1971(a). *The transparent self*. New York: Van Nostrand Co., 134–42.

————. 1971(b). *Self disclosure: An experimental analysis of the transparent self*. New York: John Wiley and Sons.

Kardener, S. M., M. Fuller, and I. Mensh. 1976. A survey of physicians' attitudes and practices regarding erotic and non-erotic contact with patients. *American Journal of Psychiatry* 130:1077–81.

Katz, M., and P. Zimbardo. 1977. Making it as a mental patient. *Psychology To-day*, Apr., 123–126.

Kernberg, O. 1965. Notes on countertransference. *Journal of American Psychoanalytic Association* 13:38–56.

Langberg, R. E. 1979. Therapists' avoidance of patient hostility during psychotherapy as a function of therapist and patient sex. (Dissertation Abstracts International, 1977.) Quoted in M. J. Lambert, *The effects of psychotherapy*, vol. 1. Montreal: Eden Press, 44–45.

Laythrop, D. 1979. Money, money, money. *Voices* (Journal of American Academy of Psychotherapists) 14:31–33.

Levine, M. 1952. Principles of psychiatric treatment. In F. Alexander & H. Ross, eds., *Dynamic Psychiatry*, 307–68. Chicago, Ill.: University of Chicago Press.

Lewis, J. M. 1978. *To be a therapist*. New York: Bruner/Mazel, 88–89.

Little, M. 1951. Countertransference and the patient's response to it. *International Journal of Psychoanalysis* 32:32–40.

———. 1957. "R"—The analyst's total response to his patient's needs. *International Journal of Psychoanalysis* 38:240–54.

Luborsky, L., and B. Singer. 1974. The fit of the therapist's behavior into patient's negative expectations: A study of transference-countertransference contagion. School of Medicine, University of Pennsylvania. Typescript.

Mann, B., and K. C. Murphy. 1975. Timing of self-disclosure, reciprocity of self disclosure and reactions to an initial interview. *Journal of Counseling Psychology* 22:304–8.

Marmor, J. 1970. The seductive psychotherapist. *Psychiatry Digest*, Oct., 10–16.

———. 1972. Sexual acting out in psychotherapy. *American Journal of Psychoanalysis* 32:3–8.

Masters, W., and V. Johnson. 1970. *Human sexual inadequacy*. Boston: Little, Brown and Co., 389–91.

McCarthy, P., and N. Betz. 1979. Differential effects of self-disclosing vs. self-involving counselor statements. *Journal of Counseling Psychology* 25:251–56.

McCartney, J. L. 1966. Overt transference. *Journal of Sex Research* 2:227–37.

Menninger, K., and P. Holzman. 1973. *Theory of psychoanalytic technique*. New York: Basic Books, 87.

Meyer, B. 1976. Attitudes of psychiatric residents toward payment of psychotherapy fees. *American Journal of Psychiatry* 133:1460–62.

Mowrer, O. H. 1963. Payment or repayment. *American Psychologist* 18:577–80.

Mullan, H. 1964. *The therapist's contribution to the treatment process*. Springfield, Ill.: Charles C. Thomas.

Nancy, C. 1973. Psychotherapy as a rip off. In P. Brown, ed., *Radical psychology*, 490–97. New York: Harper and Row.

Orr, D. 1954. Transference and countertransference. *Journal of American Psychoanalytic Association* 2:621–70.

Pasternack, S., and P. Treigen. 1976. Psychotherapy fees and residency training. *American Journal of Psychiatry* 133:1064–66.

Patterson, C. H. 1974. *Relationship counseling and psychotherapy.* New York: Harper and Row, 80.

Peabody, S., and C. Gelso. 1982. Countertransference and empathy: The complex relationship between the divergent concepts in counseling. *Journal of Counseling Psychology* 29:240–45.

Rabiner, E. L., M. F. Reiser, H. Barr, and A. Bralnic. 1955. Therapists' attitudes and patients' clinical status. *Archives of General Psychiatry* 25:555–69.

Racker, H. 1957. Meanings and uses of countertransference. *Psychoanalytic quarterly* 26:305–57.

———. 1968. *Transference and countertransference.* London: Hogarth Press.

Reich, A. 1951. On countertransference. *International Journal of Psychoanalysis* 32:25–31.

———. 1960. Further remarks on countertransference. *International Journal of Psychoanalysis* 41:389–95.

Reynolds, C., and C. Fisher. 1983. Personal versus professional evaluations of self-disclosing and self-involving counselors. *Journal of Counseling Psychology* 30:45–54.

Rosenweig, S., and R. Folman. 1974. Patient and therapist variables affecting premature termination in group psychotherapy. *Psychotherapy: Theory, Research and Practice* 11:76–79.

Ross, D. W., and F. T. Knapp. 1962. A technique for self analysis. *Journal of American Psychoanalytic Association* 10:643–57.

Ruesch, J. 1961. *Therapeutic communication.* New York: W. W. Norton, 175.

Russell, P. D., and W. V. Snyder. 1963. Counselor anxiety in relation to amount of clinical experiences and quality of affects demonstrated by client. *Journal of Consulting Psychology* 27:358–63.

Sandler, J., A. Holder, and C. Dare. 1970. Basic psychoanalytic concepts: IV. Counter-transference. *British Journal of Psychiatry* 117:83–88.

Saul, L. 1958. *Technique and practice of psychoanalysis.* Philadelphia: J. B. Lippincott Co.

Schonbar, R. A. 1967. The fee as a focus for transference and countertransference. *American Journal of Psychotherapy* 21:275–85.

Schwartz, E., and A. Wolf. 1969. Money matters. *International Mental Health Newsletter* 2:1–7.

Shapiro, R. J. 1974. Therapists attitudes and premature termination in family and individual therapy. *Journal of Nervous and Mental Disease* 159:101–7.

Sharpe, E. F. 1947. The psychoanalyst. *International Journal of Psychoanalysis* 28:1–6.

Shepard, M. 1971. *The love treatment: Sexual intimacy between patient and therapist.* New York: P. H. Wyden, 207.

Sherman, M. 1965. Peripheral cues and the invisible countertransference. *American Journal of Psychotherapy* 19:280–92.

Singer, B., and L. Luborsky. 1977. Countertransference: The status of clinical and quantitative research. In A. S. Gurman and A. M. Razin, eds., *Effective Psychotherapy*, 433–51. New York: Pergamon Press.

Singer, E. 1965. *Key concepts in psychotherapy*. New York: Random House, 296–97.

Spitz, R. 1956. Countertransference. *Journal of American Psychoanalytic Association* 4:256–65.

Stern, A. 1924. On the countertransference in psychoanalysis. *Psychoanalytic Review* 11:164–74.

Storr, A. 1980. *The art of psychotherapy*. New York: Methuen.

Stricker, G. 1977. Implications of research for psychotherapeutic treatment of women. *American Psychologist* 32:14–22.

Strupp, H. 1958. Psychotherapists' contribution to the treatment process. *Behavioral Science* 3:34–67.

Tarachow, S. 1963. *An introduction to psychotherapy*. New York: International University Press.

Tauber, E. 1954. Exploring the therapeutic use of countertransference data. *Psychiatry* 17:331–36.

Taylor, B., and N. Wagner. 1976. Sex between therapists and clients: A review and analysis. *Professional Psychology* 6:593–601.

Tourney, G., V. Bloom, P. Lowinger, C. Schorer, F. Auld, and J. Grisell. 1966. A study of psychotherapeutic process variables in psychoneurotic and schizophrenic patients. *American Journal of Psychotherapy* 20:112–24.

Tower, L. 1956. Countertransference. *Journal of American Psychoanalytic Association* 4:224–55.

Ulanov, A. 1979. Follow up treatment in case of patient/therapist sex. *Journal of the American Academy of Psychoanalysis* 7:101–10.

Van Emde Boas, C. 1966. Some reflections on sexual relations between physician and patient. *Journal of Sex Research* 2:215–18.

Weigert, E. 1954. Countertransference and self analysis of the psychoanalyst. *International Journal of Psychoanalysis* 35:242–46.

Weiner, D. N., and O. Raths, Jr. 1960. Cultural factors in the payment for psychoanalytic therapy. *American Journal of Psychoanalysis* 20:66–72.

Weiner, I. B. 1975. *Principles of Psychotherapy*. New York: John Wiley and Sons.

Weiner, M. 1978. *Therapist disclosure: The use of self in psychotherapy*. Boston: Butterworth, 48, 101–2.

Winnicott, D. W. 1949. Hate in the countertransference. *International Journal of Psychoanalysis* 30:69–74.

Wolberg, L. 1977. *The technique of psychotherapy*. New York: Grune and Stratton, 630–34.

Wolstein, B. 1959. *Countertransference*. New York: Grune and Stratton, 49.

Yulis, S., and D. J. Kiesler. 1968. Countertransference response as a function of therapist anxiety and content of patient talk. *Journal of Consulting and Clinical Psychology* 32:413–19.

10

Insight, Interpretation, and Confrontation

For three reasons, two of which are historical in nature, considerable importance has been given to "insight" as a vehicle of change in psychotherapy. The first is a historical-philosophical reason. Since early times, philosophers have emphasized the Socratic dictum, "Know thyself" (Martin 1952; Roback 1974). Implied here is the individual's ability to develop insight into himself, to accept the truth about himself, and to change. This viewpoint was incorporated into many schools of psychotherapy.

The second reason evolved from the days of the industrial revolution. It is generally believed that the understanding of men and machines is possible through the application of insight, reason, and the rational method. In this way, not only could their functioning be understood, but whatever might go wrong with them could be repaired. If, therefore, the human being developed a malfunction, it was assumed that the application of insight and the rational method would correct it (Hobbs 1962).

The third reason is a psychoanalytic one. Psychoanalytic theory assumes that a large part of the motivation which underlies human behavior is lodged in the unconscious mind. The individual's unconscious needs, feelings, instincts, and premises about life lie beyond his awareness. One must develop insight into these forces (Kris 1956) in order to change. Thus, the concept of insight became the cornerstone of therapy, and to abandon the concept is to question the validity of psychoanalytic observations and theories (Barnett, 1978).

The belief in the power of insight to remedy the malfunctioning of human behavior became extremely important in the theory and practice of psychotherapy and psychoanalysis. So crucial has been the role assigned to the concept of insight that models of therapy claiming to utilize insight as a tool for bringing about change in a client's life are frequently referred to as insight-oriented therapies (or as uncovering or reconstructive therapies). These models contrast with other kinds of therapies which do not emphasize insight, such as supportive and nondirective therapies (Wolberg 1977; Garfield 1980).

The purported aim of psychotherapy has been to help the client develop insight into his behavior and dynamics. As Singer (1965) observes, "Since the earliest days of contemporary psychotherapy, the persistent theme running through its literature suggests that the development of insight is the basic aim of psychotherapy and that gaining of self-knowledge is somewhat synonymous with emotional well being."*

As psychotherapy and psychoanalysis became accepted by society and began to be practiced relatively widely, practitioners decided that ordinary insight was insufficient to induce behavioral changes. A certain kind of insight was required: insight into one's past, or, more precisely, into one's childhood conflicts and the unconscious as understood during the course of psychoanalysis (Baranger 1966). "Psychoanalytic insight," some called it (Segal 1962; Myerson 1965). The therapist spent much time and attention in helping the client develop insight into his unconscious fantasies and childhood conflicts. Insight was achieved through the interpretation of the client's behavior. If the

---

*Only a handful of empirical studies exist on the relationship between insight and adjustment or psychological health. Some studies are poorly conceptualized (Eskey 1958; Roback and Abramowitz 1979; Tolor and Reznikoff 1960); others are inconclusive (Sweet 1953); while others suggest a negative relationship (Appelbaum 1976).

client achieved insight into his unconscious as a result of this interpretation, it was assumed that behavioral changes would follow somewhat automatically. Thus, insight became both a vehicle and a cause of the change in human behavior; the concepts of insight and interpretation grew more and more intertwined and began to be used, albeit unwittingly, interchangeably (Hammer 1966).

Freud maintained that the client's insight and the understanding of his childhood traumas would bring change in his behavior (Singer 1965; Baranger 1966). Yalom (1980) observes that

Freud . . . to the end of his life, believed that the excavation of the past was essential, even tantamount, to successful therapy.

. . . An analyst who is not successful in helping the patient to recollect the past should, Freud suggests, nonetheless give the patient a construction of the past as the analyst sees it. Freud believed that this construction would offer the same therapeutic benefit as would actual recollection of past material.

The assumption that insight brings about a change in behavior led to circular reasoning. For example, if a client did not manifest behavioral changes during the course of therapy, then it was assumed that he had not gained insight into himself; otherwise, he would have changed. If, however, the client showed no behavioral change but did display certain verbalizations that could be construed as an indication of insight (as many clients do), then it was believed that he must have developed a false insight, sometimes called "verbal" or "intellectual" insight (Hobbs 1981). If the client changed his behavior, then he must have developed "real" insight, which was sometimes called "emotional" insight.*

Differentiating between intellectual and emotional insight usually involves a post hoc approach; a client is considered to have intellectual insight if he does not show behavioral changes after attaining self-awareness, and emotional insight if he does demonstrate the desired behavioral changes. This is essentially circular reasoning insofar as the index for achieving emotional insight is behavioral improvement (Coons 1967; Roback 1974).

The concept of insight was used in a variety of ways by both practitioners and authors. It was sometimes used interchangeably

---

*According to Zilboorg (1952), it was under the influence of psychoanalysis that the term *emotional insight* was adopted by clinical psychiatry.

with other terms, such as *understanding, awareness, interpretation, change*, and *construction*. For a beginner in the field, the concept of insight was not only confusing, even tautological, it was also a glib explanation of the client's success and/or failure in therapy.

Two Types of Insight

The literature of psychotherapy consistently makes a distinction between intellectual and emotional insight. Intellectual insight, which presumably does not affect behavior, is equated with "unreal" insight. Emotional insight, on the other hand, is assumed to bring about behavioral change, and is equated with "real" or "true" insight. As Raimy (1975) observed:

Intellectual insight is often defined as only verbal, superficial understanding. The vague concept of emotional insight implies that emotional support has somehow been welded into intellectual understanding. Intellectual insight is often viewed as flabby and unconvincing, whereas emotional insight consists of robust convictions which effectively change behavior.*

This distinction has been criticized on many counts. Richfield (1954) maintains that the distinction is redundant; Barnett (1978) says that it is a rather confused conception; Roback (1974) believes that it begs the question.

Richfield (1954) maintains that

it is primarily in the problem of "emotional" insight that the greatest difficulty is found. The contrast of "intellectual" and "emotional" insight is made repeatedly, but never with adequate clarity. How any cognition is related to its alleged affective components in "emotional" insight has not been satisfactorily stated. Generally, the contrast merely signifies a vague difference between an intellectual understanding and some kind of understanding accompanied by an emotional reaction. . . . The term "intellectual insight" is redundant, the descriptive function of the adjective being included in the generic meaning of insight. Since all insights are ultimately intellectual, "emotional insight" is not an expression of the same order as the one to which it has been opposed. It would have to be understood as an elliptical phrase signifying a cogni-

---

*Ellis (1963) attempts to define emotional insight more precisely, but his definition includes action and behavior: "Emotional insight, in other words, is a multiple-barreled process which involves seeing—and believing; thinking—and acting; wishing—and practicing. Quantitatively, it includes more kinds of behaviors than does 'intellectual' insight. Qualitatively, it is a radically different, essentially more forcefully effective and committed kind of behavior."

tion whose content was an emotion. . . . As we have seen, the content or the object of the cognition is not an adequate basis on which to explain the distinctions. . . .

In spite of this, Richfield goes on to show, in a somewhat confusing way, why the so-called emotional insight brings change, while intellectual insight does not:

Two patients may know that their excessive dependence upon certain forms of emotional reassurance from their wives is caused by repressed oedipal drives. But the insight of one of these patients may be a cognition about these dynamic factors which never themselves emerged into the consciousness of the patient as direct objects of his awareness. In the other patient, the cognition which is said to be the patient's insight into dynamic forces may consist of a direct presentation of the unconscious emotion to the patient's awareness. Only when knowledge takes this form is it possible for the cognitive object to receive the necessary integration into the ego. . . . But the awareness must have the need itself as its object and not merely facts about it, before changes in the distribution of cathexes are brought about.

Reid and Finesinger (1952) believe that there are three rather distinct categories of insight. First is the intellectual insight, a cognition which does not pertain to any emotion. Since any insight is by definition an intellectual one, this variant is called "neutral." The insight is neutral with respect to emotion. The second kind of insight, one in which some relevant emotion is a part of the subject matter under scrutiny, is called "emotional" insight. Reid and Finesinger call the third type "dynamic insight," which they deem the "intellectual summum bonum of analysis." They hold that "insight is 'dynamic' in the systematic Freudian sense of penetrating the repressive barrier and making the ego aware of certain hyper-cathected wishes that were previously unconscious. . . . In short, as here defined, there would be no dynamic insight, if there were no Freudian unconscious." Dynamic insight produces "therapeutic effects . . . through the 'economic' shifts brought about with their consequent alterations in the unconscious cathexes on 'thought contents' at various levels of organization in the symbolic behavior of the patient."

Brady (1967) states that the concept of insight is used by clinicians in four different ways, which he designates as four levels of insight.

Most clinicians include in the term insight the patient's awareness that he is ill, i.e., the patient has insight into the fact that he recognizes his feelings, thoughts and/or behavior are abnormal. The term is also used to refer to the patient's cognition of the nature of his disorder; in particular, the consequences it has for his satisfaction and adjustment and its effect on others. A third use of the term concerns still another level of self-awareness, viz., knowledge of specific dynamic factors which give rise to various symptoms and now operate to maintain them. It's chiefly in this sense that the term is used to describe a favorable development in psychotherapy. That is why we say that a patient has gained insight if he comes to recognize some of the previously unconscious roots of his attitudes, beliefs, feelings, conflicts or behavior. It should be added that there is a fourth level of insight which is emphasized chiefly by more traditionally psychoanalytic writers. This is insight into the unconscious roots of the original conflict, i.e., the inadequately resolved infantile conflicts of which the present neurotic difficulties are a product.

This brief but representative survey of the literature suggests the obscure and somewhat confused discussion of the concept. Authors and therapists have become dissatisfied with the usefulness of insight in the process of therapy. Their doubts were strengthened by the fact that many seriously disturbed clients, as well as clients receiving behavior modification or similar forms of therapy, would improve without gaining insight. Many began to question the validity of the concept, either as an operational tool or as an agent of change in therapy (Rogers 1944; Rogers 1951; Coons 1957; Hobbs 1962). Hobbs went so far as to suggest that

insight is not a cause of change but a possible result of change. It is not a source of therapeutic gain but one among a number of possible consequences of gain. It may or may not occur in therapy; whether it does or not is inconsequential, since it reflects only the preferred modes of expression of the therapist or the client. It is not a change agent, it is a by-product of change. In a word, insight is an epiphenomenon. (Hobbs 1962)

Yalom (1980) states that insight is not always necessary for change: "Individuals go through therapy in a variety of ways; some profit from insight; some from other mechanisms of change; some may even obtain insight as a result of change, rather than the other way around." He points to the fact that

though there is considerable discussion and controversy about the type of insight most likely to produce change, the literature is relatively silent about how insights affect change. Many of the traditional explanations—for example, making the unconscious conscious, undermining resistances, the working through of the past, the reintegration of dissociated material, a corrective emotional experience—all elaborate upon the problem but still beg the question and fall short of providing a precise mechanism of the influence of insight.

For him, "insight effects change through (1) facilitating the development of the therapist-patient relationship, and (2) a series of maneuvers that help the therapist liberate the patient's stifled will: these maneuvers are designed to enable patients to realize that only they can change the world they have created. . . ." In Yalom's framework, a sense of personal mastery and will are closely interlinked. In fact, a sense of personal mastery inspirits the dormant will.

Insight, Will, and Change

The concept of will (volition) and determination has been ignored in modern psychotherapy. It has lost its position as a primary mental function and has become an epiphenomenon. It has been replaced by such concepts as (conscious or unconscious) motivation, need, and instincts. Will is explained away as "nothing but magical thinking . . . the stronger the will, the more likely it is to be labelled a 'counterphobic maneuver.' The unconscious is heir to the prestige of will. As one's fate was formally determined by will, now it is determined by the repressed in the mental life" (Wheelis 1956). It is obvious, however, that sustained effort is a function of will and determination. Those who are deficient in will find it extremely difficult to bring about certain changes in their lives, while those who possess will and determination are able to do so (Rank 1945).* Therefore, therapists frequently bemoan the fact that certain clients lack determination (or long-term motivation) and the therapist can do very little to help them bring about any change in their lives. Yet therapists shy away from using the concept of will or determination.

This author believes, and clinical experience confirms, that neither intellectual nor emotional insight, by themselves, is sufficient to bring about change in a client's life. Generally, change in psychotherapy appears to result from a four-step process: gaining insight into oneself; expressing indignation or protest about what is discovered and/or the awareness that other behaviors may be more enjoyable and

---

*Rank (1945) first introduced the concept of will in modern psychotherapy; unfortunately, it has been ignored by subsequent writers.

less conflicting; forming the will and/or determination to change; and taking action in the attempt to change.* Frequently, some of these steps may be condensed into one or two operations; that is, a client may not view himself as taking each step separately.

Will or determination does not imply a kind of New Year's resolution, nor is it related to teeth-gritting resolve. The concept of will or determination is a broad one. As Yalom (1980) states it,

. . . The meaning and roots of "willing" lead us into the area of the deepest unconscious concerns. But even unconscious willing does not occur without determination and commitment. Effortless change is not possible; the patient must transport himself . . . to therapy, must pay money . . . experience conflict and the anxiety that inevitably accompany the work of therapy. In short, the therapy vehicle has no slick, noiseless automatic transmission; effort is required, and will is the "trigger of effort."

Although generally we conceive of will and/or determination more or less as conscious phenomena, Yalom (1980) maintains that

by and large patients do not change in therapy as a result of an act of conscious will. In fact, what is so often perplexing to the therapist . . . is that changes occur at a subterranean level, far out of the ken of either the therapist or the patient.

Is subterranean, "nonvolitional" change an act of will? It is precisely this question, this connection between willful acts and the unconsciously based changes that has created so much difficulty for psychologists who have tried to fashion a sufficient, workable definition of will. . . .

Farber (1965) holds that will has two realms which are somewhat distinct from each other, and each realm requires a different approach. The first realm of will, which may be said to be unconscious, is not experienced consciously during an act, and its meaning must be inferred after the event. Farber suggests that many important choices are not experienced as conscious choices at the time they are made. Only after the fact can one deduce that one has made a choice. In this realm, one will can be thought of as a subterranean life current that has direction but not distinct objects or goals.

The second realm of will is experienced during the event and has a conscious component. Here, the will presses toward a particular objective (unlike the first realm, in which will is basically propelled) and is utilitarian in character: "I do this to get that." The goal of the will

---

*Wheelis (1956) presents a similar scheme of change in psychotherapy; conflict → insight → will → action → character change.

is known from the beginning; for example, "I go to college to obtain a diploma."

The two realms of will must be approached differently in therapy. The conscious realm is approached through exhortations and appeals to willpower, effort, and determination. The unconscious realm is impervious to these enjoinders and must be approached obliquely. A serious problem occurs when one applies exhortative techniques to unconscious activities (Yalom 1980).

The subterranean level of will—what Farber refers to as the "first realm of will"—has to be approached indirectly. Yalom (1980) states that

therapists cannot create will or commitment . . . but they can influence the factors that influence willing. No one has a congenital absence of will. . . . Will is blocked by obstacles in the part of a child's development; later these obstacles are internalized, and the individual is unable to act even though no objective factors are blocking him or her. The therapist's task is to help remove those obstacles. Once that is done, the individual will naturally develop. . . . Thus, the therapist's task is not to create will but to disencumber it.

. . . The therapists must first help the patient become aware of the inevitability and the omnipresence of decision. The therapist helps the patient "frame" or gain perspective upon a particular decision, and then assists in laying bare the implications [the "meaning"] of that decision. Finally through the leverage of insight the therapist attempts to awaken the dormant will.

A twenty-six-year old, single unemployed male came to therapy because he saw no purpose in doing anything. He lived with his mother. His daily routine was to get up in the morning, drink coffee, look at the newspaper, have lunch, and take an afternoon nap. In the early evening he would go to a bar for a drink or two. He patronized two or three bars in particular. He would sit at the bar and start conversations with other customers. He would listen to them attentively and ask questions. When others would ask him for his opinions about their personal troubles, he would give a succinct summary of their conflicts and troubles and his opinion of why they might be having difficulty in resolving their conflicts. People were grateful to him; frequently they would tell him, "You must have your act together or you couldn't be so insightful about my problems." When the therapist asked if he could apply the same advice in his own life, he said, "I have insight into myself, just as I have insight into others; but I can't change." When asked why he couldn't change, he said, "I have no will to change."

The therapist then asked, "Looking back on your life, when do you think you lost the will to change?" It was difficult for him to remember, offhand, any incident or event. Gradually, during subsequent sessions, he began to recall various incidents and events which had led him to abandon his will to act. During his preadolescent and adolescent years, he had begun to feel that his actions did not bring the approbation, the rewards, or the direction in his life that he desired. His parents were too involved in fighting with each other to pay much attention to him. His sister, one year his senior, ran away from home after some incestuous episodes. Gradually, he withdrew, played sadistically with pet animals, and let himself drift listlessly through life.

Change in psychotherapy requires four steps—insight, the attainment of the expression of indignation or protest about what is discovered, the will to change, and the action taken to create change.* If any of these steps are missing from a client's life, or if he is not willing to take all the steps, the possibility of change diminishes.

It should be noted that each of these steps is relatively independent; insight does not necessarily lead to indignation or protest about what is discovered, and indignaton or protest does not necessarily lead to the determination to change. However, will or determination does frequently lead one to take action in an attempt to change. A client may take any one of these steps and not the other ones. Unless he takes all four steps, either consciously or unconsciously, behavioral change is not likely.

The literature of psychotherapy, holds that only emotional insight brings change; emotions and/or affects become attached to the cognitive process of insight, which then leads to change. Psychoanalytic literature, in particular, presents change through insight as a two-step process. Insight introduces a dynamic shift in psychic balance of forces. After the development of insight, during the process of working through conflicts, the unconscious affects and emotions become attached to the cognitive insight; this welding of the two brings change (Freud 1914). If, after the development of insight, the process of working through the conflicts* is not initiated, then the possibility of change is slim. Our discussion suggests that even emotional insight, whether before or after the working-through process, does not necessarily lead to change unless it is mediated by the mechanism of indignation and protest and further converted through will into change.

---

*Wheelis (1950) and Yalom (1980) assert that there is no personality change without action. Wheelis states, "A real change occuring in the absence of action is a practical and theoretical impossibility."

*Fine (1971) states that "by working through is meant the persistent investigation of conflicts until they are resolved. The emphasis is on time on the one hand and

Emotional insight, by itself, can provide catharsis. This may bring a certain relief but not necessarily change.

The fact that people change without first developing insight is by now well substantiated (Rogers 1944; Hobbs 1962; Roback 1974). It is also well established that insight may develop after behavioral change (Cautela 1965). In short, insight is not necessary for behavioral change.

How does insight come about? Generally, it seems to emerge through three processes. First, when a client talks and expresses himself relatively freely, he may encounter in himself many hitherto unknown or unfamiliar feelings, attitudes, and values. He may be vaguely aware of some of them, while he may be totally unaware of others. With the progression of therapy, he may piece together or make sense of many previously isolated bits of feelings and behavior. This may bring about a new awareness of certain problems or conflicts.

The second avenue for achieving insight is through behavioral change or through a change in the client's self-perception. Many authors believe that after a client's behavior changes he begins to perceive himself differently. This shift in perspective gives him insight. Thus, insight is not a cause but a result of change (Rogers 1944; Hobbs 1962; Cautela 1965). The third avenue through which insight is achieved is via the interpretations which the therapist gives to the client during the course of therapy. This brings us to the issue of interpretations. What is an interpretation, and how should it be given? How does one know whether the interpretation is correct or incorrect? Is interpretation necessary for successful therapy?

The Concept of Interpretation

Most therapists, particularly those of psychoanalytic orientation, believe that interpretation of the client's behavior is the most important tool for creating insight and change. The existing literature maintains and most practicing therapists believe that what a therapist interprets during the course of therapy is self-evident. Yet, like many other concepts in psychotherapy and psychoanalysis, the concept of interpretation remains nebulous. It is difficult to say what the concept

---

on thoroughness on the other. . . . Working through is the opposite of the naive image that one or two interpretations are going to 'explode the neurosis.'"

means and what a therapist interprets. A series of factors contribute to the vagueness of the concept.

First, schools of therapy either totally accept or reject the concept of interpretation as a vehicle of change in psychotherapy; consequently it is difficult to assess its place and importance in the therapeutic process. Levy (1963) notes the range of opinion:

At one extreme we find Rogers, who has been constant [1942, 1951, 1961] in his proscriptions against the use of interpretation in psychotherapy and in his warnings that "interpretations are usually threatening and tend to slow rather than speed the progress of therapy" [1961], while at the other end we find, among others, Fenichel [1945], Fromm-Reichman [1950] and Rosen [1953], for whom interpretations represent one of the nodal points of the entire psychotherapeutic process. Precisely what role interpretation does or should play in psychotherapy is a difficult question to answer because of the sparsity of research evaluating the effectiveness of specific therapeutic procedures.

The second reason for the ambiguity is a semantic one. The term *interpretation* has been used synonymously and interchangeably with many other terms which may or may not carry the same meanings for different people. In his earlier writings, Freud (1907) frequently used the words *interpretation* and *explanation* interchangeably. In his later writings, however, he differentiates between interpretation and construction:

"Interpretation" applies to something that one does to some single element of the material, such as an association or a parapraxis. But it is a "construction" when one lays before the subject of the analysis a piece of his early history that he has forgotten, in some such way as this: "Up to your nth year you regarded yourself as the sole and unlimited possessor of your mother; then came another baby and brought you grave disillusionment. Your mother left you for some time, and even after her reappearance she was never again devoted to you exclusively. Your feelings toward your mother became ambivalent, your father gained a new importance for you," . . . and so on. (Freud 1937)

Frequently, other psychoanalytic writers also use the terms *interpretation* and *explanation* interchangeably (Healy et al. 1930; Lowenstein 1963; Glover 1968). Some writers use the term *intervention* instead of *interpretation*. They maintain that interpretation is only one of the many forms of intervention which a therapist uses during the course of his work. Therefore, the concept of interpretation should be treated as an aspect of intervention and should not be singled out for special study (Menninger and Holzman 1973).

The third reason for the term's nebulousness appears to be that authors have attempted to create, on an ad hoc and subjective basis, various categories of interpretation to explain and justify what they do in therapy. The result is that few authors agree with each other with regard to the categories of interpretation. For instance, Colby creates three categories of interpretation: (1) clarification interpretations— statements made by the therapist to crystallize the patient's thoughts and feelings around a particular subject, to focus his attention on something requiring further investigation and interpretation, or to sort out a theme from apparently diversified material; (2) comparison interpretations—statements in which the therapist places two (or more) sets of events, thoughts, or feelings side by side for comparison; and (3) wish-defense interpretations—statements made by the therapist which directly point to the wish-defense components of a neurotic conflict (Colby 1951).

Paul (1963) states that a therapist uses two kinds of interpretation—the causal interpretation and the noncausal interpretation. Causal interpretation deals with the reasons for the behavior; it accounts for the client's behavior by describing an antecedent emotional state. Noncausal interpretations pertain to what the behavior is, and include processes of reflecting the client's behavior, enumerating multiple instances of a certain kind of behavior, and connecting or correlating noncausally several instances of behavior.

In the same vein, classical psychoanalysis makes a distinction between four kinds of interpretations, depending upon the behavior being interpreted. These are (1) dynamic interpretations, dealing with the mental forces of the client; (2) genetic interpretations, dealing with the childhood history of the client; (3) structural interpretations, dealing with the mental structure of the client, namely, the id, ego, and the superego; and (4) transference interpretations, dealing with the (erotic) feelings of the client toward the therapist.

The fourth reason for the ambiguity of the term is the definition of *interpretation*. Some authors define it as only those statements (interventions) of the therapist which pertain to the cause and/or meaning of the client's behavior; while others define it loosely, subsuming under interpretation many other aspects of the behavior, namely, clarification, confrontation, naming, description, restructuring, motivation, and so forth. For instance, Rausch et al. (1956) define interpretation as "any behavior on the part of the therapist that is an expression of his view of the patient's emotions and motivations—either wholly or in part—[and which] is considered an interpretation." Levy (1963) states that

when we engage in psychological interpretation we are, in effect, saying: "The way in which we have been looking at this situation has led us to a dead end. Let's see if there isn't some other way of looking at this thing." And this is precisely what the psychological interpretation of content consists of: a redefining or restructuring of the situation through the presentation of an alternate description of some behavioral datum.

More specifically, interpretation occurs when a new or different frame of reference, or language, is brought to bear upon some problem or event. . . . Psychological interpretation consists of bringing into play in a particular situation a new frame of reference, a new language system, a new theory.

Specificity of the Definition of Interpretation

While, on the one hand, a great deal of surplus meaning and nebulousness surrounds the concept of interpretation, at the same time many authors have tried to give specific meaning and specific definition to the term *interpretation*. Some representative examples of such a definition are presented below.

Chessick (1974) declares that "to interpret is to make an unconscious psychic event conscious, to give it meaning and causality." Greenson (1967) states: "To interpret means to make an unconscious phenomenon conscious. More precisely, it means to make conscious the unconscious meaning, source, history, mode or cause of a given psychic event. . . . By interpreting we go beyond what is really observed and we assign meaning and causality to a psychological phenomenon." Wolberg (1977) says that in making interpretations, "the more unconscious elements of the psyche are brought to the patient's awareness. . . . Interpretation consists of seeing beyond the facade of manifest thinking, feelings, and behavior into less obvious meaning and motivations."

Ruesch's definition (1961) is as follows: "To interpret means to connect the past with the present, the inside experience with the outside effect, the self with the group. Such connections produce a feeling of relief in the patient, things begin to make sense, growth is experienced, and the patient endows the therapist with leverage because he made such an experience possible."

Slater (1956) asks, "What is an interpretation? It is a suggestion by the analyst to the patient as the possible meaning of what the patient says and does. . . . When he [the therapist] tries to convey his understanding, or some part of it, to the patient, he is making an interpretation." Meltzoff and Kornreich (1970) declare that "interpretations are designed forcibly to bring to the patient's conscious awareness the causal relations between aspects of this current behavior, attitudes and feelings and their antecedent motivations."

Colby (1963) states,

The more general [and hence vague] definition of an interpretation describes it as a statement which connects a referent known and observable to the patient with another reference unknown and/or only partially known to the patient. So that we may be clear about what the definition excludes as well as includes, I would propose a more restricted definition in which an interpretation is defined according to the nature of the connective between the observable and unobservable, namely a causal link. From this standpoint, interpretation statements intend to show a patient causal correlation.

In summarizing his book on psychoanalytic clinical interpretation, Paul maintains that "a clinical interpretation is defined as a statement or set of related statements to the patient which point to and name, even though vaguely, and sometimes loosely causally accounts for, his present operative, most prepotent unrecognized behavior or the most prepotent unrecognized or warded off elements in the external world" (1963).

Fenichel (1946) says:

Knowing that the utterances of the patient are really allusions to other things, the psychoanalyst tries to deduce what lies behind the allusions and imparts this information to the patient. When there is a minimum of distance between allusion and what is alluded to, the analyst gives the patient words to express feelings just rising to the surface and thereby facilitates their becoming conscious.

This procedure of deducing what the patient actually means and telling it to him is called interpretation. Since interpretation means helping something unconscious to become conscious by naming it at the moment it is striving to break through, effective interpretations can be given only at one specific point, namely, where the patient's immediate interest is momentarily concerned.

For Bibring (1954),

interpretation . . . refers exclusively to unconscious material: To the unconscious defensive operations [motives and mechanisms of defense], to the unconscious, warded-off instinctual tendencies, to the hidden meanings of the patient's behavior patterns to their unconscious interconnections, etc. . . . In contrast to clarification, interpretation by its very nature transgresses the clinical data, the phenomenological-descriptive level. . . .

These definitions clearly suggest that a therapist interprets the cause, the meaning, or the motivation of the client's behavior. As some of the definitions state, and as most of them clearly imply, the reasons for the client's behavior are lodged in the preconscious or unconscious mind, and therefore do not fully exist within his awareness. For this reason, a client's behavior must be interpreted to him. A client, on his own, would not be able to arrive at the meaning of his behavior.

For these authors, an interpretation is a statement that connects a referent which is known and observable to the patient with another referent which is unknown or partially known to the patient. It is an inference which provides a causal link between the observable and unobservable. While making an interpretation, "if only manifest elements are connected, it is the inter-connection itself [rather than the elements] of which the patient is deemed to be unconscious" (Garduk and Haggard 1972). Therefore, an interpretation deals with unconscious rather than manifest material; it seeks to explain rather than describe the client's behavior; it consists of inferences, probabilities, and alternate hypotheses rather than observations and facts (Weiner 1975).*

---

*For numerous reasons, the existing empirical studies do not support or refute these assumptions about interpretation. The comprehensive study by Garduk and Haggard (1972) does not easily lend itself to clear conclusions. First, the study attempts to answer too many questions; second, there was low inter-rater reliability; third, the number of judges was too small; fourth, the N was too small. In their own words, "Partly because of the small N's, most of these did not yield statistically significant results; there were 10 nonchance findings in 56 tests. Furthermore, only four of these 10 significant findings were based on reliable ratings. Thus our statistical evidence did not point to any great effectiveness of interpretations in the individual case." They add further, "Our summary comments on separate cases must be tempered by the lack of reliability of much of our evidence. Nevertheless, it seems reasonably clear that interpretations tend to be consistently effective elicitors of a few patients' reactions, but their effectiveness in relation to other reactions depends to some extent on the particular case under consideration."

Similarly, two other empirical studies on interpretation by Adams et al. (1962) and Noblin et al. (1963) are difficult to evaluate. First, they are analogue studies; second, their conception or definition of interpretation is not the same as that of a practicing therapist; third, both the conditions under which interpretations are presented are artificial and contrived. In their own words, "It is probably not wise to generalize from the present rather artificial situation to the psychotherapeutic situation" (Adams et al. 1962).

For these writers, all of the therapist's statements which do not allude to the reason or of the client's behavior are not to be considered part of the category of interpretation. They are assigned to other categories of statements, such as those of clarification, information gathering, interrogative statements, confrontation, and so forth.

Many writers and practitioners maintain that interpretation is "seldom evaluative" (Schonbar 1965) and that it is essentially a deduction of "facts" from the client's life. A therapist casts the deductions into a technical or semitechnical form, called "interpretation," and presents it to the client. Therefore, interpretations do not introduce any value judgment, predetermined causality, or meaning into the client's behavior (Fenichel 1941; Greenson 1967; Menninger and Holzman 1973).

The assumption that an interpretation is "value free" is a naive one. It presupposes a value-free interaction between the therapist and client; it assumes that the theories and techniques of psychotherapy upon which the therapist's interpretations are based have no valuative assumption about the causality of human behavior; and finally, it assumes that the theory and techniques of psychotherapy which the therapist uses to arrive at an interpretation are scientifically valid, that is, that they have been proven by empirical facts and are beyond the therapist's personal bias and moral and ethical predilections.

An interpretation is by no means a neutral or value-free construction of the data presented by the client. It is steeped in the valuative assumptions of the theory of therapy, and it is bound up with the therapist's own morality and values system. This point is rather vividly demonstrated in cases where therapists of different theoretical orientations ascribe different causality, meaning, and motivation to the same or similar behavior manifested by the client.* The question of why clients improve at approximately the same rate, even when they are offered different interpretations of similar behavior, is discussed by Hobbs (1962), Frank (1974), and Garfield (1980).

Principles of Interpretation

For a therapist to make an interpretation—to ascribe causality, meaning, and/or motivation to the client's behavior—much data and information about the client's life is required. To obtain such data, a

---

*For example, see case studies and their interpretations reported by Greenson (1967) and Bugental (1965). See also Gatch and Temerlin (1965).

therapist will have to do a considerable amount of preliminary work; he must clarify the client's feelings and conflicts, learn about the client's defensive system, explore the various issues which he wants to interpret, become familiar with the client's modus operandi, and so forth. Therapists who follow psychoanalytic theory believe that the cause and meaning of the client's behavior are buried in his unconscious. Before a therapist can make an interpretation, he will have to uncover many of the hidden forces to the client's attention. Piecing together diverse behaviors requires considerable patience and work, which may then be presented to the client in the form of an interpretation.

Any interpretation of behavior should be convincing to the client in order to bring about insight and, ultimately, change. The therapist must convince the client of his interpretations by backing them up with supportive evidence from the client's life. An interpretation without supporting evidence will not only be unconvincing to him, but it will do little to elucidate the client's conflicts. Slater (1956) uses the term *premature interpretation* to refer to "those interpretations given too early in the therapeutic work; the patient cannot make constructive use of them at that time. Such interpretations are usually the result of the analyst's failure to be clear as to what he is tackling." Furthermore, a premature interpretation forecloses the exploration of the conflicts in question, since the therapist has already provided the causation, meaning, and/or motivation of the client's behavior. Therefore, there is little left for the client to elaborate upon or to explore. A therapist should not make an interpretation too quickly, or too early in therapy.

For various reasons, however, many therapists (especially beginning therapists) are eager to make interpretations early in therapy, rather than clarify feelings and conflicts, gather information, provide support, reduce resistances, confront, and so on. They feel that an early interpretation of the client's behavior will demonstrate to him the therapist's acumen. Or they believe that an early interpretation is the true work of therapy. They may wish to test the strength of the client's ego by making an early interpretation. These motivations have little beneficial effect upon therapy; if anything, they produce an adverse effect.

With this background, we turn to general principles of interpretation that may help the beginning therapist. Many of these principles have been discussed in the literature and are supported by clinical evidence.

First, some form of emotional bond must develop between the therapist and the client before an interpretation can prove effective. As Alexander has stated (1961),

The only generalization which at the present state of this study I would venture to make is that the patient's emotional experiences in relationship to the therapist precede his cognitive insight. I find in this time sequence the possible answer for one of the most puzzling observations . . . that the same interpretations which have been repeatedly offered to the patient in the course of the treatment one day suddenly sink in and take effect.

In other words, interpretations given by the therapist before a strong rapport has developed with the participant are not likely to bring much change in a client's life (Garfield 1968; Menaker 1968).

Second, an interpretation given by a therapist should not attempt to delve too deeply. An interpretation is too deep "when a patient cannot recognize its correctness by experiencing the impulse in question" (Fenichel 1941). In other words, the greater the disparity between the therapist's view and the client's own awareness, the deeper the interpretation (Levy 1963). Or the less disparity there is between the therapist's formulations and the client's view and feelings, the less deep the interpretation will be.

Studies suggest that deep interpretations lead to and are followed by the highest level of resistance. Moderate interpretations, on the other hand, are followed by more exploration and fewer resistances. Superficial interpretations are followed by explorations, but by a moderate level of resistance (Speisman 1959; Browning 1966; Claiborn et al. 1981). Therapeutic movement thus seems to be associated with interpretations that are not too deep and yet, at the same time, go somewhat deeper than pure reflection. Additionally, when both the client's feelings and behavior are interpreted, the probability of the progressive movement of therapy becomes greater (Dittman 1952).

Third, an interpretation should be presented concretely. A therapist should use concrete material from the client's life, which has been presented during the course of therapy. In addition, a therapist should support his interpretations from material in the client's life. The language of the interpretation should also be concrete so that the client is able to relate the interpretation to the experiences in his life. Abstract or cliché-ridden language tends to remove the client from his concrete life struggles and affective states.

Fourth, an interpretation should be offered by the therapist as a hypothesis of behavior which is yet to be confirmed or refuted by the client. A therapist may preface his remarks or observations by saying, "Is it possible that . . ."; or "It appears to me that . . ."; or "In light of what you have said, wouldn't it look more like. . . ." Not much should be made of interpretations; they should be presented like any other observation or formulation.

Fifth, an interpretation is more effective if it is elicited from the client (Saul 1958). The client will view it as a self-discovery, become more ego-involved, and therefore will be more likely to change. This could be accomplished by a therapist in various ways. After presenting to the client data from his life (which the client has provided during the course of therapy), a therapist may ask, "Can you make something of this?" or "Does this make sense to you?"

Sixth, a therapist should avoid offering too many interpretations during a session. They seem to confound the client; they do not give him an opportunity to work through them and therefore are less likely to be assimilated by him. As Alexander and French (1946) state, "it is best to choose and time interpretations in such a way as to focus the patient's attention upon only one problem at a time. Until the patient has utilized the insight contained in one interpretation by finding a better solution for the conflict that has been reopened by it, it is better to keep his attention focused upon analyzing the resistance to it and not stir up quite new and unresolved problems."

Seventh, the interpretation of resistance should precede its content. In other words, if a client is negative or evasive (resistant) this should be interpreted before interpreting what the client is negative or evasive about (Fenichel 1941). Otherwise, a client is likely to ignore what the therapist has to say.

Confirmation and Disconfirmation of Interpretations

How does a therapist know that the interpretation he has made is correct? Several criteria, based upon clinical observations, have been offered in the literature. Generally, in testing an interpretation one looks for the emergence of, and the client's conscious recognition of, his subsequent behavior (Paul 1963). Subsequent behavior may include new memories on a particular topic or conflict, the client's ability to talk more freely about that topic, or an association that contains something similar or analogous to the subject matter being discussed (Freud 1939).

Other responses to the interpretation that confirm it, which may occur during the same session or in subsequent sessions, include a reduction of specific anxiety (Issacs 1939). Generally, the more specific the therapist's interpretation, the more it is likely to reduce the client's anxiety (Pope and Siegman 1962). If the client shows more clarity and less confusion in his feelings and thoughts after the interpretation, then it should be taken as a confirmatory response. Frequently, clients express surprise or a feeling of mastery through recognition of the interpretation's veracity. Such reactions may be expressed: "I never saw it that way before," "Yes, that fits," "Now it all makes sense," and so on. Sudden laughter is not an uncommon expression of surprise in some clients (Paul 1963).

What if a client objects to the interpretation made by the therapist? Is the interpretation then considered to be correct or incorrect? Generally, when a client argues with or rejects an interpretation, therapists assume that their interpretation is correct but that the client is resisting it,* or that the interpretation is correct but their timing may be wrong (Fenichel 1941; Fromm-Reichman 1950; Wolberg 1977). In his own good time, the client will see the interpretation as valid and correct.

In rejecting the criticism of a sympathetic critic of psychoanalysis, Freud (1937) declared, "He [the critic] said that in giving an interpretation to a patient we treat him upon the famous principle of 'Heads I win, tails you lose.' That is to say, if the patient agrees with us, then the interpretation is right; but if he contradicts us, that is only a sign of his resistance, which again shows that we are right." Later in the same article, he says:

A "No" from a person in analysis is no more unambiguous than a "Yes," and is indeed of even less value. In some rare cases it turns out to be the expression of a legitimate dissent. Far more frequently it expresses a resistance which may have been evoked by the subject matter of the construction that has been put forward but which may just as easily have arisen from some other factor in the complex analytic situation. Thus a patient's "No" is no evidence of the correctness of a construction, though it is perfectly compatible with it.

---

*On this point, Fine (1971) states, "Many analysts have been so impressed by the negativistic element in every patient's neurosis that they have set up a rule that an interpretation cannot be considered successful unless the patient disagrees with it. The rationale behind this statement is that if the interpretation is sufficiently important, it will run up against deep-seated anxiety that the patient cannot be expected to bring to the fore; hence, on the surface there is resistance and rejection."

Fromm-Reichman (1950) maintains that "if a patient gets angry or upset about an interpretation, this is usually indicative of its being correct or at least in the immediate neighborhood of correctness."

Contrary to what is presented above, this author proposes the following guidelines for a beginning therapist to check the validity of his interpretations. First, if a client objects or does not agree with the therapist's interpretations, the interpretation is incorrect either in content or in timing. The prevalent belief that the client's objection is only a resistance to the therapist's interpretation is logically untenable. If a client objects, the therapist must either withdraw his interpretation, reexamine it, or consider the possibility that it is incorrect.

Second, when an interpretation arouses more resistance or hostility in the client, it is again incorrect either in its content or in its timing. Third, when a client becomes more confused rather than more clear in his comprehension of his troubles and conflicts, the interpretation is incorrect. An interpretation should clarify things for the client rather than make them more confused. Finally, when an interpretation revives the so-called symptoms, it is incorrect.

Does this mean that clients accept correct interpretations without anxiety or protest? Obviously not. An interpretation generally conveys something different or new to the client about his behavior. To accept it, a client has to give up his old beliefs or change his viewpoint. Therefore, it tends to generate a certain degree of discomfort or even anxiety in the client (Weiner 1975). However, the discomfort or anxiety produced by a correct interpretation is qualitatively different from the one generated by an incorrect interpretation. It is not tied to the client's resistance, hostility, or negativism toward the therapist; rather, it is more of a puzzling, bewildering kind of searching in which the client attempts to assimilate or accommodate the new information.

Are Interpretations Necessary for Successful Therapy?

To an experienced therapist it is obvious that interpretations are not necessary for successful therapy, since many clients, especially the seriously disturbed ones, improve without interpretations from the therapist. However, the literature frequently states that with less-disturbed clients, who use repression and other nonprimitive defense mechanisms, interpretations are necessary to bring out the unconscious motivations of the client's behavior. Without such interpretations, therapy would not be successful. This theory implies that in treating neurotic clients a therapist begins to deal more with the unconscious material as therapy unfolds. Since the meaning of the client's behavior is lodged in his unconscious, a therapist has to make more interpretations to be successful.

Contrary to the general belief that a therapist deals more with the unconscious or preconscious as therapy proceeds, studies suggest that the "therapist inreases the percentage for the intervention that is directly pertinent at the manifest level . . . [and] therapists do not significantly increase their total depth interpretation" (Slansky et al. 1966). Rogers's study (1944) seems to support the theory that the therapist deals primarily with conscious material during the course of therapy.

In addition, the general belief that with interpretations a deeper level of material will emerge does not seem to be substantiated. Slansky et al. (1966) declare: "No one kind of therapist intervention seems associated with patients' shift in awareness from unconscious to conscious level. However, in our data, immediate shifts in level of meaning were such rare occurrences that we would be unjustified to draw any generalizations at all in relation to them."*

What seems to happen in therapy is that as the therapist clarifies the client's confusions, provides him with support and sympathy, and confronts him with some of his behaviors, the hidden (the unconscious or preconscious) material becomes more available to the client. In other words, by discussing, exploring, and clarifying the reasons for his behavior, the client begins to become more aware of the hitherto hidden material. A therapist then deals with those feelings, attitudes, and conflicts that have begun to emerge in the client's consciousness. A therapist may or may not deal with the cause of the client's behavior.

Does this mean that a therapist does not have to, or should not, make interpretations or determine the causality, meaning, and motivation of the client's behavior? Certainly not. In many situations a client is either unable or unwilling to interpret his own behavior, in spite of the available data. Under such conditions, it is the therapist's task to do so.

It is true that a therapist cannot help but interpret the client's

---

*Colby's study (1961a) suggests that clients associate more freely after a therapist has made a "causal-correlative" statement. Yet other kinds of statements seem to produce a similar effect as the causal-correlative statements (Colby 1961b).

behavior within the framework of the values and the morality of his theory of therapy. However, a therapist must try to minimize these values in the interpretation itself. This can best be achieved by accumulating as much supportive evidence as possible for an interpretation of the client's life.

Confrontation

The concept of confrontation has gained considerable popularity in the recent literature of psychotherapy. The term *confrontation* evokes the image of clash, challenge, or antagonism between two adversaries. One may wonder, under what circumstances and for what reason do the therapist and the client, who are supposed to be allies, confront each other? Various authors have delineated the reasons and circumstances that lead to the therapist's confrontation with the client and what the therapist expects to achieve.

Webster's Dictionary defines *Confront* in this way: "to face, especially in challenge; oppose; to cause to meet; bring face to face." In psychotherapy, the term *confrontation* is generally used in the last sense. The question is, What does a therapist bring a client face to face with?

Weisman (1973) states that "perforce, confrontation is an effort to penetrate a screen of denial, aversion, or deception." He calls it "the tactics of undenial" and says that "when we try to expose an area of denial, to challenge a belief, or to influence the direction of behavior, we confront."

Levin (1973) declares:

The process of confrontation is essentially communicative. A therapist might point out to a patient something he does not know about himself, something he knows only vaguely, or something he knows but thinks others don't know. He might point out aspects of reality that are being denied. . . . But when we refer to these communications as confrontations, we imply not only that the patient is being made aware of certain aspects of his neurosis that require exploration and analysis; we also imply that pressure is being exerted on the patient to give up certain neurotic patterns of behavior.

A confrontation, then, "is a forceful way to intervene. When a therapist intervenes he has in mind getting the patient's attention, producing a reaction in him, and demanding that he change. In confrontation, the therapist presents a unilateral view of what he considers to be reality" (Adler and Myerson 1973).

In what ways is interpretation different from confrontation? Stocking (1973) maintains that there are three basic differences between interpretation and confrontation. First, "the therapist who interprets shares a hypothesis with his patient. . . . The therapist who confronts brings the patient face to face with 'a reality.' He presents a view he accepts as real or factual. . . ." Second, "interpretation is based on a body of association or evidence arising from the patient's activity and initiative at times when he has been successful, either alone or with his therapist, in overcoming his inner resistances. . . . Confrontation is used when the therapist and patient have not succeeded in diminishing the patient's resistance. . . . The therapist assumes the therapeutic initiative and bypasses the patient's inner resistances to bring him in touch with an underlying reality of his functioning."

Third, "the therapist who interprets presents the patient with a hypothesis. The validation of the hypothesis is obtained through continuing joint work by therapist and patient. . . . In confrontation . . . the therapist presents a view of the patient's world or function for which he feels he already has sufficient validation. At the point when a confrontation is initiated, validation of the reality considered will seem unilateral, the therapist's alone" (Stocking 1973).

Anderson (1968) states that confrontation may be distinguished from interpretation in that confrontation stems primarily from the therapist himself; it is an expression of his own counter viewpoint rather than simply an explanation or elucidation based on one of the client's views. Confrontation focuses on present feelings and behavior; whereas an interpretation is usually directed toward the past."

Devereux (1951) believes that

confrontation, which differs appreciably from interpretation, consists essentially in a rewording of the patient's own statements, especially in the form of "calling a spade a spade." Nothing is added to the patient's statements, nor is anything subtracted therefrom, with the exception of the actual wording, which is viewed as an attempt to gloss over the obvious. . . .

Perhaps the most fundamental difference between a confrontation and an interpretation is the fact that the former is usually a starting point for the bringing up of new problems or associations, whereas the latter is, in a way, a means of bringing to a head and resolving some hitherto unsolvable problems. A further difference is that in confrontation the analyst utilizes primarily his secondary thought process. Consequently, confrontation is an analytic device only in so far as it leads to the production, or to the mulling over, of some new material, which is, eventually interpreted in terms of the logic of the unconscious.

Some researchers have divided confrontation into two categories: confrontation based on patients' strengths and resources, and "confrontation based on patients' weaknesses or pathology" (Anderson 1968; Mitchell and Berenson 1970). These authors, along with others, state that therapists who advocate an approach using empathy, positive regard, genuineness, concreteness, and self-disclosure confront the client more directly with their own resources. Therapists who do not use this positive approach confront their clients more often with their limitations (Anderson 1968; Berenson, Mitchell, and Moravec 1968; Mitchell and Berenson 1970; Mitchell and Hall 1971). In terms of frequency, the former type of therapist confronts his clients more frequently than the latter (Anderson 1968; Berenson, Mitchell, and Laney 1968).

At first glance, these studies appear promising for therapeutic technique, yet on a closer look one has to agree with Bordin (1974), who believes that "this research seems highly superficial since it is confined to a single interview [generally, the initial interview] and, often, to very contrived situations." While Bordin's criticisms seem to be correct from a philosophical viewpoint these studies do warrant some attention, simply because so many therapists habitually confront a client with his limitations and liabilities. Whenever a therapeutic situation permits, the therapist should confront the client with his strengths and assets, an approach that would help balance the client's limitations and his strengths.*

Juxtaposing the Contradictions

This author prefers to regard the issue of confrontation somewhat differently than the way it is presented in the literature. The concept of contradiction, or rather the juxtaposition of contradictions in the client, seems a far more useful concept for psychotherapeutic purposes.

---

*Studies show that of the four categories of therapists' interventions (reflection, interpretation, interrogation, and confrontation), confrontation generates the highest amplitude of autonomic response (GSR), both in the therapist and the client, with interpretation creating the next highest. Further, the frequency with which a therapist confronts a client is much lower as compared to the frequency of interpretation, 4 percent versus 23 percent (McCarron and Appel 1971).

In juxtaposing contradictions, the therapist offers the two opposing aspects of the client's behavior or feelings for his observation and consideration, thereby helping the client confront himself. The client and the therapist are not placed in an adversary relationship; the therapist does not have to force the client to pay attention to anything. In a confrontation, however, a therapist advances his own views, unilaterally, in opposition to the client's view. The therapist has to be forceful to prevail over the client.

Juxtaposing the contradictions has many advantages. First, as discussed above, the concept of confrontation carries with it the quality of challenge. Juxtaposing the contradictions, however, simply presents to the client, without making any assumptions, the opposing forces that are operating in his life.

Second, the contradictions which the client may be facing or avoiding could be either external or internal, and the concept of juxtaposed contradictions can be used to delineate both the internal and external conditions. In the psychotherapy literature, the term *conflict* refers to the internal contradictions, while the term *situational conflict* (or *reality conflict*) refers to external ones. The concept of contradiction is broader and can be applid to both conditions.

Third, the concept of juxtaposed contradictions can be presented quite early in therapy without threatening the client. This may not be true of a confrontation.

Fourth, the concept of contradiction (and its resolution) suggests a hierarchy of levels or stages. If and when one set of contradictions is resolved, a different set of contradictions emerges which the client will need to resolve at a different level or stage of his development. Thus, a client continuously remains an active agent in resolving the contradictions in his life as they emerge, one at a time.

Generally a client presents five types of contradictions in therapy:

1. Contradictions between ideology and practice, or between the client's statements and his actions. Example: "You say you are generous, yet when you have to give something to someone you always manage to find excuses."

2. Contradictions between opposing sets of feelings and emotions. Example: "You have two sets of feelings toward your girlfriend; you want to be with her, yet when you are with her you feel like leaving as soon as possible."

3. Contradictions between actions of the client. Example: "You have put away money to buy a house; yet you cannot stop squandering it when you go to a bar."

4. Contradictions of perception. Example: "Sometimes you perceive your spouse as affectionate and friendly, while at other times you perceive her as angry and hostile, although she generally behaves much the same on any occasion."

5. Contradictions between inner and outer conditions. Example: "You believe you have power or control over others; yet when you exercise your power, nothing happens."

Juxtaposing the client's contradictions serves many useful purposes during the course of therapy. First, it brings together for the client many disparate and/or unrelated aspects of his behavior. For instance, a client may not have correlated his statements about certain things or people and his behavior toward them. In his perceptions they may seem unrelated to each other. Juxtaposing the disparate aspects of his life helps to bring them together. Second, juxtaposing the contradictions brings into focus conflicting forces of which the client may not be aware. Third, it begins to clarify the client's role in the conflicts since contradictions originate in him, at least to some extent. Finally, the concept provides the therapist, within limits, with a certain degree of freedom. He can juxtapose more than one set of contradictions during a single session; he can do so in any aspect of the client's life which both or either of them choose to discuss during a session; and he can do so without the feeling that he may be threatening, opposing, or forcing the client.

How does the therapist juxtapose the contradictions for the client? This could be done in a straightforward manner by simply presenting the contradictions, as he sees them. Nothing much should be made of them other than offering them to the client for his consideration.

Another method (not necessarily accomplished in the same session) is for the therapist to ask the client if such contradictions create any difficulty or conflict in his life, and if so, in what ways? The therapist could ask the client if he wishes to resolve the contradictions which may be generating difficulties for him. If the client seems inclined to do so, then the issue of how he wishes to resolve them could be raised.

There are various ways in which the client may choose to resolve a single contradiction. He may wish to eschew one of the two aspects of the contradiction, or he may wish to take parts from each aspect of the contradiction and thus emerge with a new synthesis. For example, a married client who is having an extramarital affair may state that he wishes to preserve the marriage. Here the two aspects of the contradiction are the extramarital affair and the desire to preserve the marriage. The client may resolve it by (1) getting a divorce and assuming the status of a bachelor where affairs are acceptable; (2) giving up the affair; or (3) preserving the marriage but developing some form of friendly relationship with the person with whom he was having the extramarital affair, thereby synthesizing the contradiction.

It should be made clear to the client that resolving one contradiction at the present stage of his life (or therapy) may bring him to different kinds of contradictions. He may have to resolve in much the same manner as he did the previous one in order to move on with his life. Thus, the process is ongoing.

This technique is based upon the assumption that clients would like to resolve the contradictions in their lives, since the resolutions may provide them with some harmony which may not be otherwise available. Yet it is possible that some client may choose to live within the forces of a contradiction, and take the consequences. In such a circumstance, there is little a therapist can do for the client except to point out to him that since he has chosen to live with the contradiction and not resolve it he should not complain about it.

There are many occasions and situations when it is more useful for a therapist to confront a client. The life of a seriously disturbed client is full of contradictions at various levels. In fact, it is such contradictions that make him disturbed. To resolve his contradictions, a client is likely to distort reality. With such a client, juxtaposing the contradictions has little utility; the therapist frequently must forcefully present a realistic view of the situation. In fact, for such a client the therapist is a representative of reality, which frequently has to be imposed upon the client.

Another group of clients with whom the therapist has to use confrontation are those who have a propensity to ignore or play down the demands of social reality.

A twenty-eight-year-old Caucasian bachelor came to therapy because he was having trouble in getting along with people and in developing and maintaining any friendship, male or female. He had a college degree and was employed in a professional position. Since his college days he had been politically active, and he believed that the income tax structure of the society

was unjust because it benefited the rich and exploited the poor. He regis-
tered his protest by not paying his income tax for many years. One day, as
he walked into the therapist's office, he saw income-tax forms on the
therapist's desk and said that he wished to discuss the issue of income tax. It
was then that he expounded his viewpoint on the tax system. In general, the
therapist agreed with him but said that the client was also a beneficiary of
the system and was aspiring to become more so. Hence, it behooved the
client to pay his taxes. If he were one of the exploited poor his protest would
have some merit; but as it was, he was simply trying not to pay taxes in the
name of egalitarianism. The client didn't agree, but said that he would
think about it.

Summary

The concept of insight is deeply ingrained in the conceptual structure of psychotherapy. Most therapists believe that if a client develops insight he will change his feelings, reactions, and behavior. Therefore, therapists try to elicit insight from clients during the course of therapy. As a general rule, however, clients do not change simply by developing insight. A few other factors have to be present: the expression of indignation or protest about what is discovered, the will to change, and the decision to act in the attempt to change one's behavior.

Some therapists believe that insight can be imparted to the client through interpretations. Interpretation has been defined in various ways in the literature, and these definitions involve a great variety of interventions on the part of the therapist. Strictly speaking, an interpretation is intervention by the therapist which ascribes causality, meaning, and/or motivation to the client's behavior, but to attribute them, a therapist must first know a good deal about the client.

Another form of intervention is called "confrontation." This is a forceful way of bringing the client's behavior to his attention. In unilaterally presenting the client with his reality—the essence of the confrontational mode—the therapist intends to expose an area or a tactic of the client's denial.

This author prefers to use another technique, the juxtaposition of contradictions. Here, the therapist simply presents to the client, for his observation and examination, the various forms of contradictions in his life. Next, the therapist may ask the client if he wishes to resolve some of these contradictions. This method possesses advantages that the use of confrontation does not have.

References

Adams, H. E., J. R. Butler, and C. D. Noblin. 1962. Effects of psychoanalytically derived interpretations: A verbal conditioning paradigm. *Psychological Reports* 10:691–94.

Adler, G., and P. G. Myerson, eds. 1973. *Confrontation in psychotherapy.* New York: Science House, 11–13.

Alexander, F. 1961. Research in experimental psychiatry. In H. W. Brosin, ed., *Lectures on experimental psychiatry.* Pittsburgh: University of Pittsburgh Press.

Alexander, F., and T. French. 1946. *Psychoanalytic therapy.* New York: Ronald Press, 91.

Anderson, S. 1968. Effects of confrontation by high and low functioning therapists. *Journal of Counseling Psychology* 15:411–16.

Appelbaum, S. 1976. The dangerous edge of insight. *Psychotherapy: Theory, Research and Practice* 13:202–6.

Baranger, M., and W. Baranger. 1966. Insight in the analytic situation. In R. E. Litman, ed., *Psychoanalysis in America*, 56–72. New York: International University Press.

Barnett, J. 1978. Insight and therapeutic change. *Contemporary Psychoanalysis* 14:534–44.

Berenson, B., K. Mitchell, and R. Laney. 1968. Level of therapist functioning, type of confrontation and type of patient. *Journal of Clinical Psychology* 24:111–13.

Berenson, B., K. Mitchell, and J. Moravec. 1968. Level of therapist functioning, patient depth of self exploration, and type of confrontation. *Journal of Counseling Psychology* 15:136–39.

Bibring, I. 1954. Psychoanalysis and dynamic therapies. *Journal of American Psychoanalytic Association* 2:745–70.

Bordin, E. 1974. *Research strategies in psychotherapy.* New York: John Wiley and Sons, 138.

Brady, J. P. 1967. Psychotherapy, learning theory, and insight. *Archives of General Psychiatry* 16:304–11.

Browning, G. J. 1966. *An analysis of the effects of therapist prestige and level of interpretation on client response in the initial phase of psychotherapy* (Ph.D. diss., University of Houston, 1965). *Dissertation Abstracts International* 26:4803. Ann Arbor, Mich.: University Microfilms, no. 66–7.

Bugental, J. 1965. *Search for authenticity.* New York: Holt, Rinehart and Winston, 127, 140–41, 302–3.

Cautela, J. H. 1965. Desensitization and insight. *Behavior Research and Therapy* 3:59–64.

Chessick, R. 1974. Technique and practice of intensive psychotherapy. New York: Jason Aronson, 201.

Claiborn, C., S. Ward, and S. Strong. 1981. Effects of congruence between counselor interpretation and client belief. *Journal of Consulting Psychology* 28:101–9.

Colby, K. M. 1963. Causal correlations in clinical interpretation. In L. Paul, ed., *Psychoanalytic clinical interpretation*, 190. London: Free Press of Glencoe.

———. 1951. *A primer for psychotherapists*. New York: Ronald Press Company.

———. 1961a. On the greater amplifying power of causal-correlative over interrogative inputs on free association in an experimental psychoanalytic situation. *Journal of Nervous and Mental Disease* 133:233–39.

Coons, W. H. 1967. Dynamics of change in psychotherapy. *Canadian Psychiatric Association Journal* 12:239–45.

———. 1957. Interaction and insight in group psychotherapy. *Canadian Journal of Psychology* 11:1–8.

Devereux, G. 1951. Some criteria for the timing of confrontations and interpretations. *International Journal of Psychoanalysis* 32:19–24.

Dittman, A. 1952. The interpersonal process in psychotherapy: Development of a research method. *Journal of Abnormal and Social Psychology* 47:236–44.

Ellis, A. 1963. Towards a more precise definition of "emotional" and intellectual insight. *Psychological Reports* 13:125–26.

Eskey, A. 1958. Insight and prognosis. *Journal of Clinical Psychology* 14:426–29.

Farber, L. H. 1965. The two realms of will. *Review of Existential Psychology and Psychiatry* 5:210–27.

Fenichel, O. 1941. *Problems of psychoanalytic technique*. New York: Psychoanalytic Quarterly, 25, 45.

———. 1945. *The psychoanalytic theory of neurosis*. New York: Psychoanalytic Quarterly.

Fine, R. 1971. *The healing of the mind*. New York: David McKay Company, 201, 225.

Frank, J. D. 1974. Therapeutic components of psychotherapy. A 25-year progress report of research. *Journal of Nervous and Mental Disease* 159:325–42.

Freud, S. 1955. Construction in analysis (1938). In *Collected papers*, vol. 5, 358–71. London: Hogarth Press.

———. 1950. Further recommendations in the technique of psychoanalysis. Recollection, repetition and working through (1914), 366–76. In E. Jones, ed., *Collected Papers*, vol. 2. London: Hogarth Press.

———. 1955. Original record of the case (of obsessional neurosis—The rat man) (1907–8), standard ed., vol. 10, 251–318. London: Hogarth Press.

Fromm-Reichman, F. 1950. *Principles of intensive psychotherapy*. Chicago: University of Chicago Press, 151.

Garduk, E. L., and E. A. Haggard. 1972. The immediate effects on patients of psychoanalytic interpretations. *Psychological Issues* (monograph 28) 7:58–59.

Garfield, S. 1968. Interpretation and the interpersonal interaction in psychotherapy. In E. F. Hammer, ed., *Use of interpretation in treatment*, 59–62. New York: Grune and Stratton.

———. 1980. *Psychotherapy: An eclectic approach*. New York: Wiley.

Gatch, V. M., and M. K. Temerlin. 1965. The belief in psychic determinism and the behavior of the psychotherapist. *Review of Existential Psychology and Psychiatry* 5:16–34.

Glover, E. 1968. *The technique of psycho-analysis.* New York: International University Press.

Greenson, R. 1967. *The technique and practice of psychoanalysis.* New York: International University Press, 29–32, 39–41.

Hammer, E. 1966. Interpretations in treatment: Their place, role, timing and art. *Psychoanalytic Review* 53:139, (463)–144(468) [sic].

Healy, W., A. Bronner, and A. Bowers. 1930. *The structure and meaning of psychoanalysis.* New York: A. A. Knopf.

Hobbs, N. 1981. The role of insight in behavior change: A Commentary. *American Journal of Orthopsychiatry* 56:632–35.

———. 1962. Sources of gain in psychotherapy. *American Psychologist* 17:714–34.

Issacs, S. 1939. Criteria for interpretation. *International Journal of Psychoanalysis* 20:148–60.

Kris, E. 1956. On some vicissitudes of insight in psychoanalysis. *International Journal of Psychoanalysis* 37:445–55.

Levin, S. 1973. Confrontation as a demand for change. In G. Adler and P. G. Meyerson, eds., *Confrontation in Psychotherapy,* 303–19. New York: Science House.

Levy, L. 1963. Psychological interpretation. New York: Holt, Rinehart and Winston, 5, 18, 245.

Lowenstein, R. 1963. Some thoughts on interpretation in the theory and practice of psychoanalysis. In L. Paul, ed., *Psychoanalytic clinical interpretation,* 162–88. New York: Free Press.

Martin, A. 1952. The dynamics of insight. *American Journal of Psychoanalysis* 12:24–38.

McCarron, L. T., and V. H. Appel. 1971. Categories of therapist verbalization and patient-therapist autonomic response. *Journal of Consulting and Clinical Psychology* 37:123–34.

Meltzoff, J., and M. Kornreich. 1970. *Research in psychotherapy.* New York: Atherton Press, 419.

Menaker, E. 1968. Interpretation and ego function. In E. F. Hammer, ed., *Use of interpretation in treatment,* 67–71. New York: Grune and Stratton.

Menninger, K., and P. Holzman. 1973. *Theory of psychoanalytic technique.* New York: Basic Books.

Mitchell, K., and B. Berenson. 1970. Differential use of confrontation by high and low facilitative therapists. *Journal of Nervous and Mental Disease* 151:303–9.

Mitchell, K., and L. Hall. 1971. Frequency and type of confrontation over time within the first therapy interview. *Journal of Consulting and Clinical Psychology* 37:437–42.

Myerson, P. G. 1965. Modes of insight. *Journal of American Psychoanalytic Association* 13:771–92.

Noblin, C. D., E. O. Timmons, and M. C. Reynard. 1963. Psychoanalytic interpretations as verbal reinforcers: Importance of interpretation content.
Journal of Clinical Psychology 19:479–81.

Paul, L. 1963. The logic of psychoanalytic interpretation. In L. Paul, ed., *Psychoanalytic clinical interpretation*, 249–73. New York: Free Press.

Pope, B., and A. W. Siegman. 1962. The effects of therapist verbal activity level
and specificity on patient productivity and speech disturbance in the initial interview. *Journal of Consulting Psychology* 26:489.

Raimy, V. 1975. *Misunderstandings of the self.* San Francisco: Jossey-Bass, 95.

Rank, O. 1945. *Will therapy: Truth and reality.* New York: Alfred Knopf.

Rausch, H. L., Z. Sperber, D. Rigler, N. Wilhaus, N. Harway, E. Bordin, A. Dittman, and W. Hays. 1956. A dimensional analysis of depth of interpretation. *Journal of Consulting Psychology* 20:43–48.

Reid, J., and J. Finesinger. 1952. The role of insight in psychotherapy. *American Journal of Psychiatry* 108:726–34.

Richfield, J. 1954. An analysis of the concept of insight. *Psychoanalytic Quarterly* 23:390–408.

Roback, H. B. 1974. Insight: A bridging of the theoretical and research literature. *The Canadian Psychologist* 15:61–88.

Roback, H., and S. Abramowitz. 1979. Insight and hospital adjustment. *Canadian Journal of Psychiatry* 24:233–36.

Rogers, C. R. 1951. *Client-Centered Therapy.* Boston: Houghton Mifflin
Company.

———. 1942. Counseling and Psychotherapy. Boston: Houghton Mifflin.

———. 1944. The development of insight in a counseling relationship. *Journal of Consulting Psychology* 6:331–42.

———. 1961. A theory of psychotherapy with schizophrenics and a proposal
for its empirical investigation. In J. G. Dawson, H. K. Stone, and N. P.
Dellis, eds., *Psychotherapy with schizophrenics.* Baton Rouge: Louisiana
State University Press.

Rosen, J. N. 1953. *Direct analysis.* New York: Grune and Stratton.

Ruesch, J. 1961. *Therapeutic Communication.* New York: W. W. Norton.

Saul, L. J. 1958. *Technic and practice of psychoanalysis.* Philadelphia: J. B.
Lippincott Co.

Schonbar, R. 1965. Interpretation and insight in psychotherapy. *Psychotherapy:
Theory, Research and Practice* 2:78–83.

Segal, H. 1962. The curative factors in psychoanalysis. *International Journal
of Psychoanalysis* 43:212–17.

Singer, E. 1965. *Key concepts in psychotherapy.* New York: Random House, 313.

Slansky, M., K. Issacs, E. Levitov, and C. Haggard. 1966. Verbal interaction
and levels of meaning in psychotherapy. *Archives of General Psychiatry*
14:158–70.

Slater, R. 1956. Interpretation. *American Journal of Psychoanalysis*
16:118–24.

Speisman, J. 1959. Depth of interpretation and verbal resistance in psychotherapy. *Journal of Consulting Psychology* 23:93–99.

Stocking, M. 1973. Confrontation in psychotherapy: Consideration arising from the psychoanalytic treatment of a child. In G. Adler and P. G. Myerson, eds., *Confrontation in psychotherapy*, 319–47. New York: Science House.

Sweet, B. S. 1953. A study of insight: Its operational definition and its relationship to psychological health. Ph.D. diss., University of California.

Tolor, A., and M. Reznikoff. 1960. A new approach to insight: A preliminary report. *Journal of Nervous and Mental Disease* 130:286–96.

Weiner, I. B. 1975. *Principles of psychotherapy*. New York: John Wiley and Sons, 118.

Weisman, A. D. 1973. Confrontation, countertransference and context. In G. Adler & P. G. Meyerson, eds., *Confrontation in psychotherapy*, 97–123. New York: Science House.

Wheelis, A. 1950. The place of action in psychotherapy. *Psychiatry* 13:135–48.

———. 1956. Will and psychoanalysis. *Journal of American Psychoanalytic Association* 4:285–303.

Wolberg, L. 1977. *The technique of psychotherapy* (pt. 1). New York: Grune and Stratton, 588.

Yalom, I. D. 1980. *Existential psychotherapy*. New York: Basic Books, 298–99, 302, 332–33, 343, 339, 347.

Zilboorg, G. 1952. The emotional problem and the therapeutic role of insight. *Psychoanalytic Quarterly* 21:1–24.

11

The Nature of Termination and Its Procedures

In Chapter 6 we discussed clients who drop out of therapy without the consent or the recommendation of the therapist. In this chapter we will discuss termination of therapy when it is carried out with the mutual consent of the therapist and the client. This implies, by and large, that therapy has been completed.*

The termination of relationships is a common human occurrence. Friends and lovers, children and parents, leaders and followers all separate from each other. Separation is difficult because both parties must continue without the supportive relationship. For this reason, some authors believe that, from the client's perspective, termination is equated with depression. Just as the main reason for depression is separation from or the loss of a loved or esteemed person, the client usually feels loss at the termination of a therapeutic relationship, which

---

*Sometimes the client and the therapist may agree to terminate because therapy has reached a stalemate, that is, no progress is being made by the client; or both may agree that therapy should continue with another therapist. This manner of termination is not discussed in this chapter.

is more meaningful to him than to the therapist. Hence, he is likely to experience separation anxiety or depression.

Yet termination can also be an experience that provides growth. In successful therapy, when termination is handled properly, clients frequently begin to look forward to termination. They start to feel a certain mastery over their lives, a greater ease and skill in their interpersonal relationships, and a sense of autonomy which they may wish to exercise independently. It is not unusual for a client to tell the therapist toward the end of therapy: "Today when I was driving here I asked myself, why am I going there? I don't need him anymore. I can handle things on my own."

Goals of Therapy and Criteria of Termination

Generally, the literature of psychotherapy and practicing therapists make it seem that termination constitutes a separate phase of therapy; hence, they do not attach much importance to termination, nor do they grant much significance to the client's feelings about it. Ticho (1972) observes that "problems of termination are sometimes discussed as if they were a sudden annex to the psychoanalytic treatment. Termination problems so intimately connected with the goals of psychoanalysis have to be kept in the analyst's mind right from the beginning of the analysis." In other words, termination becomes a part of the structure of psychotherapy when the client and the therapist set the goals of therapy. Indeed, the goals of therapy determine when and how termination will take place.

For example, the goals of psychoanalysis (or psychoanalytic therapy) include, from a structural point of view, Freud's dictum (1933), "Where id was, there shall ego be" (Wallerstein 1965; Rangell 1966); the achievement of insight into the unconscious (Hoffer 1950; Saul 1958; Firestein 1978); the resolution of the transference neurosis (Hoffer 1950; Loewald 1962; Kubie 1968; Firestein 1978; Hurn 1971); and the attainment of genitality or orgiastic potency (Fenichel 1941; Reich 1949). A psychoanalyst will think of termination when most (or some) of these goals have been reached in therapy. Otherwise, he may consider the therapy itself unsuccessful and termination premature.[*]

---

[*]Ekstein (1965) states "that this ideal ending—for example, the complete resolution of transference neurosis, the disappearance of all symptoms, the structural changes, the perfectly integrated personality, etc.,—is an over-idealized goal hardly ever reached. . . ."

Similarly, the goal of client-centered therapy is a fully functioning individual, who is congruent with himself, has positive regard for himself, posesses an openness to experience, and perceives himself as the locus of control (Patterson 1973). When some of these conditions have been met through therapy, or when the client perceives that he is developing some of these traits, it is time for termination.

Other authors describe the criteria of termination rather than the goals of therapy. They assume that these criteria constitute therapy's goal and that both become intertwined. Menninger and Holzman (1973) state that satisfactory adjustment provides the criteria of termination. They maintain that, "in a general way, we can say that better utilization of work, play, and other sublimations indicate such a satisfactory adjustment." Singer (1965) believes that "this leads to the obvious conclusion that the readiness to engage in a genuine search and to shoulder its burden is the hallmark of therapeutic success, and, therefore, the ultimate criterion for termination of therapy." He goes on to say: "With the development of the patient's intense desire to break the chains of self-alienation and its attending alienation from others, and with the initiation of this self-expanding process, formal therapy may terminate."

Weiner (1975) says that therapy should terminate "when the goals of treatment have been achieved. In actual practice, however, the goals of psychotherapy are seldom sufficiently delineated for either the patient or therapist to identify precisely when they have been achieved." Therefore, he advocates

three minimum criteria that should be satisfied before termination is even considered as a possibility. First, some substantial progress should have been made toward achieving the goals of the treatment. Second, the patient should appear capable of continuing to work independently on understanding and alleviating his problems. Third, the patient's transference relationship to the therapist should have been resolved sufficiently for the real relationship between them to gain ascendance. . . .

Therefore the goals of therapy are sometimes explicitly stated in the theory of psychotherapy that the therapist follows, while at other times they are implied in the criteria of termination. However, a simple rule of termination could be that whenever the client's troubles and conflicts (his symptoms) diminish or disappear therapy should be terminated. Yet most therapists and analysts believe that the disappearance of symptoms does not necessarily constitute a "cure." Nacht (1965) observes, "There can be no real cure as long as the disappearance of one symptom gives rise to its substitution by another—as long as the neurosis itself has not been entirely eliminated."

Weigert (1952) maintains that "symptoms often disappear rather early in analysis, in response to a positive transference, without deeper changes in the structure of the character. Symptoms may reappear in phases of negative transference or, even after profound changes of character, they may be remobilized to prevent the ultimate separation from the analyst." For this reason, it is believed that the criterion for termination should be the removal of the underlying causes of the symptoms.

At this point, a brief discussion of the concept of symptoms and "symptom substitution" is warranted, since it appears to play a significant role in the termination process.

Symptoms, Symptom Substitution, and Termination

Kazdin (1982) states that "symptom substitution refers generally to the possibility that a successful elimination of a particular presenting problem or symptom in therapy, without treating the underlying cause, may result in the appearance of a new (substitute) symptom." It, therefore, assumes an underlying causal unity of various symptoms. Unless the underlying cause of the symptoms is cured, therapy should not be terminated, for new and equivalent symptoms are likely to develop.

For many reasons, the issue of symptoms and symptom substitution has become a confusing one. Many authors state that the confusion resides in the ambiguity and vagueness of the term *symptom* (Yates 1958; Bookbinder 1962; Cahoon 1968; Montgomery and Crowder 1972). They have tried to provide a more precise definition of the term, but the confusion persists.

The reason for the confusion is not the lack of a precise definition but the presentation of precise definitions within the framework of the medical model, which implicitly assumes the validity of the concept of symptom and symptom substitution. (See Chapter 2.) Hence, a more precise definition within the same conceptual model—which created the concept of symptom and symptom substitution in the first place—simply begs the question and becomes circular in nature.

Other authors state that the concept of symptom substitution is difficult to investigate empirically; hence, it is not possible to validate the concept. The result is that the confusion surrounding the concept cannot be clarified. Drawing on various sources, Kazdin (1982) lists six difficulties of an empirical investigation of symptom substitution:

The first difficulty is identifying symptoms and distinguishing them from underlying disorders—the underlying disorder is difficult to identify independently of the symptoms. . . .

A second difficulty resides in the connection between original and substitute symptoms. When a new problem emerges after treatment, how can one determine whether it is a substitute symptom? . . .

A third difficulty arises from the time frame associated with the development of substitute symptoms. No clear time boundaries exist within which substitute symptoms necessarily emerge. . . .

A fourth difficulty is to determine if a new problem (symptom) that emerges after treatment is a substitute symptom or a separate problem that emerges independently . . . (Gale and Carlsson 1976).

A fifth problem is whether apparently "new" symptoms were not already present in some form before treatment. The new symptoms may not be substitutes for the symptom that was eliminated. Rather, they may be more readily detected once the patient's major problem has been eliminated (Balson 1973).

A final difficulty arises from the now widely acknowledged view that substitute symptoms are not inevitable products of "symptomatic" treatment. Some symptoms may become functionally autonomous; that is, free from the underlying disorder (Holte 1976). Thus, symptom substitution may not occur because the underlying disorder may be resolved.

Later in his article, Kazdin implies a seventh difficulty: therapy occasionally produces a negative outcome effect; that is, clients deteriorate rather than improve in therapy. In their deterioration clients may show new symptoms that can be interpreted as "symptom substitutes." Kazdin says: "In a sense, symptom substitution is a special subclass of deterioration effects. . . . These salient issues have led many authors to reject substitution as a verifiable concept."

Perhaps the basic source of confusion about the issue of symptom and symptom substitution is a conceptual one. In psychotherapy, the term *symptom* refers to the personal troubles, the interpersonal conflicts, and the undesirable social behavior of the client. The client's personal troubles and interpersonal conflicts are translated or conceptualized by the therapist within the framework of the disease or the medical model of mental illness, and they are then called "symptoms," like those of any other physical disease (see Chapter 2). If therapists did not use the medical model to conceptualize a client's troubles and conflicts, the issue of symptoms and symptom substitution would not arise. The therapist would deal with those behaviors that trouble the client rather than with his symptoms. The source of confusion, therefore, is the transposition of concepts from an interpersonal to a medical framework and an assumption of equivalence and interchangeability between the two frameworks.

Here, from a well-known psychoanalyst and author, is a somewhat typical example of such confusion. In discussing the problem of symptom substitution, Reider (1976) states: "Clearly, I have used the term *symptom substitution* so loosely as to indicate substitution not only of one symptom for another on the same level, but also an exchange of behavior for a symptom. A switch from symptom to behavior may actually be a description of a spontaneous cure. . . ." Here the terms *symptom*, *symptom substitution*, *behavior*, and *cure* are used interchangeably and leave the reader baffled.

The confusion is compounded when investigators using the medical model attempt to search for and validate the diagnostic categories (the mental illnesses) which show the greatest and the least proclivity for symptom substitution. These investigators report that hysteria (or conversion) shows the greatest propensity for symptom substitution (Rosen 1953; Seitz 1953; Eysenck 1969; Blanchard and Hersen 1975; Wallace and Rothstein 1975).* Such an attempt creates the impression that symptoms and symptom substitution are authentic and verifiable phenomena—symptoms embedded in a disease entity.

Studies of behavior therapies suggest that successful treatment of tics (Yates 1958b), phobias (Lazrus 1961; Marks and Gelder 1965; Bandura 1968), enuresis (Mowrer and Mowrer 1938; Martin and Kubly 1955; Freyman 1963; Lovibond 1964; Baker 1969), and stuttering (Goldiamond 1966; Brady 1971) is followed by little or no symptom substitution. Therefore, behavior therapists maintain that symptom

---

*It should be noted that the diagnostic category of hysteria has been historically a catchall, and a vague one; it is defined by "shifting symptomatology" (Szasz 1966; Ellenberger 1970). So elusive and unreliable has been this category that it is not included in the Diagnostic Statistical Manual III, of the American Psychiatric Association (1980). (The Manual does list "conversion" as a diagnostic category.) This fact becomes even more glaring when we realize that DSM III is both larger and more comprehensive than DSM II, published in 1968, "encompassing half again as many separate diagnostic descriptions as does DSM II" (Schacht and Nathan 1977). For more on the diagnosis of hysteria, see Goshen 1952; Ziegler and Paul 1954; Reichard 1956; and Temoshok and Attkisson 1977.

substitution is not a valid phenomenon (Lazrus 1965; Wolpe 1968; Nurnberger and Hington 1973).

It is worth mentioning, in passing, that in classical psycho-pathology, tics and phobias are classified as forms of hysteria. Some studies find that symptom substitution is quite common in certain forms of hysteria, while other studies show that in other forms of hysteria (tics and phobias) it is rather uncommon.

Symptom substitution, therefore, seems to be a spurious issue, one which should not enter into the consideration of termination. As far as the process of termination is concerned, Szasz (1965) seems correct when he says that it is the client who, in two ways, provides the criteria of termination of therapy.

First, as argued here, psychotherapy is not like a medical treatment. "The client, in contrast to the therapist, knows his life situation, his feelings, and his conflicts well. He has a better idea how he is functioning. Therefore, a therapist should let a client initiate the process of termination" (Szasz 1965). Whenever the client presents direct or indirect communication pertaining to termination, a therapist should openly discuss the process.

The second criterion for termination could be formulated in the following way. In Chapter 5 it was noted that during the first few sessions, the therapist must ask the client what he wishes to change in his life, or in what ways he would like to live differently. The client's answer to this inquiry indicates the general goals for both client and therapist.*

When either the therapist or the client feels that many (or some) of the stated goals have been reached, one of the parties may raise the issue of termination. When the therapist raises the issue of termination, the client may or may not agree with his assessment and observations about termination. If the client agrees with the therapist that therapy should be terminated, the next issue to be settled is the method of termination—whether to decrease the frequency of therapy sessions and then terminate, or to set a date on which therapy will be terminated, while meeting regularly until that time. For their own reasons, clients prefer one method of termination over the other. Some

---

*As therapy unfolds a client may modify and expand the goals he wishes to accomplish in therapy; yet the expanded goals are usually related to the goals stated initially.

wish to terminate on a particular date; others wish to taper off; still others wish to set their own "rhythm" of termination. In choosing the method of termination, the client's preference should be accorded priority, for the client is generally aware of the reasons for his preference.

If the client does not agree with the therapist that therapy should be terminated, the therapist should continue seeing the client.* This does not mean that the therapist should not raise the issue of termination in the future when he feels that the client has made further progress. When the issue of termination is raised again, the therapist should present once more the evidence of further progress (or the lack of it) in the client's life.

How should the issue of termination be raised with the client? There are advisable and inadvisable ways of broaching the issue. The two different ways of handling termination seem to have a different impact upon the client in subsequent therapy sessions, and even after the termination of therapy. Both methods are discussed below.

Improper and/or Unsatisfactory Handling of Termination

Numerous situations exist in which a therapist may improperly or unsatisfactorily handle the termination process. Many of them are frequently encountered in the work of a beginning therapist. Some of the more common situations include the following examples.

The first example occurs when a client wishes to discuss termination of therapy, and the therapist either refuses to discuss it openly with the client or considers it a resistance. This method of treating termination is likely to make the client feel that the therapist is not aware of the progress he has made; the client feels that the therapist is insensitive to his desire to handle his own affairs now and to terminate. When this situation develops, the client and the therapist implicitly begin to work at cross-purposes.* The client begins to look for oppor-

---

*Ferenczi (1955) and Szasz (1965) maintain that it is the task of a therapist to continue to provide therapy as long as the client wishes to come. Ferenczi states: "The proper ending of an analysis is when neither the physician nor the patient puts an end to it, but when it dies of exhaustion, so to speak, though even when this occurs, the physician must be more than suspicious of the two and must think of the possibility that behind the patient's wish to take his departure some neurotic factors may still be concealed."

*This point was brought to my attention by Charles Meyers of the Sharma Center for Psychological Services, Sacramento, California.

tunities and excuses to drop out of therapy. To avoid this situation, the therapist should pay serious attention to the client's hints or indirect communications and seriously discuss them with him.

If the therapist feels that the client's wish to terminate emerges from some form of resistance, then he must reveal the resistance and demonstrate it to the client by relating it to his wish to terminate. In every event, all of the client's direct and/or indirect communications about termination must be openly discussed.

Frequently, the client keeps coming to therapy, but no movement or change occurs in his life; therapy reaches a stalemate.* For whatever reasons, the therapist may fail to raise the issue of termination. The client begins to feel that although there may be no progress he should continue in therapy because the therapist may have some hidden insight which he has not yet imparted to the client, and this may be the reason that termination has not been suggested. If this happens, the stalemate will continue until extraneous factors bring a change in the situation, or until the client realizes that termination may be warranted and raises the issue.

A second instance of improper and unsatisfactory handling of termination occurs when the therapist somewhat suddenly announces termination to the client, thus failing to give the client time to adjust to the idea. The client's feelings and reactions about termination are not explored and resolved before the therapist sets the termination date. This practice is frequently encountered in clinics and institutions where the therapist is a trainee on a time-limited basis, or when the institution closes down for several months of the year (during the summer session, for example).

The client is usually surprised and feels betrayed and deserted by the therapist. He feels that the therapist has not confided in him by discussing termination in advance. He may react in a number of ways: he may become worse (revive his "symptoms"); he may quit therapy before the termination date; he may retaliate by not paying his bills or delaying payment; he may malign the therapist to his friends. From then on the client begins to distrust the therapist.

---

*Lewis (1978) points out that "a surprisingly common finding, however, in stalemated therapy was the therapist's failure to attend to the patient's affects. In many such interviews, patients communicated intense feelings that were disregarded by the therapist who focused almost exclusively on the content of their fantasies, thoughts, or dreams." See also Weiner (1982), who discusses therapeutic impasse as a failure of psychotherapy.

A twenty-eight-year-old, twice-married young man was being seen in psychotherapy at the university clinic which closes down for the summer. His therapist was a forty-two-year-old, second-year female graduate student. The client had a turbulent and tragic background. He was one of six children in a Mexican-American family, all of whom had been brought up in orphanages. The client spent his early years in seven different orphanages until he joined the army at seventeen years of age. After placing the children in orphanages, the mother became a prostitute; the father remarried and became an alcoholic. After his discharge from the army, the client married a girl in Florida. The marriage lasted for four months. He then decided to come to California, where some of his army buddies had settled. After a year in California he married the woman he had been living with. She, too, had had a difficult family background full of conflict. Soon after the marriage, she began to urge the husband to find out about his parents and siblings whom he had not seen since his orphanage days. It was then that he found out what had happened to his parents; and he did not wish to see them again.

The client got a job with the state of California. The marriage became turbulent, with each person displaying considerable abuse toward the other. The client made good progress in therapy. Two months prior to the beginning of summer, when the clinic closes, the supevisor asked the therapist to discuss termination with the client. By this time, he had been seen for about eighteen sessions. The therapist mentioned termination to the client only in passing, stating that the clinic would close when the summer session began. Two weeks before the closing of the clinic, she began to make arrangements to transfer the client to another therapist. At that point, the client agreed to see the new therapist.

When he saw the new therapist, he was very upset and bitter about being transferred. He said that it was unjust that he should be removed from a situation where for the first time in his life he had developed a trusting relationship with someone, and that it was very difficult for him to start again because he was just beginning to open up with the previous therapist. He was sad and troubled and did not know if he could work with the new therapist; he felt betrayed and deserted.

At this point, making a special dispensation, the client was reassigned to the first therapist. She was asked to see him during the summer and advised that her main thrust in therapy should be to help the client resolve his feelings about termination, to detach him from her, and to help him accept a new therapist who could then start with him in the fall semester (since the therapist was graduating during the summer session and would not be returning). It took three months to work through many of the client's feelings so that he became somewhat comfortable with the subsequent therapist.

Another situation frequently encountered in supervision occurs when a therapist continues to focus upon the client's past or his unconscious conflicts and to analyze his defenses after both have discussed termination and agreed upon a date. Technically, this may be considered an improper and unsatisfactory method of handling termination.

The client usually perceives the therapist's moves as indicating that therapy should not be terminated because he still has many unresolved conflicts. This creates doubts and confusion in the client's mind, for although an agreement has been reached about termination, he is shown that he still has a series of unresolved conflicts.

A fourth situation occurs when the therapist does not encourage the client to discuss his feelings and reactions about termination after an agreement to terminate is reached; nor does he attempt to relate what goes on in therapy to the termination process. The client senses that since he does have feelings and reactions about termination the therapist does not think they are important. At first, the client may not acknowledge a strong feeling or reaction to termination; however, if the issue of his feelings about termination is raised in a supportive environment, he will begin to express his feelings.

Contrary to prevailing theories that clients have only certain feelings about termination, the client actually manifests a myriad of feelings, such as sadness, irritation, anger, exhilaration, autonomy, relief, a feeling of closure, the desire to be on his own, and concern about missing the therapist and/or the therapy sessions.

Classical psychoanalytic literature is almost adamant in maintaining that the most prominent feelings that a client experiences at termination are depression or mourning (Weigert 1952; Reich 1950; Loewald 1962; Edelman 1963; Miller 1965; Feder and Pineda 1966; Chessick 1974). As Feder and Pineda (1966) state, "The review of the literature demonstrates almost total agreement on at least one point. The termination of the analysis is equivalent to the process of mourning. Call it separation anxiety, finality symptoms with death, loss of the object, or what you will; the concordance appears to be uniform on this point." In the same vein, Chessick (1974) states that "in the termination phase we must provide the patient with an opportunity to elaborate and work through the grief and mourning reaction in whatever intensity the patient will experience it. If there is no such reaction, something has gone wrong, something is being repressed, or most likely, we are terminating the patient prematurely."

A strong reaction of grief or mourning is rarely mentioned by either clients or psychotherapists, especially after a satisfactory completion of therapy. But psychoanalysts claim that classical psychoanalysis, in contrast to psychotherapy, is a long and emotionally intense process. Hence, it is assumed that many reactions at termination—mourning, grief, separation anxiety—are much more intense and discernible in psychoanalysis than in psychotherapy. This claim by psychoanalysts appears to be of doubtful validity.

A study of patients at the Boston Psychoanalytic Institute shows that the average number of sessions per patient was 675 (the number of meetings per week is not mentioned) (Shashin et al. 1975). If the parties met four times a week (including interruptions, vacations, and breaks), therapy lasts, roughly, five years. Frequently psychotherapy also lasts four or five years, especially with seriously disturbed clients. It is a moot point whether seeing a client once or twice a week within a period of four or five years produces a weaker attachment than if the client were seen four or five times a week. The weight of existing clinical and empirical evidence suggests that the length of time, rather than the frequency of meetings, is more important in determining the degree of attachment and, hence, the client's reactions at termination (Thompson 1950; Lorr 1962; Strupp et al. 1964; Marmor 1975). Generally, the feelings of the client at termination become intertwined or alternate with each other as he continues to try to put them into perspective at the time of termination and long afterward (Firestein 1978).

Satisfactory and/or Proper Handling of Termination

In handling termination properly and satisfactorily, termination should be discussed with, not announced to, the client many weeks in advance. When the therapist raises the issue of termination or of bringing therapy to a close, his assessment of the client's progress, and his rationale for it, should be presented. The therapist's rationale may be that most or some of the goals of therapy have been reached, that the changes which the client wanted to make in his life have been made, that the therapy has reached a stalemate, or that the client's dreams and/or associations (as in classical analysis) suggest that termination may be warranted. Whatever the therapist's reasons, they should be presented as issues for discussion and not as a pronouncement by the therapist.

If the client resists termination, it is best to continue therapy. This does not mean that the therapist should not raise the issue again when he feels that the client has made further progress. If, on the other hand, the client agrees with the therapist's observations, a date should then be set either for the tapering off or for terminating outright. Again, the client should be given the choice.

Many classical psychoanalysts advocate against a gradual reduction of therapy. They believe that a firm date should be set for termination, which should be adhered to strictly, regardless of the client's reactions (Freud 1950; Orens 1955; Rangell 1966; Kubie 1968). From this writer's point of view, such a practice is not only too rigid and categorical, but it implicitly accepts the medical model. It assumes that just as a medical patient is discharged from a hospital or from treatment on a particular date because he is cured of his illness, psychotherapy should also stop on the day that the patient is deemed "cured." This practice overlooks the basic fact that psychotherapy, or psychoanalysis, is based upon an intimate and delicate interpersonal relationship, which cannot be dissolved so quickly and so simply.

Frequently, the client may raise the issue of termination before the therapist does. In this situation, the therapist should listen carefully and sympathetically to the client's reasons, feelings, and assessment of his life situation. Both parties may go over what has or has not been accomplished in therapy. If both agree that the time has come to terminate, a date should then be set. If, however, the therapist's observations and assessment do not agree with those of the client, the therapist should present them clearly to the client and state his rationale for continuing therapy. The client may still insist upon termination, in which case the therapist should agree with the client's wishes but continue to work with him, with the same sincerity as before, until the date of termination or of the beginning of closure. Nevertheless, the therapist should be satisfied, for he has stated his case openly.

A forty-eight-year-old black woman, the mother of four children, came to therapy because of anxiety and a feeling that things were not going well in her life. She was employed in a middle management position in the state bureaucracy. She had married at a young age. A few years after the marriage she discovered that her husband had tuberculosis. He spent about six years, off and on, in a sanatorium. During these years, the burden of bringing up the children and running the household fell upon her. She was also enrolled in school to complete a master's degree. She had a great deal of fortitude and was successful in accomplishing many of these tasks. When her husband recovered, he went into the printing business, but at the same time he developed deviant sexual practices: masturbating in front of nude pictures, making incestuous advances toward his daughter, and so on. She asked her husband to move out, which he did.

The daughter became a lesbian, and one of the sons returned from Vietnam addicted to drugs. Although the husband and wife were living separately and were economically independent, she could not bring herself to ask for a divorce, for she had vowed to be with him "for better or for worse." She wished he would ask for a divorce so that she would not have to break her vows. She claimed she had developed a dislike for men and sex. Yet, at the same time, she had developed a relationship (a platonic one, she claimed) with another man, which she enjoyed considerably.

After nine months of therapy many of the problems became manageable. One day, she stated that she wished to terminate since her life had become less tense and relatively more pleasant and enjoyable. The therapist, however, mentioned that he did not feel she should terminate at that time since the issue of sexuality, her guilt feelings, and her reactions toward her husband still remained bothersome to her. Those were a few aspects of her life which the therapist felt should be explored. She, on the other hand, felt that since she had a boyfriend and was becoming bolder about discussing divorce with her husband these aspects of her life would work themselves out. Thereupon, a date was set to taper off therapy. She came for four more sessions and terminated.

After a date has been agreed on, the focus of the therapy should begin to shift. Discussion of the client's past or of his unconscious should be deemphasized. Therapy sessions should focus more upon the client's future (Szasz 1965).* Focusing upon the client's present and future prepares the client for termination and his life without the therapist.

Sometimes, after a date has been set, the client may bring up what have been called "new conflicts or symptoms"; the process of termination seems to uncover many of the client's latent fears and doubts. For instance, soon after the termination date is established, the client may say that for many weeks he has been making plans to take a trip abroad after therapy ends, but now he has discovered that he is afraid of flying and is very upset that he cannot take the trip. He is not sure that therapy should be terminated. In general, the new conflicts or symptoms are not very different from those the client has already pre-

---

*Szasz (1965) maintains that the contradiction between the past and the future is built into psychoanalysis. When the client goes for psychoanalysis, "the prospective analysand focuses on the future. However, the analyst practicing in the traditional fashion will focus on the past. The patient wants to know what will happen to him [in analysis], whereas the analyst wants to know what has happened to him [in his childhood]. Hence, the interest of the analyst and the analysand are likely to conflict soon after they meet."

sented during the course of therapy and successfully resolved. Therefore, when they reappear they are not insurmountable. A therapist should bring to the client's attention that he has already resolved his conflicts and can do so once again.

In classical psychoanalytic literature, such reactions of the client have been labeled as "revival," or as the "return of the symptoms." A great deal of emphasis has been placed upon these reactions in relation to termination. Most analysts believe that a revival of symptoms is a regular phenomenon in any classical analysis (Buxbaum 1950; Payne 1950; Reich 1950; Pfeffer 1963; Ekstein 1965; Miller 1965; Atkins 1966). Various reasons have been given for the revival of symptoms. Payne (1950) believes that these symptoms can be compared with "the anxieties of growing up and leaving school, leaving the university, rebirth, weaning, the end of mourning; all being critical times involving a reorganization of ego and libidinal interests." Reich (1950) and Buxbaum (1950) maintain that the patient is attempting to hold onto the analyst or to delay the final leave-taking (Ekstein 1965; Ticho 1972). Miller (1965) maintains that the revival of symptoms is due to mourning the loss of omnipotence.

It should be noted that the return of symptoms is not a regular phenomenon in psychoanalysis or in psychotherapy (Robbins 1975; Witenberg 1976). Generally, the revival of symptoms depends upon the following factors:

1. Who initiates the termination—the therapist or the client. There is some evidence to suggest that if the client initiates termination, he will feel more in control of his own fate; he is less likely to feel subservient or rejected, and thus he is less likely to experience the revival of symptoms.

2. The degree and the extent of openness with which tapering-off or termination has been discussed with the client in advance of the date. If the issue of termination is not openly discussed between the parties, the client may well revive his symptoms.

3. The amount of progress made by the client. If the client feels that he has been able to fulfill most of his goals in therapy, tapering-off or termination will not be upsetting for him. It is encouraging for him to learn that the therapist also believes that he has made good progress. Hence, the probability of the revival of symptoms is considerably reduced.

4. The degree of counter-transference of the therapist. The fact that therapists develop counter-transference and wish to keep their clients in therapy is well known (Ticho 1972; Menninger and Holzman 1973). For this reason, the therapist may revive the client's symptoms so that he does not terminate. Hence, the less counter-transference occurs and the more supportive and sympathetic the therapist is toward the client's feelings surrounding termination, the less likely the revival of symptoms becomes.

Therapists' Reactions to Termination

As discussed in Chapter 9, a therapist also becomes attached to the client and can have various reactions to the process of termination and to the client leaving therapy. Therapists' reactions to termination have been described by various authors (Ticho 1966; Menninger and Holzman 1973; Firestein 1978). Some therapists become possessive of their clients and do not wish to let go of them. Some are attracted to their clients and want to develop an ongoing relationship with them. Some therapists "interfere with the patient's attempt to live a life of his own" (Ticho 1972). Some like to have clients around them for their own narcissistic satisfaction. Monetary considerations may influence the therapist in deciding not to terminate therapy. If the therapist is not doing well financially, he may wish to hold on to a paying client. Certain therapists have an ideal picture of a successfully analyzed client that must be realized before therapy can be terminated. Hence, they prolong therapy even though the client's life may become satisfactory and manageable and yet not ideal according to the therapist's criteria.

In order to be as effective as possible, the therapist must guard against such prejudices and predilections. He should occasionally examine what kinds of feelings and reactions termination provokes in him. Each terminating client evokes different emotions in the therapist, and the therapist should know how to manage them when they occur. If the therapist is not very aware of his feelings, then it is likely that he will handle termination improperly and unsatisfactorily.

Generally, toward the end of therapy, the relationship between the client and the therapist should begin to change from what has been described as an "as if" relationship to a "real" relationship (Weiner 1975)—from a therapist-client relationship to a relationship between two human beings. This is difficult to achieve because for a long time the therapist has held a superior position of power and control, and it is difficult for him to shed this role. It is also difficult for the client because for a long time he has accepted his subservient and dependent role. In addition, "he is frequently told and generally made to feel that he doesn't know what he is talking about; and if, stung to reprisal, he criticizes the analyst, he is informed that he is just projecting self criticism . . ." (Glover 1955). For him to feel equal to the therapist, he must also readjust his behavior. This role switch should be attempted by both the client and the therapist.

There are no prescribed rules for how this is to be achieved. Different therapists use different methods. Analysts who use the couch, asking the client to lie down while they sit behind the client throughout the course of analysis, believe that during the last phase of analysis the patient should be seated face-to-face with the analyst. "In short, we shall try to establish a less rigid, less artificial relationship between patient and therapist by putting them on the new level of adult to adult" (Nacht 1965). They believe this procedure helps achieve a relationship between equals. Some therapists begin to answer more personal questions and try to be more informal with their clients. Some therapists begin to take clients out for coffee so that they meet in an atmosphere where the client can talk more as an equal and where the focus is removed from the client's conflicts. The client and the therapist may discuss more neutral subjects which interest both of them, such as movies, sports, and travel. The therapist might also ask the client what kinds of interaction (within certain limits) between them might produce a semblance of equality.* Apparently, there are no empirical studies that show whether such practices do indeed reduce the client's feeling of inequality and/or make the client feel more like the therapist's equal. Yet these practices have been frequently recommended.

After the termination of therapy sessions, a client does not immediately forget feelings he has experienced in therapy and at the time of termination; they may continue for many months or even years. The client attempts to understand and resolve his new conflicts in the same manner which he learned in therapy. In other words, the open and supportive atmosphere of therapy enabled him to encounter

---

*This point was brought to my attention by Joyce Ballard Wexler of Los Angeles.

many of his inner secrets and conflicts, and imitate and identify with the therapist; this new form of learning becomes a part of the client's life and helps him face his problems relatively more effectively after therapy is terminated.

Summary

The criteria of termination are closely tied up with the goals of therapy. When the client and therapist set the goals of therapy, they also agree implicitly when to terminate therapy. When the client or therapist feels that some (or most) of the goals of therapy have been attained, the issue of termination may be raised by either party. If they both agree, a date for termination should then be set.

If, however, the client raises the issue of termination before the therapist does, the therapist should pay serious attention to the client's reasons for termination. The therapist may or may not agree with the client's reasons. If he does not, the therapist should clearly state why.

Many methods of handling termination have a deleterious effect upon the client; they include: when the client wishes to discuss termination and the therapist pays no heed; when the therapist announces termination precipitously and does not allow the client enough time to resolve his feelings and reactions about termination; when both parties have agreed upon termination but the therapist continues to focus upon the client's past or his unconscious; when both parties have agreed upon termination but the therapist does not discuss the client's feelings and reactions about termination; when the therapist, because of his own counter-transference, becomes uncomfortable and terminates the client without sufficient notice.

To avoid problems with termination, a therapist should openly discuss it with the client well in advance; he should point out to the client why he thinks termination is warranted. If the client agrees with the therapist's assessment, a termination date should be set. After the termination is agreed upon, a therapist should help the client express his feelings and reactions to termination; he should focus on the client's present and future rather than his past; and he should try to assist the client in developing a feeling of equality with the therapist.

References

American Psychiatric Association. 1968. *Diagnostic and Statistical Manual of Mental Disorders.* 2d ed. DSM II. Washington, D.C.

―――. 1980. Diagnostic and Statistical Manual of Mental Disorders. DSM III. Washington, D.C.

Atkins, S. 1966. Discussion. In R. E. Litman, ed., *Psychoanalysis in the Americas,* 240–46. New York: International University Press.

Baker, B. 1969. Symptom treatment and symptom substitution in enuresis. *Journal of Abnormal Psychology* 74(1):42–49.

Balson, P. M. 1973. Case Study: Encopresis: A case study with symptom substitution. *Behavior Therapy* 4:134–36.

Bandura, A. 1968. Modeling approaches to the modification of phobic disorders. In R. Porter, ed., *The Role of Learning in Psychotherapy.* Boston: Little, Brown and Co.

Blanchard, E., and M. Hersen. 1975. Behavioral treatment of hysterical neurosis: Symptom substitution and symptom return reconsidered. *Psychiatry* 39:118–29.

Bookbinder, L. 1962. Simple conditioning versus the dynamic approach to symptom and symptom substitution: A reply to Yates. *Psychological Reports* 10:71–77.

Brady, J. P. 1971. Metronome-conditioned speech training for stuttering. *Behavior Therapy* 2:129.

Buxbaum, E. 1950. Technique of terminating analysis. *International Journal of Psychoanalysis* 31:184–90.

Cahoon, D. 1968. Sympton substitution and the behavior therapies: A reappraisal. *Psychological Bulletin* 69:149–56.

Chessick, R. 1974. *Technique and practice of intensive psychotherapy.* New York: Jason Aronson, 323.

Edelman, M. 1963. *Termination of intensive psychotherapy.* Springfield, Ill.: Charles C. Thomas.

Ekstein, R. 1965. Working through and termination of analysis. *Journal of American Psychoanalytic Association* 13:57–77.

Ellenberger, H. 1970. *The discovery of the unconscious.* New York: Basic Books.

Eysenck, H. 1969. Relapse and symptom substitution after different types of psychotherapy. *Behavior Research and Therapy* 7:283–87.

Feder, L., and F. G. Pineda. 1966. Discussion. In R. E. Litman, ed., *Psychoanalysis in the Americas,* 268. New York: International University Press.

Fenichel, O. 1941. Problems of psychoanalytic techniques. *Psychoanalytic Quarterly.*

Ferenczi, S. 1955. The problem of the termination of the analysis. In Ferenczi, *Final contributions to the problems and methods of psychoanalysis,* 85. New York: Basic Books.

Firestein, S. 1978. *Termination in psychoanalysis.* New York: International University Press.

Freud, S. 1950. Analysis: Terminable and interminable. In J. Strachey, ed., *Collected papers*, vol. 5, 316–58. London: Hogarth Press.

Freyman, R. 1963. Follow-up study of enuresis treatment of a bell apparatus. *Journal of Child Psychology and Psychiatry* 4:199.

Gale, E., and S. Carlsson. 1976. Look carefully: A short note on symptom substitution. *Behavior Research and Therapy* 14:77.

Glover, E. 1955. *The technique of psychoanalysis*. New York: International University Press, 147.

Goldiamond, I. 1966. Stuttering and fluency as manipulatable operant response classes. In L. Krasner and L. P. Ullman, eds., *Research in behavior modification* 106–56. New York: Holt, Rinehart and Winston.

Goshen, C. 1952. The original case material of psychoanalysis. *American Journal of Psychiatry* 108:829–34.

Hall, M. 1979. Symptom substitution concept revisited. *Hypnosis Quarterly* 22:19–22.

Hoffer, W. 1950. Three psychological criteria for the termination of treatment. *International Journal of Psychoanalysis* 31(3):194–95.

Holte, A. 1976. The role of symptom in psychopathological states. *Scandinavian Journal of Psychology* 17:161–70.

Hurn, H. T. 1971. Toward a paradigm of the terminal phase: The current status of the terminal phase. *Journal of American Psychoanalytic Association* 19:332.

Kazdin, A. 1982. Symptom substitution, generalization, and response covariation: Implication for psychotherapy outcome. *Psychological Bulletin* 92(2):349–66.

Kubie, L. 1968. Unsolved problems in the resolution of the transference. *Psychoanalytic Quarterly* 37:331–52.

Lazrus, A. A. 1965. Behavior therapy, incomplete treatment, and symptom substitution. *Journal of Nervous and Mental Disease* 140:80.

———. 1961. Group therapy of phobic disorders by systematic desensitization. *Journal of Social & Abnormal Psychology* 63:504.

Lewis, J. 1978. *To be a therapist*. New York: Brunner-Mazel, 6.

Lipton, S. 1961. The last hour. *Journal of American Psychoanalytic Association* 9:325–30.

Loewald, H. 1962. Internalization, separation, mourning and the superego. *Psychoanalytic Quarterly* 31:483–504.

Lorr, M. 1962. Relation of treatment frequency and duration to psychotherapy outcome. In H. H. Strupp and L. Luborsky, eds., *Research In Psychotherapy*, vol. 2, 134–42. Washington, D.C.: American Psychological Association.

Lovibond, S. 1964. *Conditioning and Enuresis*. London: Pergamon.

Marks, I., and Gelder, M. 1965. A controlled retrospective study of behaviour therapy in phobic patients. *British Journal of Psychiatry* 3:571–73.

Marmor, J. 1975. *Psychiatrists and their patients*. The Joint Information Services of the American Psychiatric Association and the National Association for Mental Health, Washington, D.C., 75.

Martin, B., and D. Kubly. 1955. Results of treatment of enuresis by a conditioned response method. *Journal of Consulting Psychology* 19:71.

Menninger, K., and P. Holzman. 1973. *Theory of psychoanalytic technique.* New York: Basic Books, 168.

Miller, I. 1965. On the return of symptom in the terminal phase of psychoanalysis. *International Journal of Psychoanalysis* 46:487–501.

Milner, M. 1950. A note on the ending of analysis. *International Journal of Psychoanalysis* 31:191–93.

Montgomery, G., and J. Crowden. 1972. Symptom substitution: Hypothesis and the evidence. *Psychotherapy: Theory, Research, and Practice* 9:98–102.

Mowrer, O. H., and W. M. Mowrer. 1938. Enuresis—a method for its study and treatment. *American Journal of Orthopsychiatry* 8:436.

Nacht, S. 1965. Criteria and technique for the termination of analysis. *International Journal of Psychoanalysis* 46:107–16.

Nurnberger, J., and J. Hington. 1973. Is symptom substitution an important issue in behavior therapy? *Biological Psychiatry* 7:221–36.

Orens, J. 1955. Setting a termination date—an impetus to analysis. *Journal of American Psychoanalytic Association* 3:651–65.

Patterson, C. H. 1973. *Theories of counseling and psychotherapy.* New York: Harper and Row, 390.

Payne, S. 1950. Short communication on criteria for terminating analysis. *International Journal of Psychoanalysis* 31:205.

Pfeffer, A. 1963. Analysis: Terminable and interminable—twenty-five years later. *Journal of American Psychoanalytic Association* 11:131–42.

Rangell, L. 1966. An overview of the ending of an analysis. In R. E. Litman, ed., *Psychoanalysis in the Americas,* 141–65. New York: International University Press.

Reich, A. 1950. On the termination of analysis. *International Journal of Psychoanalysis* 31:179–83.

Reich, W. 1949. *Character analysis.* New York: Orgone Institute Press.

Reichard, S. 1956. A re-examination of "studies in hysteria." *Psychoanalytic Quarterly* 25:155–77.

Reider, N. 1976. Symptom substitution. *Bulletin of the Menninger Clinic* 46(6):629–40.

Rickman, J. 1950. On the criteria for the termination of analysis. *International Journal of Psychoanalysis* 31:200–201.

Robbins, W. S. 1975. Termination: Problems and technique. *Journal of American Psychoanalytic Association* 23:166–76.

Rosen, H. 1953. Discussion of Seitz' "Experiment in the substitution of symptoms by hypnosis." *Psychosomatic Medicine* 15:422–24.

Saul, L. 1958. *Technique and practice of psychoanalysis.* Philadelphia: J. B. Lippincott Co.

Schacht, T., and P. Nathan. 1977. But is it good for the psychologists? *American Psychologist* 32:1017–25.

Seitz, P. F. 1953. Experiments in the substitution of symptoms by hypnosis: II. *Psychosomatic Medicine* 15:405–24.

Shashin, J., S. Eldred, and S. van Amerongen. 1975. A search for predictive factors in institute supervised cases: A retrospective study of 183 cases from 1959–1966 at the Boston Psychoanalytic Society and Institute. *International Journal of Psychoanalysis* 56:343–59.

Singer, E. 1965. *Key concepts in psychotherapy*. New York: Random House, 353.

Strupp, H., M. Wallach, and M. Wogan. 1964. Psychotherapy experience in retrospect: Questionnaire survey of former patients and their therapists. *Psychological Monograph* 78(11):1–45.

Szasz, T. 1965. *Ethics of Psychoanalysis*. New York, Basic Books, 138–39, 141.

———. 1966. Mental illness is a myth. *New York Times Magazine*, June 12, 30–31, 90–92.

Temoshok, L., and C. Attkisson. 1977. Epidemiology of hysterical phenomena: Evidence for a psychosocial theory. In M. J. Howowitz, ed., *Hysterical Personality*, 145–222. New York: Jason Aronson.

Ticho, E. 1966. Discussion. In R. E. Litman, ed., *Psychoanalysis in the Americas*. New York: International University Press.

———. 1972. Termination of psychoanalysis: Treatment goals, life goals. *Psychoanalytic Quarterly* 41:315–33.

Thompson, C. 1960. *Psychoanalysis: Evolution and Development*. New York: Hermitage House, 234–35.

Wallace, E., and W. Rothstein. 1975. Symptom substitution in a male hysteric. *The American Journal of Psychoanalysis* 35:355–57.

Wallerstein, R. 1965. The goals of psychoanalysis. *Journal of American Psychoanalytic Association* 13:748–70.

Weigert, E. 1952. Contribution to the problems of terminating psychoanalysis. *Psychoanalytic Quarterly* 21:465–80.

Weiner, I. 1975. *Principles of psychotherapy*. New York: John Wiley and Sons, 263–64, 270–71.

Weiner, M. 1982. *The therapeutic impasse*. New York: The Free Press.

Witenberg, E. 1976. Problems in terminating psychoanalysis (A symposium). *Contemporary Psychoanalysis* 12:335–65.

Wolpe, J. 1968. *The practice of behavior therapy*. New York: Pergamon Press.

Yates, A. 1958b. The application of learning theory to the treatment of tics. *Journal of Abnormal and Social Psychology* 56:175.

———. 1958. Symptoms and symptom substitution. *Psychological Review* 65:371–74.

Ziegler, D. K., and N. Paul. 1954. On the natural history of hysteria in women. *Disease of the Nervous System* 15:301–6.

12

Growth of a Therapist: Practice, Reflection, and Self-Scrutiny

The therapist's psychological and emotional growth should be an unending process. A therapist can never honestly state that he has acquired all, or most, of the necessary knowledge and acumen sufficient to help the client effectively. Like knowledge, growth has no limits or bounds.

From a theoretical point of view, at least, a therapist should grow as he practices his profession, and he should become progressively more helpful to his clients. The characteristics and qualities that presumably make a "good" and/or competent therapist are not innate. Many of them have to be learned through prolonged and laborious self-struggle. In the process of becoming a "good" therapist, one not only has to acquire various skills, but he must also shed and curb many of the traits which detract from his ability to be helpful and effective with a client, such as arrogance, argumentativeness, and extreme supportiveness. All of this means that the therapist's growth and development are his personal struggle to change, which involves self-

319

reflection and self-scrutiny. It is a long and arduous process, which some are willing to undertake, no matter how painful it may become. Some become discouraged and give up, while still others make various compromises.

Struggles of a Beginning Therapist

A beginning therapist, quite understandably, is diffident and anxious in his work* (Schlict 1968; Chessick 1971; Book 1973). There are many reasons that make him feel this way. First are the questions about the therapist's proper role in relation to the client, to other professionals, and to society in general. When a beginning therapist enters his profession his conception of his own role is somewhat diffuse. Many aspects of his role and the implications of his role-related actions are not clear to him, since generally they are not taught to him during his academic training. He has to learn through experience how to perform satisfactorily in relation to the client, to other professionals, and to society at large (Roback et al. 1971; Cherniss 1976; Lamb et al. 1982). This is a source of anxiety.

As a beginner, generally he has a "preoccupation with self in his role of a therapist" (Auerbach and Johnson 1977). This preoccupation and lack of a clear concept of his position generate anxiety.

Another reason for his anxiety is a lack of quick and tangible evidence of his effectiveness and competence as a therapist. In psychotherapy, changes and improvements in a client's life are slow, intangible, and frequently almost imperceptible. Slow progress does not help the beginning therapist develop a feeling of competence and worthwhileness as a therapist, for he cannot see the tangible effects of his work during the therapy sessions. He may feel that he lacks knowledge, acumen, and competence. He may have an underlying fear that the client will discover how incompetent he is (Whitaker 1972). If he could have tangible and immediate confirmation that his efforts are helping the client to resolve his conflicts and to improve, then some of his fears and lack of self-confidence might be alleviated.

A third reason for a novice therapist's anxiety is the relationship between the theory and the practice of psychotherapy. The beginning

---

*There are, however, some beginning therapists who present themselves to their supervisors and colleagues as cocky, knowledgeable, and confident about the field, as if they have little to learn from anyone.

therapist has read many books, has tried to familiarize himself with the existing literature on psychotherapy, and has tried to espouse a particular school or system of psychotherapy that he is eager to apply in therapy sessions. However, he soon finds that the relationship between the theory and practice of psychotherapy is not a direct one. Clients do not fit neatly the dynamic structure or the diagnostic categories that the therapist has read about in books. Nor do the "treatment modalities" or therapeutic techniques that he has studied operate in reality as they do in theory. At best, the relationship between the theory and practice of psychotherapy is indirect and/or curvilinear. The therapist must struggle to find a pattern of relationship between theory and practice, and this may take a long time. Strupp (1977) implies that the theory and techniques of psychotherapy are hardly related, and the techniques should be taught separately from theory. The beginning therapist, therefore, must bridge the gap between theory and practice. If he is not successful in this task, it will undermine his confidence in his studies, in his knowledge, and in his training generally.

A further source of anxiety stems from the fact that since he is generally supervised, a beginning therapist must expose and make himself vulnerable to his supervisors, his colleagues, and his classmates. Self-exposure is particularly difficult for him because he wishes to appear competent. Interactions with the supervisor are important to him since the supervisor is usually his role model. A beginning therapist is dependent upon the supervisor's approval and derives his professional self-esteem from it. He sometimes feels that he may have made certain errors in his therapeutic work which the supervisor may discover. He may try too hard to please and/or appease him, even to the point of diminishing his autonomy and initiative. Hence, he may not feel free with clients during the therapy sessions. He may find it difficult to listen to the clients with ease. It may become difficult for him to recall what the client said in the preceding sessions without making his own projections and interpretations. Such a situation leads to what Kepecs (1979) calls "tracking errors," which are "incorrect statements to the patient that get him off his track. A correct statement, or silence, is one which facilitates the patient's self-understanding and encourages him to reveal himself to the therapist." Kepecs maintains that tracking errors, in small part, are due to inexperience and lack of knowledge, and in large part, to personal factors—essentially the therapist's anxiety.

Matarazzo, Weins, and Saslow (1966) maintain that the beginning therapist makes four kinds of errors in his work: (1) errors of focus (narrow focus, or focus on irrelevant material); (2) faulty role definition (authoritarian, dogmatic or argumentative); (3) faulty facilitation of communication (asking "yes" or "no" or brief-answer questions); and (4) other errors (irrelevant or unprofessional statements).

Lewis (1978) observes that frequently the beginning therapist makes the errors of intimacy and detachment. It is not unusual for him to become psychologically involved or intimate with his clients. He may become involved to the point of giving up his neutrality, his nonjudgmental role, and his relatively value-free posture. Or, in the name of objectivity and science, he may become too detached and distant. He may lose his warmth and sympathy for the client's struggles. In either case, his usefulness as a therapist begins to diminish.

Despite these quandaries and struggles of the beginning therapist, he is still eager to learn and dedicated to understanding and helping his clients. Most beginning therapists strive to achieve excellence in their future work with clients. They are willing to study and work hard to acquire knowledge and skill in their chosen profession, which involves the understanding of the psychological motives of behavior in others as well as in themselves (Henry 1977).

Experience versus Growth

The longer a therapist stays in his field, the more experience he gains. He works with different kinds of clients, frequently in diverse institutional settings. He gains experience in terms of the length of time he may see clients in therapy, and he interacts with professionals in related fields. Because of such experiences, he begins to develop a better sense of what to expect in therapy. He learns to anticipate possible eventualities in the course of therapy. He vaguely suspects how the story of a client may turn out, and fewer stories upset or shock him (Auerbach and Johnson 1977).

Through experiences with different clients in different situations, a beginning therapist learns new methods and techniques to handle conflicts. Gradually, he begins to establish the role as a therapist that is most comfortable for him. As experience increases, his preoccupation with self will decrease. He begins to rely less on rules set either by a system of psychotherapy or by his supervisor, and more on his own experience, his own assessment of the client's situation, and his spontaneity and ingenuity (Sundland 1977).

With experience, the therapist grows more at ease, more confident, and more flexible in his approach to clients (Parloff et al. 1978; Farber 1980). The single most common effect of experience upon the therapist seems to be the development of a belief in the diversity and flexibility of therapeutic intervention (Fey 1958; Strupp 1958; Rice et al. 1972; Rice et al. 1974). As a therapist becomes more experienced he begins to reveal more of himself, make more interpretations, become more flexible, joke and laugh more, and yet become more direct in his observations of a client's behavior.

Some studies suggest that the experienced therapist establishes a better therapeutic relationship so that the client can explore himself more. Inexperienced therapists are also capable of offering such conditions, but with them there seems to be a great deal of variability. It follows, then, that experienced therapists achieve better results than those who are inexperienced. Yet empirical studies suggest that experienced therapists do not consistently achieve better results. After a thorough review of empirical studies on the success rate of experienced and inexperienced therapists, Auerbach and Johnson (1977) state that "the studies we have reviewed are generally supportive of the lore on the subject of therapist experience with one exception—the view that experienced therapists achieve better results, while it may be true, does not find the unequivocal support that we expected." Parloff et al. (1978) also reviewed studies on the relationship between the therapist's experience and success, and declare, "Our conclusions are even more pessimistic than those of Auerbach and Johnson."

Why don't experienced therapists achieve unequivocally better results than inexperienced ones? Auerbach and Johnson (1977) cite three reasons. The first reason involves the client's contribution to the outcome.

There are probably some clients for whom the choice of a therapist is not crucial. The least healthy will be difficult for anyone to help, and the healthiest can, in many cases, adjust to an inexperienced therapist who perhaps makes up in interest and enthusiasm what he lacks in skill. For example, this adjustment to an inexperienced therapist would seem quite possible for a client with a basically sound personality who is going through a crisis or loss. With those clients in the middle range of ego-strength, the outcome is more uncertain, and it is here that experience probably makes a difference."

Second is the interpretation of the question, "Is a better therapeutic relationship established by experienced therapists?" Auerbach and Johnson maintain that the therapist's mastery of his role is likely to be confused with his influence on the client.

With experience, mastery undoubtedly develops, and it is most gratifying to lose one's early feelings of uncertainty, anxiety, and preoccupation with self in the role of therapist. We naturally assume that this greater sense of competence and well-being will be accompanied by a proportional facility in influencing clients. With some clients, this occurs, but only with some.

Third is the uncertainty in measuring outcome. "The outcome measurements often include an uncomfortable degree of error variance which would tend to minimize differences between experienced and inexperienced therapists. . . ."

In addition to these three reasons, other factors operate in the therapist's professional life which are likely to detract from his growth. Thus, experienced therapists do not consistently achieve better results than those who are inexperienced. These factors are discussed below.

Experience and Lack of Growth

Although the therapist may gain experience in his field, this does not automatically lead to his growth as a therapist. Experience alone is not a sufficient condition of growth. To grow in his role, the therapist must engage in other activities, such as self-scrutiny and reading. If he does not develop himself in these ways, in certain instances experience can and does detract from his effectiveness as a therapist.

Some therapists, as they become more experienced, tend to become dogmatic in their theoretical beliefs and techniques and acquire a stereotypical approach toward clients. They begin to believe that because their approach has been successful for so many years with various clients there is no reason for them either to critically assess it or to incorporate newer approaches. If the client does not improve, perhaps it is the client's fault. Strupp et al. (1963) found that more experienced therapists are more likely to have and to express negative attitudes toward patients. Such stasis of growth does not necessarily lead to effectiveness as a therapist.

Other therapists, as they stay longer in the field, "become skeptical in the value of their work and in the validity of their concepts. They do not study or write" (Wheelis 1958). They attempt to hide their skepticism by the use of various devices. Because of the intangible and amorphous nature of psychotherapy, some therapists, especially medical therapists, begin to believe in and search for more certain cures, like pills, electroshock, neurology, pharmacology, and so forth (Book 1973). Nonmedical therapists who harbor a similar skepticism also begin to wish that they had access to concrete cures; they, too, begin to search for tangible results in, for example, certain forms of exercise, certain gimmicks, and special kinds of therapies—all of which give the impression of tangibility. With these attitudes and approaches toward psychotherapy, such therapists, although they gain experience in the field, do not grow in their work.

Some therapists, as they gain in experience, begin to develop certain personality patterns which may interfere with growth. Bugental (1965) calls them "pseudo-maturity" patterns. Such therapists mistake pseudo-maturity patterns for real maturity. Pseudo-maturity patterns include the following manifestations:

Pontificating—This includes the therapists who pontificate, speaking as though they are the infallible intermediary between God and the patient; pronouncing judgments, giving instructions, and acting out a certainty that is the therapist's own resistance to contingency. Whatever the patient says is the occasion for the therapist to give a lecturette. . . .

Acting-out giving—A more frequent sign of pseudo-maturity, one in which the therapist's own needs are more covert and unconscious is that form of acting-out giving by the therapist which is actually a substitute for his genuine presence in the interview. The therapists who are caught up in the delusion of the curative power of unstinting love . . . would be the primary examples of this type of acting out. Genuine presence with the patient, encounter and engagement with him, seldom will be expressed through continual and unilateral giving. . . .

Enacted openness—A variation of this same pattern of acting-out giving as a substitute for genuine presence occurs in the kind of enacted openness which is really exhibitionism on the therapist's part. I had a patient who went to a psychotherapist who in the second session undressed himself completely as a demonstration of his openness and lack of pretense to the patient. . . .

Submergence in a theory—Another sort of pseudo-maturity that is often somewhat subtle and difficult to recognize is that in which a theory or system displaces the person of the therapist. Such a therapist becomes, as it were, an embodiment of a particular viewpoint, rather than a person in his own right. . . .

Encouragement of impulsivity—A final kind of pseudo-maturity pattern . . . is . . . the encouragement of the patient in his acting-out impulsivity and overthrow of the superego. This attempt to free the patient to be that which he "naturally" is by raising no question or responsibility about the patient's impulses is an all too frequent type of therapeutic pseudo-maturity. (Bugental, 1965)

Other therapists, although they gain experience, begin to "burn out" from the demands, duties, and expectations of the professional role performance, and as a result they "lose all concern, all emotional feelings for the persons they work with and come to treat them in detached or even dehumanized ways" (Maslach 1976). Other observers list the following characteristics or symptoms of "burnout": exhaustion, detachment, or psychological withdrawal; boredom and cynicism; impatience and heightened irritability; feelings of being unappreciated; and psychosomatic complaints (Cherniss 1980; Freudenberger 1980; Kahn 1978). Burnout is reported to be a relatively slow process which may take many years to reach its culmination (Freudenberger 1980).

Farber and Heifetz (1981, 1982), in their empirical investigations of "burned-out" therapists, found the following factors contributing to the therapists' exhaustion. The first factor reported by therapists was physical and emotional depletion. Therapists feel that they are constantly "giving" without enough in return. Thus, they are not emotionally replenished, and over time they begin to burn out. Second, the inherent tension built into the profession of therapy, such as the tension between intimacy and restraint, contributes to the burnout. Third, if the therapist is working in an institutional setting, the extratherapeutic impediments to the conduct of effective and satisfying therapy begin to contribute toward the therapist's burnout. Another reason given for burnout is the difficulty in working with disturbed people—for example, suicidal clients, agitated and anxious clients, clients with paranoid delusions, hostile clients—all of whom take an emotional toll on the therapist.*

To sum up, all such feelings and reactions of the therapist—dogmatism and rigidity, skepticism about the validity of one's work, development of pseudo-maturity patterns, and burnout—are not conducive to better results with clients, no matter how experienced a therapist may become. In fact, in such cases the therapist will have a negative effect on the client, who will begin to deteriorate in therapy.

---

*Norcross and Prochaska's (1983) and Tyron's (1983) survey of private practitioners of psychotherapy does not support these studies. Their finding is that after ten years of full-time private practice, most of the respondents were relatively satisfied with their work.

Deterioration, or the Negative Effects

"Deterioration implies an impairment of vigor, resilience, or usefulness from a previously higher state. Generally, it has been regarded as a worsening of the patient's symptomatic picture, the exaggeration of existing symptoms, or the development of new symptoms, as assessed before and after treatment" (Bergin and Lambert 1978). Generally, two reasons have been mentioned for the negative effect: (1) the preexisting condition of the client (Lieberman et al. 1973; Hartley et al. 1976) and (2) the deterioration related to the therapist and the therapeutic process. In this chapter we shall focus only upon the latter.

Literature frequently states, and ample evidence seems to substantiate, that some of the therapists and their therapeutic techniques generate a deterioration or negative effect on a portion of the very clients whom they intend to help. The reported rate of deterioration in psychotherapy varies considerably. In encounter groups the rate of deterioration, or casualty rate, has been reported between less than 1 percent to almost 50 percent, averaging around 6 percent. In individual therapy, a deterioration rate of 10 percent has been frequently reported* (Bergin and Suinn 1975; Lambert et al. 1977). Bergin (1975) states that "ten percent of the therapy cases deteriorate significantly after treatment, twice as many as in the untreated groups. That means that one of every ten therapy patients ended up in worse condition that when he or she began treatment. In half of those cases the deterioration can fairly well be blamed on the therapy itself."

The deterioration effect is quite widespread and is not confined to any particular school of therapy. Lambert, Bergin, and Collins (1977) and Bergin and Lambert (1978) reviewed exhaustively the literature on this topic. Their conclusions seem to be in agreement. Bergin and Lambert (1978) state that "deterioration can and does occur in a wide variety of the patient population with an equally wide variety of treatment techniques." It occurs in severely disturbed patients (Fairweather et al. 1960), in predelinquent boys (Powers and Witmer

---

*In their thorough study on the outcome of psychotherapy, Smith, Glass, and Miller (1980) report that "only 9% of the effect-size measures were negative (where the mean for the control group was higher than the mean for the psychotherapy group.)"

1951), in normal persons (Lieberman, Yalom, and Miles 1973), and in neurotic outpatients (Baron and Leary 1955). Deterioration also seems to be reported in studies that employed therapists who differ sharply in training and experience, such as medical students (Uhlenhuth and Duncan 1968), psychiatric residents (Gottschalk, Mayerson, and Gottlieb 1967), paraprofessionals (Carkhuff and Truax 1965), social caseworkers (McCabe 1967; Segal 1972; Fisher 1973), and combinations of experienced and inexperienced therapists (Rogers and Dymond 1954; Feifel and Eells 1963). Bergin and Lambert (1978) go on to state "that there is evidence of client worsening within all the major therapy systems, including behavioral, humanistic, psychoanalytic, and cognitive approaches."

Our interest, however, is in the therapist's contribution to the client's deterioration. Many writers contend that the therapist is mainly responsible for the negative effects in therapy (Robertiello 1975; Strupp et al. 1977; Parloff et al. 1978). Fiske (1977) declares that "any overall negative effect is due to the fallibility of the therapist. Ideally, he should be able to tell when the treatment is harming the patient, even changing the therapist if necessary. . . ." We should ask, How does a therapist contribute to the client's deterioration? Two separate yet related characteristics or traits of the therapist have been mentioned as contributory factors. The first is deficiency in training and skills. Part of the problem with training in psychotherapy and the mental-health field is simply the relative lack of knowledge within the field (Hadley and Strupp 1976). The second factor is the therapist's personality and therapeutic style.

Deficiency in the therapist's training and skills can result from many sources. These may include poor training facilities, poor supervision, poor background in understanding certain kinds of clients (such as minority clients), lack of rigor in instructions and education, limited experience with clients, rigidity and stereotyping of the techniques taught and learned, and so on. Hadley and Strupp (1976) observe that "deficiencies in therapists' skills may produce particularly severe negative effects in dealing with borderline patients, due to therapists' stimulating the release of primitive aggression without quite knowing how to deal with it in psychotherapy. Such negative effects may be exacerbated by the therapist who masochistically participates in the patient's acting out."

With regard to the therapist's personality and his therapeutic style, various authors have noted different individual characteristics and traits. Truax and Carkhuff (1967) and Truax and Mitchell (1971) maintain that therapists who do not possess three basic personality ingredients—empathy, warmth, and genuineness—are more likely to produce deterioration in the client during the course of therapy.*

Therapists whose personal lives are unsettled or in turmoil are more likely to produce a deteriorating effect. Vandenbos and Karon (1971) found that those therapists who consciously or unconsciously use clients to satisfy their own needs (in their study, dependency needs) are likely to cause deterioration in the client. (They label such therapists as "pathogenic" therapists.)

On the basis of existing studies, we could draw a composite picture of the personality and style of such therapists (Feiffel and Eells 1963; Truax and Carkhuff 1967; Yalom and Lieberman 1971; Lieberman, Yalom, and Miles 1973; Ricks 1974; Ellis 1977). First are those therapists (or leaders), as described in the study by Lieberman et al. (1973). In this study the high-risk groups—those groups which produced the greatest number of casualties—were led by a person whose style is characterized by high aggressive stimulation, high charisma, high individual focus, high support, and high confrontation. "The various mechanisms of injury include: (1) attack by leader or by group, (2) rejection by leader or by group, (3) failure to attain unrealistic goals, (4) coercive expectations, and (5) input overload or value shuffle."

The study goes on to point out that "high attack leaders shared several characteristics; an unwavering faith in themselves, their product, and their technique; a sense of impatience (changes must be made); a tendency to impose their values on their subjects; a failure to recognize signals that vital defenses are prematurely crumbling; and a failure to differentiate between individuals."

Other studies support these findings. Powers and Witmer (1951) also noted that counselors who either reject their clients or are punitive toward them are likely to generate a negative effect. Feifel and Eells (1963) found that therapists who show irritation, anger, or boredom, or who use interpretation and confrontation excessively are likely to generate a negative effect in the client. Ellis (1977) states that

---

*For a thorough discussion of the interrelationship and independence of these three personality traits, see Mitchell, Bozarth and Krauft (1977).

the main factors responsible for negative effects would be the "ignorance and stupidity of the therapist, the incompetence of the therapist, and the need of the therapist to depend on clients emotionally or exploit them. . . ."

Another category of therapists who produce negative effects are those who during the course of therapy focus predominantly upon the client's "psychopathology," "symptomatology," and unconscious conflicts and anxieties, such as the fear of going crazy or the fear of committing suicide. These therapists encourage and instigate the client to express such fears and concerns. However, when the client does express his fears, the therapist becomes frightened and upset and begins to withdraw from the client (Ricks 1974).* The client begins to feel as though the rug has been pulled out from under him: he has been encouraged to express his fears and conflicts, and when he does the therapist does not help him resolve his conflicts. The client feels overwhelmed and abandoned at a critical moment in his struggles. Soon, the client either drops out or begins to deteriorate.

Ingredients of Growth

How does a therapist grow into a competent and mature therapist? The answer to this question is very difficult, since there is neither a prescribed path nor a shortcut to growth. The existing literature describes a number of personality characteristics of a "good" or "competent" therapist.

Parloff, Waskow, and Wolf (1978) state that

the various prescriptions for the ideal psychotherapist have included a litany of virtues more suited, perhaps, to the most honored biblical figures than to any of their descendants. A partial listing of the qualities that have been advanced as those to which all prospective therapists should aspire include objectivity, honesty, capacity for relatedness, emotional freedom, security, integrity, humanity, commitment to the patient, intuitiveness, patience, perceptiveness, empathy, creativity, and imaginativeness. (Krasner 1962; Salvson 1964; Swenson 1971).

Matarazzo (1978) says that

---

*In many instances, such a therapist may have his own anxieties regarding the very same issues presented by the client, which the therapist may be trying to resolve or avoid by focusing upon the client's psychopathology.

so far, we can probably safely say that psychological good health, flexibility, open-mindedness, positive attitudes toward people, and interpersonal skills are associated with success as a psychotherapist. These desirable characteristics, of course, are presumably associated with success in any endeavor in which human interaction is a large component. Lack of these attributes, or personality disturbances, is very likely to hinder the student's growth as a therapist.

Rogers (1957), Truax and Carkhuff (1967), and Tyler (1969) all seem to agree that the three basic characteristics of a "good" therapist are empathy, nonpossessive warmth, and authenticity or genuineness. The more one possesses these qualities, the better therapist he is likely to be. Conversely, the less he possesses them, the poorer therapist he is likely to be.

Holt and Luborsky (1958) found that "better" residents in psychiatry, as compared to relatively "poor" ones, were characterized by "genuineness" (as opposed to "facade"), better in adjustment to co-workers, and freer from "status-mindedness."

Wilcox (1960) describes what goes into the making of a good therapist. He lists four characteristics: "formal training, broad experience in living, desirable personality characteristics, and personal therapy." Hartlage and Sperr (1980) asked outpatient psychotherapy patients to describe the attributes of an ideal therapist. Most patients agreed upon the following characteristics: making a good impression; being frank, honest, and appreciative, self-respecting and able to take care of oneself; being firm, cooperative, friendly, self-confident; showing leadership and respect for others. It is toward these characteristics that a beginning therapist strives in his professional career.

Incorporating these traits into one's style of work is a continuous process. A therapist may be more successful in developing some of these traits, while not so successful in developing or acquiring others. Yet it would seem that the incorporation of these traits and characteristics is not a superhuman task. It is a task that can be accomplished by those who wish to struggle with themselves. In fact, one may say that the struggle to incorporate these traits is, in itself, a process of growth for the therapist.

A growing therapist should be able to create more and more of the facilitative conditions for the client during the therapy session. The therapist's growth is reflected by his ability to create such facilitative conditions for most of his clients, regardless of their condition.

Obviously, it is not easy to create such facilitative conditions with every client and over a long period of time. Studies suggest that therapists vary in their ability to create them for long-term clients; yet therapists who are able to provide acceptance, empathy, and genuineness in the first place are those who are able to maintain them over a long period of time.

The development of traits that help create facilitative conditions can be learned or taught to a therapist (Carkhuff 1972; Perlman 1973; Sherer and Rogers 1980). Therapists who are deficient in learning and/or incorporating these traits into their work are likely to be deficient in their growth as therapists and are less likely to be successful with their clients (Strupp, Wallach, and Wogan 1964). Therapists who lack the facilitative traits will have a difficult time making therapy move beyond a certain point, simply because many clients are likely to pull back and become "closed," while others may become resistive, and still others may drop out of therapy.

"Openness" is another important personality characteristic for the growth of a therapist. Openness has two aspects, which are somewhat arbitrarily created. The first aspect is being open to oneself, that is, the ability and willingness to acknowledge and accept one's emotions and be aware of one's values, prejudices, and assumptions about life. The second aspect of openness is a sensitivity or psychological permeability to the external world, namely, the ability to take in and assimilate external stimuli. Such stimuli may include the viewpoints and criticisms of others, including those of the client. Some therapists are open to themselves but not to the outside world; others are open to the external world but not to themselves. Openness in both respects helps the therapist.

Openness is important on many counts. Every client has a certain impact upon the therapist, especially in his narration and description of turmoil and conflicts, and the emotions and affects associated with it. The client's conflicts and turmoils are rooted in his life's values and assumptions, which may be quite different from and even alien to those of the therapist. Thus, when the two sets of values and assumptions are juxtaposed, they evoke in the therapist innumerable thoughts and feelings, reactions and prejudices, memories and images. If the therapist does not openly acknowledge them within himself, or shuts them off, he is likely to lose touch with himself and reduce the possibility of his further growth.

The client's discussion of his conflicts and troubles may stimulate and/or rekindle many of the therapist's latent (and sometimes overt) conflicts, anxieties, temptations, and wishes. Once stimulated, the therapist has to acknowledge or deny them. If he acknowledges them, he must then handle them without adversely affecting the therapeutic process. If he denies them, the possibility of an authentic encounter and relationship with the client is lost. Thus, if a therapist is open to himself and to others, he must constantly struggle with his feelings, reactions, temptations, prejudices, and values. He must evaluate and manage them so they are helpful to both the client and himself. Therapists who are reluctant to being open are not likely to grow in their role as therapist, simply because they will have to stifle or blunt one of the main instruments of psychotherapy, namely, themselves.

The third important factor in a therapist's growth is self-reflection and self-scrutiny. Nondefensively, the therapist assesses and examines himself (his feelings and emotions, his biases and prejudice, his fears and temptations) and how these may affect his work with the client. There are many reasons why self-reflection and self-scrutiny are important for the therapist's growth.

First, if a therapist does not engage in self-reflection and self-scrutiny, there is little likelihood that he will become aware of, let alone channel and control, those feelings and emotions that may affect and influence behavior in therapy. Self-reflection and self-scrutiny are especially important, considering that in the process of psychotherapy a therapist does not use instruments external to himself, like pills, drugs, shock, or any mechanical devices. It is through himself alone that a therapist helps and influences the client. In other words, the therapist is his own instrument. Like any other instrument, it has to be kept clean, sharp, and unencumbered.

Many therapists are reluctant to engage in self-reflection and self-scrutiny, even when they are encouraged to do so. They somehow feel these activities are more appropriate to a trainee-subordinate. Now that they are no longer in this position, they feel that they do not have to engage in such activities. Such an attitude and approach toward oneself, toward the client, and toward the therapeutic process is rarely conducive to growth. Without engaging in such activities, a therapist rarely learns his strengths and deficiencies; hence, he does not know what to "work on" in himself. For the same reason, he will have considerable difficulty in learning alternative ways to approach the client. When a therapist shys away from self-reflection and self-scrutiny, he may become defensive and/or secretive about his work and develop excuses about its shortcomings rather than face them directly.

Truax and Carkhuff (1967) suggest a method for a therapist to initiate self-reflection.

The client can be asked to mail to the therapist his own brief subjective account of those moments that were most meaningful—both the helpful and hurtful moments. Such post-therapy, subjective accounts by the client, though perhaps somewhat distorted, offer a meaningful learning experience to any therapist or counselor. The authors, in reading such accounts from their own clients, have learned something new about themselves from every patient.

The fourth characteristic in the growth process of a therapist is modesty. It seems reasonable to assume that if the therapist maintains a certain openness and engages in self-scrutiny and self-criticism, modesty should develop automatically in him. Yet this does not seem to be the case because in a therapeutic situation the therapist has a superior position, with power and authority. The client has placed a certain faith and hope in him to help him to improve his condition. The client relies on the therapist's expert opinion. In this situation, the therapist is likely to develop feelings of arrogance and pomposity. He may begin to feel that his experience has earned him the right to feel superior. He may believe that he understands the complexities and conflicts in life and is knowledgeable about these matters; therefore, he may pontificate to others on how to live their lives. This condition is the opposite of modesty.

Hence, we may say that modesty does not develop spontaneously in the therapist, even though he may be open and self-reflecting. Generally, it has to be acquired and cultivated through a constant struggle to remind oneself that life-forces and social forces are far too complex, too numerous, and too unpredictable for a therapist to understand completely, especially in weekly meetings with the client. The therapist's understanding of the client's life and his struggles remains somewhat limited; therefore, no therapist should presume to understand his client fully.

The awareness of one's limitations as a person as well as the limitations of the psychotherapeutic process is another aspect of the therapist's growth. The therapist has limitations of time; he can spend only a limited amount with each client, however much he may wish to devote all of himself to the task of reducing the client's anguish. As a human being, he can endure the pain and anguish of others only up to a point. Going beyond that point is counterproductive. A growing therapist must realize the extent of his endurance.

Further, the therapist can only help the client live his life; he cannot live it for him. Frequently, a therapist may identify strongly with the client's dilemmas. He may feel that if only he could make the client see, do, or undo certain things in his life, the client would be better off. To the therapist it may seem obvious what needs to happen to make the client's life effective and comfortable. As much as the therapist would like to act for the client, the client must act for himself. The client may or may not wish to follow his advice. This is the limitation of the therapist's role. In trying to help others live more effectively, he can only stand by and watch.

A therapist cannot bring direct material gains to clients who may badly need them. Nor can he change the harmful and deleterious social and material conditions in which a client may live. Finally, the knowledge and techniques of therapy have limitations. A therapist cannot help all the clients who come to see him. His therapeutic techniques may not be applicable to all of them. Hence, his realizations about whom he can help and to what extent comprise another aspect in his growth.

Reading and studying are important in continued therapist's growth. Generally, they are underplayed or overlooked by both beginning and experienced therapists. One would assume that each client's struggles are carefully and thoroughly studied by the therapist. Yet this may not be the case. Studying the pertinent literature and case histories and engaging in professional discussions help the therapist learn from the experiences of others who have worked with similar clients and who may have been in a situation similar to his own. It may help him to find new or different approaches toward his clients. In addition, reading, study, and consultation are likely to provide the therapist with a certain distance and objectivity toward his work, which will ensure that he does not get too involved with the client.

Study widens the intellectual horizons of the therapist and helps him to accept his own limitations. It may familiarize him with certain things beforehand which otherwise might bewilder and shock him during the course of therapy. For instance, it is not unusual for the beginning therapist to be upset by stories of clients who have been involved in incest. Studying the literature on this topic, or reading case histories of clients involved in incestuous relationships, may help him to be less shocked and more understanding of the client's dilemmas.

Summary

The growth of a therapist is a long and arduous process which involves a continuous struggle with himself. A beginning therapist is generally diffident and anxious in his work and about his role as a therapist. There are stresses and conflicts for which he is not well prepared, and quick and tangible evidence of his effectiveness with clients is lacking. The relationship between the theory of psychotherapy and its practice is generally an indirect and unclear one. Finally, the beginning therapist may worry about exposing his errors and ignorance to his supervisors.

The longer a therapist stays in the field, the more experience he gains with diverse clients. He learns new techniques, becomes more confident and flexible, and begins to shape a role as a therapist which is comfortable for him. However, more experienced therapists do not consistently attain better results than inexperienced ones.

Experience alone does not appear to be a sufficient condition for growth in a therapist. Rather, many experienced therapists become rigid and dogmatic. Some give up on reading and writing in their field and become skeptical about the validity of their work. Some develop personality traits which do not allow growth, while others burn out as therapists. These therapists may create negative therapeutic effects, which cause the client to deteriorate rather than improve in therapy.

The basic ingredients for growth in a therapist are the development of an ability to create facilitative conditions for the client in therapy sessions, he should display acceptance, warmth, empathy, and genuineness; openness with himself and with others; self-reflection and self-scrutiny; modesty; the realization of his limitations; and an interest in reading and studying further.

References

Auerbach, A., and M. Johnson. 1977. Research on the therapist's level of experience. In A. S. Gurman and A. M. Razin, eds., *Effective Psychotherapy*, 84–103. New York: Pergamon Press.

Baron, F., and T. Leary. 1955. Changes in psychoneurotic patients with and without psychotherapy. *Journal of Consulting Psychology* 19:239–45.

Bergin, A. E. 1975. Psychotherapy can be dangerous. *Psychology Today*, Nov., 96–98, 100–104.

Bergin, A. E., and M. J. Lambert. 1978. The evaluation of therapeutic outcomes. In S. L. Garfield and A. E. Bergin, eds., *Handbook of Psychotherapy and Behavior Change* (2d ed.), 139–89, 154–55. New York: John Wiley and Sons.

Bergin, A. E., and R. M. Suinn. 1975. Individual therapy and behavior therapy. In M. R. Rosenweig and L. W. Porter, eds., *Annual Review of Psychology*, 509–57. Palo Alto: Anmed Reviews.

Book, H. 1973. On maybe becoming a psychotherapist, perhaps. *Canadian Psychiatric Association Journal* 18(6):487–93.

Bugental, J. 1965. *The Search for Authenticity*. New York: Holt, Rinehart and Winston, 369–71.

Carkhuff, R. 1972. New directions in training for the helping professions: Toward a technology for human and community resource development. *The Counseling Psychologist* 3:12–30.

Carkhuff, R., and C. Truax. 1965. Lay mental health counseling: The effects of lay group counseling. *Journal of Consulting Psychology* 29:426–31.

Cherniss, C. 1980. *Professional burnout in human service organizations*. New York: Praeger Publishers, 209–10.

Cherniss, C., E. Egnation, and S. Wacker. 1976. Job stress and career development in new public professionals. *Professional Psychology* 7:428–36.

Chessick, R. 1971. How the resident and the supervisor disappoint each other. *American Journal of Psychotherapy* 25:272–83.

Ellis, A. 1977. Quoted in H. Strupp, S. Hadley, and B. Gomez-Schwartz, *Psychotherapy for better or worse*, 248. New York: Jason Aronson.

Fairweather, G., R. Simon, M. Gebhard, E. Weingarton, J. Holland, R. Sanders, G. Stone, and J. Reahl. 1960. Relative effectiveness of psychotherapeutic programs: A multicriteria comparison of four programs for three different patient groups. *Psychological Monographs* (General and applied) 74:5 (whole no. 492).

Farber, B. A. 1980. The effects of psychotherapeutic practice upon psychotherapists. *Psychotherapy: Theory, Research and Practice* 20:174–82.

Farber, B. A., and L. J. Heifetz. 1982. The process and dimensions of burnouts in psychotherapists. *Professional Psychology* 13:293–301.

———. 1981. Satisfactions and stresses of psychotherapeutic work: A factor-analytic study. *Professional Psychology* 12:621–30.

Feifel, H., and J. Eells. 1963. Patients and therapists assess the same psychotherapy. *Journal of Consulting Psychology* 27:310–18.

Fey, W. F. 1958. Doctrine and experience: Their influence upon the psychotherapist. *Journal of Consulting Psychology* 22:403–9.

Fisher, J. 1973. Is casework effective: A review. *Social Work* 1(5):314–15.

Fiske, D. 1977. Quoted in H. Strupp, S. Hadley, and B. Gomez-Schwartz, *Psychotherapy for Better or Worse*, 255. New York: Jason Aronson.

Freudenberger, H. 1980. *Burn Out*. Garden City, N.Y.: Anchor Press, 61–65.

Gottschalk, L., P. Mayerson, and A. Gottlieb. 1967. Prediction and evaluation of outcome in an emergency brief psychotherapy clinic. *Journal of Nervous & Mental Disease* 144:77–96.

Hadley, S., and H. Strupp. 1976. Contemporary views of negative effects in psychotherapy. *Archives of General Psychiatry* 33:1291–1302.

Hartlage, L., and E. Sperr. 1980. Patient preferences with regard to ideal therapists. *Journal of Clinical Psychology* 36:288–91.

Hartley, D., H. Roback, and S. Abramowitz. 1976. Deterioration effects in encounter groups. *American Psychologist* 31:247–55.

Henry, W. 1977. Personal and social identities of psychotherapists. In A. S. Burman and A. M. Razin, eds., In *Effective Psychotherapy*, 47–63. New York: Pergamon Press.

Holt, R., and L. Lubrosky. 1958. *Personality patterns of psychiatrists*. New York: Basic Books.

Kepecs, J. 1979. Tracking errors in psychotherapy. *American Journal of Psychotherapy* 3:365–77.

Krasner, L. 1962. The therapist as a social reinforcement machine. In H. H. Strupp and L. Luborsky, eds., *Research in psychotherapy*, vol. 2. Washington, D.C.: American Psychological Association.

Kahn, R. 1978. Job burn out: Prevention and remedies. *Public Welfare*, Spring, 61–63.

Lamb, D., J. Baker, M. Jennings, and E. Yarris. 1982. Passage of an internship in professional psychology. *Professional Psychology* 5:661–70.

Lambert, M., A. Bergin, and J. Collins. 1977. Therapist-induced deterioration in psychotherapy. In A. S. Gurman and A. M. Razin, eds., *Effective Psychotherapy*, 452–82. New York: Pergamon Press.

Lewis, J. M. 1978. *To Be A Therapist*. New York: Brunner-Mazel.

Lieberman, M., I. Yalom, and M. Miles. 1973. *Encounter Groups: First Facts*. New York: Basic Books, 174, 194, 436.

McCabe, A. 1967. *The Pursuit of Promise*. New York: Community Service Society.

Maslach, C. 1976. Burned-out. *Human Behavior* 5:16–22.

Matarazzo, R. G. 1978. Research on the teaching and learning of psychotherapeutic skills. In S. L. Garfield and A. S. Bergin, eds., *Handbook of Psychotherapy and Behavior Change*, 941–67. New York: John Wiley.

Matarazzo, R., A. Weins, and G. Saslow. 1966. Experimentation in the teaching and learning of psychotherapy skills. In L. Gottschalk and A. Auerbach, eds., *Methods of Research in Psychotherapy*, 597–635. New York: Appleton-Century-Crofts.

Mitchell, K. M., J. D. Bozarth, and C. C. Krauft. 1977. A reappraisal of the effectiveness of accurate empathy, nonpossessive warmth, and genuineness. In A. S. Gurman and A. M. Razin, eds., *Effective Psychotherapy*, 482–503. New York: Pergamon Press.

Norcross, J., and J. Prochaska. 1983. Psychotherapists in independent practice:

Some findings and issues. *Professional Psychology: Research and Practice* 14:869–81.

Parloff, M., I. Waskow, and B. Wolfe. 1978. Research on therapist variables in relation to process and outcome. In S. L. Garfield and A. E. Bergin, eds., *Handbook of Psychotherapy and Behavior Change*, 233–83. New York: John Wiley.

Parloff, M., B. Wolfe, S. Hadley, and I. Waskow. 1978. Assessment of psychosocial treatment of mental disorders: Current status and prospectus. *National Technical Service Information Services.* Springfield, Va.: U.S. Department of Commerce.

Perlman, G. 1973. Change in central therapeutic ingredients of beginning psychotherapists. *Psychotherapy: Theory, Research, and Practice* 10:48–51.

Powers, E., and H. Witmer. 1951. *An Experiment in the Prevention of Delinquency.* New York: Columbia University Press.

Rice, D. G., W. F. Fey, and J. G. Kepecs. 1972. Therapist experience and style as factors in co-therapy. *Family Process* 11:1–12.

Rice, D. G., A. S. Gurman, and A. M. Razin. 1974. Therapist sex, "style," and theoretical orientation. *Journal of Nervous and Mental Disease* 159:413–21.

Ricks, D. 1974. Supershrink: Methods of a therapist judged successful on the basis of adult outcome of adolescent patients. In D. Ricks, M. Roff, and A. Thomas, eds., *Life History Research In Psychopathology*, vol. 3, 251–95. Minneapolis: University of Minnesota Press.

Roback, H., A. Webersinn, and H. Guion. 1971. Effects of the therapeutic experience on emerging psychotherapists. *Mental Hygiene* 55:228–29.

Robertiello, R. C. 1975. Iatrogenic psychiatric illness. *Journal of Contemporary Psychotherapy* 7:3–8.

Rogers, C. R. 1957. The necessary and sufficient conditions of therapeutic personality change. *Journal of Consulting Psychology* 21:95–103.

Rogers, C., and R. Diamond. 1954. *Psychotherapy and Personality Change.* Chicago, Ill.: University of Chicago Press.

Schlict, W. S. 1968. The anxieties of the psychotherapist. *Mental Hygiene* 52:439–44.

Segal, S. 1972. Research on the outcome of social work therapeutic intervention: A review of the literature. *Journal of Health and Social Behavior* 13:3–17.

Sherer, M., and R. Rogers. 1980. Effects of therapists' nonverbal communication on rated skill and effectiveness. *Journal of Clinical Psychology* 36:696–700.

Slawson, S. 1964. *A Textbook in Analytic Group Psychotherapy.* New York: International University Press.

Smith, M., G. Glass, and T. Miller. 1980. *The benefits of psychotherapy.* Baltimore: Johns Hopkins University Press, 88.

Strupp, H. 1977. A reformulation of the dynamics of the therapist's contribution. In A. S. Gurman and A. M. Razin, eds., *Effective Psychotherapy*, 1–23. New York: Pergamon Press.

———. 1958. The psychotherapist's contribution to the treatment process. *Behavioral Science* 3:34–67.

Strupp, H., S. Hadley, and B. Gomez-Schwartz. 1977. *Psychotherapy for Better or Worse*. New York: Jason Aronson.

Strupp, H., M. Wallach, and M. Wogan. 1964. Psychotherapy experience in retrospect: Questionnaire survey of former patients and their therapists. *Psychological Monograph* 78(11):26, 30.

Strupp, H., M. Wallach, M. Wogan, and J. Jenkins. 1963. Psychotherapists' assessment of former patients. *Journal of Nervous and Mental Disease* 137:220–30.

Sundland, D. 1977. Theoretical orientations of psychotherapists. In A. S. Gurman and A. M. Razin, eds., *Effective Psychotherapy*, 189–219. New York: Pergamon Press.

Swenson, C. 1971. Committment and the personality of the successful therapist. *Psychotherapy: Theory, Research, and Practice* 8:31–36.

Truax, C. B., and R. R. Carkhuff. 1967. *Toward effective counseling and psychotherapy*. Chicago: Aldine Publications, 374.

Truax, C. B., and K. M. Mitchell. 1971. Research on certain therapists' interpersonal skills in relation to process and outcome. In A. E. Bergin and S. L. Garfield, eds., *Handbook of Psychotherapy and Behavior Change*, 299–334. New York: John Wiley.

Tyler, L. E. 1969. *The Work of the Counselor* (3d ed.). New York: Appleton-Century-Crofts.

Tyron, G. 1983. The pleasures and displeasures of private practice. *The Clinical Psychologist* 36:45–48.

Uhlenhuth, E., and D. Duncan. 1968. Subjective changes in psychoneurotic outpatients with medical students: The kind, amount, and course of change. Johns Hopkins University. In manuscript.

Vandenbos, G. R., and B. P. Karon. 1971. Pathogenesis: A new therapist personality dimension related to therapeutic effectiveness. *Journal of Personality Assessment* 35:252–60.

Wheelis, A. 1958. *The Quest For Identity*. New York: W. W. Norton and Co., 232.

Whitaker, C. 1972. A longitudinal view of therapy style where N=1. *Family Process* 11:13–15.

Wilcox, R. 1960. The relationship of personal background variables to psychotherapists' orientation. Master's thesis, Ohio State University.

Yalom, I., and M. Lieberman. 1971. A study of encounter group casualties. *Archives of General Psychiatry* 25:16–30.

Index